ENCYCLOPAEDIA
OF
INDIAN ART AND ARCHITECTURE

ENCYCLOPAEDIA
OF
INDIAN ART AND ARCHITECTURE

Patanjali Nandan Chaturvedi

MD PUBLICATIONS PVT LTD
NEW DELHI
www.mdppl.com

Copyright © 2009 by MD Publications Pvt Ltd.

Published by :

 MD Publications Pvt Ltd
'MD House', 11, Darya Ganj
New Delhi - 110 002
Phone : +91-11-41563325 (Customer Service)
        +91-11-41562846 (Editorial)
E-mail (orders): contact@mdppl.com
Website: www.mdppl.com

ISBN : 978-81-7533-186-0

Published and Printed by Mrs. Rajni Gupta on behalf of **MD Publications Pvt Ltd** at Times Press, New Delhi.

CONTENTS

Preface .... *vii*

1. Architecture: An Introduction 1

2. Indian Art and Architecture 38

3. Types of Indian Architecture 61

4. Hindu Architecture in India 101

5. Buddhist Art and Architecture in India 145

6. Islamic Art and Architecture in India 223

7. Jain Art and Architecture in India 272

8. Sikh Architecture in India 286

9. Colonial Architecture in India 296

10. Philosophical Contents of Indian Art and Architecture 310

11. Contemporary Architecture 325

    Bibliography 341

    Index 345

PREFACE

Indian art has been very rich. There have been many forms of Indian art over the years. Indian art has attracted millions of people. The art of ancient India brings before us a vision of great compassion. It is a view of the world that sees a harmony in the whole of creation. It sees the same that is in each of us, in the animals, the flowers, the trees, the leaves and even in the breeze that moves the leaves. All that there is, is seen to be a reflection of the one.

Similarly Indian architecture has also been very rich in style. The diversity of India is truly reflected in Indian architecture. There are many styles of architecture in India, like the Temple architecture, Rajput style of architecture, Southern architecture, Mughal architecture, Colonial architecture. The art and architecture of India must be understood and judged in the context of the ideological, aesthetic, and ritual assumptions and needs of the Indian civilization. These assumptions were formed as early as the 1st century BC and have shown a remarkable tenacity through the ages.

The Indian artist deftly uses certain primeval motifs, such as the feminine figure, the tree, water, the lion, and the elephant. In a given composition, although the result is sometimes conceptually unsettling, the qualities of sensuous vitality, earthiness, muscular energy, and rhythmic movement remain unmistakable. The form of the Hindu temple; the contours of the bodies of the Hindu gods and goddesses; and the light, shade, composition, and volume in Indian painting are all used to glorify the mystery that resolves the conflict between life and death, time and eternity. This book traces these various aspects of Indian art and architecture.

I am very grateful to Mr. Pranav Gupta, Director, MD Publications Pvt Ltd for his cooperation and support for this book.

Patanjali Nandan Chaturvedi

1

ARCHITECTURE

AN INTRODUCTION

The term architecture can be used to mean a process, a profession or documentation. As a process, architecture is the activity of designing and constructing buildings and other physical structures by a person or a machine, primarily to provide socially purposeful shelter. A wider definition often includes the design of the total built environment, from the macro level of how a building integrates with its surrounding man made landscape to the micro level of architectural or construction details and, sometimes, furniture. Wider still, architecture is the activity of designing any kind of system.

As a profession, architecture is the role of those persons or machines providing architectural services. As documentation, usually based on drawings, architecture defines the structure and/or behavior of a building or any other kind of system that is to be or has been constructed.

Architects have as their primary object providing for the spatial and shelter needs of people in groups of some kind (families, schools, churches, businesses, etc.) by the creative organisation of materials and components in a land- or city-scape, dealing with mass, space, form, volume, texture, structure, light, shadow, materials, program, and pragmatic elements such as cost, construction limitations and technology, to achieve an end which is functional, economical, practical and often with artistic and aesthetic aspects. This distinguishes architecture from engineering design, which has as its primary object the creative manipulation of materials and forms using mathematical and scientific principles.

Separate from the design process, architecture is also experienced through the senses, which therefore gives rise to aural, visual, olfactory, and tactile architecture. As people move through a space, architecture is experienced as a time sequence. Even though our culture considers architecture to be a visual experience, the other senses play a role in how we experience both natural and built environments. Attitudes towards the senses depend on culture. The design process and the sensory experience of a space are distinctly separate views, each with its own language and assumptions.

Architectural works are perceived as cultural and political symbols and works of art. Historical civilizations are often known primarily through their architectural achievements. Such buildings as the pyramids of Egypt and the Roman Colosseum are cultural symbols, and are an important link in public consciousness, even when scholars have discovered much about a past civilization through other means. Cities, regions and cultures continue to identify themselves with (and are known by) their architectural monuments.

The question 'What is architecture?' may at one level seem so obvious that it hardly warrants a whole chapter. Yet there has been and continues to be considerable debate about what should be included in the term and we all have our own ideas and preconceptions. So this analysis is about the problems of defining architecture as a subject and giving boundaries to it, by looking at some of the ways in which it has been defined in the past. It is also concerned with some of the reasons for studying architecture and with breaking down some preconceptions.

Architecture is the art and science of designing buildings and other physical structures. A wider definition often includes the design of the total built environment, from the macro level of how a building integrates with its surrounding manmade landscape to the micro level of architectural or construction details and, sometimes, furniture. The term "Architecture" is also used for the profession of providing architectural services.

Architects are primarily driven by the creative manipulation of mass, space, volume, texture, light, shadow, materials, program, and pragmatic elements such as cost, construction and technology, in order to achieve an end which is aesthetic, functional and often artistic. This distinguishes architecture from engineering design, which is driven primarily by the creative manipulation of materials and forms using mathematical and scientific principles.

Separate from the design process, architecture is also experienced through the senses, which therefore gives rise to aural, visual, olfactory, and tactile architecture. As people move through a space, architecture is experienced as a time sequence. Even though our culture considers architecture to be a visual experience, the other senses play a role in how we experience both natural and built environments. Attitudes towards the senses depend on culture. The design process and the sensory experience of a space are distinctly separate views, each with its own language and assumptions.

Architectural works are perceived as cultural and political symbols and works of art. Historical civilizations are often known primarily through their architectural achievements. Such buildings as the pyramids of Egypt and the Roman Colosseum are cultural symbols, and are an important link in public consciousness, even when scholars have discovered much about a past civilization through other means. Cities, regions and cultures continue to identify themselves with (and are known by) their architectural monuments.

According to Le Corbusier, 'Architecture is the masterly, correct and magnificent play of masses seen in light.' For him Architecture with a capital A was an emotional and aesthetic experience, but if we restrict our definition of architecture solely to those buildings that raise our spirits, then we would end up with rather a short list. According to which dictionary you use, architecture is defined as the art, or science, of building, or as one of the fine arts, that is to say it is concerned with the aesthetic arts as opposed to the useful or industrial arts such as engineering. When the Crystal Palace was erected in Hyde Park, London, in 1851 it was praised for its space, lightness and brilliancy and for its 'truthfulness and reality of construction', but 'the conviction has grown on us that it is not architecture: it is engineering of the highest merit and excellence, but not architecture', The foremost critics and theorists of the day such as John Ruskin and William Morris contributed to the debate. Generally they agreed that the distinction between architecture and building could be summarised as:

BUILDING+ART=ARCHITECTURE

It is a definition that some people would still agree with today, but this dualism between art on the one hand and utility or function on the other is an unsatisfactory one. It does not tell us about the relationship between art and utility, and it omits our experience of the reality and meaning of architecture.

If we consider the enormous variety of types of building that exist in different parts of the world, we still find that there is considerable debate about what should be included in the term 'architecture' and what should not. Many would agree that important buildings such as palaces, temples, cathedrals and castles should be included, but would disagree about the inclusion of cottages, garages or railway stations. So although we may take great delight in the moss-covered thatched roofs and mellow walls of country cottages, or the way that pole and *dhaka* (mud) homesteads blend into the African landscape, some would argue that they are not architecture because they were not designed by architects.

So although such buildings may be visually pleasing, they were not deemed worth studying as architecture. These cottages and homesteads are examples of traditional or vernacular architecture, which embodies particular ideas and aesthetic notions. They were consciously designed, following traditional patterns that evolved and were handed down from generation to generation. Although vernacular architecture has influenced individual architects and indeed was the inspiration behind both the British and American domestic revivals of the 1880s, it has generally been studied separately from polite, or monumental architecture and has been seen as a branch of anthropology, of construction history, or of social history. Bernard Rudofsky's *Architecture without Architects* was a pioneering study of traditional architecture, and the title is revealing.

Because architecture is such a vast subject there have been many attempts to limit it, or to break it down into more manageable areas. Limiting the definition of architecture to polite or monumental works such as castles, palaces or cathedrals is a way of defining the boundaries of the subject, and many of the older books adopted this stance. The narrow definition of architecture which limits it to polite architecture, or to the works of those considered to be key architects, has meant that those who wished to study other building types have had to do so outside what was defined as architecture. Factory buildings were studied as industrial archaeology and as an aspect of labour and industrial history; railway stations as part of engineering and transport history; and steel-framed buildings such as skyscrapers, or iron and glass buildings such as the Crystal Palace, as construction history. Grouping buildings according to their use, such as castles, palaces, factories or railway stations, is another way of breaking the subject down, as is grouping them according to the methods or materials of construction.

THE ROLE OF THE ARCHITECT

Most of us would agree that the term 'architecture' includes the great medieval cathedrals that were built in western Europe, but were they designed by architects? From the evidence available some argue that these cathedrals were designed by the monks as builders and as patrons. Others stress the role of the master masons and emphasise the mechanics of construction, particularly of large and complicated churches, so that the architect is seen in effect as a practising engineer. Another interpretation is to see the creation of cathedrals as the achievement of collectives of craftsmen contributing their individual skills and working cooperatively. There is still controversy about even the existence of architects in the Middle Ages. Although historians have different interpretations of the evidence as to who built these cathedrals, we still appreciate them as architecture, whether or not an architect was involved. We perceive these magnificent buildings as art and recognise the resources that enabled them to be built and the purpose that they served.

The word architect derives from the Greek work for 'builder' (*archi* meaning 'chief' and *tecton* meaning 'builder') and until quite recently, within the last 150 years, the role of the architect included surveying and building, as well as military and civil engineering. Vitruvius, the Roman architect active in the first century BC, included a whole range of examples of civil and military engineering in his influential ten-volume book, *De Architecture*. Similarly the important renaissance architect Palladio included designs for civil engineering as well as for churches, palaces, farms and villas in his *Quattro Libri dell' Architectura*. It was only with the increase of specialisation within the building industry that the architect ceased being a tradesman and achieved professional status, a process that in the west had its roots in the eighteenth century. In China there are records of named architects dating from the tenth century and the earliest surviving manual by Li Chieh, *The Treatise on Architectural Methods*, was published in 1103. Li Chieh was in the Directorate of Buildings and Construction c.1092 and was a distinguished practising builder as well as a writer.

In France the separation of civil and military engineering as disciplines distinct from architecture dates from 1747 when a school of civil engineering was set up in Paris, organised by Rudolphe Perronet. In Britain the Society of Civil Engineers was set up in 1771, the Surveyors' Club in 1792 and the Institution of Mechanical Engineers in 1847. Howard M. Colvin's *A Biographical Dictionary of British Architects 1600-1840* lists some 1,500 architects. Of these only about forty were involved in building the factories that we associate with the early stages of the industrial revolution. It was the engineers who designed the machinery and it was mainly they who designed the structures to house them. The reasons for these changes relate not only to the changing practice of building which was occurring in the mid-eighteenth century, but also to the increasing division of labour, the changes taking place in building technology and the development of new types of building. In the process of these changes what we understand by the term 'architect' changed its meaning.

The development of the architectural profession in Britain is marked by the foundation of the Institute of British Architects launched by T.L. Donaldson in 1834, and the setting up of the first chairs of architecture in the universities. Donaldson held the first chair of architecture when it was set up at University College, London, in 1841. The Royal Institute of British Architects (RIBA), as it subsequently became, was designed to prevent 'the great contaminating trade element' such as builders, carpenters, cabinet makers, ironmongers, painters and undertakers from undermining the professional status of architects. The aim of Donaldson, the Institute's first secretary, was 'To uphold in ourselves the character of Architects as men of taste, men of science and men of honour'. The use of the term 'men' is significant, for women were not admitted to the architectural profession until the late nineteenth century, when Ethel Mary Charles became the first woman member of the RIBA in 1898. Women have nevertheless practised architecture throughout history although their contribution has been largely unrecognised. In peasant communities they were often both architect and builder and we can still see examples of this in some developing countries today.

HEROIC ARCHITECTS AND HEROIC ARCHITECTURE

The professionalisation of architecture brought with it an increased emphasis on the importance of the individual architect, an emphasis that continues today. It is in the studio that architectural students learn how to shape the spaces we live in and how to form our environment, and it is in the studio that the practice of architecture as a solitary creative activity is inculcated. Great architects are seen as heroes who create sculptural objects alone, often in the face of incomprehension and opposition. This focus on architects as heroes also entails the disparagement of those who do not understand them, namely the clients, town planners and the public. Teamwork and collaboration between architects and other disciplines, or between architect and client, are rarely emphasised and this attitude is reinforced by a whole range of professional architectural publications. The results of this privileging tendency is to emphasise originality and novelty, and this is also evident in current practice and in histories of architecture. It creates a predominantly aesthetic emphasis, with much less stress on the teams of people involved in the production of buildings, or appreciating the needs of prospective users.

Architecture is not an isolated activity: today it can only be carried out within a network of other political, social and economic institutions such as local authority planning, housing and environmental health departments, financial institutions such as banks and insurance companies and the changing legislation which may at one time promote development and at another seek to control it. It is necessary to understand these institutions in order to understand the factors which affect the built environment. If architecture is seen solely as the province of architects, whether heroic or not, then it is likely that people may not only misunderstand their role in creating the built environment, but also become suspicious of their activities and blame them if they do not like the results.

The ideology of individualism and art that surrounds architecture is often in sharp contrast to the realities of practice, in which architects work as part of a team. From the seventeenth century onwards in Britain those who designed buildings were either wealthy amateurs or highly skilled building craftspeople such as masons or carpenters. By 1788 John Soane was able to describe the architect's work as not only designing, but making estimates, directing works, controlling costs, acting as agent between the patron and builders and even promoting speculative development. In the nineteenth century the work of many architectural practices consisted more of surveying, providing bills of quantities, arranging leases and assessing rents than designing.

With the demise in the nineteenth century of the building trades and the rise of the general building contractor, such as Cubitts in London, architects took on the important role of supervising works on site and communicating to builders the full details of the building work required. These architects could be self-employed, or salaried and working for large architectural practices, local authorities or commercial and industrial companies. Philip Hardwick was a salaried architect working for the London and Birmingham Railway in the late 1830s. He was required to design and provide specifications for all new buildings, advertise for tenders, enter into contracts, measure buildings and superintend building work, examine and certify building accounts, direct and superintend all repairs and alterations to company buildings, collect rents and prepare plans of company property and any additional property that might be acquired, value all property being purchased or sold, attend meetings of committees and report on all business.

In the late twentieth century there are again great variations in the architect's role. In some 'design and build' projects the work of the architect has declined to that of supplying outline drawings, the final detail being developed by the builder during construction. Some architects may be little more than technicians or draughts people, while at the other end of the scale they may act as entrepreneurs and developers, particularly in the United States. A developer raises capital, acquires and assembles the site, hires a development team and when the project is complete sells the site, often at a considerable profit. In contrast to the prevailing ideology of professionalism, architects in this role are more like business managers.

The nature of patronage and the relationship of architects to users is also important in understanding the role of the architect. Until the eighteenth century patrons had a strong involvement in the design of buildings, which were usually to be used by them. By the nineteenth century the clients of civic and commercial buildings might be committees of people with little knowledge of architecture. The buildings that they commissioned ranged from town halls, hospitals and prisons to office buildings, warehouses and factories. With the rise of developers and the involvement of pensions funds and investment trusts in financing building development, many buildings are constructed speculatively.

In such projects those who commission the building may be far removed from the users and this raises particular problems for the architect who also has little or no contact with the users. Underlying all projects is the need for finance, and in many cases this will determine whether or not a scheme goes ahead. It can be quite difficult unravelling the contributions of all the individuals and organisations involved in the production of buildings, but it is important in order to understand the final form of the building and the processes involved. The notion of the architect as hero and supreme artist is somewhat diminished when we consider the role of the architect in the context of these realities.

The idea of the heroic architect relates partly to the romantic view of architects as artists, partly to the ideology of individualism and partly to the perception that promoting individual architects is good for business. Indeed several American architects, including Michael Graves and Robert Venturi, have built up reputations as signature architects, who are brought in after an important building has been designed inside and out, to add their recognisable signature to the façade.

The heroic approach to architecture reinforces the idea that it is the individual architect who makes history and consequently that the history of architecture is the history of great architects and great buildings. Memoirs, monographs, biographies, exhibitions and films all reinforce this tendency. New research on an important but neglected building, or architect, remains unpublished because commercial publishers like safe, recognised subjects and do not want to risk investing in a topic hitherto unknown. The strength of this approach lies in its clearly defined subject, the individual architect; but a weakness could lie in the tendency to isolate the architect and neglect the context within which the individual worked, the influences that were significant, the clients and patrons, the needs of the prospective users and the development of the architectural language that they used. While it is important to recognise that some architects are more important and more influential than others, it is also important to recognise that individuals are products of their society and it is only by fully exploring that context that we can begin to understand their work. There are many exemplary studies of individual architects which place their subject fully within their contexts.

The counterpart to the heroic architect is the heroic building, presented as an individual star. If a sufficient number of publications focus on the same buildings the process becomes self-reinforcing and it becomes very difficult to alter. With sufficient exposure to this approach there is a danger that we almost cease to see the building concerned. The Eiffel Tower is so closely linked in our minds with Paris that we cease to think about it as a building constructed for a particular purpose and greeted with outrage initially. The Sydney Opera House, Australia, which was completed by Ove Arup in 1972, six years after its architect Jorn Utzon left the project, has been voted one of the wonders of the twentieth century by readers of the London *Times Saturday Review*, and it remains one of Australia's most potent symbols. Tower Bridge in London and the Taj Mahal in Agra, Central India, are other examples of cultural monuments isolated from the context in which they developed. We tend to view them uncritically and yet accept the strength of their symbolism.

The idea of heroic or notable buildings is in one sense obvious, for some buildings do stand out more than others. Lewis Mumford in his important book *The City in History* argued that cities always reflect the societies that built them. The buildings that dominated a medieval city, the church and the castle, reflected the power structure of society at that time. The major buildings in renaissance and baroque cities similarly reflected the power of church, state and royalty. Heroic architecture visually reinforces the power structure in any period, today and yesterday. Concentrating on heroic buildings, or applying the star system to architecture leads to a very partial view of our subject, comparable to studying history only in terms of kings and queens.

One of the most extensive surveys of notable buildings ever undertaken is the forty-six-volume *Buildings of England* series undertaken by Nikolaus Pevsner, which took forty-five years to complete. Pevsner and his assistants did not restrict themselves only to such obviously notable buildings as churches and palaces: nevertheless they had to evolve criteria to enable them to decide which buildings to include and which to omit. Bridget Cherry and her team are now resurveying British buildings for revised editions and they are having to make similar decisions about what to include.

The key buildings that form what we call heroic architecture are only a small part of our built environment, as are the works of heroic architects. Most of the urban environment has not been designed by heroic architects and clearly a view of architecture which ignores where the vast majority of people live and where they work and play is extraordinarily limited. If we want to try to understand architecture and the built environment generally, then we need to begin to determine what is significant and what is not. For most of us where we live is very important, yet unless we live in a palace, or in a house designed by a major architect, the heroic approach would not see this as a suitable topic.

It is essential to consider the full range of buildings in any society and indeed to examine also those societies which at certain periods produced little architecture. In ancient Sparta there was little if any monumental architecture and the city had no city wall; yet Andrew Ballantyne has argued that this is a most telling expression of the formidable military might of the Spartans who required no protective architecture and lacked 'vanity and indulgence'. He has contrasted this with the 'conspicuous consumption' of the contemporary ancient Athenians whose city is well known for its vast numbers of magnificent buildings for every civic function. The lacunae and the everyday offer as much insight into architecture as the grand monuments and they are essential to enable us to make informed judgements about a society's priorities and achievements.

Studying any type of building is revealing whether or not it was designed by an architect. Every building had to be paid for, whether by a patron, the builder or a commercial organisation. All buildings stand in a particular relationship to their site and to neighbouring buildings. Their form relates to their use and to the materials of which they are constructed. Their success as buildings relates to their form, construction, materials and physical context, and to how well they accommodate the functions required by those using them. They proclaim symbolic and metaphorical messages to which we respond on a variety of levels. The scope of the subject is enormous and buildings do not need to be aesthetically pleasing, intellectually stimulating or architect-designed to warrant further study.

THE PROBLEM OF TASTE

Often we are drawn into studying architecture because we have strong feelings about our environment and about what we like and dislike. Among the most popular contemporary buildings today in western Europe in terms of the numbers of people visiting them are the Pompidou Centre in Paris, Lloyds Insurance, London and the Staatsgalerie Extension in Stuttgart. When local citizens were given the opportunity to vote on rival plans for Richmond Riverside, west of London, Quinlan Terry's classical design (1988) was three times more popular than the modernist alternative. The demonstrated popularity of these buildings is important in that it underlies the growing public interest in architecture, but taste can prove fickle. When the National Theatre opened in London in 1975, it was thought by critics to be possibly the greatest modern building in Britain. Some fifteen years later Prince Charles thought it was 'a clever way of building a nuclear power station in the middle of London without anyone objecting'.

We all have our preferences and prejudices in architecture as in anything else and our experiences determine our attitude. All of us are different, but it is important not to draw historical conclusions from personal likes and dislikes. Because we do not like a particular building style, it does not mean that that style was not historically important, or that the architects involved in producing such work were totally mistaken in their aims. This is particularly important now, for many architectural critics, writers and historians are so against any form of modernism that to try to understand such buildings in an objective way becomes very difficult. If we are to try to understand the National Theatre as a building it is no use averting our eyes and saying it is horrible. We would have to look at the ideas and ideals which inspired Lasdun at the time the building was being designed. We would have to look at the brief of the client, at the funding, at the way crucial decisions were taken at various times during the long-drawn-out process of the building's construction. We would have to look at the way the building performs, that is to say how theatregoers, actors and other staff respond to it. We would also have to question the now almost pathological hatred of concrete in order to distance ourselves from today's prejudices and try to reach an understanding of the building that is as objective as possible.

It is true that interpretations do change and we look at the past quite differently according to our present concerns and outlook. Different facts from the past become significant and affect our interpretations, and these in turn affect how we see and understand the present. We need to try to be as objective as possible, while recognising that our ability to be so is affected by our present assumptions and the limits of our historical period and place. Later historians may well see our interpretations quite differently and what we find difficult to understand, or impossible to see as pleasing, may prove a delight to later generations.

ARCHITECTURAL TERMINOLOGY

If we are to understand buildings and communicate our understanding to others we need to be able to identify particular details and give them their correct name. Learning architectural terminology is like learning a new language and unfortunately there are no shortcuts. There are a number of architectural dictionaries, including illustrated ones which are particularly useful for acquiring the vocabulary necessary to discuss buildings in detail. Owning your own copy is essential in order to be able to look terms up as you come across them. Acquiring an architectural vocabulary not only enables us to read about and discuss the details of buildings, it is also an essential part of acquiring the confidence to do so. One of the most direct and enjoyable ways of building up this new language is to visit buildings with a good guide book. This will direct your attention to the most significant features to look at and, with the correct terminology, will enable you to identify them. Many of us in Britain who developed a passion for architecture acquired our architectural vocabulary largely through travelling around the country with the appropriate Pevsner *Buildings of England* in our hands.

Another aspect of architectural terminology concerns the way in which architecture is discussed in books, or by architects and architectural critics. When we hear people discussing buildings that have movement, that have masculine or feminine characteristics, buildings that are sick and buildings that speak, we may wonder if we do indeed speak the same language. Buildings that have movement may mean that they are suffering from subsidence, or are crumbling away, but when architects and architectural writers talk about a building having movement, they could mean something quite different. If we compare a baroque exterior with a Georgian one, we see that the latter has a facade that is flat. The door and windows are set into the wall so that they are almost level with the wall plane.

In other words, they do not break the overall flatness of the façade and this enables one's eye to run over it without interruption. The baroque church, with its columns and pilasters, ornate doorway and bold mouldings over the windows, has a façade that is elaborately modelled. The windows and doors are deeply recessed, the detailing around them is very sculptural and projects from the wall plane, casting shadows which vary according to the time of day and time of year. There are also columns and pilasters which project from the wall plane. The Georgian terrace with its symmetrical flat façade looks static and in repose, in comparison to the façade of the baroque church, whose varied forms and undulations give it movement.

The implication behind the application of terms such as 'masculine' and 'feminine' to buildings is that we can equate particular forms with a particular gender. Thus the straight lines and qualities of massiveness that we might see in a fortified castle connote masculinity, whereas curves such as those we associate with the style of art nouveau connote femininity. Some see masculine and feminine attributes in a variety of architectural features: towers are phallic and masculine; domes represent breasts and are feminine. The use of this sort of terminology and this type of interpretation does not add very much to our understanding of architecture. Moreover, it promotes a stereotyped view of what constitutes masculinity and femininity, and is therefore something of which to be very aware.

A 'sick building' is shorthand for sick building syndrome (SBS), meaning that users become sick by being in a particular building. The indoor environment of such buildings causes malaise to people while they are in them and this ceases when they leave. Allergies, asthma, headaches and lethargy are the symptoms of SBS and they can result from a number of causes. Ventilation systems, the chemicals used in the building fabric, in the furnishings or in the equipment, dust, mould and fumes may all play a part and airconditioned office buildings seem particularly prone.

'Buildings that speak' is another phrase that is often used about architecture today. Some architectural writers argue that there is a building syntax with words, phrases and grammar and they imply that buildings speak a language comparable to that which we speak. Language is about communication and expression and buildings do indeed embody ideas which they express and communicate by a variety of means.

MEANING AND METAPHOR

We experience buildings in terms of their form, their structure, their aesthetics and how we and others use them. This constitutes the reality of our physical experience, but buildings not only have an existence in reality, they also have a metaphorical existence. They express meaning and give certain messages, just as the way we dress or furnish our homes gives people certain messages about us. The dramatic roof lines of Sydney Opera House have been described variously as looking like sea-shells and sails. Its physical form, in other words, also has a symbolic message which refers to the building's maritime position and to the sailing boats in Sydney Harbour. When Adolf Loos entered the competition for a building to house the offices of the *Chicago Tribune* newspaper, his design took the form of a column, a pun on the idea of a newspaper column.

Buildings are central to our need for shelter and security, and they symbolise aspects of these needs in their form. A house not only provides shelter and warmth, it also symbolises home on a very deep level. A young English child drawing a house will characterise it very simply, with a pitched roof and maybe a door and windows. In the north European climate the pitched roof evolved because this was the form that shed rain and snow most effectively. This form came to symbolise shelter, just as the chimney came to symbolise the existence of warmth. Together their message is home. Many architects have exploited this symbolism in their work, among them the American architect Frank Lloyd Wright. In his prairie houses of the early twentieth century, the dominant features were the centrally placed hearth and chimney, symbolising the heart of the home and the dramatic roofs with large overhanging eaves symbolising shelter.

Buildings have intrinsic meanings which result from their spatial and visible forms and extrinsic meanings which have evolved out of tradition and social use. A doorway is a means of gaining access to a building: its significance and function can be recognised from its scale and type. Thus the meaning of a door is intrinsic to it. In the housing of certain periods and places we can recognise which rooms are the most socially significant by the size of their windows. In the Georgian terrace the windows at the first-floor level are larger than the rest and indicate the importance of the reception rooms on this floor. The exterior indicates how the interior of the building functions and this intrinsic meaning becomes part of the architectural language of the period.

The ways in which the form of particular buildings relates to their function is part of their extrinsic meaning. Because north European houses traditionally had pitched roofs, this form has come to mean home and if a flat roof is introduced it will appear alien and may be disliked because of its lack of meaning and semantic content. This dislike may be rationalised in practical terms, with the argument that such roofs are inappropriate and not weatherproof, but this may not be the real reason for the dislike.

Architecture provides the environment for our lives. Buildings are not just places of physical shelter, but places in which our social rituals are enacted. During the nineteenth century a range of new building types evolved to house the new developments of that prodigiously inventive century. Banks, railway stations, theatres, law courts, shops, town halls, apartment blocks and offices developed forms that were not rigidly fixed, but were nevertheless recognisable. You did not enter a theatre expecting to see the bank manager, nor did you confuse the town hall with the railway station. The overall form of these buildings communicated their purpose. Over a period of time the buildings which housed social, legal, religious and other rituals evolved into forms that we subsequently have come to recognise and associate with those buildings' function.

This is a two-way process, the building provides the physical environment and setting for a particular social ritual such as travelling by train or going to the theatre, as well as the symbolic setting. The meaning of buildings evolves and becomes established by experience and we in turn read our experience into buildings. Buildings evoke an empathetic reaction in us through these projected experiences, and the strength of these reactions is determined by our culture, our beliefs and our expectations. They tell stories, for their form and spatial organisation give us hints about how they should be used. Their physical layout encourages some uses and inhibits others; we do not go backstage in a theatre unless especially invited. Inside a law court the precise location of those involved in the legal process is an integral part of the design and an essential part of ensuring that the law is upheld. If a building gives us an incorrect message about its role and function then we are liable to become confused or irritated.

The postmodern architecture of today is essentially about communication. Postmodernism was initially a reaction against the high-rise apartment blocks, the commercial developments and the use of concrete that is associated with modernism in the 1960s. Such architecture alienated people, said the postmodernists, because it did not communicate; so postmodernism set out to communicate. This it does by borrowing styles from previous periods, or by 'quoting' details from adjacent buildings and the surrounding environment. New housing developments may be neo-Georgian, or they may incorporate elements such as gables, dormers and tile hanging which are derived from the traditional architecture of the preindustrial era. Postmodern commercial buildings feature classical, gothic and many other styles on their façades as a means of communicating and as a way of attracting prestigious clients. These elements are restricted to the exterior of the building only and are in effect masks which have little or nothing to do with what goes on inside.

One of the aims of modernism in the 1920s and 1930s was to try to evolve a new architecture fitted to the twentieth century, based on new materials, new techniques of construction and a rethinking of the uses of buildings. It tried to liberate architecture from an obsession with style and its aims were universal. Modernism became an international force, but in so doing modernist buildings tended not to respond to particular cultures or to particular environments. By contrast postmodernism is trying to reassert a sense of local identity, as one example illustrates. Richmond Riverside is an office development by Quinlan Terry on the river Thames, that is widely liked by the local residents of Richmond. They like its scale, which is in harmony with the adjacent townscape, the variety of the materials used and the traditional feel to the whole complex.

This has been achieved by using a classical vocabulary which is claimed by the architect to constitute 'real architecture'. Real architecture in this particular instance means solid brick walls and slate roofs, or roofs hidden behind parapets and classical elements which according to the architect are eternal and universal, and therefore appropriate to all periods. The complex looks like a series of eighteenth-century town houses, but Terry has applied these recognisable classical models to new buildings and a new purpose: commercial offices. He did not evolve a new classical language out of the past, as happened in the time of the renaissance, and many critics think that the ultimate effect of his design is one of pastiche, a stage set which clashes discordantly with the clearly visible open-plan offices within. Others, including many Richmond residents, argue that Richmond Riverside is a series of 'real' neo-Georgian buildings and since Richmond is a largely eighteenth-century town, Terry's design is true to its context and appropriate, although it would not be appropriate for the modern commercial centre of New York or Paris.

ARCHITECTURE TODAY

The whole subject of architecture is acquiring a thorough overhaul as a result of current concerns for today and for the future. Its content and the approaches to it are being widened. Today we accept that it is just as valid to examine an industrial building such as a gasholder as it is to examine castles, cathedrals and dwellings of all types. Stylistic analysis and the search for the principles of beauty are still with us and we all want to improve our environments, but we no longer seek to do this in isolation or just in terms of individual buildings, but in terms of the built environment as a whole. Greater awareness of what architecture is about is vital if we are to develop an environment that means something to us all. We need to understand how we have arrived at today and that means that we need to see today within the context and perspective of the past.

Understanding history helps us to understand how we have arrived at today, it empowers us to work for a better future and prevents us from passively accepting what we find unacceptable, whether as the users of architecture, as architects or as architectural critics. Architecture affects everyone and so we all need to take responsibility for it, but we can only do so when we understand more about it. Architecture is something to be enjoyed and shared. If it is shared more widely because more people understand it, take it seriously and are not frightened by it, then the chances are that the urban environment will improve and architects will no longer be seen as responsible for all that we dislike but as part of a team which enables us to achieve our ideals.

ARCHITECTURAL HISTORY

Architectural history is like other histories in that it is concerned with understanding and finding explanations for the past. Where it differs is in the nature of the evidence available and in the techniques that have been developed to evaluate that evidence. In its initial stages any historical study involves collecting facts, but facts by themselves tell us nothing. In order to make any sense of those facts they must be selected, ordered, evaluated, interpreted and placed in context. E.H. Carr in *What is History?* explains this very clearly. History begins today, but one of the main difficulties about studying the recent past is the sheer volume of information available and the problem of determining what is significant and what is not.

Architectural history is different from antiquarianism, nostalgia and the heritage industry. Antiquarians love ancient objects and buildings, and facts about them, because they are ancient, but they may not necessarily be interested in the reasons that lie behind their development. Nostalgia and the heritage industry are about escaping into the past in order to enter a different world, a world that may be of beauty and interest, but one which could have little to do with the realities of that past. Now we are not suggesting that it is wrong to want to have a heritage experience, or to visit a beautiful historic house, rather that we should be aware that we may be seeing only a partial or distorted picture of the past.

History is about trying to understand the past in a critical way, its negative as well as its positive features. It is a dynamic process, not a static one, and the history unfolding before our eyes, the present, is part of that process and informs our understanding of the past. History is not a jigsaw puzzle which can be completed and put away, and the accuracy of any historical interpretation is always open to reinterprelation. There will never come a time when we can claim we know all there is to know about, say, medieval architecture. That is not the purpose of the discipline. We believe that the purpose of studying architecture and its history is not only to try to understand the past, but also to try to understand how the past and the present engage. Studying architectural history, as with any historical study, relates to our need to understand the present.

It is based on the belief that this understanding is impossible without a knowledge of the past, for it is only by studying the past that we can hope to understand how we have arrived at today, and something of the complex choices and decisions that were involved. The study of history, whether contemporary history or the distant past, encourages us to think critically about both today and yesterday. It is only by understanding the past that we can understand the present that has grown out of it and it is only by understanding how past and present interact that we can hope to build a better future. Without that perspective we become prisoners of the present, for our understanding will be limited, so we will be unable to foresee alternatives, or recognise the possibilities of choice.

Architectural history is not isolated in the past: it takes on an active role in improving our contemporary and future architecture, town planning and urban environment. Indeed some would argue that a passionate interest in architectural history can only come from an intense commitment to current architectural practice and that without a commitment to attaining the highest ideals in architecture and the urban environment today, one's ability to study the past is limited. If architecture embraces the whole of the built environment, as we think it does, then its history concerns us all. Because studying history encourages us to think critically, one of the objections voiced against the study of contemporary history in any area, including architectural history, is that it could be controversial or even dangerous. If people start to think critically about the recent past, they will then be in a more informed position to do something positive and this could be construed as dangerous.

Historians use evidence from the past in order to reconstruct what happened and why it happened. In architectural history this evidence may take the form of the buildings themselves or their remains, and documents such as plans, drawings, descriptions, diaries or bills. Our picture of any period of history is derived from a multitude of sources, such as the paintings, literature, buildings and other artefacts that have survived. The problem of survival lies at the root of many of the historian's problems, for what has survived may not be more significant than what has not survived. The Egyptian pyramids have survived thousands of years, but historical significance is not just a question of durability. These buildings were part of a rich and diverse culture. They are historical facts, but facts by themselves, even such massive facts as the pyramids, are just the first stage in any historical study, and until they have been evaluated, placed in context and interpreted they tell us little. Different historians may place different values on the same facts and the discovery of new evidence may modify or change existing theories and interpretations.

HISTORIOGRAPHY

Architectural history, like any other branch of history, is not a static subject; interpretations often change quite radically, for we see things in a new light from new evidence and from the changing perspectives of the day. Historiography is the study of the ways in which historical interpretations have changed over a period. The changing tastes of one period may lead to once great architecture being completely reinterpreted. In the 1950s and 1960s Victorian architecture was despised, particularly by modernists who could see nothing to commend it. Yet today we take great delight in the richness and complexity of Victorian architecture and seek to preserve it wherever possible; and now modernism is anathema to many people. It is not just a question of changing tastes. New issues encourage us to ask different questions, questions that had hardly been thought of a century ago, or if they were, it was only by a very few. Today our concern for the environment makes us question the use of energy both in the production and in the maintenance and use of buildings. Feminist issues lead us to question the role of women in the built environment and the ways in which design assumptions have reflected gender. Recognition of these issues may encourage us to look at different strategies for design and building today.

Asking different questions about the past can lead to changes of emphasis and new interpretations. When Tim Mowl was researching Bath for his book *John Wood: Architect of Obsession*, he found that John Wood (the elder) had surveyed Stonehenge and the moon temple at Stanton Drew. The diameter of the Circus at Bath is 318 feet, the same as that of Stonehenge and this was, so Wood argued, equal to 60 Jewish cubits, that is to say the dimensions of the second temple at Jerusalem. Bath was the first Masonic city of England and John Wood was a typical member of the Society of Freemasons. He was convinced that Bath had been the principal Druid centre of Britain and he based his design of the Circus not on the Roman Colosseum, as previous writers had assumed, which in any case was elliptical, but on the most important remaining Druidic edifice in the west of England, Stonehenge. By looking at the historical evidence and asking questions of that evidence, Tim Mowl arrived at a new interpretation of one of the most important architectural features of Bath, yet he was advised by other well-established figures in this field not to mention Wood's emphasis on Druids as his book might then not be treated seriously.

As different facts become significant they affect our interpretation of both past and present, for as we appreciate the past differently, so this affects our understanding of the present. In other words the process is dialectical. Our perceptions of both past and present are determined by the period we are living in and our ability to understand our period and situation. Objectivity is relative to the period in which we live and to the sort of people we are. Some people have a broader understanding than others and some are better able to question the assumptions of their period than others, but this does not mean that we should not try to be as objective as possible.

THE DEVELOPMENT OF ARCHITECTURAL HISTORY

Architectural history is concerned with understanding all types of building and studying the built environment in its historic context. The subject is in a sense as old as architecture itself, but in another sense it is a comparatively new one. The first Society of Architectural Historians was founded in the United States as recently as 1940. Because the separation of architectural history as a discipline distinct from that of architecture is comparatively recent, architectural histories have in the past tended to be written mainly by architects. Moreover, from the period of ancient Greece and Rome until the sixteenth century, architectural critics wrote about contemporary architecture. It was not until the sixteenth century that this changed. When the renaissance architect and painter Vasari wrote about the architecture of the past, it was in relation to the architecture of his day and as a justification of its superiority.

The idea that architecture progresses and that the buildings of one period are better than their predecessors is a theme that runs through much of the writings on architecture from the sixteenth century onwards and is still evident today. The stance taken by architects in their historical writings tended to be a polemical one, in which they used the past in order to justify and validate the present. In many periods architects have been strongly influenced by the architecture of the past. That influence may take the form of reacting against the past in order to establish a new and 'better' architecture, or finding inspiration from the architecture of the past. The surviving remains of ancient Roman buildings in Italy provided a positive inspiration to the architects of the early renaissance there. By contrast, to A.W.N. Pugin, intent on re-establishing gothic architecture in Britain at the beginning of the nineteenth century, classical architecture was pagan, barbaric and particularly inappropriate for Christian churches. Pugin's negative attitude towards classical architecture was an important part of his argument for the merits of the gothic, which led to the development of the gothic revival. In each of these examples the new contemporary architecture was seen as an improvement on what had preceded it.

The eighteenth century was an important period for the development of architectural history. Instead of simply seeing contemporary architecture as the latest or best expression of a tradition of architecture inherited from the past, some architects and intellectuals began to appreciate past periods and styles of architecture as discrete phases with distinct merits. They began systematically to explore earlier architecture in order to identify the principles and criteria by which to measure great architecture. In doing so they embarked on the road to understanding architecture rather than simply using it to support current practice. Johann Joachim Winckelmann is sometimes called the father of modern art and architectural history. His *History of the Arts of Antiquity* was published in Dresden in 1767, but it was not the first work of its kind. J.B. Fischer von Erlach, one of the leading baroque architects in Austria and designer of the Karlskirche in Vienna, published an earlier history, *The Design of Historic Architecture*, in Vienna in 1721. This was the first book to include Egyptian, Chinese and Islamic buildings and could indeed claim to be the first comparative history of world architecture.

In France the earliest group of architectural historians was to be found in the circle connected with the Académie Royale d'Architecture, which was founded in 1671. In 1687 J.F. Félibien, who was secretary of the Académie, published *The History of the Life and Works of the Most Celebrated Architects*. Unlike Vasari, this provided an account of past architecture which did not interpret it as a prelude to the superior architecture of the present day.

The eighteenth-century enlightenment encouraged the development of architectural history. During this period many intellectuals questioned the rational basis of society and everything that had been taken for granted, religion, the monarchy, aesthetics, and history. It was this questioning which ultimately gave birth to the French revolution and to the industrial revolution. The enlightenment examined the past in order to discover why the world was as it was and what the alternatives were. Excavations of Pompeii and Herculaneum began to reveal something of the past, as did visits to ancient classical sites and to Egypt. The newly developing subject of architectural history tended to be encyclopaedic in scope and to concentrate on form, styles and heroic building types such as palaces, castles, churches and temples. In the United States the development of architectural history in the nineteenth and twentieth centuries was strongly influenced by both Germany and France. Hundreds of American students studied architecture in Paris at the Ecole des Beaux-Arts and associated studios, and took that influence home with them. The close ties between American and German scholarship in the area of architectural history persisted during the major part of both centuries.

SCOPE

In any new and developing subject the first problem is to identify and catalogue the material that forms the core of the subject. Early architectural histories sought to identify and differentiate between the architecture of different periods and different geographical areas primarily through an analysis of architectural form and style. One book based on this approach is still in print after almost a century and is familiar to generations of architectural students as 'Bannister Fletcher'. *A History of Architecture for the Student, Craftsman and Amateur, being a Comparative View of the Historical Styles from the Earliest Period* was first published in 1896. With the fifth edition in 1905 it changed its title to *A History of Architecture on the Comparative Method;* and the nineteenth edition was published in 1987. The method adopted by the father and son team was to apply the techniques of comparative anatomy and comparative biology to architecture.

Comparing and contrasting buildings in order to reveal similarities and differences is still a technique that is applied today by both critics and historians and it can be a useful one if the buildings being compared have something in common. For example it can be revealing to compare a medieval church with a Victorian gothic revival one, or a Roman arena with a modern football stadium, since each pair is concerned with similar functions. There would, however, be little point in comparing buildings that had nothing in common, such as a Roman arena with a Victorian church.

The technique has also been used very successfully for didactic purposes. A.W.N. Pugin's *Contrasts* was a polemical blast against what he saw as the horrors of the architecture and urban environment of the time. In his book Pugin juxtaposed illustrations contrasting the negative qualities of contemporary cities and their architecture with the positive qualities of the medieval equivalent. In so doing he celebrated the virtues of gothic architecture and at the same time drew attention to the 'barbarism' of the classical architecture of the day. The walled medieval town with church spires punctuating the skyline is surrounded by open countryside. In the nineteenth-century town, factories and factory chimneys vie with the spires. The open fields now feature a lunatic asylum, a gas works and a radially planned prison, and the medieval gothic church has been replaced by a classical one.

Architectural history developed in Europe and although Fischer von Erlach included non-European architecture in his early history of the subject the main focus of study has been and continues to be on European architecture. Indeed until 1959 Bannister Fletcher omitted any reference to African architecture. Furthermore if the architecture of continents other than Europe or north America was discussed, it tended to be from a Eurocentric point of view and vernacular architecture was regarded as primitive, unchanging and therefore non-historical. To those sharing this overwhelming European focus it was impossible to believe that a major African building such as the thirteenth-century Great Zimbabwe ruins could have been built by the local people; it was argued that they must have been built by early Arab or European traders and explorers.

APPROACHES

Since the history of architecture spans a chronology of thousands of years, embraces the whole world and all types of building, it is not surprising to find that a wide variety of approaches to it have developed. Some see the subject in terms of three main approaches: practical, historical and aesthetic. The practical aim seeks to establish what was built, when it was built and by whom, so it would include the architect, the patron and system of patronage. The historical aim seeks to establish why a building was built and its relationship to the social, economic, political, cultural and religious environment. The aesthetic aim seeks to account for visual and stylistic differences and to explain how styles change and why they do so. Older histories of architecture tended to focus on the practical and the aesthetic approaches.

We believe that architecture is an all-embracing subject, but many of the approaches that have been developed for studying it have tended to be reductionist in attitude. That is to say there has been a tendency for the subject to be broken up into a myriad specialisms, some with their own society and journal. This was partly the result of the way in which architectural history was identified in the early stages of its development. Today architectural history reflects the impact of feminist, Marxist, structuralist, psychological, semiological and socio-political ideas. It is responding to the linguistic theories of Althusser, Barthes, Saussure and Derrida, just as much as it is to the historical and anthropological models of Foucault and Levi-Strauss, and to the cultural psychoanalyses of post-Freudian critics such as Lacan. Part of its aim is to deconstruct tradition and to question the most familiar and unquestioned ideas. Here we can only introduce the first steps in various approaches to understanding architecture. Every approach has added to the richness of the subject. By including an analysis on periods and styles we might appear to be advocating that particular approach, but this is not so. We have included it because it is one of the most widespread of approaches and our aim is to examine, clarify and deconstruct some of its concepts. Our approach is one which is concerned about both practical and aesthetic needs and this includes both a green and a feminist stance.

EXPLANATIONS OF ARCHITECTURAL HISTORY

The quest for understanding why the architecture of any place or period developed as it did has led to many explanations. These explanations have helped historians to understand the period being studied and they have helped to define organising principles for selecting and differentiating between the wealth of information, but they can also lead to serious problems. Explanations for architectural change generally fall into four main groups: rational, technological and constructional; social and religious; economic, cultural and political; and the spirit of the age. The technical and rational explanation of architecture may seek answers simply in terms of new technological or constructional developments, or it may see the development of architecture in any period as the result of applying logic to technological or practical problems. If we look at the medieval cathedral according to this logic, then the reason why gothic cathedrals evolved their complex forms was in response to the practical problems posed by building high buildings, spanning wide spaces and incorporating increasingly large glass windows. The rational explanation of architecture was an approach largely developed by French architects and theorists such as Laugier and Viollet-le-Duc.

The explanation that architecture expresses the social, moral and philosophical conditions of the period implies that a sufficient knowledge of those conditions should make it possible to forecast what the architecture will be. But in a sense this begs the question, for what is sufficient knowledge? It also implies a simple, direct, relationship between architecture and these conditions, rather than acknowledging that all societies are complex organisms. If there is a moral justification for architecture then it becomes possible to argue that some architecture is moral and truthful and some is not. From A.W.N. Pugin came the idea of architectural morality and truth. In *True Principles of Pointed or Christian Architecture* he analysed gothic buildings and equated architectural truth with religious truth.

He argued that gothic was not a style, but a principle of building and that those principles were as relevant to the 1840s as they were to the medieval period. All buildings reflect the society in which they are built, but the gothic had particular lessons to teach us, said Pugin, which concerned constructional truth and material truth. Constructional truth meant that the construction of a building should be evident: ornament could be used, but it should not obscure the construction and it should be appropriate in form and meaning. Truth to materials meant that all materials should be chosen for their particular qualities and they should not be painted to look like other materials. Pugin's ideas were developed by John Ruskin, William Morris and others and provided one of the inspirations for the arts and crafts movement and for modernism.

The explanation that architecture reflects the material, economic and cultural conditions of the time seeks to set architecture in the broadest sense in its material context, by focusing on buildings, either singly or in groups, and placing them firmly within their economic, social and political context. Then by characterising their function, form, construction, materials and location, this approach attempts to explain how and why they came to be built and the critical responses to them at the time that they were built.

The explanation that sees architecture as reflecting the spirit of the age, or *Zeitgeist*, comes from Hegel and has provided a conceptual framework for understanding the historical development of art and architecture for the major part of this century. Central to the concept of the *Zeitgeist* is the idea of history as a progressive process. The motor underlying the processes of history and giving rise to each period was thought to be an evolving 'spirit', which pervades and gives unity to every area of human endeavour- religion, law, customs, morality, technology, science, art and architecture. Any historian must identify and classify material, and in the process of doing so common ideas and themes will become apparent.

Those who accepted the concept of the *Zeitgeist* suggested that because styles such as neo-classicism in the mid-eighteenth century, modernism in the 1920s or postmodernism today have shown themselves in different areas of the arts such as architecture, painting, furniture, ceramics, dress and literature they are manifestations of the *Zeitgeist*. The similarities in the work of architects, painters, designers and writers were the result of living in the same period. Another interpretation might be that each period and place, with their evolving material and spiritual conditions, give rise to their own unique cultural forms and that although many styles may coexist at any one time, only one major style truly reflects the *Zeitgeist*. The danger of this explanation is that it encourages the search for consistency in order to build a coherent picture. Anything that does not fit into this picture would then tend to be ignored or to be undervalued as it does not show the all-pervading *Zeitgeist* spirit.

In an attempt to establish modernism as the only true style, early twentieth-century historians such as Nikolaus Pevsner and Siegfried Giedion employed the concept of the *Zeitgeist*. Well before modernism had reached the pre-eminence that it achieved after the Second World War, they identified mass production, glass, steel, reinforced concrete, new forms of transport and increasing urbanisation as the main features that distinguished the modern world of the twentieth century from preceding ages. They went on to argue that modernism was the only style which accorded with these features and thus with the spirit of the age. The modernist architects and designers were committed to the use of new materials and technology, and explored forms appropriate to them.

They questioned the function of architecture in order to arrive at novel and socially progressive plans and designs, and they particularly welcomed projects for mass housing, health centres, industrial buildings and town planning. At the time, that is between the wars, modernism was practised by only a small group of avant-garde architects and designers, located mainly in Germany and France. Modernism coexisted in Europe with art deco, classicism, the vernacular revival and national romanticism. These styles were not seen by modernist historians as genuine products of the age but rather as the result of crass commercialism, wayward individualism or as the archaic remnants of styles belonging to previous periods.

The concept of the *Zeitgeist* seems to have informed Dennis Sharp's approach in *A Visual History of Twentieth Century Architecture* (London) which was first published in 1972. From the title we might expect a survey of building in the twentieth century, but this is not the case. The works that Sharp selected were those produced by one stylistic movement only, modernism. Like his predecessors Pevsner and Giedion, Sharp found in modernism a style that he believed was the true and ultimately hegemonic style of the period. Few would find it satisfactory that all the other building styles produced throughout the world in this century have been ignored.

All approaches and explanations of architecture and architectural change have a grain of truth. Buildings reflect moral values and the economic, social and political context of the period in which they are produced. They may, for example, be the product of rationalism or of new technology, but in each building and in each period the balance of influences varies.

BUILDINGS AND ARCHITECTURAL HISTORY

Buildings themselves provide evidence of their history but the problem of disentangling that evidence may prove very complex. Most buildings that have existed for more than a few decades have been altered and the longer a building has been in existence, the more likely it is to have been altered a number of times. If drawings have been made they may provide clues to some of the alterations, but if there are no drawings the evidence is restricted to the fabric of the building itself, including its foundations and drains. Some large building projects such as the great medieval castles and cathedrals were built over many years or centuries. During that time their plan and form changed as resources became available, as technology, materials, need and tastes changed, or as a result of damage by fire or from war. Evidence of these changes can be seen in the construction and a visit to any of the larger cathedrals will almost certainly reveal parts from very different periods: perhaps a Normans-style nave, a decorated-style transept, and a perpendicular-style chancel.

Throughout history people have sought to alter and convert buildings to new uses as the situation demanded. As the methods for importing and exporting goods by sea have changed, so old docks and warehouses have become redundant. Rather than being demolished they have been converted into apartments, museums, shops and restaurants. During our lives our family size changes and if it is not convenient to move house we may accommodate those changes by altering our houses, adding extensions and making rooms in the attic. We may be able to identify some of these changes by examining a building's fabric. We may notice variations in the ornament, changes in the brickwork, windows that have been blocked off or are of a different size, and changes in the roof pitch and form. We may discover, for example, that a church chancel was not just a late addition, but was rebuilt at a later date.

Churches in the twelfth century had steeply pitched, high roofs, but by the fifteenth century the roof pitch had become shallow. If we look at a twelfth-century church with a fifteenth-century chancel, we may see in the stonework of the wall at the east end of the nave, above the chancel, traces of an earlier higher, steeper chancel roof. In a Victorian terraced house, the two living rooms on the ground floor may have been made into one through room by knocking down the wall separating them. If we look where the wall used to be we may see a large beam or RSJ (reinforced steel joist) spanning the opening and resting on the end walls. This was inserted to carry the weight of the upper floors. With the advent of central heating chimneys became redundant and in order to give more internal space, they may have been removed.

Today many churches have become redundant, as congregations have dwindled. Some have been subdivided to cater for smaller congregations, and others have been converted to new uses. If the conversion makes use of the original large space, then something of the quality of the original church may have been retained, but if the whole building is divided up into flats, then the whole significance of the church is lost, except perhaps for its exterior silhouette. The awesome space of the nave, the aisles used for processions, the stained glass windows and the chancel with its sacred altar will all have been destroyed. The tower might provide an eccentric, if somewhat poky, living space, but the bells will no longer broadcast the presence of the church to the neighbourhood.

Inside isolated floriated capitals and angel corbels may end up decorating the walls of individual flats, where they will seem quite out of place. Outside the traces of the new use will inevitably scar the exterior, with new windows for the new floor levels, skylights in the roof for the upper floors and a car park, garden and garages instead of the churchyard. Identifying the alterations and changes will place us in a better position to understand the design of the original buildings, but it might take a great leap of the imagination to appreciate the character of the original spaces and forms that no longer exist. Examining buildings for evidence of alteration and change of use provides the starting point from which to explore the reasons for these changes. These in turn provide the context from which we can begin to understand a building's history.

Many buildings have been completely destroyed, but occasionally one that has been destroyed is reconstructed. Reconstructions provide an interesting problem, for although drawings of the original may be in existence so that the reconstruction is accurate in form and measurement, there may nevertheless be differences between the two. As part of the celebrations for the Barcelona Olympics, 1992, it was decided to reconstruct Mies van der Rohe's original Barcelona Pavilion in its original location on the site of the Barcelona International Exhibition of 1929. No detailed drawings of the original existed and the reconstruction was worked out from photographs and with the help of the architect.

This proved a mixed blessing for Mies saw the reconstruction as an opportunity to improve upon the original. When the reconstruction was built it was so accurate that the location of the pillars fitted exactly with those in the original foundations. There are, however, a number of significant differences between the two. The original building did not have a basement and was subject to flooding; the reconstruction has a basement to house the heating and water. Onyx, travertine, marble and stone from the same quarries as the original were used, but it was not possible to manufacture glass of the exact tint of the original, so clear glass is used in the reconstruction.

ARCHITECTS AND ARCHITECTURAL HISTORY

'The study of architecture without its historical bearings would be truly frightful in its results.' Since the latter part of the nineteenth century the teaching of architectural history in architectural schools in England has been seen as an essential part of the curriculum, but the way in which it has been taught has varied widely. At the beginning of this century W.R. Lethaby at the Central School of Arts and Crafts and the School of Building in Brixton, London, argued against a concern with style and instead presented architectural history as a series of experiments in construction. He looked at the conditions and materials which gave rise to Roman vaulted structures or to gothic cathedrals, and saw architecture as the rational solution to structural problems.

At the English universities a different approach was initiated and Reginald Blomfield was its most strident exponent. Blomfield was an advocate of the system taught at the Ecole des Beaux Arts, Paris. He argued that the masterpieces of the past should be studied in order to understand how they achieved their beauty. He analysed the principles of composition of these masterpieces, in terms of the disposition of planes, masses, form, proportion and treatment of materials, and he thought that from such analyses students could learn to make pleasing forms themselves. Blomfield was concerned with a limited range of building types and he was not interested in how buildings were constructed or why they were built.

After the Second World War the main influence on architectural schools was the approach initiated by Walter Gropius at the Bauhaus, set up in Weimar in 1919. There history was seen as an obstacle inhibiting the development of creativity, so it initially had no place in the curriculum. Principles of design were to evolve from the practical activity of designing and making. However, after three years, architectural history was introduced at the Bauhaus, as a means of verifying the principles that the students discovered. Gropius saw the architecture of specific periods of the past as the product of the unique social and material conditions of that period. From them students could verify what they had discovered about their own period, that is that designing for modern needs and using modern materials would lead to the development of new appropriate forms. Each of these approaches offered a partial view of the architecture of the past and prejudged the architecture of the future. The past was used to confirm a particular view of how to proceed into the future, instead of being explored in as open-minded a way as possible.

Recently there has been a change in how the history of architecture has been seen in relation to the training of architects. The tendency of using a selective study of the past in order to support a particular design approach that occurred in schools influenced by the Beaux Arts system, and in post-Second World War modernist courses, is now no longer seen as valid. Today architectural history is seen as a subject in its own right, but nevertheless attitudes towards it vary. Some see the architecture of the past as a continuum and argue that studies should concentrate on recurring ideas and themes, for similarities of approach can be found between the past and current architectural practice. Others argue the opposite, that history should be interpreted as a process of continual change and that it is important to emphasise the ways in which the past differs from the present. Seeing architectural history as part of a wider social process implies a rigorous historical approach which does not focus primarily on architects and their ideas. Other architectural schools such as those in France emphasise sociology and urbanism in their architectural history.

The role of architectural history in architecture today is evident from the variety of styles that are used in contemporary buildings. Architects, architectural critics, developers and planners have strong and conflicting views on the role of architectural history and on the appropriateness to today of particular styles from the past. In order for architects to respond to the past knowledgeably, they need a good understanding of it and they need to be able to place current architectural ideas within a larger historical framework. To those of us who have lived most of our lives in large cities, with their wealth of architectural history, it may come as something of a surprise to find that there are people in certain rural states in the USA who may never have come across buildings that are more than fifty years old and who may never have seen a large city. Such people have an even greater need for adequate experience of architectural history.

THEORY OF ARCHITECTURE

HISTORIC TREATISES

The earliest written work on the subject of architecture is *De architectura*, by the Roman architect Vitruvius in the early 1st century CE. According to Vitruvius, a good building should satisfy the three principles of *firmitatis utilitatis venustatis*, which translates roughly as:

- Durability - it should stand up robustly and remain in good condition.
- Utility - it should be useful and function well for the people using it.
- Beauty - it should delight people and raise their spirits.

According to Vitruvius, the architect should strive to fulfill each of these three attributes as well as possible. Leone Battista Alberti, who elaborates on the ideas of Vitruvius in his treatise, De Re Aedificatoria, saw beauty primarily as a matter of proportion, although ornament also played a part. For Alberti, the rules of proportion were those that governed the idealised human figure, the Golden Mean. The most important aspect of beauty was therefore an inherent part of an object, rather than something applied superficially; and was based on universal, recognisable truths. The notion of style in the arts was not developed until the 16th century, with the writing of Vasari. The treatises, by the 18th century, had been translated into Italian, French, Spanish and English.

In the early nineteenth century, Augustus Welby Northmore Pugin wrote Contrasts (1836) that, as the titled suggested, contrasted the modern, industrial world, which he disparaged, with an idealized image of neo-medieval world. Gothic architecture, Pugin believed, was the only "true Christian form of architecture."

The 19th century English art critic, John Ruskin, in his *Seven Lamps of Architecture*, published 1849, was much narrower in his view of what constituted architecture. Architecture was the "art which so disposes and adorns the edifices raised by men... that the sight of them" contributes "to his mental health, power, and pleasure". For Ruskin, the aesthetic was of overriding significance. His work goes on to state that a building is not truly a work of architecture unless it is in some way "adorned". For Ruskin, a well-constructed, well-proportioned, functional building needed string courses or rustication, at the very least.

On the difference between the ideals of "architecture" and mere "construction", the renowned 20th C. architect Le Corbusier wrote: "You employ stone, wood, and concrete, and with these materials you build houses and palaces: that is construction. Ingenuity is at work. But suddenly you touch my heart, you do me good. I am happy and I say: This is beautiful. That is Architecture".

MODERN CONCEPTS OF ARCHITECTURE

The great 19th century architect of skyscrapers, Louis Sullivan, promoted an overriding precept to architectural design: "Form follows function". While the notion that structural and aesthetic considerations should be entirely subject to functionality was met with both popularity and skepticism, it had the effect of introducing the concept of "function" in place of Vitruvius "utility". "Function" came to be seen as encompassing all criteria of the use, perception and enjoyment of a building, not only practical but also aesthetic, psychological and cultural.

Nunzia Rondanini stated, "Through its aesthetic dimension architecture goes beyond the functional aspects that it has in common with other human sciences. Through its own particular way of expressing values, architecture can stimulate and influence social life without presuming that, in and of itself, it will promote social development. To restrict the meaning of (architectural) formalism to art for art's sake is not only reactionary; it can also be a purposeless quest for perfection or originality which degrades form into a mere instrumentality".

Among the philosophies that have influenced modern architects and their approach to building design are rationalism, empiricism, structuralism, poststructuralism, and phenomenology.

In the late 20th century a new concept was added to those included in the compass of both structure and function, the consideration of sustainability. To satisfy the modern ethos a building should be constructed in a manner which is environmentally friendly in terms of the production of its materials, its impact upon the natural and built environment of its surrounding area and the demands that it makes upon non-sustainable power sources for heating, cooling, water and waste management and lighting.

ORIGINS AND THE ANCIENT WORLD

Architecture first evolved out of the dynamics between needs (shelter, security, worship, etc.) and means (available building materials and attendant skills). As human cultures developed and knowledge began to be formalized through oral traditions and practices, architecture became a craft. Here there is first a process of trial and error, and later improvisation or replication of a successful trial. What is termed Vernacular architecture continues to be produced in many parts of the world. Indeed, vernacular buildings make up most of the built world that people experience every day.

Early human settlements were mostly rural. Due to a surplus in production the economy began to expand resulting in urbanization thus creating urban areas which grew and evolved very rapidly in some cases, such as that of Catal Huyuk in Anatolia and Mohenjo-daro in Pakistan. In many ancient civilizations, like the Egyptians' and Mesopotamians', architecture and urbanism reflected the constant engagement with the divine and the supernatural, while in other ancient cultures such as Persia architecture and urban planning was used to exemplify the power of the state.

The architecture and urbanism of the Classical civilizations such as the Greek and the Roman evolved from civic ideals rather than religious or empirical ones and new building types emerged. Architectural styles developed. Texts on architecture began to be written in the Classical period. These became canons to be followed in important works, especially religious architecture. Some examples of canons are found in the writings of Vitruvius, the *Kao Gong Ji* of ancient China and Vaastu Shastra of ancient India.

The architecture of different parts of Asia developed along different lines to that of Europe, Buddhist, Hindu and Sikh architecture each having different characteristics. Buddhist architecture, in particular, showed great regional diversity. In many Asian countries a pantheistic religion led to architectural forms that were designed specifically to enhance the natural landscape.

THE MEDIEVAL BUILDER

Islamic architecture began in the 7th century CE, developing from the architectural forms of the ancient Middle East but developing features to suit the religious and social needs of the society. Examples can be found throughout the Middle East, North Africa and Spain, and were to become a significant stylistic influence on European architecture during the Medieval period.

In Europe, in both the Classical and Medieval periods, buildings were not attributed to specific individuals and the names of the architects frequently unknown, despite the vast scale of the many religious buildings extant from this period. During the Medieval period guilds were formed by craftsmen to organise their trade and written contracts have survived, particularly in relation to ecclesiastical buildings. The role of architect was usually one with master builder, except in the case where a cleric, such as the Abbot Suger at Saint Denis, Paris, provided the design. Over time the complexity of buildings and their types increased. General civil construction such as roads and bridges began to be built. Many new building types such as schools, hospitals, and recreational facilities emerged.

RENAISSANCE AND THE ARCHITECT

With the Renaissance and its emphasis on the individual and humanity rather than religion, and with all its attendant progress and achievements, a new chapter began. Buildings were ascribed to specific architects - Brunelleschi, Alberti, Michelangelo,

Palladio - and the cult of the individual had begun. But there was no dividing line between artist, architect and engineer, or any of the related vocations. At this stage, it was still possible for an artist to design a bridge as the level of structural calculations involved was within the scope of the generalist.

With the emerging knowledge in scientific fields and the rise of new materials and technology, architecture and engineering began to separate, and the architect began to lose ground on some technical aspects of building design. He therefore concentrated on aesthetics and the humanist aspects.

There was also the rise of the "gentleman architect" who usually dealt with wealthy clients and concentrated predominantly on visual qualities derived usually from historical prototypes, typified by the many country houses of Great Britain that were created in the Neo Gothic or Scottish Baronial styles.

Formal architectural training, in the 19th century, at, for example Ecole des Beaux Arts in France, gave much emphasis to the production of beautiful drawings and little to context and feasibility. Effective architects generally received their training in the offices of other architects, graduating to the role from draughtsmen or clerks.

Meanwhile, the Industrial Revolution laid open the door for mass production and consumption. Aesthetics became a criterion for the middle class as ornamented products, once within the province of expensive craftsmanship, became cheaper under machine production. Vernacular architecture became increasingly ornamental. House builders could access current architectural design in their work by combining features found in pattern books and architectural journals.

MODERNISM AND REACTION OF ARCHITECTURE

The dissatisfaction with such a general situation at the turn of the twentieth century gave rise to many new lines of thought that served as precursors to Modern Architecture. Notable among these is the Deutscher Werkbund, formed in 1907 to produce better quality machine made objects. The rise of the profession of industrial design is usually placed here.

Following this lead, the Bauhaus school, founded in Germany in 1919, consciously rejected history and looked at architecture as a synthesis of art, craft, and technology. When Modern architecture was first practiced, it was an avant-garde movement with moral, philosophical, and aesthetic underpinnings. Immediately after World War I, pioneering modernist architects sought to develop a completely new style appropriate for a new post-war social and economic order, focused on meeting the needs of the middle and working classes. They rejected the architectural practice of the academic refinement of historical styles which served the rapidly declining aristocratic order.

The approach of the Modernist architects was to reduce buildings to pure forms, removing historical references and ornament in favor of functionalist details. Buildings that displayed their construction and structure, exposing steel beams and concrete surfaces instead of hiding them behind traditional forms, were seen as beautiful in their own right. Architects such as Mies van der Rohe worked to create beauty based on the inherent qualities of building materials and modern construction techniques, trading traditional historic forms for simplified geometric forms, celebrating the new means and methods made possible by the Industrial Revolution.

Many architects resisted Modernism, finding it devoid of the decorative richness of ornamented styles. As the founders of the International Style lost influence in the late 1970s, Postmodernism developed as a reaction against the austerity of Modernism. Robert Venturi's contention that a "decorated shed" (an ordinary building which is functionally designed inside and embellished on the outside) was better than a "duck" (a building in which the whole form and its function are tied together) gives an idea of this approach.

MODERN ARCHITECTURE

Modern architecture is a term given to a number of building styles with similar characteristics, primarily the simplification of form and the elimination of ornament. The style was conceived early in the 20th century. Modern architecture was adopted by many influential architects and architectural educators, however very few "Modern buildings" were built in the first half of the century. It gained popularity after the Second World War and became the dominant architectural style for institutional and corporate buildings for three decades. The exact characteristics and origins of Modern architecture are still open to interpretation and debate.

Some historians see the evolution of Modern architecture as a social matter, closely tied to the project of Modernity and thus the Enlightenment. The Modern style developed, in their opinion, as a result of social and political revolutions. Others see Modern architecture as primarily driven by technological and engineering developments, and it is true that the availability of new building materials such as iron, steel, concrete and glass drove the invention of new building techniques as part of the Industrial Revolution. In 1796, Shrewsbury mill owner Charles Bage first used his 'fireproof' design, which relied on cast iron and brick with flag stone floors. Such construction greatly strengthened the structure of mills, which enabled them to accommodate much bigger machines. Due to poor knowledge of iron's properties as a construction material, a number of early mills collapsed. It was not until the early 1830s that Eaton Hodgkinson introduced the section beam, leading to widespread use of iron construction, this kind of austere industrial architecture utterly transformed the landscape of northern Britain, leading to the description of places like Manchester and parts of West Yorkshire as "Dark satanic mills".

The Crystal Palace by Joseph Paxton at the Great Exhibition of 1851 was an early example of iron and glass construction; possibly the best example is the development of the tall steel skyscraper in Chicago around 1890 by William Le Baron Jenney and Louis Sullivan. Early structures to employ concrete as the chief means of architectural expression (rather than for purely utilitarian structure) include Frank Lloyd Wright's Unity Temple, built in 1906 near Chicago, and Rudolf Steiner's Second Goetheanum, built from 1926 near Basel, Switzerland.

Other historians regard Modernism as a matter of taste, a reaction against eclecticism and the lavish stylistic excesses of Victorian Era and Edwardian Art Nouveau. Note that the Russian word for Art Nouveau, *"Modeph"*, and the Spanish word for Art Nouveau, *"Modernismo"* are cognates of English word "Modern" though they carry different meanings.

Whatever the cause, around 1900 a number of architects around the world began developing new architectural solutions to integrate traditional precedents (Gothic, for instance) with new technological possibilities. The work of Louis Sullivan and Frank Lloyd Wright in Chicago, Victor Horta in Brussels, Antoni Gaudi in Barcelona, Otto Wagner in Vienna and Charles Rennie Mackintosh in Glasgow, among many others, can be seen as a common struggle between old and new. An early use of the term in print around this time, approaching its later meaning, was in the title of a book by Otto Wagner.

A key organization that spans the ideals of the Arts and Crafts and Modernism as it developed in the 1920s was the Deutscher Werkbund (German Work Federation) a German association of architects, designers and industrialists. It was founded in 1907 in Munich at the instigation of Hermann Muthesius. Muthesius was the author of a three-volume "The English House" of 1905, a survey of the practical lessons of the English Arts and Crafts movement and a leading political and cultural commentator. The purpose of the Werkbund was to sponsor the attempt to integrate traditional crafts with the techniques of industrial mass production. The organization originally included twelve architects and twelve business firms, but quickly expanded. The architects include Peter Behrens, Theodor Fischer (who served as its first president), Josef Hoffmann and Richard Riemerschmid. Joseph August Lux, an Austrian-born critic, helped formulate its agenda.

MODERNISM AS DOMINANT STYLE

By the 1920s the most important figures in Modern architecture had established their reputations. The big three are commonly recognized as Le Corbusier in France, and Ludwig Mies van der Rohe and Walter Gropius in Germany. Mies van der Rohe and Gropius were both directors of the Bauhaus, one of a number of European schools and associations concerned with reconciling craft tradition and industrial technology.

Frank Lloyd Wright's career parallels and influences the work of the European modernists, particularly via the Wasmuth Portfolio, but he refused to be categorized with them. Wright was a major influence on both Gropius and van der Rohe, however, as well as on the whole of organic architecture.

In 1932 came the important MOMA exhibition, the International Exhibition of Modern Architecture, curated by Philip Johnson. Johnson and collaborator Henry-Russell Hitchcock drew together many distinct threads and trends, identified them as stylistically similar and having a common purpose, and consolidated them into the International style.

This was an important turning point. With World War II the important figures of the Bauhaus fled to the United States, to Chicago, to the Harvard Graduate School of Design, and to Black Mountain College. While Modern architectural design never became a dominant style in single-dwelling residential buildings, in institutional and commercial architecture Modernism became the pre-eminent, and in the schools (for leaders of the profession) the only acceptable, design solution from about 1932 to about 1984.

Architects who worked in the International style wanted to break with architectural tradition and design simple, unornamented buildings. The most commonly used materials are glass for the facade, steel for exterior support, and concrete for the floors and interior supports; floor plans were functional and logical. The style became most evident in the design of skyscrapers. Perhaps its most famous manifestations include the United Nations headquarters (Le Corbusier, Oscar Niemeyer, Sir Howard Robertson), the Seagram Building (Ludwig Mies van der Rohe), and Lever House (Skidmore, Owings, and Merrill), all in New York. A prominent residential example is the Lovell House (Richard Neutra) in Los Angeles.

Detractors of the International style claim that its stark, uncompromisingly rectangular geometry is dehumanising. Le Corbusier once described buildings as "machines for living", but people are not machines and it was suggested that they do not want to live in machines. Even Philip Johnson admitted he was "bored with the box." Since the early 1980s many architects have deliberately sought to move away from rectilinear designs, towards more eclectic styles. During the middle of the century, some architects began experimenting in organic forms that they felt were more human and accessible. Mid-century modernism, or organic modernism, was very popular, due to its democratic and playful nature. Alvar Aalto and Eero Saarinen were two of the most prolific architects and designers in this movement, which has influenced contemporary modernism.

Although there is debate as to when and why the decline of the modern movement occurred, criticism of Modern architecture began in the 1960s on the grounds that it was universal, sterile, elitist and lacked meaning. Its approach had become ossified in a "style" that threatened to degenerate into a set of mannerisms. Siegfried Giedion in the 1961 introduction to his evolving text, *Space, Time and Architecture* (first written in 1941), could begin "At the moment a certain confusion exists in contemporary architecture, as in painting; a kind of pause, even a kind of exhaustion." At the Metropolitan Museum of Art, a 1961 symposium discussed the question "Modern Architecture: Death or Metamorphosis?" In New York, the coup d'état appeared to materialize in controversy around the Pan Am Building that loomed over Grand Central Station, taking advantage of the modernist real estate concept of "air rights".

In criticism by Ada Louise Huxtable and Douglass Haskell it was seen to "sever" the Park Avenue streetscape and "tarnish" the reputations of its consortium of architects: Walter Gropius, Pietro Belluschi and the builders Emery Roth & Sons. The rise of postmodernism was attributed to disenchantment with Modern architecture. By the 1980s, postmodern architecture appeared triumphant over modernism; however, postmodern aesthetics lacked traction and by the mid-1990s, a neo-modern (or hypermodern) architecture had once again established international pre-eminence. As part of this revival, much of the criticism of the modernists has been revisited, refuted, and re-evaluated; and a modernistic idiom once again dominates in institutional and commercial contemporary practice, but must now compete with the revival of traditional architectural design in commercial and institutional architecture; residential design continues to be dominated by a traditional aesthetic.

CHARACTERISTICS

Modern architecture is usually characterized by:

- an adoption of the principle that the materials and functional requirements determine the result
- an adoption of the machine aesthetic
- a rejection of ornament
- a simplification of form and elimination of "unnecessary detail"
- an adoption of expressed structure
- Form follows function

PRESERVATION

Although relatively young, works of Modern architecture may be lost because of demolition, neglect, or alterations. While an awareness of the plight of endangered Modern buildings is growing, the threats continue. Non-profit groups such as the

World Monuments Fund, Docomomo International and the Recent Past Preservation Network are working to safeguard and document imperiled Modern architecture. In 2006, the World Monuments Fund launched Modernism at Risk, an advocacy and conservation program. Since Hurricane Katrina, New Orleans modernist structures have been increasingly slated for demolition. Currently plans are underway to demolish many of the city's modernist public schools, as well as large portions of the city's Civic Plaza. FEMA funds will contribute to razing the State Office Building and State Supreme Court Building, both designed by the collaborating architectural firms of August Perez and Associates; Goldstein, Parham and Labouisse; and Favrot, Reed, Mathes and Bergman. The New Orleans Recovery School District has proposed demolitions of schools designed by Charles R. Colbert, Curtis and Davis, and Ricciuti Associates. The 1959 Lawrence and Saunders building for the New Orleans International Longshoremen's Association Local 1419 is currently threatened with demolition although the union supports its conservation.

ARCHITECTURE TODAY

Part of the architectural profession, and also some non-architects, responded to Modernism and Postmodernism by going to what they considered the root of the problem. They felt that architecture was not a personal philosophical or aesthetic pursuit by individualists; rather it had to consider everyday needs of people and use technology to give a livable environment. The *Design Methodology Movement* involving people such as Christopher Alexander started searching for more people-oriented designs. Extensive studies on areas such as behavioral, environmental, and social sciences were done and started informing the design process.

As the complexity of buildings began to increase (in terms of structural systems, services, energy and technologies), architecture started becoming more multi-disciplinary. Architecture today usually requires a team of specialist professionals, with the architect being one of many, although usually the team leader.

During the last two decades of the twentieth century and into the new millennium, the field of architecture saw the rise of specializations by project type, technological expertise or project delivery methods. In addition, there has been an increased separation of the 'design' architect from the 'project' architect.

Moving the issues of environmental sustainability into the mainstream is a significant development in the architecture profession. Sustainability in architecture was pioneered in the 1970s by architects such as Ian McHarg in the US and Brenda and Robert Vale in the UK and New Zealand. There has been an acceleration in the number of buildings which seek to meet green building sustainable design principles.

It is now expected that architects will integrate sustainable principles into their projects. The American Institute of Architects acknowledges that half of today's global warming greenhouse gas emissions come from buildings - more than transportation or industry. AIA states that immediate action by the building sector is essential to avoid hazardous man-made climate change. They have an "Architecture 2030" plan to reduce new building energy consumption by 90% in 2030, and net zero greenhouse gas emissions by 2035. Passive solar building design has been demonstrating essential elements of 70% to 90% energy consumption reduction in roughly 300,000 buildings since the 1978 U.S. Solar Energy Tax Incentives. Many of these energy efficiency features can be added at little-or-no additional net cost during construction. Newer zero energy buildings have reduced net annual energy consumption, producing excess energy and selling it back to the power company during moderate months. The demand for zero energy buildings is growing rapidly - subsidies are available for this type of building - The supply of zero energy buildings has fallen far short of current demand. Off-the-grid buildings are now demonstrating total self sufficiency. The 2009 Bank of America Tower (New York) has many innovative energy features.

President George W. Bush's 2006 Solar America Initiative expects architects and builders to design and construct new zero energy buildings by 2015. The U.S. Energy Independence and Security Act of 2007 funded the new Solar Air Conditioning Research and Development Program, to develop technology innovations and mass production economies of scale. The U.S. Department of Energy and the National Renewable Energy Laboratory (NREL) also sponsor The Solar Decathlon, an international competition among universities for solar energy alternatives when it comes to houses. The houses built by the team are exhibited on the National Mall for the public to experience.

2

INDIAN ART AND ARCHITECTURE

Works of art and architecture produced on the Indian subcontinent, which is now divided among India, Pakistan, and Bangladesh. In the Western world, notable collections of Indian art can be seen in the British Museum, in the Victoria and Albert Museum, and in the Museum of Fine Arts, Boston.

Although a great deal of Indian secular art was produced, it was essentially made of perishable material and has not survived. What has survived in the medium of stone is religious art. In both Buddhist and Hindu art, symbolism in gesture, posture, and attribute contains many levels of meaning. In images of the Buddha, different hand positions (mudras) signify religious states, such as the Enlightenment (Nirvana), Meditation, and Preaching. In Hindu sculpture, deities are frequently represented with many hands to indicate their power to perform multiple deeds at the same time, and the hands each carry their characteristic attributes.

INDUS VALLEY CIVILIZATION

The earliest Indian art emerged from the valley of the Indus River during the second half of the 3rd millennium b.c. The best-known sites are Harappa, destroyed in the 19th cent., and Mohenjo-daro; these are among the earliest examples of civic planning. Houses, markets, storage facilities, offices, and public baths were arranged in a gridlike scheme. There was also a highly developed drainage system.

The Indus civilization produced many statuettes made of steatite and limestone. Some statuettes resemble the hieratic style of contemporary Mesopotamia, while others are done in the smooth, sinuous style that is the prototype of later Indian sculpture, in which the plastic modeling reveals the animating breath of life (prana). Also found in this region are square steatite seals adorned with a range of animals, including naturalistically rendered bulls; ceramic storage jars with simple, stylized designs; toys with wheels; and figurines, which may be mother goddesses. Bronze weapons, tools, and sculptures indicate a sophistication in craftsmanship rather than a major aesthetic development.

POST-INDUS CIVILIZATION THROUGH THE MAURYA DYNASTY

Of the period from the end of the Indus civilization (c.1500 b.c.) until Alexander the Great crossed (325 b.c.) the Indus, few traces remain. However, the principles of Indian architecture were developed in wooden buildings, long since disintegrated.

From the great Maurya dynasty the most famous remains are the edict pillars, erected throughout North India by the Emperor Asoka to proclaim his devotion to Buddhism. The monolithic, smooth columns are over 50 ft (15 m) high and are surmounted by lotus capitals and animal figures. Some of the pillar capitals reveal forms that suggest Persepolitan influences. Also dating from the reign of Asoka is the earliest stone ogival chaitya window, found on the portal of a small rock-cut sanctuary near Bodh Gaya. The chaitya halls were monastic sanctuaries hewn out of rock. As they evolved, from the 3rd cent. b.c. through the 1st millennium a.d., they became elaborate colonnaded halls, or walls embellished with painting or sculpture.

SUNGA AND ANDHRA DYNASTIES

The earliest extant stupas date from the Sunga dynasty (2nd–1st cent. b.c.) and early Andhra dynasty (1st cent. b.c.). These relic mounds are surrounded by railings and gateways covered with carved ornament. One of the main stupas is at Bharhut, where the sculpture is archaic in character. Relief medallions of the Buddha's life or of the jatakas (tales of his previous lives) are shallow cut, with all the incidents of each story arranged within a single composition. The bodies of semidivine beings including yakshis (female tree spirits) are flattened against the pillar of which they form part; prana is still emphasized.

The important stupa at Sanchi shows a similar style. Important carvings on the gateways of another stupa at Sanchi date from the early Andhra period. The yakshis have acquired full, graceful forms, and high-relief compositions are frequently conceived in a continuous method of narration. The carved railing from Bodh Gaya, the place of the Buddha's enlightenment, and the earliest surviving wall paintings are also early Andhra; paintings in the rock-cut cave at Ajanta narrate the Buddha's birth as an elephant and the entire synopsis of historic life. In the far south, in the Deccan, the later Andhra dynasty continued to flourish into the 1st cent. a.d. Its greatest monument is the carving at the Great Stupa at Amaravati, c.a.d. 200. The complex but coherent composition, the chiaroscuro, and the liveliness of the crowded surfaces distinguish these bas-reliefs.

GANDHARA AND MATHURA

Under the Kushans, conquerors from central Asia, two of India's most important styles were developed between the 2nd and 5th cent. a.d.: Gandhara art and art of Mathura. Gandhara art, named after the region of Gandhara now in Pakistan, presents some of the earliest images of the Buddha. Earlier at Bharhut and Sanchi, the Buddha's presence was represented by symbols, such as the pipal tree, the wheel of life, footprints, and an empty throne. The Gandhara style was profoundly influenced by 2d-century Hellenistic art and was itself highly influential in central and eastern Asia. Ivories and imported glass and lacquerware attest to the cosmopolitan tastes and extensive trade that characterized the period. Stupas and monasteries were adorned with relief friezes, often carved in dark schist, showing figures in classical poses with flowing Hellenistic draperies.

Farther east and south, contemporary Mathura, also under Kushan rule, created a wholly Indian sculptural art. Reddish limestone was the usual medium. More sensuous, heavier Buddhas whose limbs are created according to canonical instructions, smile directly at their worshipers. Reliefs of the yakshis carved against railing pillars are more frankly sensual and erotic than those at Sanchi. Buddhist iconography was developed in Gandhara. Mathura, however, preserved and developed Indian forms for three centuries.

THE GUPTA PERIOD

Buddhist art flourished during this period, which has often been described as a golden age. A famous rock-cut monastery at Ajanta consists of several chaitya halls and numerous residential viharas. Both facades and interiors contain elegant relief sculpture, while interiors are covered with painted murals that feature superb figures drawn with a gracefully sinuous line. As in all periods, there is little difference in the images of the major Indian religions, Buddhist, Hindu, and Jain. Large stone figures, stone and terra-cotta reliefs, and large and small bronzes are made in the refined Gupta style; the level of production is uniformly high. After the 7th cent., although the rulers of the Pala and Sena dynasties (730–1197) were Hindu, significant Buddhist art was created. Images in bronze and in hard black stone from Nalanda and elsewhere reveal a development of the Gupta manner, with extensive attention to ornamental details.

ARCHITECTURE AND SCULPTURE OF THE HINDU DYNASTIES

From the 6th century on, with the resurgence of Hindu dynasties throughout India, a characteristic temple plan was developed. An entrance portico led to a pillared hall (mandapa) into the cella. The shrine was often crowned by a large tower known as the shikhara. In South India the Dravida tower rose in a series of terraces, each symbolizing a different divinity; in the north, *nagara* spires ascended in a massive conical shape.

Innumerable temples were built that were so exuberantly embellished with sculpture that their style is called "sculptural architecture." The Khajuraho temples in central India (c.1000) represent one of the high points of the *nagara* buildings, and the damaged Temple of the Sun at Konarak (c.1250) reveals, in its famous erotic sculptures, carvings that combine balanced mass with delicate execution. The Jain temples at Mt. Abu, constructed entirely of imported white marble and dating from the 10th and 13th cent., have plain exteriors but are ornately carved inside.

In South India the 7th-century Pallava dynasty introduced the *dravida* style temple in a number of pyramidal *raths* (temples) at Mahabalipuram; an enormous cliff-face at the site is carved with a life-size representation of gods, men, and beasts, including the elephant family. The *dravida* style plan was used also in the 8th cent. in the quarried temple at Ellora. The Chola dynasty of South India further developed this form in the 11th cent., when they probably also cast most of large numbers of South Indian bronzes, of which the *Nataraja* (dancing Shiva) images are perhaps the best known.

The *dravida* style culminated in a series of expanded "temple townships," of which the largest is Srirangam, consisting of seven concentric enclosures. These ended in the comparatively crude stucco sculptured architecture of 17th-century Mandura. Medieval bronze sculpture was highly developed in South India. The chief subjects were the deities, figures of whom were used for processional and home ritual. Skilled cire-perdue sculptures were produced until the late 19th cent. in many regions of India.

INDIAN PAINTING

Adverse climate and other conditions have injured what wall painting existed. The most famous surviving Buddhist paintings are from the caves at Ajanta. Little is known of Hindu wall painting except for fragments at Ellora and Tanjore. The earliest Indian manuscript paintings are Buddhist, of the Pala dynasty; they have a delicate color. The 13th- to 15th-century Jain manuscript illuminations, painted in vivid red, blue, and gold, are most easily recognized by the characteristic protruding farther eye. Rajput miniature painting, which was practiced in N India from the 16th through the 19th cent., is related both to Mughal painting and to earlier Indian styles. It illustrates a variety of Hindu subjects: the *ragamala* series (musical modes), the legendary epics and romances, and particularly Krishna's deeds. Rajput painting is characterized by lyrical landscapes, sinuous grace in the depiction of the human form, and an interest in perspective.

THE MODERN ERA

Little of the glorious tradition of Indian artistic achievement survived British rule. Indian artists adapted Western techniques and produced gouache paintings to suit the tastes of European buyers. Patua scrolls, containing swiftly executed watercolor illustrations of many subjects, became one source for the revival of Indian themes during the 20th cent. A growing nationalist sentiment pervaded Indian art in the early decades of the 20th century along with the conscious assimilation of Western styles. Major modern artists include Abanindranath Tagore, Nandalal Bose, Jamini Roy, Amrita Sher Gil, N. S. Bendre, M. B. Samant, Francis Souza, Bhagwan Kapoor, M. F. Husain, Bhupen Khakhar, Ram Kinker, Dhanraj Bhagat, Amar Nath Seghal, Chintamoni Kar, and Amina Ahmad.

INDIAN ARCHITECTURE

One of the most enduring achievements of Indian civilization is undoubtedly its architecture, which extends to a great deal more than the Taj Mahal or the temple complexes of Khajuraho and Vijayanagara. Though the Indus Valley sites of Harappa, Mohenjo-daro, and Lothal provide substantial evidence of extensive town planning, the beginnings of Indian architecture are more properly to be dated to the advent of Buddhism in India, in the reign of Ashoka (c. 270-232), and the construction of Buddhist monasteries and stupas. Buddhist architecture was predominant for several centuries, and there are few remains of Hindu temples from even late antiquity. Among the many highlights of Buddhist art and architecture are the Great Stupa at Sanchi and the rock-cut caves at Ajanta.

By the eighth century, with the consolidation of Hindu kingdoms, the southern Hindu school of architecture was beginning to flourish. The most notable achievements of the Pallavas were the rock-cut temples of Mahabalipuram and the temples of Kanchipuram. The subsequent history of South Indian temple architecture takes us, over the next eight centuries, to Thanjavur (Tanjore), to the brilliant achievements of the Hoysalas (as seen in the temples at Belur and Halebid), and the temple complexes, which represent the flowering of the Vijayanagara empire, of Kanchipuram, Thiruvannamalai, and Vellore. The most stellar achievement of the later Vijayanagara period may well be the Meenakshi temple in Madurai. In Kerala, however, a distinct style of architecture took shape. In Ellora in western India, Hindus added a new series of temples and carvings at what had once been Buddhist caves, culminating in the majestic Kailasa temple, constructed in the reign of the Rashtrakuta monarch Krishna I (757-73), while the rock-cut caves in Elephanta and Jogeshvari, in the proximity of Bombay, were most likely executed in the sixth century.

In north India, meanwhile, architecture was to be a more contentious matter. The fabled temple at Somnath, renowned for its purported riches, is said to have been destroyed by the Muslim invader Mahmud of Ghazni, and after the attainment of Indian independence, the restoration of this temple became a matter of national pride for more ardent defenders of the faith. The story of Somnath points to the manner in which histories, whether political, cultural, or architectural, have become communalized. But the period from 1000-1300 was, in any case, a time when Hindu architecture flourished throughout India. In central India, the Chandellas built a magnificent complex of temples at their capital, Khajuraho, between 950-1030 A.D.

These temples, which show Vaishnavite, Shaivite, and Tantric influence, have acquired a renewed reputation today as indices of India's libertine past, allegedly indicative of India's relaxed sexual mores before puritanical Muslims made India a sexually repressed society. The sexual postures depicted in many of the sculptures that adorn some of the temples appear equally on the posters of the Government of India's Tourist Office and the pages of gay and lesbian magazines. The cultural politics of Khajuraho, as indeed of Indian architecture, still remains to be written. In the north-west, the Solanki kings spent lavishly on buildings, and the Surya or Sun temple in Modhera, some 3 hours from Ahmedabad, stills provides striking testimony to their achievements. More stupendous still is the Surya temple at Konarak, built by Narasimha-deva Ganga (c. 1238-64), though masterpieces of Orissan architecture from the reign of the Gangas are to be found in Bhubaneshwar and Puri as well. The weakness of Muslim dynasties in the north enabled Rajput kings to assert their independence; the results of this Hindu revival are to be seen in Chittor, and elsewhere in Rajasthan where massive forts dot the landscape.

The Mughal emperors of India, most particularly Humayun, Akbar, Jahangir, and Shah Jahan, were heavily invested in monumental architecture and spent lavishly on the construction of mosques, mausoleums, forts, palaces, and other buildings. The principal sites of Mughal architecture are Lahore, Delhi, Agra, and Fatehpur Sikri, though dazzling specimens of Mughal architecture are to be found elsewhere. Shah Jahan constructed a new capital, then to be known as Shahjahanabad, and now a part of Old Delhi. Its most famous buildings include the Jama Masjid, one of the largest mosques in the world, and the Red Fort (*Lal Qila*), which over the last four hundred years has become uniquely emblematic of state power. Akbar likewise built a new capital at Fatehpur Sikri, a few miles outside Agra, but it was abandoned on account of insuperable difficulties in obtaining a water supply. Some have described the complex of buildings at Fatehpur Sikri, which include the majestic Buland Darwaza and Salim Chisti's tomb, as the most splendrous accomplishment of Mughal architecture. Among the most exquisite of the Mughal works of architecture are various mausoleums, including Humayun's Tomb in Delhi, Akbar's Tomb in Sikandra on the outskirts of Agra, and the Taj Mahal, an edifice of such ravishing beauty that it has now become iconic of India itself. Mughal emperors also laid down elaborate gardens, the finest of which are to be found in Srinagar, and built elaborate forts, principally at Agra (1564), Ajmer (1570), Lahore (1580), and Allahabad.

Unlike the Mughals, the British contributed little to India's architectural history. Their rule is associated mainly with monumental civic buildings, such as the Victoria Terminus in Bombay, or commemorative exercises typified by the Victoria Memorial in Calcutta. There are some notable specimens of church architecture, such as St. James's Church in Delhi, but the principal regal contribution of the British appears to be the construction of a new capital in Delhi. Meanwhile, indigenous styles of architecture did not entirely suffer a demise, and step-wells continued to be built in Gujarat throughout the nineteenth century. In Rajasthan rich merchants constructed large havelis or residences in which the window work defies description. The most striking of these havelis are to be found in Jaisalmer, also notable for Rajasthan's finest, certainly most romantic, fort. Though few people associate India with modern architecture, the work of many Indian architects, such as Charles Correa and Balkrishna Doshi, is renowned internationally. Other prominent architects include Satish Gujral, also known as a painter, and Laurie Baker, an Englishman settled in India who first became known for designing low-cost housing and using only local materials. It is also noteworthy that the city of Chandigarh was designed by Le Corbusier.

The Indus civilization or the Harappan civilization, which flourished during the Bronze Age i.e. 2500-2000 BC is ranked among the four widely known civilizations of the old world. Extensive excavation work that has been done since Independence has so far identified more than 100 sites belonging to this civilization. A few prominent among them are Dholavira (Gujarat), Kalibangan (Rajasthan), Lothal (Gujarat), Sarkotada (Gujarat), Diamabad (Maharashtra), Alamgirpur (U.P.), Bhagwanpura (Haryana), Banawali (Haryana), Kuntasi, Padri (Gujarat) and Mauda (Jammu).

Extensive town planning was the characteristic of this civilization, which is evident from the gridiron pattern for the layout of cities, some with fortifications and the elaborate drainage and water management systems. The houses were built of baked bricks, which is rare in contemporary civilizations at Mesopotamia and Egypt. Bricks of fixed sizes, as well as stone and wood were also used for building. Buildings in the lower area are rather monotonous, being mainly functional rather than decorative. But many houses are two storeyed. The most imposing of the buildings is the Great Bath of Mohenjo-daro. It is 54.86 metres long and 32.91 metres wide and with 2.43 metres thick outer walls. The Bath had galleries and rooms on all sides. Another important structure was the Granary complex comprising of blocks with an overall area of 55 x

43 metres. The granaries were intelligently constructed, with strategic air ducts and platforms divided into units.

THE MAURYAN PERIOD

If the remnants of the Indus culture are excluded, the earliest surviving architectural heritage in India is that of the Mauryans. The Mauryan period was a great landmark in the history of Indian art. Some of the monuments and pillars belonging to this period are considered as the finest specimens of Indian art. The Mauryan architecture was embalmed in timber, for rocks and stones were not as freely in use then. The art of polishing of wood reached so much perfection during the Mauryan period that master craftsmen used to make wood glisten like a mirror. Chandra Gupta Maurya had built many buildings, palaces and monuments with wood, most of which perished with time. In 300 B.C., Chandragupta Maurya constructed a wooden fort 14.48 km long and 2.41 km wide, along the Ganges in Bihar. However, only a couple of teak beams have survived from this fort.

Ashoka was the first Mauryan Emperor who began to "think in stone". The stonework of the Ashokan Period (3rd century B.C.) was of a highly diversified order and comprised of lofty free-standing pillars, railings of the stupas, lion thrones and other colossal figures. The use of stone had reached such great perfection during this time that even small fragments of stone art was given a high lustrous polish resembling fine enamel. While most of the shapes and decorative forms employed were indigenous in origin, some exotic forms show the influence of Greek, Persian and Egyptian cultures.

The Ashokan period marked the beginning of the Buddhist School of architecture in India. It witnessed the construction of many rock-cut caves, pillars, *stupas* and palaces. A number of cave-shrines belonging to this period have been excavated in the Barabar and Nagarjuni hills and Sitamarhi in Bihar. These rock-cut sanctuaries, quarried from large masses of rocks called *gneisses*, are simple in plan and are devoid of all interior decorative carvings. The caves served as the residences of the monks. There are several inscriptions, which indicate that these rock-cut sanctuaries were constructed by Emperor Ashoka for the monks of the Ajivika sect, who are more closely related to the Jains than to the Buddhists.

The Ashokan rock-edict at Dhauli, near Bhubaneshwar, is considered to be the earliest rock-cut sculpture in India. It has a sculpted elephant on the top, which signifies the Emperor's conversion to Buddhism after his Kalinga victory. The monolithic Ashokan pillars are marvels of architecture and sculpture. These were lofty free standing monolithic columns erected on sacred sites. Originally there were about thirty pillars but now only ten are in existence, of which only two with lion capitals stand *in situ* in good condition at Kolhua and Laurya Nandangarh respectively. Each pillar was about

15.24 metres high and weighed about 50 tonnes and was made out of fine sandstone. The pillar consisted of three parts-the prop, the shaft and the capitol. The capitol consisted of fine polished stone containing one or more animal figures in the round. Made of bricks, they carried declarations from the king regarding Buddhism or any other topic. The pillars did not stand in isolation and were usually found near stupas in a spot either unknowingly marked by the Buddha himself or along the royal route to Magadha, the capital. The Sarnath pillar is one of the finest pieces of sculpture of the Ashokan period. The Ashokan pillars also throw light on the contacts India had with Persia and other countries. Two of the Ashokan edicts have also been found at Laghman, near Jalalabad in modern Afghanistan.

Ashoka was responsible for the construction of several *stupas*, which were large halls, capped with domes and bore symbols of the Buddha. The most important ones are located at Bharhut, Bodhgaya, Sanchi, Amravati and Nagarjunakonda. The Buddhist shrines or the monasteries were built in somewhat irregular designs following the Gandhara style of architecture. Built on the patterns of a fort and defended by a stone wall, the monastery evolved from the site of an ancient *stupa*. The principle buildings were housed within a rectangular courtyard with a *stupa* in the south and the monastery in the north.

Ashoka had also built a number of palaces, but most of them have perished. Ashoka's palace near Patna was a masterpiece. Enclosed by a high brick wall, the highlight of the palace was an immense 76.2 metres high pillared-hall having three storeys. The Chinese traveller Fahien was so impressed by this palace that he stated that "it was made by spirits" and that its carvings are so elegantly executed "which no human hands of this world could accomplish". Made mostly of wood, it seems to have been destroyed by fire. Its existence was pointed out during the excavations at Kumrahar, near Patna, where its ashes have been found preserved for several thousand years.

THE STUPAS

Sanchi Stupas: The early *stupas* were hemispherical in shape with a low base. The hemispherical shape symbolized the cosmic mountain. The later *stupas* assumed an increasingly cylindrical form. The early *stupas* were known for their simplicity. Apart from the than ruins of *stupa* at Piprahwa (Nepal), the core of *stupa* No 1 at Sanchi can be considered as the oldest of the *stupas*. Originally built by Asoka, it was enlarged in subsequent centuries. An inscription by the ivory carvers of Vidisha on the southern gateway throws light on the transference of building material from perishable wood and ivory to the more durable stone.

Amaravati Stupa: Amaravati *stupa*, built in 2nd or 1st century BC was probably like the one at Sanchi, but in later centuries it was transformed from a Hinayana shrine to a

Mahayana shrine. The diameter of the dome of the *stupa* at ground level was about 48.76 metres and its height was about 30 metres. Amaravati *stupa* is different from the Bharhut and Sanchi *stupas*. It had free-standing columns surmounted by lions near the gateways. The dome was covered with sculptured panels. The *stupa* had an upper circumambulatory path on the drum as at Sanchi. This path had two intricately carved railings. The stone is greenish-white limestone of the region.

Gandhara stupa: The Gandhara *stupa* is a further development of *stupas* at Sanchi and Bharhut. In Gandhara *stupas* the base, dome and the hemisphere dome are sculpted. The *stupa* tapers upward to form a tower like structure. The *stupas* of Nagarjunakonda in Krishna valley were very large. At the base there were brick walls forming wheel and spokes, whish were filled with earth. The Maha Chaitya of Nagarjunakonda has a base in the form of *Swastika*, which is a sun symbol.

THE SUNGAS, KUSHANS AND SATAVAHANAS

The Mauryan dynasty crumbled after Asoka's death in 232 B.C. In its wake came the Sungas and Kushans in the north and the Satavahanas in the south. The period between 2nd century B.C. and 3rd century A.D. marked the beginning of the sculptural idiom in Indian sculpture where the elements of physical form were evolving into a more refined, realistic and expressive style. The sculptors strived at mastering their art, especially of the human body, which was carved in high relief and bore heaviness and vigour. These dynasties made advances in art and architecture in areas like stone construction, stone carving, symbolism and beginning of temple (or *chaitya hall*) and the monastery (or *vihara*) constructions.

Under these dynasties the Asokan *stupas* were enlarged and the earlier brick and wood works were replaced with stone-works. For instance, the Sanchi Stupa was enlarged to nearly twice its size in 150 B.C. and elaborate gateways were added later. The Sungas also reconstructed the railings around the Barhut Stupa. The Sungas also built the *toranas* or the gateways to the stupas. An inscription at the Barhut Stupa indicates that the *torana* was built during the reign of Sungas i.e. 184-72 B.C. These *toranas* indicate the influence of Hellenistic and other foreign schools in the Sunga architecture.

The Satavahanas constructed a large number of *stupas* at Goli, Jaggiahpeta, Bhattiprolu, Gantasala, Nagarjunakonda and Amravati. During the Kushan period (1-3 A.D.), the Buddha was represented in human form instead of symbols. Buddha's image in endless forms and replicas became the principal element in Buddhist sculpture during the Kushan period. Another feature of this period was that the Emperor himself was shown as a divine person. The Kushans were the pioneers of the Gandhara School of Art and a large number of monasteries; stupas and statues were constructed during the reign of Kanishka.

THE SCHOOLS OF ART

The Gandhara School of Art (50 B.C. to 500 A.D.): The Gadhara region extending from Punjab to the borders of Afghanistan was an important centre of Mahayana Buddhism up to the 5th century A.D. The region became famous throughout the world since a new school of Indian sculpture known as the Gandhara School developed during that period. Owing to its strategic location the Gandhara School imbibed all kinds of foreign influences like Persian, Greek, Roman, Saka and Kushan. The origin of Gandhara art can be traced to the Greek rulers of Bactria and Northwest India. But it was during the reign of Kanishka that the art received great patronage.

The Gandhara School of Art is also known as the Graeco-Buddhist School of Art since Greek techniques of Art were applied to Buddhist subjects. The most important contribution of the Gandhara School of Art was the evolution of beautiful images of the Buddha and Bodhisattavas, which were executed in black stone and modelled on identical characters of Graeco-Roman pantheon. Hence it is said, "the Gandhara artist had the hand of a Greek but the heart of an Indian." The most characteristic trait of Gandhara sculpture is the depiction of Lord Buddha in the standing or seated positions. The seated Buddha is always shown cross-legged in the traditional Indian way. Another typical feature of the Gandhara Art is the rich carving, elaborate ornamentation and complex symbolism. The best specimens of Gandhara art are from Jaulian and Dharmarajika *stupa* at Taxila and from Hadda near Jalalabad in modern Afghanistan. The tallest rock-cut statue of Lord Buddha is also located at Bamiyan in modern Afghanistan and dates back to 3-4 century AD.

The Mathura School of Art: The Mathura School of art flourished at the holy city of Mathura, especially between 1-3 A.D. It established the tradition of transforming Buddhist symbols into human form. Buddha's first image can be traced to Kanishka's reign (about 78 A.D.). The earliest sculptures of Buddha were made keeping the *yaksha* prototype in mind. They were depicted as strongly built with the right hand raised in protection and the left hand on the waist. The figures produced by this school of art do not have moustaches and beards as in the Gandhara Art. These figures can be seen in the museum of Mathura. The standing Buddha figures resembles the *yaksha* figures and indicates the Kushan influence. The seated figures are in the *padmasana* posture. The Mathura School not only produced beautiful images of the Buddha but also of the Jain Tirthankaras and gods and goddesses of the Hindu pantheon. Many scholars believe that the Mathura School of Art, although of indigenous origin, was greatly influenced by the Gandhara School of Art. The Guptas adopted the Mathura School of Art and further improvised and perfected it.

The Amravati School of Art: This school of art developed at Amravati, on the banks of the Krishna River in modern Andhra Pradesh. It is the site for the largest Buddhist *stupa* of South India. Its construction began in 200 B.C. and was completed in 200 A.D. The diameter of the *stupa* at the base was 51 metres. The height of the dome was 31 metres and its outer railing was 5 metres wide. The stupendous *stupa* could not withstand the ravages of time and its ruins are preserved in the London Museum.

TEMPLE ARCHITECTURE OF INDIA

As temples form the backbone of Indian medieval architectural heritage, it would be appropriate to discuss their basic architectural features before we move on to different styles of Indian architecture. Despite the vastness of the land, Indian temple architecture is remarkably uniform. It is, however, often distinguished into two chief styles, each having numerous sub-styles. The Northern or Indo-Aryan style is marked by a tower with rounded top and curvilinear outline while the Southern or Dravidian style has the tower usually in the shape of a rectangular truncated pyramid.

The standard type of the Hindu temple has remained fundamentally same from the 6th century AD to the present day. The construction of temples – whether in the north in the south – essentially followed a similar pattern. There is the sanctuary or the *vimana* of which the upper and outer pyramidal and tapering portion is called the *shikhara*, or pinnacle. The *vimana* is a rather dark place that houses the divine deity. This small area is called *garbha griha*, literally meaning 'womb house'. The entrance is through a doorway, normally from the eastern side. The doorway is reached through a *mandapa* or pillared hall, where devotees congregate for prayers. However, earlier temples may have had the *mandapa* at a little distance from the main temple (the Shore Temple in Mamallapuram near Chennai, circa 700 A.D.), although this practise was done away with in later constructions. Later it became necessary to unite both buildings, making way for the *antarala* or intermediate vestibule. A porch or a smaller room called *ardha mandapa* leads up to a hall (*mandapa*), which in turn goes into a *maha mandapa*. A tower generally surmounted the shrine-room while smaller towers rose from other parts of the building. The whole conception was set in a rectangular courtyard, which sometimes contained lesser shrines and was often placed on a raised platform. The most perfect examples of temples on this structure are the Khajuraho temples. Here, each chamber has its own separate pyramidal roof rising in gradual steps so that the final sanctum's roof towers up, surrounded by smaller spires, finally forming a graceful, rising stepped pyramid.

In some parts of India, the ascending pyramid roof format was not followed. The roof in such temples was still pyramidal, but was formed of layers that gradually became narrower as they rose. A courtyard was built around the temple, and sometimes a wall would be constructed to ensure seclusion. The outer walls were treated by carving in an orderly group of repetitive miniatures. The *shikhara* or tapering roof was specifically based on this design, which may have originated from the domed huts of central and eastern India.

THE PRATHIHARAS

The Pratiharas, who ruled over an extensive empire from Ujjain during the 8th and 9th centuries, were among the significant successors of the Guptas. The Pratihara temples of Central India have their own unique designs and decorative schemes. The important temples of Ujjain include the Mahakaleshwar temple, which has one of the twelve *Jyotirlingas* of India, Kal Bhairava temple, which finds a mention in the *Skanda Purana,* and Mangalnath temple, which is regarded as the birthplace of Mars, according to the *Matsya Purana.*

THE PALAS

The Pala School of Architecture (8-13 Centuries AD) flourished in Bengal and Bihar under the Pala and the Sena rulers. Nalanda was its most active centre, whose influence was spread to Nepal, Myanmar and even Indonesia. Stone sculptures of this period are found at Nalanda, Rajagriha, Bodh Gaya, Rajashahi and other places. The Pala School of art is seen at its best at Nalanda and several sculptures belonging to this period have been unearthed in excavations.

THE CHANDELAS

The Chandelas of Jijihoti or Bundelkhand were known as great builders during the 10th-11th centuries. It is they who built the temples at Khajuraho justly famous for their graceful contours and erotic sculptures. These 22 temples (out of the original 85) are regarded as one of world's greatest artistic wonders. The Khajuraho Temples do not illustrate a development over a long period of time but were built within a short period of hundred years from 950-1050 A.D. The Khajuraho Temples have highly individualistic architectural character and are generally small in size. Each temple is divided into three main compartments - the *cella* or *garbha griha,* an assembly hall or *mandapa* and an entrance portico or *ardha mandapa.* Some temples also contain the *antarala* or vestibule to the *cella* and the transepts or *maha-mandapa.* The Kendriya Mahadev temple is the largest and most beautiful of the Khajuraho Temples. The Shiva Temple at Visvanath and the Vishnu Temple at Chaturbhanj are other important temples at Khajuraho.

CAVE ARCHITECTURE OF INDIA

The earliest man-made caves date back to the 2 century BC while the latest date to the 7 century AD. The splendid sculpture and lovely frescoes adorning these caves make them one of the glorious monuments of India's past.

AJANTA CAVES

The cave temples of Ajanta, situated north of Aurangabad, were first mentioned in the writings of the Chinese pilgrim Huen Tsang who visited India between 629 AD and 645 AD. These caves were discovered by the British officers in 1819 AD. The thirty temples at Ajanta are set into the rocky sides of a crescent shaped gorge in the Inhyadri hills of the Sahyadri ranges. At the head of the gorge is a natural pool which is fed by a waterfall. The excavations spanned a period of about six centuries. The earlier monuments include both *chaitya* halls and monasteries. These date from the 2nd to 1st centuries B.C. After a period of more than six centuries, excavations once again revived during the reign of the Vakataka ruler Harishena. The sculptures contain an impressive array of votive figures, accessory figures, narrative episodes and decorative motifs. The series of paintings is unparalleled in the history of Indian art, both for the wide range of subjects and the medium. The caves depict a large number of incidents from the life of the Buddha (Jataka Tales). Overlapping figures suggest that the perspective and colors are harmoniously blended and that the line work is sinuous. However, the identities of the artists responsible for the execution of the Ajanta caves are unknown.

BHIMBETAKA CAVES

Bhimbetaka is located in the Raisen District of Madhya Pradesh about 45 km to the southeast of Bhopal near a hill village called 'Bhiyanpur'. Bhimbetaka, discovered in 1958 by V.S. Wakanker, is the biggest prehistoric art depository in India. A top the hill a large number of rock-shelters have been discovered, of which more than 130 contain paintings. Excavations in some of the rock-shelters revealed history of continuous habitation from early stone age (about 10000 years) to the end of stone age (c. 10,000 to 2,000 years) as seen from artificially made stone tools and implements like hand-axes, cleavers, scrappers and knives. Neolithic tools like points, trapezes and lunates made of chert and chalcedony, besides stone querns and grinders, decorated bone objects, pieces of ochre and human burials were also found here.

ELEPHANTA CAVES

The 6th century Shiva temple in the Elephanta caves is one of the most exquisitely carved temples in India. The central attraction here is a twenty-foot high bust of the deity in three-headed form. The Maheshamurti is built deep into a recess and looms up from the darkness to fill the full height of the cave. This image symbolizes the fierce, feminine and meditative aspects of the great ascetic and the three heads represent Lord Shiva as *Aghori, Ardhanarishvara* and *Mahayogi.* Aghori is the aggressive form of Shiva where he is intent on destruction. Ardhanarishvara depicts Lord Shiva as half-man/half-woman signifying the essential unity of the sexes. The Mahayogi posture symbolises the meditative aspect of the God and here Lord Shiva is shown in his most quiet and serene form. Other sculptures in these caves depict Shiva's cosmic dance of primordial creation and destruction and his marriage to Parvati.

MAHAKALI CAVES

These are rock-cut Buddhist caves situated in the Udayagiri hills, about 6.5 km from Mumbai. These were excavated during 200 BC to 600 AD and are now in ruins. They comprise of 4 caves on the southeastern face and 15 caves on the northwestern face. Cave 9 is the chief cave and is the oldest and consists of a stupa and figures of Lord Buddha.

JOGESHWAR AND KANHERI CAVES

Located in the western suburbs of Bombay, it is second largest known cave after the Kailasa cave in Ellora and houses a Brahmanical temple dating back to the 6 century AD.

Excavated between the 1st and 2nd centuries, the Kanheri is a 109-cave complex located near Borivili National Park in Bombay. The Kanheri caves contain illustrations from Hinayana and Mahayana Buddhism and show carvings dating back to 200 BC.

KARLA AND BHAJA CAVES

About 50-60 kms away from Pune, these are rock-cut Buddhist caves dating back to the 1st and 2nd centuries BC. The caves consist of several *viharas* and *chaityas*.

RAJPUT ARCHITECTURE

The Rajputs were great patrons of art and architecture, the finest examples being their forts and palaces. The Rajput palaces are complex compositions built as inner citadels surrounded by the city and enclosed by a fortified wall as at Chittorgarh and Jaisalmer. Some forts, such as those at Bharatpur and Deeg, were protected by wide moats.

The oldest surviving palaces date from the mid-fifteenth century and are found at Chittor and Gwalior. The *Man Mandir*, the largest palace in Gwalior, was built by Raja Man Singh Tomar (1486-1516). The *Man Mandir* has two storeys above, and two below, ground level overhanging a sandstone cliff. This gigantic cliff is punctuated by five massive round towers, crowned by domed cupolas and linked by delicately carved parapets. The whole facade is enriched with brilliant blue tiles.

The palaces of Jaisalmer, Bikaner, Jodhpur, Udaipur and Kota represent the maturity of the Rajput style. All of these palaces were built predominantly in the 17th and early 18th centuries. The huge fortified city of Jaisalmer is situated far out in the Thar Desert. The buildings are constructed with the local yellow-brown stone and they have been remarkably preserved owing to their remote location.

The city of Bikaner is encircled by 5.63 km long stone wall in rich pink sandstone. There are five gates and three sally ports. The Jodhpur Fort dominates the city, which is surrounded by a huge wall with 101 bastions, nearly 9.5 km long. The Meherangarh fort stands on a cliff with a sheer drop of over 36 metres.

The foundation of Jaipur, the fabled "pink city", in 1727 AD represents the final phase of Rajput architecture. Built by Jai Singh, Jaipur represents a fusion of Eastern and Western ideas of town planning. The city is enclosed by a wall and has bastions and towers at regular intervals. The City Palace is at the center of the walled city and is a spectacular synthesis of Rajput and Mughal architectural styles. The famous building *Hawa Mahal*, or Palace of Winds, (1799) has a five-storeyed symmetrical facade composed of 953 small casements in a huge curve each with a projecting balcony and crowning arch. The *Jantar Mantar*, the largest of five observatories built by Jai Singh II in the early eighteenth century, is another interesting example of Rajput architecture.

JAIN ARCHITECTURE

The contribution of Jain art to the mainstream art in India has been considerable. Every phase of Indian art is represented by a Jain version and each one of them is worthy of meticulous study and understanding. Jain architecture cannot be accredited with a style of its own, for in the first place it was almost an offshoot of Hindu and Buddhist styles. In the initial years, many Jain temples were made adjoining the Buddhist temples following the Buddhist rock-cut style. Initially these temples were mainly carved out of rock faces and the use of bricks was almost negligible. However, in later years Jains started building temple-cities on hills based on the concept of 'mountains of immortality'.

Compared to the number of Hindu temples in India, Jain temples are few and spaced out. Surrounded by embattled walls, the temples are divided into wards, guarded by massive bastions at its ends, with fortified gateways as the main entrances. These temple-cities were not built on a specific plan; instead they were the results of sporadic construction. Natural levels of the hill on which the 'city' was being built accommodated various levels so that as one goes higher the architecture and grandeur increases. The only variation in these temples was in the form of frequent chamukhs or four-faced temples. In these the image of a Tirthankara faces the four sides, or four Tirthankars are be placed back to back to face four cardinal points. Entry into this temple is also from four doors. The Chamukh temple of Adinath (1618 AD) is a characteristic example of the four-door temple.

The great Jain temples and sculptured monuments of Karnataka, Maharashtra and Rajasthan are world-renowned. The most spectacular of all Jain temples are found at Ranakpur and Mount Abu in Rajasthan. Deogarh (Lalitpur, U.P.), Ellora, Badami and Aihole also have some of the important specimens of Jain Art.

THE INDO-ISLAMIC ARCHITECTURE

Indian architecture took new shape with the advent of Islamic rule in India towards the end of the 12 century AD. New elements were introduced into the Indian architecture that include: use of shapes (instead of natural forms); inscriptional art using decorative lettering or calligraphy; inlay decoration and use of coloured marble, painted plaster and brilliantly glazed tiles. In contrast to the indigenous Indian architecture which was of the *trabeate* order i.e. all spaces were spanned by means of horizontal beams, the Islamic architecture was *arcuate* i.e. an arch or dome was adopted as a method of bridging a space. The concept of arch or dome was not invented by the Muslims but was, in fact, borrowed and was further perfected by them from the architectural styles of the post-Roman period. The Muslims used the cementing agent in the form of mortar for the first time in the construction of buildings in India. They further put to use certain scientific and mechanical formulae, which were derived by experience of other civilizations, in their constructions in India. Such use of scientific principles helped not only in obtaining greater strength and stability of the construction materials but also provided greater flexibility to the architects and builders. This amalgamation of the Indian and the Islamic elements led to the emergence of a new style of architecture called the *Indo-Islamic Architecture*.

One fact that must be stressed here is that, the Islamic elements of architecture had already passed through different experimental phases in other countries like Egypt, Iran and Iraq before these were introduced in India. Unlike most Islamic monuments of these countries, which were largely constructed in brick, plaster and rubble, the Indo-Islamic monuments were typical mortar-masonry works formed of dressed stones. It must be emphasized that the development of the Indo-Islamic architecture was greatly facilitated by the knowledge and skill possessed by the Indian craftsmen, who had mastered the art of stonework for centuries and used their experience while constructing Islamic monuments in India.

In simple terms the Islamic architecture in India can be divided into religious and secular. Mosques and Tombs represent the religious architecture, while palaces and forts are examples of secular Islamic architecture. Forts were essentially functional, complete with a little township within and various fortifications to engage and repel the enemy.

MOSQUES

The mosque or *masjid* is a representation of Muslim art in its simplest form. The mosque is basically an open courtyard surrounded by a pillared verandah, crowned off with a dome. A *mihrab* indicates the direction of the *qibla* for prayer. Towards the right of the *mihrab* stands the *mimbar* or pulpit from where the *Imam* presides over the proceedings. An elevated platform, usually a minaret from where the Faithful are summoned to attend the prayers is an invariable part of a mosque. Large mosques where the faithful assemble for the Friday prayers are called the Jama Masjids.

TOMBS

Although not actually religious in nature, the tomb or *maqbara* introduced an entirely new architectural concept. While the *masjid* was mainly known for its simplicity, a tomb could range from being a simple affair (Aurangazeb's grave) to an awesome structure enveloped in grandeur (Taj Mahal). The tomb usually consists of solitary compartment or tomb chamber known as the *huzrah* in whose centre is the cenotaph or *zarih*. This entire structure is covered with an elaborate dome. In the underground chamber lies the mortuary or the *maqbara*, in which the corpse is buried in a grave or *qabr*. Smaller tombs may have a *mihrab*, although larger mausoleums have a separate mosque located separately from the main tomb. Normally the whole tomb complex or *rauza* is surrounded by an enclosure. The tomb of a Muslim saint is called a *dargah*. Almost all Islamic monuments were subjected to free use of verses from the Holy Koran and a great amount of time was spent in carving out minute details on walls, ceilings, pillars and domes.

COLONIAL ARCHITECTURE

European colonists brought with them to India concepts of their "world view" and a whole baggage of the history of European architecture — Neo-Classical, Romanesque, Gothic and Renaissance. The initial structures were utilitarian warehouses and walled trading posts, giving way to fortified towns along the coastline. The Portuguese adapted to India the climatically appropriate Iberian galleried patio house and the Baroque churches of Goa. *Se Cathedral* and *Arch of Conception* of Goa were built in the typical Portuguese-Gothic style. The St. Francis Church at Cochin, built by the Portuguese in 1510, is believed to be the first church built by the Europeans in India. The Portuguese also built the fort of *Castella de Aguanda* near Mumbai and added fortifications to the Bassein fort built by Bahadur Shah, the Sultan of Gujarat, in 1532 AD. The Bassein fort is famous for the *Matriz* (Cathedral of St Joseph), the Corinthian pillared hall and the *Porte da Mer* (sea gate).

The Danish influence is evident in Nagapatnam, which was laid out in squares and canals and also in Tranquebar and Serampore. The French gave a distinct urban design to its settlement in Pondicherry by applying the Cartesian grid plans and classical architectural patterns. The *Church of Sacred Heart of Jesus (Eglise De Sacre Coeur De Jesus)*, the *Eglise de Notre Dame de Anges* and the *Eglise de Notre Dame de Lourdes* at Pondicherry have a distinct French influence.

However, it was the British who left a lasting impact on the India architecture. They saw themselves as the successors to the Mughals and used architecture as a symbol of power. The British followed various architectural styles – Gothic, Imperial, Christian, English Renaissance and Victorian being the essentials.

The first buildings were factories but later courts, schools, municipal halls and *dak* bungalows came up, which were ordinary structures built by garrison engineers. A deeper concern with architecture was exhibited in churches and other public buildings. Most of the buildings were adaptations of the buildings designed by leading British architects of that time like Wren, Adam, Nash and others in London and other places. For instance, the Church of St. John at Calcutta was built in 1787 inspired by St. Stephens Church at Walbrooks, the Government House in Calcutta was built by Capt. Charles Wyatt modelled on the Kedleston Hall of Derbyshire, the Indian Government Mint in Calcutta is a half-scale replica of the Temple of Minerva at Athens and the Pachaiyappa's Hall in Chennai was modelled on the Athenium Temple of Theseus. Unlike Europe, however, these buildings were built mostly of brick and stuccoed with lime or *chunam*, sometimes "facades" incised to look like stones. Some later buildings were, however, built with stones. Churches, which were symbols of colonialism, were built in great style. Based on London prototypes, several churches evolved with variations as highly original works. The earliest example is the St. Mary's Church in Fort St. George in Chennai.

Neo-Gothic architecture flourished in different parts of India under the British, inspired by the Houses of Parliament in London. Colonel Thomas Cowper built the town hall in Bombay during 1820 to 1835. Governor Sir Bartle Frere tried to give a truly imperial ambience to the city of Bombay. During his reign the old town walls were broken down and the Gateway of India was built in the Gothic style of architecture. The Secretariat, University Library, Rajabai Tower, Telegraph Office and the Victoria Terminus all followed the Victorian Gothic style, similar to buildings in London. Undoubtedly, the Victoria Terminus, designed by the architect Frederick Willaim Stevens modelled on the St. Pancras Station, is the finest example of Gothic architecture with a subtle hint of the Indo-Saracenic motifs, an extravaganza of polychromatic stone, decorated tile marble and stained glass. Stevens also designed other buildings like the Churchgate Terminus and the Municipal Building opposite the Victoria Terminus.

In Varanasi, one of the true Gothic monuments is Queen's College, built in a perpendicular style by Major Kitoe from 1847 to 1852. In Allahabad, the British built a series of edifices including the University, All Saints Cathedral, the High Court and the Mayo College. In Calcutta, a High Court was constructed following the Gothic style. The Howrah Bridge (1943), with its red brick facade surrounded by eight square towers represents a combination of the Oriental and Roman styles. Fort William, the stronghold of the British in mid 19 century that took 13 years to construct at a cost of more than $3.5 million and the Victoria Memorial in Calcutta (1921), designed by Sir William Emerson, are probably the most imposing of all British structures in India.

The passing of power from the East India Company to the British Crown, the rise of Indian nationalism and the introduction of Railways were the watersheds in the British Colonial Indian architectural history. New materials like concrete, glass, wrought and cast iron opened up new architectural possibilities. The British also started assimilating and adopting the native Indian styles in the architecture. All these factors led to the development of Indo-Saracenic architecture towards the end of the 19 century. Victorian in essence, it borrowed heavily from the Islamic style of Mughal and Afghan rulers. In fact it was a *pot pouri* of architectural styles; a hybrid style that combined in a wonderful manner diverse architectural elements of Hindu and Mughal with gothic cusped arches, domes, spires, tracery, minarets and stained glass.

The Indo-Saracenic style was Indian on the outside and British inside since the facade was built with an Indian touch while the interior was solely Victorian. F.S.Growse, Sir Swinton Jacob, R.F.Chisholm and H.Irwin were the pioneers of this style of architecture. The Chepauk Palace in Chennai designed by Paul Benfield is said to be the first Indo-Saracenic building in India. Other outstanding examples of this style of architecture include the Law Courts, Victoria Memorial Hall, Presidency College and Senate House of Chennai, Muir College at Allahabad, Napier Museum at Thiruvanthapuram, the Post Office, Prince of Wales Museum and the Gateway of India in Mumbai, the Maharaja's Palace at Mysore and M.S.University and Lakshmi Villas Palace at Baroda.

The architecture of New Delhi was the crowning glory of the British Raj. Robert Byron described New Delhi as "The Rome of Hindostan". The British built New Delhi as a systematically planned city after it was made the capital in 1911. The British Viceroy made Sir Edward Lutyens responsible for the overall plan of Delhi. He was specifically directed to "harmonise externally with the traditions of Indian art". Thus, the Western architecture with Oriental motif was realised with *chajjas, jalis* and *chhattris*, as stylistic devices in the Viceroy's House (now Rashtrapati Bhawan). Herbert Baker added the imposing buildings of the South Block and the North Block, which flank the Rashtrapati Bhawan. Another Englishman called Robert Tor Tussell built the Connaught Place and the Eastern and Western Courts.

St Martin's Garrison Church marks the culmination of the British architectural ventures in India. The Church is a huge monolith with a high square tower and deeply sunken window ledges reminiscent of Dutch and German architecture.

MODERN ARCHITECTURE OF INDIA

After the British left India in 1947, Indian architecture dropped into an abyss. Indian architects, who were relegated to the role of being assistants to the British architects under the British Raj, took their own time to express their ingenuity. Perhaps, there was an identity crisis, a dilemma whether to bask in the glory of the past or move forward with times using new ideas, images and techniques. While in other fields like art, music and culture, the distinct Indian imprint was more enhanced in the post-Independence period; no such thing was discernible in the case of architecture. It is no doubt that the Indian architects were unable to achieve a transformative architecture despite the existence of great potential at the time of Indian Independence.

The post-Independence period saw the emergence of two schools of thought in architecture—the Revivalist and the Modernist. The Revivalists, who advocated "continuity with the past", could not break the shackles of the colonial legacy and left no significant impact on the neo-Indian architecture. The Modernists too depended heavily on the European and American models and tried to adopt them in India without taking into consideration the regional aspirations, diversities and requirements. The contemporary Indian architecture was also beset with problems like population explosion, lack of vision among the planners, lack of support from the government and a less than satisfactory standard of architecture education. The result was that during the initial years after the Independence, foreign architects continued to play a leading role in Indian architecture.

Jawaharlal Nehru, the first Prime Minister, had called for an open architectural competition for the design of the Ashoka Hotel in 1956, which was won by B.E. Doctor, an architect from Bombay. Using technology to create large pillar-less spaces, Doctor created a facade that borrowed from Islamic, Hindu, British and modern architecture.

Indian architecture witnessed a revolution when the Punjab government engaged Le Corbusier to design the new city of Chandigarh. Built in three stages, Corbusier divided the city into three sections. The 'head' consisted of political, bureaucratic and judicial buildings, the administrative parts of the city. The 'body' housed the university and residential complexes in the heart of the city. The 'feet' consisted of industrial sectors and the railway station. Apart from the initial layout of the city, Corbusier also designed several buildings in Chandigarh. The High Court building has a sloping roof, supported by concrete walls which allow air to pass through them. The Assembly is a squarish structure topped with a huge industrial chimney while the Secretariat is made up of hundreds of rooms with an airy exterior.

Taking inspiration from Le Corbusier's creativity, a young Indian architect D.V. Joshi designed the Institute of Indology in Ahmedabad. Charles Mark Correa, Doshi's contemporary, designed the Hindustan Lever pavilion for the India International Trade Fair in 1961. The pavilion was an exposed concrete structure resembling a crumpled packing case made of concrete with a zigzag ramp to walk along. Correa also designed the Gandhi Sanghralaya in Ahmedabad as a tribute to Mahatma Gandhi.

The Asiad Village in New Delhi, designed by Raj Rewell and built as a colossal complex with more than 800 residential units, landscaped courts, streets, restaurants and shops, all catering to sports persons who had assembled for the 1982 Asian Games, is one of the architectural landmarks of modern India. The lotus-shaped Bahai temple in New Delhi, designed by Fariburz Sabha in 1980 and completed in December 1986, is an awe-inspiring example of the ingenuity of the Indian architects.

However, the fact remains that the contemporary architecture in India has failed to inspire. Even after 50 years of Independence our cities are still symbolised by pre-independence buildings. For instance, Calcutta is symbolised by the Victoria Memorial, New Delhi by the Rashtrapati Bhawan, Mumbai by the Victoria Terminus and the Gateway of India and Chennai by the Victoria Memorial Hall. The post-independence buildings such as the New Secretariat building in Calcutta or the Vigyan Bhawan in New Delhi has nothing much to offer in terms of architectural style.

In contrast most major cities in the world have splendid modern buildings to boast off, like Sydney has its Sydney Opera House, Paris has new Grand Arch and the Georges Pompidos Centre, New York has its World Trade Centre, Chicago has the Sears Tower and Toronto has the C.N.Tower. Even cities in other Third World countries have several buildings to feel proud about, like Kuala Lumpur has its Petronas Tower, Shangai has the TV Tower, Hong Kong has its Hongkong and Shanghai Corporation building and the Bank of China Building and even Colombo has its new Parliament building.

In November 1998, the media reported that the foundation stone of World Centre of Vedic Learning, the world's tallest building would be laid at Karondi village, in Jabalpur in Madhya Pradesh. The building, which will be built by the Maharishi Mahesh Yogi Vedic University, is being designed according to the Maharishi Sthapatya Veda symbolising the victory of India's ancient knowledge of Vastu Vidya. The proposed centre for Vedic consciousness, which is modelled on Sao Paulo Tower of Brazil, would be 677 metres (2222 feet) high and 339 metres (1111 feet) wide at the square base. Once completed it will be more than 213 metres (700 feet) taller than the Petronas Tower in Kuala Lumpur and will achieve the distinction of being the world's tallest building. It was also reported that a consortium of architects and engineers who have designed several of the tallest structures in the world is undertaking the design of the building. Indeed, India will have something to cheer about if this building materializes!

Madhya Pradesh seems to be the only state in India which has several grand public buildings and international award winning projects. The New Assembly building in Bhopal and the Madhya Pradesh State Electricity Board office in Jabalpur, The Judicial Academy in Bhopal, the Rajiv Gandhi Jal Grahan Mission in Raipur and the proposed "White House" in Bhopal are some fascinating examples which show that global aesthetics is moving very fast into the smaller Indian cities. Paradoxically, it is the smaller cities and towns like Indore, Raipur, Rajkot, Baroda and Bhopal, with no greatly visible architectural traditions like that of Jaipur, Hyderabad or Lucknow, that are displaying unprecedented alacrity in adapting to 'international styles'. There is a growing brand of young and dynamic architects, which include Charles Correa, Prashant Diwakriti, Ajay Kataria, Anjum Gupta, Vineet Chadha, Nikhil Sompura and others, who do not shy away from experimentation. Most often these architects employ a hybrid style that is a free mix of Roman, English, Gothic, Rajasthani and Mughal styles. This new-age architectural aesthetics has redefined the idea of space. The emphasis now seems to be on having more open spaces, green spaces and natural lighting. It is, however, not possible to term this new trend as a 'representative' architecture of our times as it is highly restricted in geographic terms and also confined to the affluent lot.

3

TYPES OF INDIAN ARCHITECTURE

The architecture of India encompasses a wide variety of geographically and historically spread structures, and was transformed by the long history of India. The result is an evolving range of architectural production that, in spite of the difficulty to identify it with any single representative style, retains a certain amount of continuity across history. The diversity of Indian culture is represented in its architecture. Indian architecture comprises a blend of ancient and varied native traditions, with building types, forms and technologies from West and Central Asia and Europe.

Studies of Indian architecture normally begin with the ancient Indus Valley Civilisation that flourished in the basin of River Indus, moving through the late Vedic period, the Maurya-Gupta age of Buddhist and Hindu monuments, monasteries and Indian rock-cut architecture, followed by the great temple-building of the medieval era. Turk and Afghan rulers in the north, during medieval times brought with them West Asian traditions of the arch, the dome and the vault. With the rise of the Rajputs in north-western India, a distinctive form of Indian architectural design developed. The rise of the Mughal Empire in the 16th century established a sophisticated synthesis of Indian regional elements with ideas from Persia and West Asia, a style that was adopted across the subcontinent even by post-Mughal rulers and recognized today as Mughal architecture. The subsequent European colonization of India paved the way for the entry of styles from that continent, including Mannerist, Baroque, Neo-Classical and Neo-Gothic styles, which were followed in the late 19th-century by the hybrid Indo-European style called the *Indo-Saracenic*.

Architecture of India is rooted in its history. Indian architecture progressed with time and assimilated the many influences that came as a result of India's global discourse with other regions of the world throughout its millennia old past. The architectural methods practiced in India are a result of examination and implementation of its established building traditions and outside cultural interactions.

Though old, this Eastern tradition has also incorporated modern values as India became a modern nation state. The economic reforms of 1991 further bolstered the urban architecture of India as the country became more integrated with the world's economy. Traditional *Vastu Shastra* remains influential in India's architecture during the contemporary era.

MEHRGARH CULTURE—INDUS VALLEY CIVILIZATION (7000 BCE—1500 CE)

Archaeological evidence from Mehrgarh (7000 BCE) shows construction of mud brick houses and granaries. Irrigation was developed in the Indus Valley Civilization around 4500 BCE. The size and prosperity of the Indus civilization grew as a result of this innovation, which eventually lead to more planned settlements which further made use of drainage and sewers.

By 2800 BCE, private bathrooms, located on the ground floor, were found in nearly all the houses of the Indus Valley Civilization. The pottery pipes in walls allowed drainage of water and there was, in some case, provision of a crib for sitting. The Indus Valley Civilization had some of the most advanced private lavatories in the world. "Western-style" toilets were made from bricks using toilet seats made of wood on top. The waste was then transmitted to drainage systems. Sophisticated irrigation and storage systems were developed by the Indus Valley Civilization, including the artificial reservoirs at Girnar in 3000 BCE and an early canal irrigation system from circa 2600 BCE.

Large-scale sanitary sewer systems were in place in the Indus Valley by 2700 BCE. The drains were 7-10 feet wide and 2 feet (0.61 m) below ground level. The sewage was then led into cesspools, built at the intersection of two drains, which had stairs leading to them for periodic cleaning. Plumbing using earthenware plumbing pipes with broad flanges for easy joining with asphalt to stop leaks was in place by 2700 BCE.

Pramod Chandra (2008) details the Indus Valley architecture from 2500–1800 BCE: From excavated remains, it is clear that the Indus Valley civilization possessed a flourishing urban architecture. The major cities associated with the civilization, notably Mohenjo-daro, Harappâ, and Kalibangan, were laid out on a grid pattern and had provisions for an advanced drainage system. The residential buildings, which were serviceable enough, were mainly brick and consisted of an open patio flanked by rooms. For monumental architecture, the evidence is slight, the most important being a "sacred" tank (thought to be for ritual ablution) and associated structures. Corbel vaulting (arches supported by brackets projecting from the wall) was known, and, to a limited extent, timber was used together with brick; whatever architectural ornamentation existed must have been of brick or plaster.

VEDIC PERIOD—POST MAHA JANAPADAS PERIOD (1500 BCE—200 CE)

The Buddhist stupa, a dome shaped monument, was used in India as a commemorative monument associated with storing sacred relics. The stupa architecture was adopted in Southeast and East Asia, where it became prominent as a Buddhist monument used for enshrining sacred relics. Upon its discovery, this architectural became known as *pagoda* to the people from the western world. Fortified cities with stûpas, *viharas*, and temples were constructed during the Maurya empire (c. 321–185 BCE). Wooden architecture was popular and rock cut architecture became solidified. Guard rails—consisting of posts, crossbars, and a coping—became a feature of safety surrounding a stupa. Temples—build on elliptical, circular, quadrilateral, or apsidal plans—were constructed using brick and timber. The Indian gateway archs, the *torana*, reached East Asia with the spread of Buddhism. Some scholars hold that *torii* derives from the torana gates at the Buddhist historic site of Sanchi (3rd century BCE - 11 century CE).

Rock-cut stepwells in India date from 200-400 CE. Subsequently, the wells at Dhank (550-625 CE) and construction of stepped ponds at Bhinmal (850-950 CE) takes place. The city of Mohenjo-daro has wells which may be the predecessors of the step well; as many as 700 wells, constructed by 3rd millennium BCE, have been discovered in just one section of the city, leading scholars to believe that 'cylindrical brick lined wells' were invented by the people of the Indus Valley Civilization. Cave temples became prominent throughout western India, incorporating various features and material to give rise to cave architecture in places such as Ajatna and Ellora.

Walled and moated cities with large gates and multi-storied buildings which consistently used arched windows and doors are important features of the architecture during this period. The Indian emperor Ashoka (rule: 273 BCE to 232 BCE) himself established a chain of hospitals throughout the Mauryan empire by 230 BCE. One of the edicts of Ashoka (272—231 BCE) reads: "Everywhere King Piyadasi (Asoka) erected two kinds of hospitals, hospitals for people and hospitals for animals. Where there were no healing herbs for people and animals, he ordered that they be bought and planted." Buddhist architecture blended with Roman architecture and Hellenestic architecture to give rise to unique blends—such as the Greco-Buddhist school.

EARLY COMMON ERA—HIGH MIDDLE AGES (200 CE—1200 CE)

Universities—housing thousands of teachers and students—flourished at Nalanda and Valabhi between the 4th-8th centuries. South Indian temple architecture—visible as a distinct tradition during the 7th century CE—is described below:

The South Indian temple consists essentially of a square-chambered sanctuary topped by a superstructure, tower, or spire and an attached pillared porch or hall enclosed by a peristyle of cells within a rectangular court. The external walls of the temple are segmented by pilasters and carry niches housing sculpture. The superstructure or tower above the sanctuary is of the kûmina type and consists of an arrangement of gradually receding stories in a pyramidal shape. Each story is delineated by a parapet of miniature shrines, square at the corners and rectangular with barrel-vault roofs at the centre. The tower is topped by a dome-shaped cupola and a crowning pot and finial.

North Indian temples showed increased elevation of the wall and elaborate spire by the 10th century. Richly decorated temples—including the complex at Khajuraho—were constructed in Central India. Indian traders bought Indian architecture to South east Asia through various trade routes.

LATE MIDDLE AGES—EARLY MODERN ERA (1200 CE—1757 CE)

Pramod Chandra (2008) holds that the Indo-Islamic architecture of Gujarat was unique and indigenous as it 'reinterprets foreign influences with great resourcefulness and confidence, producing works notable for their integrity and unity'. Foreign influences assimilated into native traditions led to the rise of Mughal architecture. Hindu kingdoms adopted aspects of Indo-Islamic architecture to construct palaces among other structures. The first prefabricated homes and movable structures were invented in 16th century Mughal India by Akbar the Great. These structures were reported by Arif Qandahari in 1579.

Mughal tombs of sandstone and marble show Persian influence. The Red Fort at Agra (1565–74) and the walled city of Fatehpur Sikri (1569–74) are among the architectural achievements of this time—as is the Taj Mahal, built as a tomb for Queen Mumtaz Mahal by Shah Jahan (1628–58). Employing the double dome, the recessed archway, white marble and parks while stressing on symmetry and detail was visible during the reign of Shah Jahan. Quranic verses were described on the walls of the buildings. However, the depiction of any living being—and essential part of the pre-Islamic tradition of India—was forbidden under Islam.

Some scholars hold that cultural contact with Europe under Manuel I of Portugal (reign: October 25, 1495—December 13, 1521) resulted in exchange of architectural influences. Little literary evidence exists to confirm the Indian influence but some scholars have nonetheless suggested a possible relation based on proximity of architectural styles.

COLONIAL BRITISH ERA (1757 CE—1947 CE)

European colonialism bought with it a wide array of influences to further shape Indian architecture. Imperial power was stressed by using grand buildings. Local craftsmen incorporated new skills and added them to their trade. Colonial architecture became assimilated into India's diverse traditions. Other innovations made during the European Industrial Revolution came with the British Raj to India.

The European involvement in India through the 1920s and the 1930s bought architect Le Corbusier and the Art Deco movement to India. Fusion has been a consistent feature of modern Indian architecture—for example Indian elements of *chhajja* (wide roof overhangs), *jaali* (circular stone apertures) and *chhatri* (free-standing pavilions) were intermixed with European architecture during the construction of the *Rastrapati bhavan*. This neoclassical project—which also contained a *stupa* like dome—was overseen by Sir Edwin Landseer Lutyens and the Indian Institute of Architects (est. 1920).

REPUBLIC OF INDIA (1947 CE—PRESENT)

In recent times there has been a movement of population from rural areas to urban centres of industry, leading to price rise in property in various cities of India. Urban housing in India balances space constrictions and is aimed to serve the working class. Indian government has accepted World Trade Organisation's General Agreement on Trade in Services (GATS), enabling foreign architects to practice in India, and thereby adding to the plurality of Indian building traditions. Growing awareness of ecology has influenced architecture in India during modern times.

Indian buildings reflect India's culture and myths. Jawahar Kala Kendra at Jaipur—for example— represents the layout of a *mandala*. Raj Jadhav (2007) notes the position of traditional *Vastu Shastra* in modern Indian architecture. The ancient Indian architectural text of Vastu Shastra is widely used in modern Indian architecture for planning houses, residential complexes, office, commercial, industrial and other building types. The principles of Vastu Shastra regulate planning and design specifics from town planning to the furniture layout of a room. The stipulations are said to be governed by ancient empirical knowledge of the human body and its relation to the earth and the cosmos. Following these stipulations, it is said, ensures overall human well-being. Hence, a client with a belief in Vastu Shastra will choose a plot of land and locate the functions and elements of a building using the guidelines of this text. Architects and clients consult specialists in Vastu Shastra and then agree upon a design. The belief in this ancient body of knowledge is experiencing a rapid revival.

Security is a main concern in government buildings. The architecture of these buildings lays emphasis on security precautions. One method of achieving that may be designing separate entrances for separate user groups. The VIP entrances and exits can have required security arrangements for ensuring safety.

Concentricity has been employed in Indian architecture since millenia. The plan of early buildings aligned them to a spiritual motif corresponding to cosmological imagination. The concentric feature of Indian architecture is common to buildings of various regions and cultures within India—notable examples being various Hindu temples, the Taj Mahal, and buildings constructed using Rajasthani architecture. This plan is divided into various parts by the designer who uses concentric placing of these parts in his construction. Modern Indian architects continue to use and incorporate this feature in buildings—for example in the Indian Parliament Library or the *Vidhan Sabha* (Bhopal). A significant feature of India's architecture is the courtyard. Klaus-Peter Gast (2007) elaborates on the significance of courtyards in India.

The courtyards also take up an old Indian architectural motif whereby the courtyard provides light and air for the rooms directly in this hot climate, and people are able to spend time outside or inside according to the time of day. The courtyard is also the classical symbol of something shared, a place where people meet, spend time with each other and live together. This aspect is emphasised in the courtyard for the general public, which is placed immediately inside the entrance and constructed in the form of a Kund, a large area of stone steps. Here people spend their waiting time together almost as if in a state of communal meditation. A waiting area that would be completely inconceivable in Western culture functions as a "think tank" here, with the ambience of waiting stimulating communal reflection.

Climate responsive architecture has long been a feature of India's architecture but has been losing its significance as of late. Indian architecture reflects its various socio-cultural sensibilities which vary from region to region. Certain areas are traditionally held to be belonging to women. Villages in India have features such as courtyards, loggias, terraces and balconies. Calico, chintz, and palampore—of Indian origin—highlight the assimilation of Indian textiles in global interior design.

DIFFERENT TYPES OF INDIAN ARCHITECTURE

HARAPPAN ARCHITECTURE

Harappan architecture is the architecture of the Harappans, an ancient people who lived in the Indus Valley from about 3300 BCE to 1600 BCE. The Harappans were advanced for their time, especially in architecture.

City walls

Each city in the Indus Valley was surrounded by massive walls and gateways. The walls were built to control trade and also to stop the city from being flooded. Each part of the city was made up of walled sections. Each section included different buildings such as: Public buildings, houses, markets, and craft workshops.

Streets

The Harappans were great city planners. They based their city streets on a grid system. Streets were oriented east to west. Each street had a well organized drain system. If the drains were not cleaned, the water ran into the houses and silt built up. Then the Harappans would build another story on top of it. This raised the level of the city over the years, and today archaeologists call these high structures "mounds".

Wells

Although not every Harappan house had a well, there are quite common and compromise one of the most recognizable features of Harappan urbanism. Over the years, the level of streets and houses were raised owing to the accumulation of debris which necessitated raising the height of the wells. This is the reason why very tall wells are often seen at Harappa and in surrounding areas.

Houses

Houses and other buildings were made of sun-dried or kiln-fired mud brick. These bricks were so strong, that they have stood up to thousands of years of wear. Each house had an indoor and outdoor kitchen. The outdoor kitchen would be used when it was warmer (so that the oven wouldn't heat up the house), and the indoor kitchen for use when it was colder. In present day, village houses in this region (e.g. in Kachchh) have two kitchens (outdoor and indoor). They use indoor kitchen mostly as store house and use as cooking place only when there is raining outside, otherwise prefer using outdoor kitchen. This is because people use dry shrub and cow dung as cooking fuel which is very smoky and makes indoor cooking difficult.

Tools

The Harappans used chisels, pickaxes, and saws. The saws they used had undulated edges so that dust escaped from the cut that they were sawing. These tools were most likely made of copper, as copper tools and weapons have been found at Harappan sites.

Lack of Temples

So far, no unequivocal examples of temples have been found at sites belonging to the Indus Valley Civilization. Archaeologists do not know yet what religion was practiced in the Indus Valley Civilization. Community water pools (swimming or bathing) do exist, which may be linked with religion practice. Water plays an important role in Hindu sacred places, and pilgrimage to such places often involves sacred bathing (apart from Ganges). The architecture of water pools used by Hindu pilgrimage and in Harappan cities are similar, although scholars disagree whether such similarities are functional, or cultural, in nature.

BADAMI CHALUKYA ARCHITECTURE

The Badami Chalukya Architecture was a temple building idiom that evolved in the time period of 5th - 8th centuries CE in the area of Malaprabha basin, in present day Bagalkot district of Karnataka state. This style is sometimes called the Vesara style and Chalukya style. Their earliest temples date back to around 450 in Aihole when the Badami Chalukyas were feudatories of the Kadambas of Banavasi. According to historian K.V. Sounder Rajan, the Badami Chalukya contribution to temple building matched their valor and their achievements in battle.

Their style includes two types of monuments.

• The rock cut halls (caves)
• Structural temples

The rock cut halls have three basic features:

• Pillared Veranda
• Columned Hall
• A sanctum cut out deep into rock
• Early experiments in rock cut halls were attempted in Aihole where they built three cave temples, one each in Vedic, Buddhist and Jaina styles. Later they refined their style and cut out four marvellous cave temples at Badami.
• One note worthy feature of these cave temples is the running frieze of *Ganas* in various amusing postures caved in relief on each plinth.
• The outside Veranda of the cave temples are rather plain, but the inner hall contains rich and prolific sculptural symbolism. Art critic Dr. M. Sheshadri wrote of the Chalukya art that they cut rock like Titans but finished like jewellers. Critic Zimmer wrote that the Chalukya cave temples are a fine balance of versatility and restrain.

In Pattadakal are their finest structural temples. Of the ten temples in Pattadakal, six are in dravidian style and four in Rekhanagara style. The Virupaksha temple in many way holds resemblance to the Kailasanatha temple in Kanchipuram which came into existence a few years earlier.

- This is a fully inclusive temple, it has a central structure, *nandi* pavilion in front and has a walled enclosure that is entered by a gateway.
- The main sanctum has a *Pradakshinapatha* and *mantapa*. The *mantapa* is pillared and has perforated windows (pierced window screens).
- The external wall surface is divided by pilasters into well spaced ornamental niches filled with either sculptures or perforated windows. Art critic Percy brown says about the sculputres that they flow into the architecture in a continuous stream. It is said that the Virupaskha temple is one of those monuments where the spirit of the men who built it, still lives.

Many centuries later, the serene art of the Badami Chalukya reappeared in the pillared architecture of the Vijayanagar Empire. Their caves include finely engraved sculptures of *Harihara, Trivikrama, Mahisa Mardhini, Tandavamurthi, Paravasudeva, Nataraja, Varaha, Gomateshvara* and others. Plenty of animal and foliage motifs are also included.

Some important sculptors of their time were Gundan Anivaritachari, Revadi Ovajja and Narasobba.

Important Badami Chalukya Temples

Pattadakal

- Virupaksha temple
- Sangameshvara temple
- Kashivisvanatha temple (Rashtrakuta)
- Mallikarjuna temple
- Galganatha temple
- Kadasiddeshvara temple
- Jambulinga temple
- Jain Narayana temple (Rashtrakuta)
- Papanatha temple
- Museum of the Plains and Sculpture gallery
- Naganatha temple
- Chandrashekara
- Mahakuteshwara temple

Aihole

- Lad Khan temple
- Huchiappayyagudi temple
- Huchiappayya math

- Durga temple
- Meguti Jain temple
- Ravanaphadi temple
- Gowda temple
- Museum & Art Gallery
- Suryanarayana temple

Badami
- Cave 1 (Shiva)
- Cave 2 (Vishnu)
- Cave 3 (Vishnu)
- Cave 4 (Buddha)
- Bhutanatha group temples (Badami and Kalyani Chalukya)
- Mallikarjuna group temples (Kalyani Chalukya)
- Yellamma group temples (Kalyani Chalukya)

Gerusoppa
- Vardhamanaswamy temple

DRAVIDIAN ARCHITECTURE

Dravidian architecture was a style of architecture that emerged thousands of years ago in the Indian subcontinent. They consist primarily of pyramid shaped temples which are dependent on intricate carved stone in order to create a step design consisting of numerous statues of deities, warriors, kings, and dancers. The majority of the existing buildings are located in the Southern Indian states of Tamil Nadu, Andhra Pradesh, Kerala, and Karnataka. Various kingdoms and empires such as the Pallavas, Cholas, Chalukyas, Rashtrakutas, Hoysalas, Vijayanagara Empire amongst the many others have made a substantial contribution to the evolution of Dravidian architecture through the ages. Dravidian styled architecture can also be found in parts of Northeastern Sri Lanka, Maldives, and various parts of Southeast Asia.

Composition and Structure

Dravidian style temples consist almost invariably of the four following parts, arranged in various manners, as afterwards to be explained, but differing in themselves only according to the age in which they were executed:

1. The principal part, the actual temple itself, is called the *Vimana*. It is always square in plan, and surmounted by a pyramidal roof of one or more stories; and it contains the cell in which the image of the god or his emblem is placed.

2. The porches or *Mantapams*, which always cover and precede the door leading

to the cell.

3. Gate-pyramids, *Gopurams*, which are the principal features in the quadrangular enclosures that surround the more notable temples.

4. Pillard halls or *Chaultris* — *properly* Chawadis — *used for various purposes, and which are the invariable accompaniments of these temples.*

Besides these, a temple always contains tanks or wells for water — to be used either for sacred purposes or the convenience of the priests — dwellings for all the various grades of the priest-hood are attached to it, and numerous other buildings for state or convenience.

Influence from Different Periods

In Southern India seven kingdoms and empires stamped their influence on architecture during different times.

Pallavas

The Pallavas ruled from AD (600-900) and their greatest constructed accomplishments are the single rock temples in Mahabalipuram and their capital Kanchipuram, now located in Tamilnadu.

Pallavas were pioneers of south Indian architecture. The earliest examples of temples in the Dravidian style belong to the Pallava period. The earliest examples of Pallava constructions are rock-cut temples dating from 610 - 690 CE and structural temples between 690 - 900 CE. The greatest accomplishments of the Pallava architecture are the rock-cut temples at Mahabalipuram. There are excavated pillared halls and monolithic shrines known as rathas in Mahabalipuram. Early temples were mostly dedicated to Shiva. The Kailasanatha temple in Kanchipuram built by Nandhivarman is a fine example of the Pallava style temple.

Cholas

The Chola kings ruled from AD (900-1150) and included Rajaraja Chola I and his son Rajendra Chola who built temples such as the Brihadeshvara Temple and Siva temple of Thanjavur.

Temple building received great impetus from the conquests and the genius of Rajaraja Chola and his son Rajendra Chola I. The maturity and grandeur to which the Chola architecture had evolved found expression in the two temples of Tanjavur and Gangaikondacholapuram. The magnificent Siva temple of Thanjavur, completed around 1009, is a fitting memorial to the material achievements of the time of Rajaraja. The largest and tallest of all Indian temples of its time, it is at the apex of South Indian architecture.

The temple of Gangaikondacholapuram, the creation of Rajendra Chola, was intended to exceed its predecessor in every way. Completed around 1030, only two decades after the temple at Thanjavur and in much the same style, the greater elaboration in its appearance attests the more affluent state of the Chola Empire under Rajendra.

The Chola period is also remarkable for its sculptures and bronzes. Among the existing specimens in museums around the world and in the temples of South India may be seen many fine figures of Siva in various forms, such as Vishnu and his consort Lakshmi, and the Siva saints. Though conforming generally to the iconographic conventions established by long tradition, the sculptors worked with great freedom in the 11 and the 12 centuries to achieve a classic grace and grandeur. The best example of this can be seen in the form of Nataraja the Divine Dancer.

Badami Chalukyas

The Badami Chalukyas also called the Early Chalukyas, ruled from Badami, Karnataka in the period AD 543 - 753 and spawned the Vesara style called Badami Chalukya Architecture. The finest examples of their art are seen in Pattadakal, Aihole and Badami in northern Karnataka. Over 150 temples remain in the Malaprabha basin.

The most enduring legacy of the Chalukya dynasty is the architecture and art that they left behind. More than one hundred and fifty monuments attributed to the Badami Chalukya, and built between 450 and 700, remain in the Malaprabha basin in Karnataka.

The rock-cut temples of Pattadakal, a UNESCO World Heritage Site, Badami and Aihole are their most celebrated monuments. Two of the famous paintings at Ajanta cave no. 1, "The Temptation of the Buddha" and "The Persian Embassy" are attributed to them. This is the beginning of *Chalukya* style of architecture and a consolidation of South Indian style.

Rashtrakutas

The Rashtrakutas who ruled the deccan from Manyakheta, Gulbarga district, Karnataka in the period AD 753 - 973 built some of the finest dravidian monuments at Ellora (the Kailasanatha temple), in the rock cut architecture idiom. Some other fine monuments are the Jaina Narayana temple at Pattadakal and the Navalinga temples at Kuknur in Karnataka.

The Rashtrakutas contributed much to the culture of the Deccan. The Rashtrakuta contributions to art and architecture are reflected in the splendid rock-cut shrines at Ellora and Elephanta, situated in present day Maharashtra. It is said that they altogether constructed 34 rock-cut shrines, but most extensive and sumptuous of them all is the Kailasanatha temple at Ellora. The temple is a splendid achievement of Dravidian art.

The walls of the temple have marvellous sculptures from Hindu mythology including Ravana, Shiva and Parvathi while the ceilings have paintings.

The project was commissioned by King Krishna I after the Rashtrakuta rule had spread into South India from the Deccan. The architectural style used was dravidian. It does not contain any of the *Shikharas* common to the *Nagara* style and was built on the same lines as the Virupaksha temple at Pattadakal in Karnataka.

Western Chalukyas

The Western Chalukyas also called the Kalyani Chalukyas or Later Chalukyas ruled the deccan from AD 973 - 1180 from their capital Kalyani in modern Karnataka and further refined the Chalukyan style, called the Western Chalukya architecture. Over 50 temples exist in the Krishna River-Tungabhadra doab in central Karnataka. The Kasi Vishveshvara at Lakkundi, Mallikarjuna at Kuruvatii, Kalleshwara temple at Bagali and Mahadeva at Itagi are the finest examples produced by the Later Chalukya architects.

The reign of Western Chalukya dynasty was an important period in the development of architecture in the deccan. Their architectural developments acted as a conceptual link between the Badami Chalukya Architecture of the 8th century and the Hoysala architecture popularised in the 13th century. The art of Western Chalukyas is sometimes called the "Gadag style" after the number of ornate temples they built in the Tungabhadra - Krishna River doab region of present day Gadag district in Karnataka. Their temple building reached its maturity and culmination in the 12th century, with over a hundred temples built across the deccan, more than half of them in present day Karnataka. Apart from temples they are also well known for ornate stepped wells (*Pushkarni*) which served as ritual bathing places, many of which are well preserved in Lakkundi. Their stepped well designs were later incorporated by the Hoysalas and the Vijayanagara empire in the coming centuries.

Hoysalas

The Hoysala kings ruled southern India during the period AD (1100-1343) from their capital Belur and later Halebidu in Karnataka and developed a unique idiom of architecture called the Hoysala architecture in Karnataka state. The finest examples of their architecture are the Chennakesava Temple in Belur, Hoysaleswara temple in Halebidu, and the Kesava Temple in Somanathapura.

The modern interest in the Hoysalas is due to their patronage of art and architecture rather than their military conquests. The brisk temple building throughout the kingdom was accomplished despite constant threats from the Pandyas to the south and the Seunas Yadavas to the north. Their architectural style, an offshoot of the Western

Chalukya style, shows distinct Dravidian influences. The Hoysala architecture style is described as *Karnata Dravida* as distinguished from the traditional Dravida, and is considered an independent architectural tradition with many unique features.

Vijayanagar

The whole of South India was ruled by Vijayanagar Empire from AD (1343-1565), who built a number of temples and monuments in their hybrid style in their capital Vijayanagar in Karnataka. Their style was a combination of the styles developed in South India in the previous centuries. In addition, the *Yali* columns (pillar with charging horse), balustrades (parapets) and ornate pillared *manatapa* are their unique contribution. King Krishna Deva Raya and others built many famous temples all over South India in Vijayanagar Architecture style.

Vijayanagara architecture is a vibrant combination of the Chalukya, Hoysala, Pandya and Chola styles, idioms that prospered in previous centuries. Its legacy of sculpture, architecture and painting influenced the development of the arts long after the empire came to an end. Its stylistic hallmark is the ornate pillared *Kalyanamantapa* (marriage hall), *Vasanthamantapa* (open pillared halls) and the *Rayagopuram* (tower). Artisans used the locally available hard granite because of its durability since the kingdom was under constant threat of invasion. While the empire's monuments are spread over the whole of Southern India, nothing surpasses the vast open air theatre of monuments at its capital at Vijayanagara, a UNESCO World Heritage Site.

In the 14th century the kings continued to build Vesara or Deccan style monuments but later incorporated dravida-style gopurams to meet their ritualistic needs. The Prasanna Virupaksha temple (underground temple) of Bukka Raya I and the Hazare Rama temple of Deva Raya I are examples of Deccan architecture. The varied and intricate ornamentation of the pillars is a mark of their work. At Hampi, though the *Vitthala* temple is the best example of their pillared *Kalyanamantapa* style, the *Hazara Ramaswamy* temple is a modest but perfectly finished example. A visible aspect of their style is their return to the simplistic and serene art developed by the Chalukya dynasty. A grand specimen of Vijayanagara art, the *Vitthala* temple, took several decades to complete during the reign of the Tuluva kings.

HOYSALA ARCHITECTURE

Hoysala architecture is the building style developed under the rule of the Hoysala Empire, in the region known today as the Indian state of Karnataka, between the 11th and 14th centuries. Hoysala influence was at its peak in the 13th century, when it dominated the Southern Deccan Plateau region. Large and small temples built during this era remain as examples of the Hoysala architectural style, including the

Chennakesava Temple at Belur, the Hoysaleswara Temple at Halebidu, and the Kesava Temple at Somanathapura. Other examples of fine Hoysala craftsmanship are the temples at Belavadi, Amruthapura, Hosaholalu, Arasikere and Nuggehalli. Study of the Hoysala architectural style has revealed a negligible Indo-Aryan influence while the impact of Southern Indian style is more distinct.

The vigorous temple building activity of the Hoysala Empire was due to the social, cultural and political events of the period. The stylistic transformation of the *Karnata* temple building tradition reflected religious trends popularized by the Vaishnava and Virashaiva philosophers as well as the growing military prowess of the Hoysala kings who desired to surpass their Western Chalukya overlords in artistic achievement. Temples built prior to Hoysala independence in the mid-12th century reflect significant Western Chalukya influences, while later temples retain some features salient to Chalukyan art but have additional inventive decoration and ornamentation, features unique to Hoysala artisans. About one hundred temples have survived in present-day Karnataka state, mostly in the Malnad (hill) districts, the native home of the Hoysala kings.

As popular tourist destinations in Karnataka, Hoysala temples offer an opportunity for pilgrims and students of architecture to examine medieval Hindu architecture in the *Karnata Dravida* tradition. This tradition began in the 7th century under the patronage of the Chalukya dynasty of Badami, developed further under the Western Chalukyas of Basavakalyan in the 11th century and finally transformed into an independent style by the 12th century during the reign of the Hoysalas. Medieval Kannada language inscriptions displayed prominently at temple locations give details of the temples and offer information about the history of the Hoysala dynasty.

Temple Deities

Hinduism is a combination of secular and sacred beliefs, rituals, daily practices and traditions that has evolved over the course of over two thousand years and embodies complex symbolism combining the natural world with philosophy. Hindu temples began as simple shrines housing a deity and by the time of the Hoysalas had evolved into well articulated edifices in which worshippers sought transcendence of the daily world. Hoysala temples were not limited to any specific organised tradition of Hinduism and encouraged pilgrims of different Hindu devotional movements. The Hoysalas usually dedicated their temples to Lord Shiva or to Lord Vishnu (two of the major Hindu gods), but they occasionally chose a different deity. Worshippers of Shiva are called Shaivas or Lingayats and worshippers of Vishnu are called Vaishnavas. While King Vishnuvardhana and his descendants were Vaishnava by faith, records show that the Hoysalas maintained religious harmony by building as many temples dedicated to Shiva as they did to Vishnu. Most of these temples have secular features with broad themes depicted in their sculptures.

This can be seen in the famous Chennakesava Temple at Belur dedicated to Vishnu and in the Hoysaleswara temple at Halebidu dedicated to Shiva. The Kesava temple at Somanathapura is different in that its ornamentation is strictly Vaishnavan. Generally Vaishnava temples are dedicated to Keshava (or to Chennakeshava, meaning "Beautiful Vishnu") while a small number are dedicated to Lakshminarayana and Lakshminarasimha (Narayana and Narasimha both being avatars, or physical manifestations, of Vishnu) with Lakshmi, consort of Vishnu, seated at his feet. Temples dedicated to Vishnu are always named after the deity. The Shaiva temples have a Shiva linga, symbol of fertility and the universal symbol of Shiva, in the shrine. The names of Shiva temples can end with the suffix *eshwara* meaning "Lord of". The name "Hoysaleswara", for instance, means "Lord of Hoysala". The temple can also be named after the devotee who commissioned the construction of the temple, an example being the Bucesvara temple at Koravangala, named after the devotee Buci.

The most striking sculptural decorations are the horizontal rows of exquisitely detailed, intricately carved images of gods, goddesses and their attendants on the outer temple wall panels. The Doddagaddavalli Lakshmi Devi ("Goddess of Wealth") Temple is an exception as it is dedicated to neither Vishnu nor Shiva. The defeat of the Jain Western Ganga Dynasty (of present-day south Karnataka) by the Cholas in the early 11th century and the rising numbers of followers of Vaishnava Hinduism and Virashaivism in the 12th century was mirrored by a decreased interest in Jainism. However, two notable locations of Jain worship in the Hoysala territory were Shravanabelagola and Kambadahalli. The Hoysalas built Jain temples to satisfy the needs of its Jain population, a few of which have survived in Halebidu containing icons of Jain tirthankaras. They constructed stepped wells called *Pushkarni* or *Kalyani*, the ornate tank at Hulikere being an example. The tank has twelve minor shrines containing Hindu deities.

The two main deities found in Hoysala temple sculpture are Lord Shiva and Lord Vishnu in their various forms and avatars (incarnations). Shiva is usually shown with four arms holding a trident and a small drum among other emblems that symbolise objects worshiped independently of the divine image with which they are associated. Any male icon portrayed in this way is Shiva although a female icon may sometimes be portrayed with these attributes as Shiva's consort, Parvati. Various depictions of Lord Shiva show him in action, such as slaying a demon or dancing on the head of an elephant. He is often accompanied by his consort Parvati or shown with Nandi the bull. He may be represented as Bhairava, another of Shiva's many manifestations.

A male figure depicted holding certain objects such as a conch (symbol of eternal, heavenly space) and a wheel (eternal time and destructive power) is Vishnu. If a female figure is depicted holding these objects, she is seen as his consort, Lakshmi. In all the depictions Vishnu is holding four objects: a conch, a wheel, a lotus and a mace. These can be held in any of the icon's hands, making possible twenty-four different forms of Vishnu, each with a unique name. Apart from these, Vishnu is depicted in any of his ten *avataras*, which include Vishnu sitting on Anantha (the celestial snake and keeper of life energy), Vishnu with Lakshmi seated on his lap (Lakshminarayana), with the head of a lion disemboweling a demon on his lap (Lakshminarasimha), with head of a boar walking over a demon (Varaha), in the Krishna avatar (as Venugopala or the cow herder playing the Venu (flute), dancing on the head of the snake Kaliya, lifting a hill such as Govardhana), with his feet over head of a small figure (*Vamana*), with Lakshmi seated on Garuda, and the eagle (stealing the parijata tree).

Temple Complex

A Hindu temple is a place of contact between the gods or deities and man. The focus of a temple is the centre or sanctum sanctorum (garbhagriha) where the image of the deity resides, so temple architecture is designed to move the devotee from outside to the garbhagriha through ambulatory passageways for circumambulation and halls or chambers (*mantapas*) that become increasingly sacred as the deity is approached. Hoysala temples have distinct parts that are merged to form a unified organic whole, in contrast to the temples of Tamil country where different parts of a temple stand independently. Although superficially unique, Hoysala temples resemble each other structurally. They are characterised by a complex profusion of sculpture decorating all the temple parts chiseled of soft soapstone (chloritic schist), a good material for intricate carving, executed mostly by local craftsmen, and exhibit architectural features that distinguish them from other temple architectures of South India.

Most Hoysala temples have a plain covered entrance porch supported by lathe turned (circular or bell-shaped) pillars which were sometimes further carved with deep fluting and moulded with decorative motifs. The temples may be built upon a platform raised by about a metre called a "jagati". The *jagati*, apart from giving a raised look to the temple, serves as a *pradakshinapatha* or "circumambulation path" for circumambulation around the temple, as the *garbagriha* (inner sanctum) provides no such feature. Such temples will have an additional set of steps leading to an open *mantapa* (open hall) with parapet walls. A good example of this style is the Kesava Temple at Somanathapura. The *jagati* which is in unity with the rest of the temple follows a star-shaped design and the walls of the temple follow a zig-zag pattern, a Hoysala innovation, pair of small shrines, each with a deity and a miniature tower directly facing the entrance, could adorn either side of steps of the *jagati*. This would be repeated for all entrances leading to the *jagati*. Devotees can first complete a ritual circumambulation on the *jagati* starting from the main entrance by walking in a clockwise direction (towards the left) before entering the *mantapa*, following the sculptural clockwise-sequenced reliefs on the outer temple walls depicting a sequence of epic scenes from the Hindu epics. Temples that are not built on a *jagati* can have steps flanked by elephant balustrades (parapets) that lead to the *mantapa* from ground level. An example of a temple that does not exhibit the raised platform is the *Bucesvara* temple in Korvangla, Hassan District. In temples with two shrines (*dvikuta*), the *vimanas* (the shrines or cellae) may be placed either next to each other or on opposite sides. The Lakshmidevi temple at Doddagaddavalli has a minor shrine at each of the four corners of the walled temple complex in addition to five major shrines.

Architectural Elements

Mantapa

The *mantapa* is the hall where groups of people gather during prayers. The entrance to the *mantapa* normally has a highly ornate overhead lintel called a *makaratorana* (*makara* is an imaginary beast and *torana* is an overhead decoration). The open *mantapa* which serves the purpose of an outer hall (outer *mantapa*) is a regular feature in larger Hoysala temples leading to an inner small closed *mantapa* and the shrine(s). The open *mantapas* have seating areas made of stone with the *mantapa's* parapet wall acting as a back rest. The seats may follow the same staggered square shape of the parapet wall. The open *mantapa* is the largest part of the temple and is the place supporting larger congregations of people. The ceiling here is supported by numerous pillars that create many bays. The shape of the open *mantapa* is best described as staggered-square and is the style used in most Hoysala temples. Even the smallest open *mantapa* has 13 bays. The walls have parapets that have half pillars supporting the outer ends of the roof which allow plenty of light making all the sculptural details visible. The *mantapa* ceiling is generally ornate with sculptures, both mythological and floral. The ceiling consists of deep and domical surfaces and contains sculptural depictions of banana bud motifs and other such decorations. The Amruteswara temple in Chikmagalur district has forty-eight domes in the *mahamantapa* ("great open hall").

If the temple is small it will consist of only a closed *mantapa* (enclosed with walls extending all the way to the ceiling) and the shrine. The closed *mantapa*, well decorated inside and out, is larger than the vestibule connecting the shrine and the *mantapa* and has four lathe-turned pillars to support the ceiling, which may be deeply domed. The four pillars divide the hall into nine bays. The nine bays result in nine finely decorated ceilings.. Pierced stone latticework screens placed between pillars to filter the light is a characteristic Hoysala stylistic element.

A porch adorns the entrance to a closed *mantapa*, consisting of an awning supported by two half-pillars (engaged columns) and two parapets, all richly decorated. The closed *mantapa* is connected to the shrine(s) by a vestibule, a square area that also connects the shrines. Its outer walls are finely decorated, but as the size the vestibule is not large, this may not be a conspicuous part of the temple. The vestibule also has a short tower called the *sukanasi* or "nose" upon which is mounted the Hoysala emblem. In Belur and Halebidu, these sculptures are quite large and are placed at all doorways.

The outer and inner *mantapa* (open and closed) have circular lathe-turned pillars having four brackets at the top. Over each bracket stands sculptured figure(s) called *salabhanjika* or *madanika*. The pillars may also exhibit fine ornamental carvings on the surface and no two pillars are alike. This is how Hoysala art differs from the work of their early overlords, the Western Chalukyas, who added sculptural details to the circular pillar base and left the top plain. The lathe-turned pillars are 16, 32, or 64-pointed; some are bell-shaped and have properties that reflect light. The Parsvanatha Basadi at Halebidu is a good example. The shaft of the pillar is a monolith with the base left as a square and with well-sculpted figures adorning the top.

Vimana

The *vimana*, also called the cella, contains the most sacred shrine wherein resides the image of the presiding deity. The *vimana* is often topped by a tower which is quite different on the outside than on the inside. Inside, the vimana is plain and square, whereas outside it is profusely decorated and can be either stellate ("star-shaped") or shaped as a staggered square, or feature a combination of these designs, giving it many projections and recesses that seem to multiply as the light falls on it. Each projection and recess has a complete decorative articulation that is rhythmic and repetitive and comprised of blocks and mouldings, obscuring the tower profile. Depending on the number of shrines (and hence on the number of towers), the temples are classified as *ekakuta* (one), *dvikuta* (two), *trikuta* (three), *chatushkuta* (four) and *panchakuta* (five). Most Hoysala temples are *ekakuta*, *dvikuta* or *trikuta*. In temples with multiple shrines, all essential parts are duplicated for symmetry and balance. A temple's minor shrine usually has its own tower. There are cases where a temple is *trikuta* but has only one tower over the main shrine (in the middle). So the terminology *trikuta* may not be literally accurate. Smaller shrines attached to the outer walls and facing outward from a larger *vimana* are a common feature.

The highest point of the temple (*kalasa*) has the shape of a beautiful water pot and stands on top of the tower. This portion of the *vimana* is often lost due to age and has been replaced with a metallic pinnacle. Below the *kalasa* is a large, highly- sculptured structure resembling a dome which is made from large stones and looks like a helmet. It may be 2 m by 2 m in size and follows the shape of the shrine. Below this structure are domed roofs in a square plan, all of them much smaller and crowned with small *kalasas*. They are mixed with other small roofs of different shapes and are ornately decorated. The tower of the shrine usually has three or four tiers of rows of decorative roofs while the tower on top of the *sukanasi* has one less tier, making the tower look like an extension of the main tower (the "nose"). One decorated roof tier runs on top of the wall of a closed *mantapa* above the heavy eaves of an open *mantapa* and above the porches.

Below the superstructure of the *vimana* are temple "eaves" projecting half a meter from the wall. Below the eaves two different decorative schemes may be found, depending on whether a temple was built in the early or the later period of the empire. In the early temples built prior to the 13th century, there is one eave and below this are decorative miniature towers. A panel of Hindu deities and their attendants are below these towers, followed by a set of five different mouldings forming the base of the wall. In the later temples there is a second eave running about a metre below the upper eaves with decorative miniature towers placed between them. The wall images of gods are below the lower eaves, followed by six different mouldings of equal size. This is broadly termed "horizontal treatment". The six mouldings at the base are divided in two sections. Going from the very base of the wall, the first horizontal layer contains a procession of elephants, above which are horsemen and then a band of foliage. The second horizontal section has depictions of the Hindu epics and *Puranic* scenes executed with detail. Above this are two friezes of *yallis* or *makaras* (imaginary beasts) and *hamsas* (swans). The *vimana* (tower) is divided into three horizontal sections and is even more ornate than the walls.

Sculpture

Hoysala artists are famous for their sculptural detail, be it in the depiction of the Hindu epics, *yallis*, deities, *kirthimukha*(gargoyles), eroticism or aspects of daily life. Their medium, the soft chlorite schist, enabled a virtuoso carving style. Their workmanship shows an attention paid to precise detail. Every aspect down to a fingernail or toenail is perfected.

Salabhanjika, a common form of Hoysala sculpture, is an old Indian tradition going back to Buddhist sculpture. *Sala* is the sala tree and *bhanjika* is the chaste maiden. In the Hoysala idiom, *madanika* figures are decorative objects put at an angle on the outer walls of the temple near the roof so that worshipers circumambulating the temple can view them. They served the function of bracket figures to pillars inside the *mantapa*. These *madanika* were sculpted as seemingly engaged in artistic activities such as music (holding musical instruments) and dance. *Kirthimukhas* (demon faces) adorn the towers of *vimanas* in some temples. Sometimes the artists left behind their signatures on the sculptures they created.

The *sthamba buttalikas* are pillar images that show traces of Chola art in the Chalukyan touches. Some of the artists working for the Hoysalas may have been from Chola country, a result of the expansion of the empire into Tamil-speaking regions of Southern India. The image of *mohini* on one of the pillars in the *mantapa* (closed hall) of the Chennakeshava temple is a fine example of Chola art.

General life themes are portrayed on wall panels such as the way horses were reined, the type of stirrup used, the depiction of dancers, musicians, instrumentalists, and rows of animals such as lions and elephants (where no two animals are identical). Perhaps no other temple in the country depicts the Ramayana and Mahabharata epics more effectively than the Hoysaleshwara temple at Halebidu.

Erotica was a subject the Hoysala artist handled with discretion. There is no exhibitionism in this, and erotic themes were carved into recesses and niches, generally miniature in form, making them inconspicuous. These erotic representations are associated with the *Shakta* practice. The temple doorway is heavily engraved with ornamentation called *Makaratorana* (*makara* being an imaginary beast) and each side of the doorway exhibits sculptured *Salabhanjika* (maidens).

Apart from these sculptures, entire sequences from the Hindu epics (commonly the Ramayana and the Mahabharata) have been sculpted in a clockwise direction starting at the main entrance. The right to left sequence is the same direction taken by the devotees in their ritual circumambulation as they wind inward toward the inner sanctum. Depictions from mythology such as the epic hero Arjuna shooting fish, the elephant-headed god Ganesha, the Sun god Surya, the weather and war god Indra, and Brahma with Sarasvati are common. Also frequently seen in these temples is Durga, with several arms holding weapons given to her by other gods, in the act of killing a buffalo (a demon in a buffalo's form) and Harihara (a fusion of Shiva and Vishnu) holding a conch, wheel and trident. Many of these friezes were signed by the artisans, the first known instance of signed artwork in India.

Research

Surveys in modern times have indicated that 1000–1500 structures were built by the Hoysalas, of which about a hundred temples have survived to date. The Hoysala style is an offshoot of the Western Chalukya style, which was popular in the 10th and 11th centuries. It is distinctively Dravidian, and owing to its unique features, Hoysala architecture qualifies as an independent style. While the Hoysalas introduced innovative features into their architecture, they also borrowed features from the earlier great builders of *Karnata* like the Kadambas, Western Chalukyas. These features were the use of chloritic schist or soapstone as a basic building material, pierced stone window screens which were very popular in Hoysala temples, and the *vimana* which follows a stellate pattern. All these features were popular with their early overlords, the Western Chalukyas. Other features were the stepped style of *vimana* tower called the *Kadamba shikhara*, which was inherited from the Kadambas. Engrained in the craftsmanship of Hoysala sculptors was their knowledge of the effect of light and shade on carved walls, which they used to maximum effect in their sculptures in the numerous projections and recesses. The Hoysala sculpture in all its richness is said to be a challenge to photography. The artistry of the Hoysalas in stone has been compared to the finesse of an ivory worker or a goldsmith. The abundance of jewelry worn by the sculpted figures and the variety of hairstyles and headdresses depicted give a fair idea of the lifestyles of the Hoysala times.

Notable Craftsmen

While the Hoysalas had the services of great architects and sculptors, some names stand out in their history. While medieval Indian artisans preferred to remain anonymous, Hoysala artisans signed their works, which has given researchers fascinating details about their lives, families, guilds, etc. Apart from the architects and sculptors, people of other guilds such as goldsmiths, ivory carvers, carpenters, and silversmiths also contributed to the completion of temples. The artisans were from diverse geographical backgrounds and included famous locals. Prolific architects included Amarashilpi Jakanachari, a native of Kaidala in Tumkur district, who also built temples for the Western Chalukyas. Ruvari Malithamma built the Kesava Temple at Somanathapura and worked on forty other monuments, including the Amruteshwara temple at Amruthapura. Malithamma specialised in ornamentation, and his works span six decades. His sculptures were typically signed in shorthand as *Malli* or simply *Ma*. Dasoja and his son Chavana from Balligavi were the architects of Chennakesava Temple at Belur; Kedaroja was the chief architect of the Hoysaleswara Temple at Halebidu. Their influence is seen in other temples built by the Hoysalas as well. Names of other locals found in inscriptions are Maridamma, Baicoja, Caudaya, Nanjaya and Bama, Malloja, Nadoja, Siddoja, Masanithamma, Chameya and Rameya. Artists from Tamil country included Pallavachari and Cholavachari.

WESTERN CHALUKYA ARCHITECTURE

Western Chalukya architecture, also known as Kalyani Chalukya or Later Chalukya architecture, is the distinctive style of ornamented architecture that evolved during the rule of the Western Chalukya Empire in the Tungabhadra region of central Karnataka, India, in the 11th and 12th centuries. Western Chalukyan political influence was at its peak in the Deccan Plateau during this period. The centre of cultural and temple-building activity lay in the Tungabhadra region, where large medieval workshops built numerous monuments. These monuments, regional variants of pre-existing dravida (South Indian) temples, defined the *Karnata dravida* tradition. Temples of all sizes built by the Chalukyan architects during this era remain today as examples of the architectural style.

Most notable of the many buildings dating from this period are the Mahadeva Temple at Itagi in the Koppal district, the Kasivisvesvara Temple at Lakkundi in the Gadag district, and the Mallikarjuna Temple at Kuruvatti and the Kallesvara Temple at Bagali, both in the Davangere district. Other monuments notable for their craftsmanship include the Siddhesvara Temple at Haveri in the Haveri district, the Amrtesvara Temple at Annigeri in the Dharwad district, the Sarasvati Temple in Gadag, and the Dodda Basappa Temple at Dambal, both in the Gadag district.

The surviving Western Chalukya monuments are temples built in the Shaiva, Vaishnava, and Jain religious traditions. None of the military, civil, or courtly architecture has survived; being built of mud, brick and wood, such structures may not have withstood repeated invasions. The centre of these architectural developments was the region encompassing the present-day Dharwad district; it included areas of present-day Haveri and Gadag districts. In these districts, about fifty monuments have survived as evidence of the widespread temple building of the Western Chalukyan workshops. The influence of this style extended beyond the Kalyani region in the northeast to the Bellary region in the east and to the Mysore region in the south. In the Bijapur-Belgaum region to the north, the style was mixed with that of the *Hemadpanti* temples. Although a few Western Chalukyan temples can be found in the Konkan region, the presence of the Western Ghats probably prevented the style from spreading westwards.

Evolution

Though the basic plan of the Western Chalukya style originated from the older *dravida style*, many of its features were unique and peculiar to it. One of these distinguishing features of the Western Chalukyan architectural style was an articulation that can still be found throughout modern Karnataka. The only exceptions to this motif can be found in the area around Kalyani, where the temples exhibit a *nagara* (North Indian) articulation which has its own unique character.

In contrast to the buildings of the early Chalukyas of Badami, whose monuments were centred around the metropoleis of Pattadakal, Aihole, and Badami, these Western Chalukya temples are widely dispersed, reflecting a system of local government and decentralisation. The Western Chalukya temples were smaller than those of the early Chalukyas, a fact discernible in the reduced height of the superstructures which tower over the shrines.

The Western Chalukya art evolved in two phases, the first lasting approximately a quarter of a century and the second from the beginning of 11th century until the end of Western Chalukya rule in 1186 CE. During the first phase, temples were built in the Aihole-Banashankari-Mahakuta region (situated in the early Chalukyan heartland) and Ron in the Gadag district. A few provisional workshops built them in Sirval in the

Gulbarga district and Gokak in the Belgaum district. The structures at Ron bear similarities to the Rashtrakuta temples in Kuknur in the Koppal district and Mudhol in the Bijapur district, evidence that the same workshops continued their activity under the new Karnata dynasty. The mature and latter phase reached its peak at Lakkundi (Lokigundi), a principal seat of the imperial court. From the mid-11th century, the artisans from the Lakkundi school moved south of the Tungabhadra River. Thus the influence of the Lakkundi school can be seen in some of the temples of the Davangere district, and in the temples at Hirehadagalli and Huvinahadgalli in the Bellary district.

Influences of Western Chalukya architecture can be discerned in the geographically distant schools of architecture of the Hoysala Empire in southern Karnataka, and the Kakatiya dynasty in present-day Andhra Pradesh. Sometimes called the Gadag style of architecture, Western Chalukya architecture is considered a precursor to the Hoysala architecture of southern Karnataka. This influence occurred because the early builders employed by the Hoysalas came from pronounced centres of medieval Chalukyan art. Further monuments in this style were built not only by the Western Chalukya kings but also by their feudal vassals.

Temple Complexes

Basic layout

A typical Western Chalukya temple may be examined from three aspects — the basic floor plan, the architectural articulation, and the figure sculptures. The basic floor plan is defined by the size of the shrine, the size of the sanctum, the distribution of the building mass, and by the *pradakshina* (path for circumambulation), if there is one.

Architectural articulation refer to the ornamental components that give shape to the outer wall of the shrine. These include projections, recesses, and representations that can produce a variety of patterns and outlines, either stepped, stellate (star-shaped), or square. If stepped (also called "stepped diamond of projecting corners"), these components form five or seven projections on each side of the shrine, where all but the central one are projecting corners (projections with two full faces created by two recesses, left and right, that are at right angles with each other). If square (also called "square with simple projections"), these components form three or five projections on a side, only two of which are projecting corners. Stellate patterns form star points which are normally 8-, 16-, or 32-pointed and are sub-divided into interrupted and uninterrupted stellate components. In an 'interrupted' stellate plan, the stellate outline is interrupted by orthogonal (right-angle) projections in the cardinal directions, resulting in star points that have been skipped. Two basic kinds of architectural articulation are found in Indian architecture: the southern Indian *dravida* and the northern Indian *nagara*.

Figure sculptures are miniature representations that stand by themselves, including architectural components on pilasters, buildings, sculptures, and complete towers. They are generally categorised as "figure sculpture" or "other decorative features". On occasion, rich figure sculpture can obscure the articulation of a shrine, when representations of gods, goddesses, and mythical figures are in abundance.

Categories

Chalukyan temples fall into two categories — the first being temples with a common *mantapa* (a colonnaded hall) and two shrines (known as *dvikuta*), and the second being temples with one *mantapa* and a single shrine (*ekakuta*).

Both kinds of temples have two or more entrances giving access to the main hall. This format differs from both the designs of the northern Indian temples, which have a small closed *mantapa* leading to the shrine and the southern Indian temples which generally have a large, open, columned *mantapa*. The Chalukyan architects retained features from both northern and southern styles. However, in the overall arrangement of the main temple and of the subsidiary shrines, they inclined towards the northern style and tended to build one main shrine with four minor shrines, making the structure a *panchayatna* or five-shrined complex. Chalukyan temples were, almost always, built facing the east.

The sanctum (cella) is connected by a vestibule (*ardha mantapa* or ante-chamber) to the closed *mantapa* (also called the *navaranga*), which is connected to the open *mantapa*. Occasionally there can be two or more open *mantapas*. In Shaiva temples, directly opposite the sanctum and opposite the closed *mantapa* is the *nandi mantapa*, which enshrines a large image of Nandi, the bull attendant of Shiva. The shrine usually has no *pradakshina*.

The pillars that support the roof of the *mantapa* are monolithic shafts from the base up to the neck of the capital. Therefore, the height of the *mantapa* and the overall size of the temple were limited by the length of the stone shafts that the architects were able to obtain from the quarries. The height of the temple was also constrained by the weight of the superstructure on the walls and, since Chalukyan architects did not use mortar, by the use of dry masonry and bonding stones without clamps or cementing material.

The absence of mortar allows some ventilation in the innermost parts of the temple through the porous masonry used in the walls and ceilings. The modest amount of light entering the temples comes into the open halls from all directions, while the very subdued illumination in the inner closed *mantapa* comes only through its open doorway. The vestibule receives even less light, making it necessary to have some form of artificial lighting (usually, oil lamps) even during the day. This artificial source of light perhaps adds "mystry" to the image of the deity worshipped in the sanctum.

Early developments

From the 11th century, newly incorporated features were either based on the traditional *dravida* plan of the Badami Chalukyas, as found in the Virupaksha and Mallikarjuna Temples at Pattadakal, or were further elaborations of this articulation. The new features produced a closer juxtaposition of architectural components, visible as a more crowded decoration, as can be seen in the Mallikarjuna Temple at Sudi in the Gadag district and the Amrtesvara Temple at Annigeri in the Dharwad district.

The architects in the Karnataka region seem to have been inspired by architectural developments in northern India. This is evidenced by the fact that they incorporated decorative miniature towers (multi-aedicular towers depicting superstructures) of the *Sekhari* and *Bhumija* types, supported on pilasters, almost simultaneously with these developments in the temples in northern India. The miniature towers represented shrines, which in turn represented deities. Sculptural depictions of deities were generally discreet although not uncommon. Other northern ideas they incorporated were the pillar bodies that appeared as wall projections. Well-known constructions incorporating these features are found at the Kasivisvesvara Temple and the Nannesvara Temple, both at Lakkundi.

In the 11th century, temple projects began employing soapstone, a form of greenish or blueish black stone, although temples such as the Mallikarjuna Temple at Sudi, the Kallesvara Temple at Kuknur, and the temples at Konnur and Savadi were built with the formerly traditional sandstone in the *dravida* articulation.

Soapstone is found in abundance in the regions of Haveri, Savanur, Byadgi, Motebennur and Hangal. The great archaic sandstone building blocks used by the Badami Chalukyas were superseded with smaller blocks of soapstone and with smaller masonry. The first temple to be built from this material was the Amrtesvara Temple in Annigeri in the Dharwad district in 1050 CE. This building was to be the prototype for later, more articulated structures such as the Mahadeva Temple at Itagi.

Soapstone was also used for carving, modelling and chiselling of components that could be described as "chubby". However, the finish of the architectural components compared to the earlier sandstone temples is much finer, resulting in opulent shapes and creamy decorations. Stepped wells are another feature that some of the temples included.

Later enhancements

The 11th-century temple-building boom continued in the 12th century with the addition of new features. The Mahadeva Temple at Itagi and the Siddhesvara Temple in Haveri are standard constructions incorporating these developments. Based on the general plan of the Amrtesvara Temple at Annigeri, the Mahadeva Temple was built in

1112 CE and has the same architectural components as its predecessor. There are however differences in their articulation; the *sala* roof (roof under the finial of the superstructure) and the miniature towers on pilasters are chiseled instead of moulded. The difference between the two temples, built fifty years apart, is the more rigid modelling and decoration found in many components of the Mahadeva Temple. The voluptuous carvings of the 11th century were replaced with a more severe chiselling.

As developments progressed, the Chalukyan builders modified the pure *dravida* tower by reducing the height of each stepped storey and multiplying their number. From base to top, the succeeding storeys get smaller in circumference and the topmost storey is capped with a crown holding the *kalasa*, a finial in the shape of a decorative water pot. Each storey is so richly-decorated that the original *dravida* character becomes almost invisible. In the *nagara* tower the architects modified the central panels and niches on each storey, forming a more-or-less continuous vertical band and simulating the vertical bands up the centre of each face of the typical northern style tower. Old and new architectural components were juxtaposed but introduced separately. Some superstructures are essentially a combination of southern *dravida* and northern *nagara* structures and is termed "Vesara Sikhara" (also called Kadamba Sikhara).

The characteristically northern stepped-diamond plan of projecting corners was adopted in temples built with an entirely *dravida* articulation. Four 12th century structures constructed according to this plan are extant: the Basaveshwara Temple at Basavana Bagevadi, the Ramesvara Temple at Devur and the temples at Ingleshwar and Yevur, all in the vicinity of the Kalyani region, where *nagara* temples were common. This plan came into existence in northern India only in the 11th century, a sign that architectural ideas traveled fast.

Stellate plans

A major development of this period was the appearance of stellate (star-shaped) shrines in a few temples built of the traditional sandstone, such as the Trimurti Temple at Savadi, the Paramesvara Temple at Konnur and the Gauramma Temple at Hire Singgangutti. In all three cases, the shrine is a 16-pointed uninterrupted star, a ground-plan not found anywhere else in India and which entirely differentiates these temples from the 32-pointed interrupted star plans of *bhumija* shrines in northern India.

The stellate plan found popularity in the soapstone constructions such as the Dodda Basappa Temple at Dambal as well. Contemporary stellate plans in northern India were all 32-pointed interrupted types. No temples of the 6-, 12-, or 24-pointed stellate plans are known to exist anywhere in India, with the exception of the unique temple at Dambal, which can be described either as a 24-pointed uninterrupted plan, or a 48-pointed plan with large square points of 90 degrees alternating with small short points of 75 degrees. The upper tiers of the seven-tiered superstructure look like cogged wheels with 48 dents. The Dodda Basappa Temple and the Somesvara Temple at Lakshmeshwara are examples of extreme variants of a basic *dravida* articulation. These temples prove that the architects and craftsman were consciously creating new compositions of architectural components out of traditional methods.

In the early 13th century, 12th century characteristics remained prominent; however, many parts that were formerly plain became decorated. This change is observed in the Muktesvara Temple at Chavudayyadanapura and the Santesvara Temple at Tilavalli, both in the Haveri district. The Muktesvara Temple with its elegant *vimana* was renovated in the middle of the 13th century. In the Tilavalli Temple, all the architectural components are elongated, giving it an intended crowded look. Both temples are built with a *dravida* articulation. Apart from exotic *dravida* articulations, some temples of this period have *nagara* articulation, built in the stepped-diamond and the square plan natural to a *nagara* superstructure. Notable among temples with a stepped-diamond style are the Ganesha Temple at Hangal, the Banashankari Temple at Amargol (which has one *dravida* shrine and one *nagara* shrine), and a small shrine that is a part of the ensemble at the Mahadeva Temple at Itagi. At Hangal, the architects were able to provide a *sekhari* superstructure to the shrine, while the lower half received a *nagara* articulation and depictions of miniature *sekhari* towers. The style of workmanship with a square plan is found at Muttagi and Degaon.

Kalyani region

Temples built in and around the Kalyani region (in the Bidar district) were quite different from those built in other regions. Without exception, the articulation was *nagara*, and the temple plan as a rule was either stepped-diamond or stellate. The elevations corresponding to these two plans were similar because star shapes were produced by rotating the corner projections of a standard stepped plan in increments of 11.25 degrees, resulting in a 32-pointed interrupted plan in which three star points are skipped in the centre of each side of the shrine. Examples of stepped-diamond plans surviving in Karnataka are the Dattatreya Temple at Chattarki, the Somesvara Temple in Kadlewad, and the Mallikarjuna and Siddhesvara at Kalgi in the Gulbarga district. The *nagara* shrine at Chattarki is a stepped diamond of projecting corners with five projections per side. Because of the stepped-diamond plan, the wall pillars have two fully exposed sides, with a high base block decorated with a mirrored stalk motif and two large wall images above. The shapes and decorations on the rest of the wall pillar have a striking resemblance to the actual pillars supporting the ceiling.

The other type is the square plan with simple projections and recesses but with a possibility of both *sekhari* and *bhumija* superstructures. The plan does not have any additional elements save those that derive from the ground plan. The recesses are simple and have just one large wall image. The important characteristic of these *nagara* temples in the Kalyani region is that they not only differ from the *dravida* temples in the north Karnataka region but from the *nagara* temples north of the Kalyani region as well. These differences are manifest in the articulation and in the shapes and ornamentation of individual architectural components, giving them a unique place in Chalukyan architecture. Temples that fall in this category are the Mahadeva Temple at Jalsingi and the Suryanarayana Temple at Kalgi in the modern-day Gulbarga district. The plan and the *nagara* articulation of these temples are the same as found to the north of the Kalyani region, but the details are different, producing a different look.

Architectural Elements

Overview

The Western Chalukya decorative inventiveness focused on the pillars, door panels, lintels (*torana*), domical roofs in bays, outer wall decorations such as Kirthimukha (common in Western Chalukya architecture), and miniature towers on pilasters. Although the art form of these artisans does not have any distinguishing features from a distance, a closer examination reveals their taste for decoration. An exuberance of carvings, bands of scroll work, figural bas-reliefs and panel sculptures are all closely packed. The doorways are highly ornamented but have an architectural framework consisting of pilasters, a moulded lintel and a cornice top. The sanctum receives diffused light through pierced window screens flanking the doorway; these features were inherited and modified by the Hoysala builders. The outer wall decorations are well rendered. The Chalukyan artisans extended the surface of the wall by means of pilasters and half pilasters. Miniature decorative towers of multiple types are supported by these pilasters. These towers are of the *dravida* tiered type, and in the *nagara* style they were made in the *latina* (mono aedicule) and its variants; the *bhumija* and *sekhari*.

Vimana

The Jain Temple at Lakkundi marked an important step in the development of Western Chalukya outer wall ornamentation, and in the Muktesvara Temple at Chavudayyadanapura the artisans introduced a double curved projecting eave (*chhajja*), used centuries later in Vijayanagara temples. The Kasivisvesvara Temple at Lakkundi embodies a more mature development of the Chalukyan architecture in which the tower has a fully expressed ascending line of niches. The artisans used northern style spires and expressed it in a modified *dravida* outline. Miniature towers of both *dravida* and *nagara* types are used as ornamentation on the walls. With further development, the divisions between storeys on the superstructure became less marked, until they almost lost their individuality. This development is exemplified in the Dodda Basappa Temple at Dambal, where the original *dravida* structure can only be identified after reading out the ornamental encrustation that covers the surface of each storey.

The walls of the *vimana* below the *dravida* superstructure are decorated with simple pilasters in low relief with boldly modeled sculptures between them. There are fully decorated surfaces with frequent recesses and projections with deeper niches and conventional sculptures. The decoration of the walls is subdued compared to that of the later Hoysala architecture. The walls, which are broken up into hundreds of projections and recesses, produce a remarkable effect of light and shade, an artistic vocabulary inherited by the Hoysala builders in the decades that followed.

Mantapa

An important feature of Western Chalukya roof art is the use of domical ceilings (not to be confused with the European types that are built of voussoirs with radiating joints) and square ceilings. Both types of ceilings originate from the square formed in the ceiling by the four beams that rest on four pillars. The dome above the four central pillars is normally the most attractive. The dome is constructed of ring upon ring of stones, each horizontally bedded ring smaller then the one below. The top is closed by a single stone slab. The rings are not cemented but held in place by the immense weight of the roofing material above them pressing down on the haunches of the dome. The triangular spaces created when the dome springs from the centre of the square are filled with arabesques. In the case of square ceilings, the ceiling is divided into compartments with images of lotus rosettes or other images from Hindu mythology.

Pillars are a major part of Western Chalukya architecture and were produced in two main types: pillars with alternate square blocks and a sculptured cylindrical section with a plain square-block base, and bell-shaped lathe-turned pillars. The former type is more vigorous and stronger than the bell-shaped type, which is made of soapstone and has a quality of its own. Inventive workmanship was used on soapstone shafts, roughly carved into the required shapes using a lathe. Instead of laboriously rotating a shaft to obtain the final finish, workers added the final touches to an upright shaft by using sharp tools. Some pillars were left unpolished, as evidenced by the presence of fine grooves made by the pointed end of the tool. In other cases, polishing resulted in pillars with fine reflective properties such as the pillars in the temples at Bankapura, Itagi and Hangal. This pillar art reached its zenith in the temples at Gadag, specifically the Sarasvati Temple in Gadag city.

Notable in Western Chalukya architecture are the decorative door panels that run along the length of the door and over on top to form a lintel. These decorations appear as bands of delicately chiseled fretwork, moulded colonettes and scrolls scribed with tiny figures. The bands are separated by deep narrow channels and grooves and run over the top of the door. The temple plan often included a heavy slanting cornice of double curvature, which projected outward from the roof of the open *mantapa*. This was intended to reduce heat from the sun, blocking the harsh sunlight and preventing rainwater from pouring in between the pillars. The underside of the cornice looks like woodwork because of the rib-work. Occasionally, a straight slabbed cornice is seen.

Figure Sculpture

Figural sculpture on friezes and panels changed during the period. The heroes from the Hindu epics Ramayana and Mahabharata, depicted often in early temples, become fewer, limited to only a few narrow friezes; there is a corresponding increase in the depiction of Hindu gods and goddesses in later temples. Depiction of deities above miniature towers in the recesses, with a decorative lintel above, is common in 12th century temples, but not in later ones. Figures of holy men and dancing girls were normally sculpted for deep niches and recesses. The use of bracket figures depicting dancing girls became common on pillars under beams and cornices. Among animal sculptures, the elephant appears more often than the horse: its broad volumes offered fields for ornamentation. Erotic sculptures are rarely seen in Chalukyan temples; the Tripurantakesvara Temple at Balligavi is an exception. Here, erotic sculpture is limited to a narrow band of friezes that run around the exterior of the temple.

Deity Sculpture

In what was a departure from convention, the Western Chalukyan figure sculptures of gods and goddesses bore stiff forms and were repeated over and over in the many temples. This was in contrast to the naturalistic and informal poses employed in the earlier temples in the region. Barring occasional exaggerations in pose, each principal deity had its own pose depending on the incarnation or form depicted. Consistent with figure sculpture in other parts of India, these figures were fluent rather than defined in their musculature, and the drapery was reduced to a few visible lines on the body of the image.

Western Chalukyan deity sculptures were well-rendered; exemplified best by that of Hindu goddess Sarasvati at the Sarasvati temple in Gadag city. Much of the drapery on the bust of the image is ornamentation comprising jewellery made of pearls around her throat. An elaborate pile of curls forms her hair, some of which trails to her shoulders. Above these curly tresses and behind the head is a tiered coronet of jewels, the curved edge of which rises to form a halo. From the waist down, the image is dressed in what seems to be the most delicate of material; except for the pattern of embroidery traced over it, it is difficult to tell where the drapery begins and where it ends.

Miniature Towers

From the 11th century, architectural articulation included icons between pilasters, miniature towers supported by pilasters in the recesses of walls, and, on occasion, the use of wall pillars to support these towers. These miniature towers were of the southern *dravida* and northern *bhumija* and *sekhari* types and were mostly used to elaborate *dravida* types of articulation. The miniatures on single pilasters were decorated with a protective floral lintel on top, a form of decoration normally provided for depiction of gods. These elaborations are observed in the Amrtesvara Temple at Annigeri. These miniatures became common in the 12th century, and the influence of this northern articulation is seen in the Kasivisvesvara Temple at Lakkundi and in the nearby Nannesvara Temple.

The miniature towers bear finer and more elegant details, indicating that architectural ideas traveled fast from the north to the south. Decoration and ornamentation had evolved from a moulded form to a chiseled form, the sharpness sometimes giving it a three-dimensional effect. The foliage decorations changed from bulky to thin, and a change in the miniature towers on dual pilasters is seen. The 11th century miniatures consisted of a cornice (*kapota*), a floor (*vyalamala*), a balustrade (*vedika*) and a roof (*kuta*) with a voluptuous moulding, while in the 12th century, detailed *dravida* miniature towers with many tiny tiers (*tala*) came into vogue. Some 12th century temples such as the Kallesvara Temple at Hirehadagalli have miniature towers that do not stand on pilasters but instead are supported by balconies, which have niches underneath that normally contain an image of a deity.

Temple Deities

The Western Chalukyan kings Shaivas (worshippers of the Hindu god Shiva) dedicated most of their temples to that God. They were however tolerant of the Vaishnava or Jain faiths and dedicated some temples to Vishnu and the Jain tirthankaras respectively. There are some cases where temples originally dedicated to one deity were converted to suit another faith. In such cases, the original presiding deity can sometimes still be identified by salient clues. While these temples shared the same basic plan and architectural sensibilities, they differed in some details, the visibility and pride of place they afforded the different deities.

As with all Indian temples, the deity in the sanctum was the most conspicuous indicator of the temple's dedication. The sanctum (Garbhagriha or cella) of Shaiva temples contain a Shiva *linga*, the universal symbol of the deity. An image of Gaja Lakshmi (consort of the Hindu god Vishnu) or an image of Vishnu riding on Garuda, or even just the Garuda, signifies a Vaishnava temple. Gaja Lakshmi however, an important deity as she was, of the Kannada-speaking regions, is found on the lintel of the entrance to the mantapa (pillared hall) in all temples irrespective of faith. The carving on the projecting lintel on the doorway to the sanctum has the image of a *linga* or sometimes of Ganapati (Ganesha), the son of Shiva in the case of Shaiva temples or of a seated or upright Jain saint (Tirthankar) in the case of Jain temples.

The great arched niche at the base of the superstructure (Sikhara or tower) also contains an image indicative of the dedicators' sect or faith. Above the lintel, in a deep and richly wrought architrave can be found images of the Hindu trimurti (the Hindu triad of deities) Brahma, Shiva and Vishnu beneath arched rolls of arabesque. Shiva or Vishnu occupies the centre depending on the sect the temple was dedicated to.

Occasionally, Ganapati and his brother Kartikeya (Kumara, Subramanya) or the *saktis*, the female counterparts, can be found at either end of this carving. Carvings of the river Goddesses Ganga and Yamuna are found at either end of the foot of the doorway to the shrine in early temples.

Appreciation

Influence

The Western Chalukya dynastic rule ended in the late 12th century, but its architectural legacy was inherited by the temple builders in southern Karnataka, a region then under the control of the Hoysala empire. Broadly speaking, Hoysala architecture is derived from a variant of Western Chalukya architecture that emerged from the Lakshmeshwar workshops. The construction of the Chennakesava Temple at Belur was the first major project commissioned by Hoysala King Vishnuvardhana in 1117 CE. This temple best exemplifies the Chalukyan taste the Hoysala artisans inherited. Avoiding overdecoration, these artists left uncarved spaces where required, although their elaborate door jams are exhibitionistic. Here, on the outer walls, the sculptures are not overdone, yet they are articulate and discretely aesthetic. The Hoysala builders used soapstone almost universally as building material, a trend that started in the middle of the 11th century with Chalukyan temples. Other common artistic features between the two Kanarese dynasties are the ornate *Salabhanjika* (pillar bracket figures), the lathe-turned pillars and the makara torana (lintel with mythical beastly figure). The tower over the shrine in a Hoysala temple is a closely moulded form of the Chalukya style tower.

When the Vijayanagara Empire was in power in the 15th and 16th centuries, its workshops preferred granite over soapstone as the building material for temples. However, an archaeological discovery within the royal center at Vijayanagara has revealed the use of soapstone for stepped wells. These stepped wells are fashioned entirely of finely finished soapstone arranged symmetrically, with steps and landings descending to the water on four sides. This design shows strong affinities to the temple tanks of the Western Chalukya–Hoysala period.

Research

Unlike the Badami Chalukyan temples featured in detailed studies by Henry Cousens (1927), Gary Tartakov (1969) and George Michell (1975), Western Chalukyan architecture suffered neglect despite its importance and wider use. Recently however, scholars have returned to the modern Karnataka region to focus on a longer chronology, investigating a larger geographical area, making detailed studies of epigraphs and giving more importance to individual monuments dating from the 11th through 13th centuries.

The first detailed study of Western Chalukya architecture was by M.A. Dhaky (1977), who used as a starting point two medieval epigraphs that claimed the architects were masters of various temple forms. This study focussed in particular on the riches of the Western Chalukya miniature wall shrines (aedicules). An important insight gained from this work was that the architects of the region learned about temple forms from other regions. These forms to them appeared "exotic", but they learned to reproduce them with more or less mastery, depending on the extent of their familiarity with the other regions' building traditions. This conscious eclectic attempt to freely use elements from other regions in India was pointed out by Sinha (1993) as well.

A seminal work by Adam Hardy (1995) examined the Karnataka temple building tradition over a period of 700 years, from the 7th century to the 13th century, and reviewed more than 200 temples built by four dynasties; Badami Chalukya, Rashtrakuta, Western Chalukya and Hoysala. The study covered *dravida* and *nagara* style monuments and the differences between the *dravida* tradition in modern Karnataka and that of neighbouring Tamil Nadu and made it possible to interpret the many architectural details as part of a larger scheme.

Today, the temples and epigraphs of the Western Chalukyas are protected by the Archaeological Survey of India and the Directorate of Archaeology and Museums–Government of Karnataka. In the words of historian S. Kamath (2001), "The Western Chalukyas left behind some of the finest monuments of artistic merit. Their creations have the pride of place in Indian art tradition".

Notable temples

The Mahadeva temple at Itagi dedicated to Shiva is among the larger temples built by the Western Chalukyas and perhaps the most famous. Inscriptions hail it as the 'Emperor among temples'. Here, the main temple, the sanctum of which has a *linga*, is surrounded by thirteen minor shrines, each with its own *linga*. The temple has two other shrines, dedicated to Murthinarayana and Chandraleshwari, parents of Mahadeva, the Chalukya commander who consecrated the temple in 1112 CE.

The Siddheshwara temple in the Haveri district has sculptures of deities of multiple faiths. The temple may have been consecrated first as a Vaishnava temple, later taken over by Jains and eventually becoming a Shaiva temple. The hall in the temple contains sculptures of *Uma Mahesvara* (Shiva with his consort Uma), Vishnu and his consort Lakshmi, Surya (the sun god), Naga-Nagini (the snake goddess), and the sons of Shiva, Ganapati and Kartikeya. Shiva is depicted with four arms, holding his attributes: the *damaru* (drum), the *aksamala* (chain of beads) and the *trishul* (trident) in three arms. His lower left arm rests on Uma, who is seated on Shiva's lap, embracing him with her right arm while gazing into his face. The sculpture of Uma is well decorated with garlands, large earrings and curly hair.

Some temples, in a departure from the norm were dedicated to deities other than Shiva or Vishnu. These include the Surya (portrayed as 'Suryanarayana') shrine at the Kasi Vishveshwara temple complex and a Jain temple dedicated to Mahavira, both at Lakkundi; the Taradevi temple (built in a Buddhist architectural style) at Dambal in the Gadag district; the Mahamaya temple dedicated to a tantric goddess at Kuknur in the Koppal district, and the Durga temple at Hirekerur in the Haveri district.

VIJAYANAGARA ARCHITECTURE

The Vijayanagara Architecture the period (1336 - 1565CE) was a notable building idiom evolved by the imperial Vijayanagar Empire that ruled the whole of South India from their regal capital at Vijayanagara on the banks of the Tungabhadra River in Karnataka, India. The empire built a number of temples, monuments, palaces and other structures over South India, with the largest concentration located in its capital. The monuments in and around Hampi, in the Vijayanagara principality, are listed as UNESCO World Heritage Sites.

In addition to building new temples, the empire also added new structures and made modifications to hundreds of existing temples across South India. Some structures at Vijayanagara are from the pre-Vijayanagara period. The Mahakuta hill temples are from the Western Chalukya era. The region around Hampi had been a popular place of worship for centuries before the Vijayanagara period with earliest records dating from 689 CE when it was known as Pampa Tirtha after the local river Goddess Pampa.

There are hundreds of extant monuments in the core area of the capital city. Of these fifty six are protected by UNESCO, six hundred and fifty-four monuments are protected by the government of Karnataka and another three hundred monuments await protection.

Salient Features

Vijayanagara architecture can be broadly classified into religious, courtly and civic architecture, as can the associated sculptures and paintings. The Vijayanagara style is a combination of the Chalukya, Hoysala, Pandya and Chola styles which evolved earlier in the centuries when these empires ruled and is characterised by a return to the simplistic and serene art of the past.

For the approximately 400 years during the rule of the Western Chalukya and the Hoysalas empires, the most popular material for temple construction was chloritic schist or soapstone. This was also true for sculpture as soapstone is soft and easily carved. During the Vijayanagar period the local hard granite was preferred in the Badami Chalukya style, although soapstone was used for a few reliefs and sculptures. While the use of granite reduced the density of sculptured works, granite was a more durable material for the temple structure. Because granite is prone to flaking, few pieces of individual sculptures reached the high levels of quality seen in previous centuries. In order to cover the unevenness of the stone used in sculptures, artists employed plaster to give the rough surface a smooth finish and then painted it with lively colours.

Temple Structures

Vijayanagara temples are usually surrounded by a strong enclosure. Small shrines are simply comprised of a *garbhagriha* (sanctum) and a porch. Medium sized temples have a *garbhagriha, shukanasi* (antechamber), a *navaranga* (*antrala*) connecting the sanctum and outer *mandapa* (hall), and a *rangamantapa* (enclosed pillared hall). Large temples have tall Rayagopuram built with wood, brick and stucco in Chola style. The term *Raya* is added to indicate a *gopura* built by Vijayanagar Rayas. The top of the *gopuram* has a *shalashikhara* resembling a barrel made to rest on its side. Large life sized figures of men, woman, Gods and Goddesses adorn the *gopuram*. This *Tamil dravida* influenced style became popular during the rule of king Krishnadevaraya and is seen in South Indian temples constructed over the next 200 years. Examples of *Rayagopuram* are the Chennakesava Temple in Belur, and the temples at Srisailam and Srirangam. In addition to these structures, medium sized temples also have a closed circumambulatory (*Pradakshinapatha*) passage around the sanctum, an open *mahamantapa* (large hall), a *kalyanamantapa* (ceremonial hall) and a temple tank to serve the needs of annual celebrations.

Temple pillars often have engravings of charging horses or hippogryphs (*Yali*) — horses standing on hind legs with their fore legs lifted and riders on their backs. The horses on some pillars stand seven to eight feet tall. On the other side of the pillar are usually carvings from Hindu mythology. Pillars that do not have such hippogryphs are generally rectangular with mythology themed decoration on all sides. Some pillars have a cluster of smaller pillars around a central pillar shaft. The bottom supports of these pillars have engravings of Gods and Goddesses. Carvings of Hippogryphs clearly show the adroitness of the artists who created them.

The *Mantapas* are built on square or polygonal plinths with carved friezes that are four to five feet high and have ornate stepped entrances on all four sides with miniature elephants or with *Yali* balustrades (parapets). The *Mantapas* are supported by ornate pillars. The thousand pillared style with large halls supported by numerous pillars was popular. The 1000 pillared Jain basadi at Mudabidri is an example. Larger temples have a separate shrine for the female deity. Some examples of this are the Hazara Rama, Balakrishna and Vitthala temples at Hampi.

Some shrines in the Vitthalapura area inside Vijayanagara were consecrated specifically for Tamil Alwar saints and for the great Vaishnava saint, Ramanujacharya. Architecturally they are different in that each shrine has an image depicting the saint for whose worship the temple was built. Each shrine has its own enclosure, and a separate kitchen and pilgrim feeding hall. The water storage tank inside the royal center, the stepped tank called *Pushkarni*, is a recent archaeological discovery. The stepped tank is fashioned with finished chlorite schist slabs arranged in a symmetrical formation with steps and landings descending to the water on all four sides. This is clearly a Western Chalukya-Hoysala style tank and is seen in many parts of present day Karnataka. The inscriptions on the slabs indicate the material was brought from outside the Vijayanagara area.

Palaces

Much of what is known today of Vijayanagara palaces is drawn from archaeological excavations at Hampi as no royal palace structures have survived. Most palaces stand within their own compound defined by high tapering walls made of stone or layered earth. Palaces are approached through a sequence of courts with passageways and doorways requiring multiple changes in direction. All palaces face east or north. The larger palaces have side extensions giving the complex a symmetrical shape. Palaces were built on raised platforms made of granite. The platforms have multiple tiers of mouldings with well decorated friezes. The decorations can be floral, *Kirtimukha* shapes (demon faces), geese, elephants and occasionally human figures. Pillars, beams and rafters inside the palace were made of wood as evidenced by ash discovered in excavations. The roof was made of brick or lime concrete, while copper and ivory were used for finials. Palaces commonly consisted of multiple levels with each flight of stairs decorated by balustrades on either side, with either *yali* (imaginary beast) or elephant sculptures. The entrance steps into palaces and temple *mantapas* were similarly decorated. Water tanks inside the palace complex have decorative water spouts such as the carved torso of the *Nandi* with a gaping mouth to allow water flow into the tank. Other structures commonly found inside a palace complex are wells and shrines.

The courtly architecture generally show secular styles with Islamic influences. Examples are the Lotus Mahal palace, Elephant stables, and watch towers. Courtly buildings and domed structures were built with mortar mixed with stone rubble.

The impact of this style of architecture was seen well into the 17th century when the various successive Nayaka kingdoms continued to encourage pillars with Hippogryphs and granite became the main building material.

Famous Temples Outside Vijayanagara

While the empire is well known for its monuments in the regal capital, Vijayanagara, it also built many temples in other areas of South India. Well known among these in Karnataka are Chaturmukha Basadi and Parshwanatheshwara Basadi (15th century) in Gerusoppa, Parshwanatheshwara Basadi, Santappanaik Tirumala Temple, Virupaksha Narayan Temple (1565), Bala Kini Raghunath Temple (1550) and Khetapai Narayan Temple at Bhatkal, Aryadurga Temple (1505) at Ankola, Partakali Jivottam Mutt (1560) at Gokarna, Mahalasa Narayan Temple (1565) at Kumta, Mahaganapati Mahamaya Temple (1560) at Shirali, Iswar Temple at Baindur, Balaram Temple at Malpe, Indrani Temple at Manipal, Vidyashankara Temple (1357) at Sringeri, Bhoganandiswara Temple and Yoganandiswara Temple at Nandi Hills, Kanakachalapathi Temple in Koppal district, Someswara Temple at Kolar, Ganesha Temple at Kurudumale, Tyaramalleshwara Temple (1466) at Hiriyur, Nandi Temple at Bangalore and others.

In Andhra Pradesh the empire built the Mallikarjuna Temple at Srisailam, Upper Narasimha Temple and Lower Narasimha Temple at Ahobilam, Veera Bhadra Temple at Lepakshi and Venkateshwara Temple at Tirupati and others. In Tamil Nadu the empire built the Vijayaraghava Permal temple modelled after the famous temples at Tirupati with statues of Krishnadevaraya in Thayar Sanithi pillars facing each other.

INDIAN VERNACULAR ARCHITECTURE

Indian vernacular architecture is the informal, functional architecture of structures, often in rural areas, of India, built of local materials and designed to meet the needs of the local people. The builders of these structures are unschooled in formal architectural design and their work reflects the rich diversity of India's climate, locally available building materials, and the intricate variations in local social customs and craftsmanship. It has been estimated that worldwide close to 90% of all building is vernacular, meaning that it is for daily use for ordinary, local people and built by local craftsmen. The term "vernacular architecture" in general refers to the informal building of structures through traditional building methods by local builders without using the services of a professional architect. It is the most widespread form of building.

CATEGORIES

Indian vernacular architecture has evolved organically over time through the skillful craftsmanship of the local people. Despite the diversity, this architecture can be broadly divided into three categories.

Kachcha

A *kachcha* is a building made of natural materials such a mud, grass, bamboo, thatch or sticks and is therefore a short-lived structure. Since it is not made for endurance it requires constant maintenance and replacement. The practical limitations of the building materials available dictate the specific form which can have a simple beauty. The advantage of a *kachcha* is that construction materials are cheap and easily available and relatively little labor is required.

Pukka

A *pukka* is a structure made from materials resistant to wear, such as forms of stone or brick, clay tiles, metal or other durable materials, sometimes using mortar to bind, that does not need to be constantly maintained or replaced. However, such structures are expensive to construct as the materials are costly and more labor is required. A *pukka* may be elaborately decorated in contrast to a *kachcha*.

Semi-pukka

A combination of the *kachcha* and *pukka* style, the semi-*pukka*, has evolved as villagers have acquired the resources to add elements constructed of the durable materials characteristic of a *pukka*. Architecture as always evolves organically as the needs and resources of people change.

REGIONAL VARIATION

Building material depends on location. In hilly country where rocky rubble, ashlar, and pieces of stone are available, these can be patched together with a mud mortar to form walls. Finer stonework veneer covers the outside. Sometimes wood beams and rafters are used with slate tiles for roofing if available. Houses on hills usually have two stories, with the livestock living on the ground floor. Often a verandah runs along the side of the house. The roof is pitched to deal with the monsoon season and the house may sit on raised plinths or bamboo poles to cope with floods.

On the flat lands, abodes are usually made of mud or sun-baked bricks, then plastered inside and out, sometimes with mud mixed with hay or even cow dung and whitewashed with lime. Where bamboo is available (mainly in the north and northeastern states) it is widely used for all parts of the home as it is flexible and resilient. Also widely used is thatch from plants such as elephant grass, paddy, and coconut. In the south, clay tiles are used for *pukka* roofing while various plant material such as coconut palm is common for *kachcha*.

4

HINDU ARCHITECTURE IN INDIA

The reference to Hindu temples in literature goes back to 5th century BC in the texts by Panini (520 BC - 460 BC) and Patanjali. Later, with increasing architectural differentiation, the southern *Dravida* and the northern *Nagara* styles emerged as dominant modes of temple architecture, differing mainly in the shape of the roofing structure, the former being a stepped pyramid while the latter has a curved profile, epitomised in productions such as the magnificent Brihadeeswara Temple, Thanjavur, and the Sun Temple, Konark.

Buddhist elements and motifs continue to influence Hindu temple architecture to a considerable extent to this day. Along with the dominant Dravida and Nagara, arose a number of varied regional styles of temples in places like Bengal, Kashmir and Kerala.

Some Hindu, as well as Buddhist and Jain, temples during the early medieval era were rock-cut. The Kailasanatha temple at Ellora was excavated from top to bottom out of a massive rock face. The structural system of temples was essentially post and beam and with massive blocks of stone being the basic raw material for the local craftsman, construction could be carried out with minimal or no mortar. Decoration was fundamental to this type of architecture and is seen often in intricate details of the figured sculpture as well as in the architectural elements. The concept of fractals has been used to examine the form of the Hindu temple, both in terms of its planning and external appearance.

The *garbhagriha* or the sanctum sanctorum forms the central focus housing the deity of the temple and is provided with a circulation passage around. There are also, however, many subsidiary shrines within temple complexes, particularly in the (Dravidian style) South Indian temples. As the Hindu temple is not intended for congregational worship, the *garbhagriha* is small in scale when compared to the whole temple complex. It is articulated externally, however, by the *vimanam* (or *sikhara*), the towering roof-structure. *Mandapas* (multiple pillared halls) are found preceding the *garbhagriha*.

The spatial experience of a Dravidian (South Indian) temple complex is considered particularly enriching and meaningful. In many, such as the Sri Ranganathaswamy Temple at Srirangam, *prakaras* (concentric enclosures) along with the series of entrance gateways (*gopurams*), reduce in scale moving towards the *garbha-griha*, setting up a rhythm of solids and voids as well as providing a ritual and visual axis.

The principles of temple architecture were codified in treatises and canons such as *Manasara*, *Mayamatam*, and *Vaastu Shastra*. These offered an ordering framework yet allowed some latitude for contextual articulation.

Notable ancient and modern Hindu temples outside India include the Angkor Wat in Cambodia, the Hindu temples in Java and Bali, including Prambanan and the Neasden Temple in United Kingdom.

HINDU TEMPLE ARCHITECTURE

A basic Hindu temple consists of an inner sanctum, the *garbha griha* or womb-chamber, in which the image is housed, often with space for its circumambulation, a congregation hall, and possibly an antechamber and porch. The sanctum is crowned by a tower-like *shikara*. At the turn of the first millennium CE two major types of temples existed, the northern or Nagara style and the southern or Dravida type of temple. They are distinguishable by the shape and decoration of their shikharas.

- Nagara style: The tower is beehive shaped.
- Dravida: The tower consists of progressively smaller storeys of pavilions.

The earliest Nagar temples are in Karnataka (e.g. Galaganath at Pattadakal) and some very early Dravida-style temples (e.g. Teli-ka-Mandir at Gwalior) are actually in North India. A complex style termed Vesara was once common in Karnataka which combined the two styles.

This may be seen in the classic Hindu temples of India and Southeast Asia, such as Angkor Wat, Brihadisvara Temple, Khajuraho, Mukteshvara, and Prambanan.

DESIGN AND HISTORY

The temple is a representation of the macrocosm (the universe) as well as the microcosm (the inner space). The Magadha empire rose with the Shishunaga dynasty in around 650 BC. The Ashtadhyayi of Panini, the great grammarian of the 5th century BC speaks of images that were used in Hindu temple worship. The ordinary images were called pratikriti and the images for worship were called archa. Patanjali, the 2nd century BC author of the Mahabhashya commentary on the Ashtadhyayi, tells us more about the images. Deity images for sale were called Shivaka etc., but an archa of Shiva was just called Shiva. Patanjali mentions Shiva and Skanda deities. There is also mention of the worship of Vasudeva (Krishna). We are also told that some images could be moved and some were immoveable. Panini also says that an archa was not to be sold and that there were people (priests) who obtained their livelihood by taking care of it.

Panini and Patanjali mention temples which were called prasadas. The earlier Shatapatha Brahmana of the period of the Vedas, informs us of an image in the shape of Purusha which was placed within the altar. The Vedic books describe the plan of the temple to be square. This plan is divided into 64 or 81 smaller square, where each of these represent a specific divinity.

Amongst the foremost interpreters of Indian art and architecture are Stella Kramrisch, Vidya Dehija, M.A. Dhaky, Lokesh Chandra and Kapila Vatsyayan. The greatest living traditional temple architect is Dr. V. Ganapati Sthapati (Chennai) the only living Shilpi Guru. He is followed by his grand nephew Santhanam Krishna Sthapati of Chennai. Both are associated with The American University of Mayonic Science and Technology.

Almost all Indian art has been religious, and almost all forms of artistic tradition have been deeply conservative. The Hindu temple developed over two thousand years and its architectural evolution took place within the boundaries of strict models derived solely from religious considerations. Therefore the architect was obliged to keep to the ancient basic proportions and rigid forms which remained unaltered over many centuries.

Even particular architectural elements and decorative details which had originated long before in early timber and thatch buildings persisted for centuries in one form or another throughout the era of stone construction even though the original purpose and context was lost. The horseshoe shaped window is a good example. Its origins lie in the caitya arch doorway first seen in the third century B.C. at the Lomas Rishi cave in the Barbar Hills. Later it was transformed into a dormer window known as a gavaksha; and eventually it became an element in a purely decorative pattern of interlaced forms seen time and time again on the towers of medieval temples. So, in its essence, Indian architecture is extremely conservative. Likewise, the simplicity of building techniques like post and beam and corbelled vaulting were preferred not necessarily because of lack of knowledge or skill, but because of religious necessity and tradition.

On the other hand, the architect and sculptor were allowed a great deal of freedom in the embellishment and decoration of the prescribed underlying principles and formulae. The result was an overwhelming wealth of architectural elements, sculptural forms and decorative exuberance that is so characteristic of Indian temple architecture and which has few parallels in the artistic expression of the entire world.

It is not surprising that the broad geographical, climatic, cultural, racial, historical and linguistic differences between the northern plains and the southern peninsula of India resulted, from early on, in distinct architectural styles. The Shastras, the ancient texts on architecture, classify temples into three different orders; the Nagara or 'northern' style, the Dravida or 'southern ' style, and the Vesara or hybrid style which is seen in the Deccan between the other two. There are also dinsinct styles in peripheral areas such as Bengal, Kerala and the Himalayan valleys. But by far the most numerous buildings are in either the Nagara or the Dravida styles and the earliest surviving structural temples can already be seen as falling into the broad classifications of either one or the other. In the early years the most obvious difference between the two styles is the shape of their superstructures.

NORTH INDIAN TEMPLES

The Nagara style which developed for the fifth century is characterized by a beehive shaped tower (called a shikhara, in northern terminology) made up of layer upon layer of architectural elements such as kapotas and gavaksas, all topped by a large round cushion-like element called an amalaka. The plan is based on a square but the walls are sometimes so broken up that the tower often gives the impression of being circular. Moreover, in later developments such as in the Chandella temples, the central shaft was surrounded by many smaller reproductions of itself, creating a spectacular visual effect resembling a fountain.

SOUTH INDIAN TEMPLES

From the seventh century the Dravida or southern style has a pyramid shaped tower consisting of progressively smaller storeys of small pavilions, a narrow throat, and a dome on the top called a shikhara (in southern terminology). The repeated storeys give a horizontal visual thrust to the southern style.

Less obvious differences between the two main temple types include the ground plan, the selection and positioning of stone carved deities on the outside walls and the interior, and the range of decorative elements that are sometimes so numerous as to almost obscure the underlying architecture.

Bearing in mind the vast areas of India dominated by the 'northern' style, i.e. from the Himalayas to the Deccan, it is to be expected that there would be distinct regional variations. For example all of the following are classified as Nagara - the simple Parasuramesvara temple at Bhubaneswar in Orissa, consisting only of a shrine and a hall; the temples at Khajuraho with their spectacular superstructures; and the exquisitely carved Surya temple at Modhera. On the other hand the 'southern' style, being restricted to a much smaller geographical area, was more consistent in its development and more predictable in its architectural features and overall appearance.

TEMPLES OF THE DECCAN

In the border areas between the two major styles, particularly in the modern states of Karnataka and Andhra Pradesh, there was a good deal of stylistic overlap as well as several distinctive architectural features. A typical example is the Hoysala temple with its multiple shrines and remarkable ornate carving. In fact such features are sometimes so significant as to justify classifying distinct sub-regional groups.

The type of raw materials available from region to region naturally had a significant impact on construction techniques, carving possibilities and consequently the overall appearance of the temple. The soft soap-stone type material used by the Hoysala architects of the twelfth and thirteenth centuries allowed sculptors working in the tradition of ivory and sandalwood carving to produce the most intricate and ornate of all Indian styles. Hard crystalline rocks like granite typical of the area around Mamallapuram prevented detailed carving and resulted in the shallow reliefs associated with Pallava temples of the seventh and with centuries. In areas without stone, such as parts of Bengal, temples constructed of brick had quite different stylistic characteristics.

Royal patronage also had a very significant effect on the stylistic development of temples, and as we have already seen, regional styles are often identified by the dynasty that produced them. For example we speak of Pallava, Chola, Hoysala, Gupta, Chalukya and Chandella temples.

It might be assumed that temple styles would be different for the various Hindu cults. In fact, this was never the case in India. Even Jain temples such as those at Khajuraho were often built in almost identical styles to the Hindu temples.

From the eighth century onward with the development of ever more sophisticated rituals and festivals, the Hindu temple especially in the south started to expand and become more elaborate. There were more mandapas for various purposes such as dancing, assembly, eating, or, for example. To house Nandi, Shiva's sacred mount; more subsidiary shrines and other structures; and more corridors and pillared halls such as the 'thousand-pillared halls'.

But the most significant visual difference between the later northern and southern styles are the gateways. In the north the shikhara remains the most prominent element of the temple and the gateway is usually modest. In the south enclosure walls were built around the whole complex and along these walls, ideally set along the east-west and north-south axes, elaborate and often magnificent gateways called gopurams led the devotees into the sacred courtyard. These gopurams led the devotees into the superstructures and capped with a barrel-shaped roofs were in fact to become the most striking feature of the south Indian temple. They become taller and taller, dwarfing the inner sanctum and its tower and dominating the whole temple site. From the Vijayanagara period (fourteenth to sixteenth century) onward, these highly embellished and often brightly painted structures become extremely numerous. The width of the storeys of pavilions and other architectural elements were carefully adjusted to create a concave contour which is a distinctive characteristic of the Dravida temples seen throughout the south, particularly in Tamil Nadu.

THE PATTERN OF TEMPLE CONSTRUCTION

The construction of Hindu temples – whether in the North or in the South – essentially followed a similar pattern. There's the sanctuary or the vimana of which the upper and outer pyramidical and tapering portion is called the shikhara, or pinnacle. The vimana is a rather dark and gloomy place and houses the divine deity. This small area is called garbha griha, literally meaning 'womb house'. The entrance is through a doorway, normally from the eastern side. The doorway is reached through a mandapa or pillared hall, where devotees congregate for prayers.

However, earlier temples may have had the mandapa at a little distance from the main Hindu temple (the Shore Temple in Mamallapuram near Chennai, circa AD 700), although this practice was done away with in later constructions. Later it became necessary to unite both buildings, making way for the antarala or intermediate vestibule. A porch or a smaller room called ardha mandapa leads up to a hall (mandapa), which in turn goes into a maha mandapa.

The most perfect example of a temple on this structure are the Khajuraho temples. Here, each chamber has its own separate pyramidical roof rising in gradual steps so that the final sanctum's roof towers up, surrounded by smaller spires, finally forming a graceful, rising stepped pyramid.

THE ROOF ARCHITECTURE

In some parts of India, the ascending pyramid roof format was not followed. The roof in such temples was still pyramidical, but was formed of layers which gradually became narrower as they rose. A courtyard was built around the religious temple, and sometimes a wall would be constructed to ensure seclusion. The outside walls were treated by carving in an orderly group of repetitive miniatures. The shikhar or tapering roof was specifically based on this design which may have originated from the domed huts of central and eastern India.

CHOLA TEMPLES IN TAMILNADU

Historically speaking, these temples are not as ancient as the 274 odd Saivite temples and the 108 Vaishnavite Shrines sung by the Nayanmars and Alwars of the 7th through the 9th centuries, however they stand out as towering monuments proclaiming the glory of the Chola regime and its committment to the arts and culture.

This issue zeroes in on the Brihadeshwara Temple in Thanjavur, Gangaikonda Choleeswarar Temple in Gangai Konda Cholapuram, the Airavateshwara Temple in Darasuram and the Kambahareshwara temple at Tribhuvanam.

Thanjavur: The districts of Thanjavur, Kumbhakonam and Nagappattinam (constituting the erstwhile Thanjavur district) boast of hundreds of ancient temples. The town of Thanjavur was the seat of the glorious Chola Empire of Tamilnadu, and was later on the seat of the Nayaks and the Marathas. True to art historian Fergusson, the Chola artists conceived like giants and finished like jewellers.

Chola History: Raja Raja Chola I, was clearly the greatest of the Chola Monarchs. During his reign (985 - 1014 AD) he brought stability to the Chola Kingdom, and restored from obscurity the brilliant Tevaram hymns of the Saivite Nayanmars from obscurity. Raja Raja was a great builder, and the Peruvudaiyar Koyil or the Big Temple at Thanjavur was his creation. His son Rajendra Chola (1014 - 1044 AD) was a greater conqueror who marched all the way to the banks of the Ganges. This march was commemorated with a new capital Gangaikonda Cholapuram and another 'Periya Koyil'. Gangai Konda Cholapuram was the capital of the Cholas for about two centuries, although it is nothing more than a village now with this rather well maintained magnificient temple. 35 Kilometers from Thanjavur lies Darasuram, once known as Rajarajapuram - a part of the Chola's secondary capital of Pazhaiyarai. Here is the Airavateshwara Temple built by Raja Raja II (1146 - 1173). It was during the reign of Kulottunga III (1178 - 1218) that the Kambahareshwara temple at Tribhuvanam was built.

These four temples under discussion stand out from the others in Tamilnadu in that, it is only in these that the Vimanam towers over the entrance Gopurams. After these four temples, the Cholas went back to their traditional style of building temples with larger Gopurams and smaller central Vimanams. These temples are fitting memorials to the glory of the rulers that built them, as well as monuments of piety and a committment to art and architecture.

Brihadeshwara Temple at Thanjavur: A 107 paragraph long inscription on the walls of the Vimanam records the contributions of Raja Raja Chola and his sister Kundavai to the Thanjavur temple. The temple stands within a fort, whose walls are later additions built in the 16th century. The towering vimanam is about 200 feet in height and is referred to as Dakshina Meru. The octogonal Shikharam rests on a single block of granite weighing 81 tons. It is believed that this block was carried up a specially built ramp built from a site 6 kilometeres away from here. Huge Nandis dot the corners of the Shikharam, and the Kalasam on top by itself is about 3.8 meteres in height. Hundreds of stucco figures bejewel the Vimanam, although it is possible that some of these may have been added on during the Maratha period. The Shivalingam - Peruvudaiyar, Rajarajeswaramudaiyar - is a huge one, set in a two storeyed sanctum, and the walls surrounding the sanctum delight visitors as a storehouse of murals and sculpture.

The long prakaram surrounds the great temple (500 feet/250 feet), and the walls surrounding the prakaram again go back to Raja Raja Cholan's period. The walls house long pillared corridors, which abound in murals, Shiva Lingams and Nandis. The Periya Nayaki temple within the temple is a later addition from the Pandya period, and so is the Subramanyar Temple sung later by the Saint poet Arunagirinathar.

Incidents from the lives of the Nayanmars, several of the 108 Bharata Natyam Dance postures, manifestations of Shiva (Aadalvallaan - Nataraja, Tripurantaka, Dakshinamurthi etc.) are depicted in sculptured panels or in exquisite Chola murals. Both the interior, and the exterior walls of the temple, are replete with images of the kind described above.

The sanctum, the ardhamandapam, the mukhamandapam and the Mahamandapam, although distinct, form a composite unit with an imposing appearance that awes visitors, forcing one to wonder how such timeless architectural feat was executed about a 1000 years ago. Entrances to the Mandapams and the towered entrances to the Prakarams are majestic. The grandeur of the architecture and the sculptural finesse speaks volumes of the skills of the Imperial Cholas.

Inscriptions refer to Shiva as Dakshina Meru Vitankar and Aadavallan. The Nandi, which dates back to the Nayak period, is housed in its own mandapam and it matches up to the grandeur and size of the temple. It is a monolithic Nandi weighing about 25 tonnes, and is about 12 feet high and 20 feet long.

HOYSALA TEMPLE ARCHITECTUR

Some of the most magnificent specimens of South Indian temples are those attributed to the Hoysala dynasty of Karnataka. How this powerful dynasty got its name is a tale that must have been narrated time and again. *Hoy Sa'la* meaning "strike Sa'la!", were the words spoken to Sa'la (legendary head of this dynasty) to kill the tiger. Since Sa'la tackled the tiger single-handed and killed him, this heroic deed took the form of the dynasty's name. The rulers of this clan were called the Yadava Kings who ruled with tremendous power after having defeated the Chalukyas and rose above all to become the paramount rulers even over the Cholas and Pandyas in South India. The Hoysala dynasty originally had their capital at Halebid (about 17 kms from Belur) where they ruled for over 150 years. However, it was attacked by invaders a couple of times during the 14th century, reducing the once grand capital to poverty and ruins. Thus, the Hoysalas shifted their seat of power to Belur which stood proud as a powerful empire back then.

At a distance of about 220 Kms from the metro city of Bangalore, Belur is considered as the Banaras of South and is thus also known as *Dakshina Varanasi*. A small town located on the banks of River Yagachi, it is but very popular for its marvellous temples which are among the best if one wants to study temple architecture. They are an architectural delight and one can spend days drinking in their beauty. The Hoysalas were brilliant builders who developed a new style of temple architecture. They conceived their shrines as star-shaped structures and not the usual cubical form. In this concept of the stellate, the main temple at Belur, is a show-stealer. Among the Hoysala rulers, King Vishnuvardhana who was also responsible for defeating the Chalukyas, built this impeccable masterpiece of a temple. The serenity of Belur is attributed to the celebrated temple of Channakeshava. According to inscriptions, the temple was built to commemorate his conversion from Jainism to Vaishnavism. He signalised his conversion by the erection of many temples of unsurpassed excellence, of which the temple of Chennakesava was no doubt the best. There is also another version where the temple is said to have been built to celebrate King Vishnuvardhana's victory of Talkad over the Cholas.

Before learning about the major assets of the Channakeshava Temple, it is essential to understand that the temples built in those days were not just limited to the cause of worship and religion. Infact a temple was built for five reasons, where apart from religion, it provided scope for a justice court, a treasure house, an institution to impart ethical education and fostered our various arts including music and dance.

The first thing that catches one's eye, is the beautiful ornamental Gopuram of the Channakeshava Temple. It stands tall, giving a feeling that one is entering a grandiose royal court. As one steps onto the temple's sacrosanct platform, in a corner of the vast courtyard are tossed a golden horse and a temple chariot. The winged figure of Garuda, Lord Vishnu's carrier, stands at the entrance, facing the temple, its palms touching in homage. The main structure of the temple, which is a stellar, stands as a homogenous architectural unit on a raised platform. The entire structure with its intricate Filigree gleams like metal. Chloritic Schist, a light greenish soapstone, hard as granite was used to create the complex. Every possible surface is covered with the most perfectly proportioned figures. The main temple is surrounded by other small ones such as those of Soumyanayaki and Ranganayaki, beloved of Sri Chennakesava.

There are also temples built for Narasimha, Anjaneya, etc. King Vishnuvardhana's senior queen Shantaladevi, a dance legend herself, built a temple in similar fashion to the main temple, which was called the Channigaraya temple. The surface of the temple exterior is intricately filled with horizontal friezes, sculptured in succession from the bottom. Stories from the Puranas, Upanishads and other mythological stories have been executed in the most authentic way. The Ramayana and the Mahabharata also have been included. There are also friezes of a variety of creepers and cornices with bead work. The lowest frieze is that of a series of 650 charging elephants around the walls and are all different from each other. They symbolise stability and tremendous strength and are considered the weight lifters of the temple. Next come the lions which symbolise courage while the horses above them are for speed. The creepers signify beauty. Thus, every piece of work is significant, having a meaning.

As you look up at the corners of the temple exterior, you are left spellbound at the ultimate sculptural beauties, that adorn it. The bracketed figurines called the *Madanikas* or celestial nymphs are no doubt the highlight of the temple's magnificent architecture. Exclusive to Belur, the *Madanikas* lift the glory of the temple to unprecedented heights of excellence. And there are as many as 42 of them, of which 38 adorn the exterior walls while the remaining four are placed inside on the ornate ceiling. The *Madanikas* are said to be inspired by the beautiful Queen Shantaladevi, epitomising the ideal feminine form. The variety of poses and subjects that these represent is something to marvel about. Each depicts a mood and all are amorous. 'The Beauty with a mirror-*Darpana Sundari*', 'The lady with the parrot', 'The Huntress', 'The *Bhasma-Mohini*' are some of the favourites. All these and more are carved with utmost care and clinical precision, making them come alive.

On entering the interiors of the Channakeshava temple, at the entrance one cannot help pausing a moment to look at the trademark of the temples of Hoysa'la dynasty, the royal emblem. The story of "Sa'la" killing the tiger as though comes to life. He has been immortalised along with the tiger and thus this heroic act has became the royal emblem of the Hoysala dynasty. This emblem is found at the entrance of almost all their temples.

If the temple's exteriors are out of this world, it is almost impossible to describe the greatness of its interiors which is even superior architecturally speaking. The presiding deity is the manifestation of lord Krishna or keshava and is called *'Vijaya Narayana'* here. The beautiful image stands six feet tall and was installed in the sanctum of the main temple in 1117 A.D. There are about 48 pillars of various sizes, shapes and designs, bearing testimony to remarkable artistry. Inside, even in the darkness, you can see the shining pillars, each unique in its own splendour. The most popular being, the *Narasimha pillar* in the *Navaranga*, unique in its filigreed splendour. It is said to have revolved on its ball bearings once. A small space has been left on it to be sculpted by anyone who has the talent. It remains untouched. The *Mohini Pillar* also deserves a special mention which has been carved with great care and proportion. Here again, the spotlight is forever focussed on the four *Madanikas* on the ceiling.

If one is willing to spend enough time at Belur, there is no end to the pleasures one experiences in gazing at the different mythological tales that these time-tested monuments have to narrate. The temples create magic during the early hours of the day, just before sunrise, when a tranquil atmosphere surrounds them. This is the best time to enjoy and understand the poetry of these stone images. The transition from dawn to after sunrise is also something not to be missed. Suddenly the temple brightens up bringing with it the liveliness of the local devotees, who begin to throng in, as part of a daily ritual. A total different mood sets in, that of colour and light.

The large temple in Belur is one of the most remarkable monuments from Hoysala times and region. It was commissioned by the Hoysala king himself to celebrate an important military victory in 1117 AD. This is exceptional, since nearly all other Hoysala temples were commissioned by rich officials or rich civilians. The king obviously wanted an extraordinary temple because it has been built in an architectural style foreign to the region. Moreover the monument is exceptionally large and its decoration very lavish. Many of the decorations were added later in the 12th century by the grandson and successor of the founder. The Cennakesava-temple stands in a compound with several smaller temples and a pond.

PLAN

The monument consists of a shrine, an open hall and a platform. The shrine (vimana, mulaprasada) is larger than usual, its pedestal measures about 10 by 10 meters while a more usual size is 5 by 5 meters. Its architectural style is Nāgara (North Indian) but this is rather difficult to see because its tower is lost. The hall (mandapa) is of the open type, originally it only had a parapet. Later on the space between parapet and roof has been closed-off with magnificent screens, together with the further embellishment of the temple. The platform (jagati) is an essential part of the over-all design of the monument. It forms a unity with the rest of the elevation because it carefully follows the outlines of the shrine and the hall. Its three flights of steps add dignity to the entrances of the hall and it provides a walkway around the shrine (pradakshinapatha). Circumambulation of the shrine is an important form of worship.

THE SHRINE

The design of the shrine was exceptional for the times and the region. It is Nāgara with a stellate plan. Both these aspects deserve separate notice. Stellate plans were new for southern Karnataka in 1117 AD but not uncommon in the north of Karnataka and in northern India. The kind of star found here differs from the northern examples because it is a 16-pointed interrupted star. Basically, the plan is a square. Including the projections that form the corners, each side of this square has five projections (bhadras, rathas). Of these, the intermediate projections are rotated through 22.5 degrees. The difference with a full star is the central projections that are not rotated but just orthogonal instead. In northern India, the most common form of stellate plan is also interrupted but 32-pointed. In that case the rotation of the projections is in steps of 11.25 degrees.

The Nāgara design of the shrine was also new to the region. The most striking element of this design is missing today because the tower of the shrine is gone. It had a curvilinear outline and consisted of a central vertical band and four columns of miniature Nāgara Ñikharas per side. This kind of tower is called Bumija and is also found on some of the miniature shrines flanking the entrances of this temple. The Nāgara design of the large shrine is still visible in the articulation of its walls: each projection is articulated as a pillar. This gives the walls a very different character compared to shrines with a Dravida (South Indian) design, the design common to all regions of southern India including southern Karnataka.

Also new is the decoration of the walls of the shrine with a row of large images. In earlier temples in southern India the walls were provided with niches, and only inside the niches there are large images of gods. The wall-images of the Cennakesava-temple are one of the large sculptural attractions of the monument. Their number is about 80, each projection and each recess of the shrine has one. It is on the southern side that the most striking depictions are found, among them Shiva dancing on a demon (Andhakasura), a horribly emaciated dancing Kali, a seated Ganesha, a pair consisting of a boy with umbrella and a king (Vamana avatara of Vishnu), Ravana shaking mount Kailasa (Ravana Anugraha murti), Durga slaying the buffalo demon (Mahisasuramardini), a straight-standing Brahma, a boar saving the goddess earth (Varaha avatara of Vishnu). The most impressive and most venerated wall-images are on the two faces of the south-western corner of the shrine: Vishnu slaying king Hiranayakasipu (Narasimha avatara) and Shiva slaying the elephant demon. On the western and northern sides the images are less impressive and show less variation. Here two times a naked Shiva (Bhairava), Surya, another Varaha and another Andhakasura are the most remarkable.

In ornate Hoysala temples depiction of numerous gods and attendants in a horizontal row of large images is usual, here in Belur this is found for the first time. Though the temple is dedicated to Vishnu, all gods of the Hindu pantheon are represented. The sculptural style of the wall-images is not yet the typical Hoysala style of later times. Comparison with other regions show that it is close to the style of similar wall-images of contemporary temples in the extreme north of Karnataka and in adjacent Maharashtra.

THE HALL

Also the hall of the temple is very large and very ornate. Originally it was an open hall without full walls, it had a parapet-wall and a roof only resting on pillars. Its plan is not a square but a stepped diamond, which is usual in this kind of open halls. The parapet-wall is very high in this case, more than two meters, and is topped with a slanting seat-back. This seat-back is decorated with panels showing mythological scenes. Below it are numerous horizontal bands with lavish sculptural decorations and depictions, some of them extremely delicate.

Above the seat-back elaborate screens are found, added later in the 12th century and making the interior of the hall dark and mysterious. Additions from the same times are the world-famous bracket-figures (mandanakai) found at the top of the pillars between the screens. These sculptures, about 40 in number, are so delicate that it seems nearly impossible that they are made of stone. Evidently the sculptors of these miniatures also considered them as a tour de force and sometimes provided them with boasting texts. Many of this bracket-figures are signed by their artist.

The hall has three majestic entrances, each with two flights of steps, one up to the platform and one up to the floor level of the hall. These flights of steps are flanked by miniature shrines. The doorways are elaborate and especially their lintels are masterpieces of delicate sculpture. They show avataras of Vishnu in the centre of an arch of foliage (torana). The arches spring from the mouths of two water monsters (makaras).

THE INTERIOR

Originally the interior received much daylight, but the added screens make it dark and mysterious. The top of the thick parapet-wall is a seat. Due to the size of the building the parapet is very high here, and therefore small steps are provided for reaching the wide top. Hundreds of people could sit here and watch dancing performances in the hall.

The many pillars of the hall again show that the Hoysala king wanted to build a temple surpassing all others. The variety among them is extremely large and one of them is even decorated with life-size figure sculpture. The four central pillars are the most heavy ones. They are very large specimens of ornate lathe-turned bell pillars, and their production also was a great technical achievement. They support a domed ceiling that is one of the most elaborately decorated ceilings in all India.

THE SANCTUM

As usual the sanctum consists of a square vestibule (antarala) and a square holy cella (garbhagiha). The entrances of both are flanked by life-size sculptures of door guardians (dvarapalas). They bear a mace (gada) and for the rest attributes characteristic for Vishnu. In the cella stands a cult-image of Vishnu, an extremely large one bearing clockwise a wheel (cakra), a mace (gada), a lotus (padma) and a conch (shankha). Indeed this is the order of attributes corresponding with the form of the god called Kesava. "Cenna" means good, respectful in Kannada, the language of Karnataka.

DATE AND STYLISTICAL POSITION

In this case, happily, there are several inscriptions telling about the erection and the consecration of the temple. This happened in 1117 AD by king Vishnuvardhana. The style of the temple is a new kind of Nāgara derived from the contemporary temples found in the region around the imperial city of Kalyana, located in the extreme north of present-day Karnataka. The Calukya of Kalyana were the overlords of the Hoysala kings. Undoubtedly, by commissioning a temple in the style of his overlords, Vishnuvardhana wanted to demonstrate claims of power and independence.

KERALA TEMPLE ARCHITECTURE

The history of ancient Kerala is closely related to that of the neighboring state of Tamilnadu. The State of Kerala was by and large a part of the Tamil cultural domain, during the rule of the *Cheras*, up to the 3rd century CE.

The earlier cave temples of Kerala were influenced by the rock cut temple styles of the Tamil region. An indigenous temple architecture based on the the utilitarian residential types of Kerala and the Konkan region originated later in Kerala. Finding expression in a mixed medium of stone, brick, laterite and wood this unique approach to temple building resulted in a distinctive form of architecture, laying stress on sanctity, simplicity and a prevailing naturalism which marked the worship in temples. This approach naturally leads to an old-world charm, not seen elsewhere in the Indian subcontinent.

Bhagawati and Sastha are the most popular of the deities enshrined in temples. So is Sankaranarayana - the Hari-Hara manifestation of Shiva and Vishnu. Bhagawati is considered to be Narayani - or the Vishnu-Maya. Sastha is considered to be the son of Hari and Hara. Shiva and Vishnu are worshipped with equal devotion in Kerala, and there are no distinctions based on the sub religions such as Saivism and Vaishnavism as seen elsewhere. In fact, Anantasaayi, or Vishnu enshrined in a reclining posture, is depicted with a Shiva lingam below his extended right arm, unlike in Tamilnadu.

The Shiva Vishnu synthesis in general modes of worship based on earlier Indian societies of the pre Christian era has been preserved in Kerala. The temple culture of Kerala also stresses the importance of the ancient Indian epics.

The temple culture in Kerala is based on Vedic moorings, in contrast to the Agamic traditions of Tamilnadu. The sustenance of ancient practices of worship, causes devotees to step into a different world upon entering the temple precincts. For instance, the use of oil lamps in contrast to electric lamps, lends an air of serenity and mysticism to all Keralite temples.

In contrast to Tamilnadu, the Keralite temple tradition focuses only on the deity enshrined in the sanctum (moola bhera) and has no importance laid on processional deities (utsava bhera). Most temples do not have shrines to the consorts of the presiding deities, although the concept of Bhoga Shakti prevails.

The earlier temples of Kerala were primarily for Shiva and Vishnu or their manifestations (Krishna, Parasurama, Rama, Vamana). Shiva is worshipped both in the iconic and the aniconic Linga form. Swayampradhana shrines to Ganesha, Kartikeya are of later origin, and are seen more in the temples of the peripheral regions of Kerala adjoining Tamilnadu or Karnataka.

Inscriptions in Kerala are mostly in the ancient Vattezhuttu script of Tamilnadu. Malayalam inscriptions are seen from the 16th century onwards. Temples have been constantly rebuilt and renovated, unlike in Tamilnadu where more permanent structures of granite were built and engraved upon.

The temples of Kerala are referenced in the works of the Tamil Alwar Saints and the Nayanmar Saints. Kulasekhara Alwar and Cheramaan Perumaal (one of the Nayanmaars) belonged to the Cheras of the ninth century CE. There are several works on temple architecture written in Kerala during the 15th and the 16th centuries. The Bhakti literature of the 16th century played an important role in the temple culture of Kerala.The Maharajas of Travancore were ardent patrons of temples.

Temple architecture in Kerala is different from that of other regions in India. Largely dictated by the geography of the region that abounds in forests blessed with the bounties of the monsoons, the structure of the temples in Kerala is distinctive. The roofs are steep and pointed, and covered with copper sheets. The Kerala roof resembles those found in the Himalayan regions and those in East Asia.

The shape of the roof is in accordance with the plan of the sanctum below. With a circular plan, one sees a conical roof, while with a square plan the roof is pyramidal. The roof is constructed with wood and is covered with copper plates. Most of the temples seen in Kerala today, have undergone several phases of renovation, given the perishable nature of the construction materials.

The central sanctum of a Keralite temple is referred to as the Sree Kovil. It is surrounded by a cloistered prakara, pierced at one or more cardinal points with a gopuradwara. The cloistered prakaram has a namaskara mandapam located directly in front of the sanctum. This prakaram also houses subsidiary shrines. A kitchen is located in the south eastern corner of ths cloistered prakaram. The mukha mandapam is integrated with the gopura entrance. The flagstaff or dwaja stambham is located outside of the dwajastambham. The balipitham may be located in the mukhamandapam or in the outer courtyard. The outer prakaram or courtyard houses other subshrines, and optionally a temple tank.

The Kuttambalam or the theater hall of the Keralite temple is located either as a part of the inner prakara, on the south east corner facing north, or as a separate hall outside the innermost prakaram, either facing into the temple or facing north. This has a stage, raised from the rest of the floor, and a backstage area. This is the site of the performance of Kathakali or Chakkiyar koothu recitals. Thus the kuttambalam plays a role in educating visitors on the rich legends of the Indian cultural fabric.

The Keralite temple is an amalgam of stonework, wood work, stucco work and painting - harmoniously blended into a structure vibrant with traditions of the region. The wood work here is of great importance, and it gives the essential verve and character to the Kerala temple silhouette. The inner skeletal framework of the temple is of wood, although the base and the structure above are of granite and laterite respectively. The roof projects out at several levels, in order to protect the inner skeletal framework from the vigorous monsoons that inundate the region.

The Kerala temple walls are of coursed laterite stone masonry plastered in mud and lime. Murals are seen on several of these temple walls. Another distictive feature of Keralite temples is the use of vilakku maadam, or the multi-tiered brass lamps in front of temples. Lakshadeepam is a spectacular celebration of traditional lighting where tiers of small oil lamps lining the outer walls of the inner prakaram are lit.

Temples have held an important place in the life of Keralites. Several temples in Kerala trace their origins to antiquity. However, they were renovated frequently and the current structures that are seen are vastly a result of the numerous renovations.

PROMINENT INDIAN TEMPLE

BRIHADISHWARA TEMPLE

The Brihadishwara Temple, also known as Rajarajeswaram, at Thanjavur is a brilliant example of the major heights achieved by Cholas in temple architecture. The temple is part of the UNESCO World Heritage Site "Great Living Chola Temples". This temple is one of India's most prized architectural sites. The temple stands amidst fortified walls that were probably added in the 16th century. The 'Vimana' or the temple tower is 216 ft (66 m) high (about 70 meters) and is among the tallest of its kind in the world. The 'Shikhara' (bulbous structure on the top) of the temple is itself very large and heavy (81.25 tons). The entire temple structure is made out of hard granite stones - hardly available in Thanjavur area where the temple is located.

The temple is an example of the architectural conception of the pure form of the dravida type of temple architecture and representative of the Chola Empire ideology and the Tamil civilisation in Southern India. The temples "testify to the brilliant achievements of the Chola in architecture, sculpture, painting and bronze casting".

The temple had its foundations laid out by the ambitious emperor Chola king Rajaraja Chola I in 1002 CE, as the first of the great Chola building projects. Although there were later modifications by the Chalukyan and Pallavas, the scale and grandeur is in the Chola tradition. An axial and symmetrical geometry rules the temple layout. Temples from this period and the following two centuries are an expression of the Chola wealth, power and artistic expertise. The emergence of such features as the multifaceted columns with projecting square capitals signal the arrival of the new Chola style.

The Brihadishwara Temple was built to be the royal temple to display the emperor's vision of his power and his relationship to the universal order. The temple was the site of the major royal ceremonies such as anointed the emperor and linking him with its deity, Shiva, and the daily rituals of the deities were mirrored by those of the king. The temple maintained a staff of 600 people in various capacities. Besides the Brahmin priest, these included record-keepers, musicians, scholars, and craftsman of every type as well as housekeeping staff. Even today, the Brihadishwara Temple remains India's largest.

Temple Complex

The temple complex sits on the banks of a river that was channeled to make a moat around the complex's outer walls, the walls being built like a fortress. The complex is made up of many structures that are aligned axially. The complex can be entered either on one axis through a five-story gopuram with a second access directly to the huge main quadrangle through a smaller free-standing gopuram. The massive size of the main sikhara (although it is hollow on the inside and not meant to be occupied), is 63 meters in height, with 16 severely articulated stories, and dominates the main quadrangle. Pilaster, piers, and attached columns are placed rhythmically covering every surface of the shikhara.

Main Temple

The main temple is in the center of the spacious quadrangle composed of a sanctuary, a Nandi, a pillared hall and an assembly hall (mandapas), and many sub-shrines. The most important part of the temple is the inner mandapa which is surrounded by massive walls that are divided into different levels by sharply cut sculptures and pilasters providing deep bays and recesses. Each side of the sanctuary has a bay emphasizing the principle cult icons. The garbhagriha, a Sanskrit word meaning the interior of the sanctum sanctorum, is the inner most sanctum and focus of the temple where an image of the primary deity, Shiva, resides. Inside is a huge stone linga, literally the word garbha griha means "womb chamber" from Sanskrit word *garbha* for womb. Only priests are allowed to enter this inner most chamber. In the Dravida style, the garbhagriha takes the form of a miniature vimana with other features exclusive to southern Indian temple architecture such as the inner wall together with the outer wall creating a pradakshina around the garbhagriha for circumambulation (pradakshina). The entrance is highly decorated. The inside chamber housing the image of the god is the sanctum sanctorum, the garbhagriha. The garbhagriha is square and sits on a plinth, its location calculated to be a point of total equilibrium and harmony as it is representative of a microcosm of the universe. In the center is placed the image of the deity. The circumambulation winds around the massive lingam in the garbhagriha and is repeated in an upper story, presenting the idea that Chola Empire freely offered access to the gods.

The inner mandapa leads out to a rectangular mandapa and then to a twenty-columned porch with three staircases leading down. Sharing the same stone plinth is a small open mandapa dedicated to Nandi, Shiva's sacred bull mount.

Adjoining Structures

Surrounding the main temple are two walled enclosures. The outer wall is high, defining the temple complex area. Here is the massive gopuram or gateway mentioned above. Within this a portico, a barrel vaulted gorpuram with over 400 pillars, is enclosed by a high wall interspersed with huge gopurams axially lined up to the main temple.

Origin of Idea

The wish to build a temple like this is said to have occured to Raja Raja while he stayed at "eezham" [today's Sri lanka] as a war head. He saw a lot of Buddha statues that were very tall, which would have made him wish to build a great temple to his cordial deity SHIVA.

Other

Not only the temple and "moolavar", [The main god of Temple (Shiva)], all other sub-lords [Koshta Moorthigal] like Dhakshinamoorthy, Sun, moon all they are very huge sized. Especially, Brihadishwara temple is one of the rare temples which is having statues for "astadiggpalakas" [Lords for the eight Direction [Indra, Varuna, Agni, Eesana, Vayu, Niruthi, Yama, Kubera], that is also like a sitting of a real man i.e approximately 6 feet.

TEMPLES OF KERALA

Kerala boasts of a hoary temple tradition. The temples of Kerala - among the best maintained in the subcontinent, are simple in construction, relying greatly on timber - a bounty of the rich forests that adorn this southern state, unlike the collossal granite structures of the neighboring state of Tamilnadu. Historically, there has been a strong link between the two southern states.

The Alwars: Sri Vaishnavism is one of the pre-eminent traditions of Hinduism. An unbroken lineage of teachers, (the Acharyas) and a wealth of literature in Tamil and in Sanskrit and the *Vishishtadvaita* philosophy form the backbone of the Sri Vaishnava religion. Twelve saint (poet) devotees - the great Alwars lived their lives dedicated to expressing their devotion to MahaVishnu - considered to be the supreme manifestation of Divinity in the Vaishnava system of beliefs. These saints composed verses in chaste tamil, and revitalized the religious spirit of the region, sparking off a renewal of devotional worship in what is generally referred to as the Bhakti movement.

Divya Desam: The poems of the Alwars address Vishnu enshrined in 108 temples and celestial abodes. 106 of these shrines are located all over the subcontinent, the majority of them being in Tamilnadu, from where the Alwars hailed. Eleven of these temples are in Kerala. These temples range from the well known Anantapadmanabhaswamy temple at Trivandrum in southern Kerala to in Northern Kerala. Each of these temples is over 1200 years old. Renovation efforts in the past millennium have altered the appearance of these temples, as in the Tiruvanandapuram temple, where much of the renovation is the result of the patronage by the Royal Travancore Maharajas. However, it remains a fact, that each of these shrines existed during the period of the Alwars, and are still flourising centers of worship.

Here are the eleven Divya Desam temples of Kerala.

- Tirunaavaai
- Tiruvithuvakkode
- Trikkakkara
- Moozhikkalam
- Tiruvalla
- Tirukkodittaanam
- Chengannur
- Tiruppuliyur
- Aranmula

- Tiruvanvandur
- Tiruvanandapuram

TIRUNAAVAAI

This is an ancient temple of Kerala - considered equivalent to Banares, located on the Bharatapuzha river. Across the river are temples to Shiva and Brahma. Tirunavaya is located on the Malabar railroad from Palakkad to Mangalore. The railhead Tirunavaya is about a mile away from the temple.

Deities: The presiding diety here is Navamukundan. There are subshrines to Ganapati on the south west corner and Bhagavati on the north east corner.

The base of the temple is built of stone, while the superstructure above is of laterite, stucco and timberwork. The temple is considered to be demonstrative of the evolved Kerala type of architecture, dating back to the 13th-14th centuries although in a comparatively poor state of existence today. There is a separate shrine for Malarmangai Naachiyaar unlike the other Divya Desam temples in Kerala.

Legends: The name Tirunaavaai is said to have stemmed from the legend that nine yogis offered worship here. Legend has it that Lakshmi and Gajendran the king of elephants worshipped Vishnu here with lotus flowers from a lake; with two devotees using flowers from the same source, supply dwindled, and Gajendran appealed to Vishnu, who took Lakshmi by his side on the same throne and accepted worship offered by Gajendran. The name of the theertham Senkamala saras arises from the legend of the lotus filled lake.

The image of Navamukundan is portrayed only from above the knee, the rest of the image being concealed within the ground. There are interesting legends associated with this state of the image. There is believed to be a bottomless unexplored pit behind the image in the sanctum.

Another legend has it that a group of nine yogis or siddhas offered worship to Vishnu at this shrine and attained moksham or salvation; hence the name Nava Narayanan. The Bharatapuzha river, the presence of temples to Brahma, Vishnu and Shiva on its banks, accords this temple town a stature equivalent to Benares. As in Benares, cremation of the dead is carried out in ghats along the river.

Legend also has it that Markandeya, fleeing the clutches of Yama appealed to Vishnu for help at this shrine and upon his direction crossed the river Bharatapuzha to worship Shiva, while Vishnu blocked the rear entrance to the temple, to prevent Yama from clutching him.

TIRUVITHUVAKKODE

This Divya Desam has been sung in a decad of 10 verses by Kulasekhara Alwar who hailed from Kerala (Chera Nadu). This temple is located at Tiruvinjikode, at a distance of 16 km from Shoranur (off of the highway), enroute to Guruvayur. The nearest railhead is Pattambi on the Malabar railway line. This temple has a shrine to Shiva and a shrine to Vishnu.

This temple is connected with legends from the Mahabharata and has four images of Vishnu believed to have been installed by the Pandavas.

Given the four Vishnu images and the sanctum enshrining Shiva this temple is popularly known as anjumoorthy koyil.

Legend has it that Vishnu appeared in four forms here (Vyuhavataram - Pradyumna, Aniruddha, Sankharshana and Para Vasudeva) in response to worship by Ambarishan and was worshipped by the Pandavas here. Ambarishan is said to have obtained salvation here. Of the four images of Vishnu seen here, Yuddhishtra is said to have worshipped the one in the center, Bhima the one on the left, Arjuna the one on the west, and Nakula and Sahadeva the other.

There is yet another temple in Karur (on the Chennai Tiruchi railroad), by name Vithuvakkodeeswaram, enshrining Abhaya Pradhana Ranganathar and Ranganayaki, also considered to be a Divya Desam by the same name. Ranganathar is enshrined in a reclining posture. This temple covers an area of about an acre and has shrines to Anjaneyar and Garudazwar.

Legend has it that Markandeyan, Mucukunda Chakravarti, Sri Devi and Bhudevi offered worship here. Two worship services are offered each day here. The annual festival is celebrated in the month of Chittirai.

TRIKKAKKARA

The Vamanamurthy Temple at Trikakkara is an ancient one, located 14 km north east of Irinjalakuda on the Thrissur Ernakulam railroad. It has been glorified by the tamil hymns (Tiruvaimozhi) of Nammalwar, of the 1st millennium CE.

This temple is associated with the Onam festival; Tiruvonam is celebrated in the Malayalam month of Chingam (Leo), the last day Onam marking the avataram of Vamana and the banishment of Mahabali Chakravarti to the netherworld. Onam is the most important festival celebrated in Kerala. Even today, an image of Trikkakkara Vamana is symbolically used in Onam celebrations in several places in Kerala.

This temple celebrates the legend of the origin of Vamana - Trivikrama and his conquest of the worlds with his massive Trivikrama form and his placing his foot on Mahabali Chakravarti's head. Local legends even associate the Kapila theertham with the source of water with which Mahabali Chakravarti symbolically made his offering of land to Vamana.

Legend has it that Mahabali returns to the earth once a year during the Onam festival and that his return is marked by celebrations involving floral decorations and more. There are interesting non-puranic local legends surrounding this place. A devout farmer, appalled by the lack of crop from his fields of plantain trees, worshipped the deity here, with an offering of a bunch of plantains fashioned out of gold, upon which, he was blessed with a more than bountiful harvest of a breed of bananas now known as Nendiram Pazham.f.

An extension to this legend has it that a yogi was accused unjustly of stealing these golden plantains; acquitted later after undue punishment, the yogi cursed the place to befall into ruins. The legend states that the yogi, thanks to his untimely death caused by the undue punishment and humiliation turned into a bhramharakshasan and that a shrine was built to propitate his spirit. The region went through wars and conquests and suffered poverty, apparently due to the yogi's curse. It was only later that the administration of the temple was taken over by the Travancore kingdom and the temple began to see better times.

Deities: The presiding deity here is Vamanamurthy. There are subshrines to Sastha and Mahalakshmi. This temple is characterized by its vritta (circular) vimanam. A Shivalingam in the temple is said to have been held in worship by Mahabali Chakravarti. There are inscriptions here from as early as the 10th century CE the period of Bhaskara Ravivarma. This temple is said to have received endowments from the Chera king Kulasekhara Perumaal of the 9th century CE.

MOOZHIKKALAM

The Lakshmana Perumaal temple is located at Tirumoozhikkalam near Alwaye and Kaaladi. The presiding deity Lakshmana Perumaal is considered to be none other than Vishnu. The Triprayar Rama temple and the Koodalmanikyam Bharata temple are related shrines located in this part of Kerala. This is an ancient temple, glorified by the tamil hymns (Tiruvaimozhi) of Nammalwar one of the 12 Vaishnavite Alwars of the 1st millenium CE.

This shrine is associated with legends from the Ramayanam. Legend has it that while Bharata the brother of Rama and Lakshmana, came to invite Rama, then in exile, to take over the reins of the kingdom, an angry Lakshmana suspecting Bharata's intentions intended to kill him; however, Bharata's innocence was very soon revealed, and then the two of them offered worship together at Tirumoozhikkalam. The name Tirumoozhikkalam is said to have originated from the phrase tiru mozhi kalam the site where sweet words were uttered.

Legend also has it that Hareetha muni the son of Viswamitra worshipped Vishnu at this site. The temple: Inscriptions from the 11th century CE (Bhaskara Ravivarman) are seen in this temple. A vritta (circular) vimanam crowns this temple whose base is of stone, and the rest of the superstructure being laterite, stucco and timber.

The image of the presiding deity is in a damage state thanks to vandalism effected by conquerors. A silver kavacam or armour was made as a covering for the image; however soon after installation of the kavacam an attempt was made to steal it, after which it has never been in use.

To the left of the sanctum is a door with no images inside. Worship is offered to Rama, Sita and Hanuman at this spot acknowledging their presence.

No music is played during worship services here, unlike other temples.

The annual festival which falls in the malayalam month of Makaram used to be an occasion of great festivity, with performances of koothu and Koodiyaattam for a 41 day period (in the temple Koothambalam).

Associated closely with this temple are temples dedicated to Bharata at Irinjalakuda (which is one of the 108 Vaishnava Divya Desam temples), Rama at Triprayar and to Satrugna at Payammel.

Legend has it that four images of the heroic brothers Rama, Lakshmana, Bharata and Satrugna were washed ashore and were discovered by a local chieftan Vakkey Kaimal and were installed at the sites mentioned above. All of these four images are those of Vishnu, but are referred to as Rama, Lakshmanaperumaal, Bharata and Satrugna. Offering worship at each of these four shrines on a given day, is considered auspicious.

TIRUVALLA

This is an ancient temple, enshrining Sri Vallabha at Tiruvalla near Kottayam. It has been glorified by the tamil hymns of Tirumangaialwar and Nammalwar of the 1st millennium CE. The name Tiruvalla originates from the presiding deity Vallabha.

Tiruvalla is an ancient town with a hoary past. It has been referenced in 7th century sanskrit literature of Dandin the sanskrit poet of Kanchi. The Tiruvalla plates contain inscriptions regarding the administration of the temple in ancient times.

The temple: The plinth and the wall of this temple are of granite while the rest of the structure is of timber and sheet roof. The shrine has a vritta (circular) vimanam. Carvings of Dakshinamurthy and Shiva - Yogiswara are seen in this temple. In front of the sanctum are a namaskaramandapam, a mukhamandapam a gopuradwaram and an agramandapam. There is a subshrine to Vishwaksena, in the north east corner of the inner prakaram, facing south.

Vallabha is portrayed as bearing a conch, a discus and a lotus.

The Sudarshana Chakram seen through the west cardinal door of the sanctum is held in worship and is believed to have been installed in the 13th century. Much of the present form of the temple dates back to the 14th century.

Sandalwood paste is offered as the prasadam in the Vallabha shrine, while vibhooti or the sacred ash is offered as prasadam in the Chakra sign on the other side of the sanctum.

The flagstaff of this temple is a monolithic structure of black granite 50 feet in height. At the top of this staff is an image of Garuda.

Interestingly, devotees offer to sponsor kathakali performances as their offering to the temple. Those whose prayers are answered offer to have a performance arranged here, as a token of acknowledgement and as a gesture of support of the arts.

Festivals: A one day festival is conducted in the month of May when images of deities (Bhagawati) from the Kavil, Padappaad and Alamthurathu temples are brought in decorated palanquins to this temple and brought in through the northern entrance of the temple in great splendor and are given offerings of new clothes and the likes prior to their return to their respective temples. It is only on this day that the northern entrance is opened.

TIRUKKODITTAANAM

Tirukkodittanam is one of the five ancient shrines in the Chengannur area of Kerala, connected with the Mahabharatam. (Chengannur - Yuddhishtra, Tiruppuliyur - Bheema, Aranmula - Arjuna, Tiruvamundur - Nakula and Tirukkadittaanam - Sahadeva). It is located near the town of Changanacheri near Kottayam. This ancient temple has been glorified by the tamil hymns (Tiruvaimozhi) of Nammalwar.

Legend has it that this temple was built by Sahadavan of the Pandavas. It is also believed that this village was ruled by Rukmangatan, a king of the Solar race.

The Temple: This temple has a vritta (circular) vimanam. Several murals (possibly from the 17th century) adorn the walls of the sanctum, portraying images of Shiva Tandavam, Karatarjuniyam, Vinayaka, Sasta, Yoganarasimha, Rama Pattabhishekam, Mahisasuramardhini, Mohini, Venugopala, Anantasayanam etc. The temple structure dates back to the 11th century. There are subshrines to Narasimha and Dakshinamurthy here. The Narasimha image is said to date back to the Vijayanagara period. The wood carvings and murals date back to the 16th through 18th centuries. Inscriptions from the period of Bhaskara Ravivarman (10th century) are seen in this temple.

High walls surround it and give it the grandeur of a fort. Stones are so carefully chiseled and joined that it is impossible to distinguish joints. There is a large 2-3 acre tank outside the temple. On the bank of the tank, near the temple gate, there is a big pillar on top of which is kept hanging a human figure in granite stone, with a crown, sacred thread and a conch. This image is related to a historic story of petty feudal warfare. Stone inscriptions found here are of significance.

Festivals: A unique custom of sprinkling rose water along the circumambulatory path is seen in this temple. Deepa Mahotsavam is celebrated in the month of Vrischikam (Nov 15 - Dec 15). This festival is said to commemorate the self immolation of Madri the mother of Sahadevan. In this unique festival, plantain leaves are arranged in the form of a pyre, and torches are inserted and lighted to the accompaniment of unique percussion instruments.

CHENGANNUR

Tiruchenkunroor is one of the five ancient shrines in the Chengannur area of Kerala, connected with the Mahabharatam. (Chengannur - Yuddhishtra, Tiruppuliyur - Bheema, Aranmula - Arjuna, Tiruvamundur - Nakula and Tirukkadittaanam - Sahadeva). Nammalwar describes Chenkunrur as a town where the smoke emanating from the vedic ritual yagnas fills the sky and as a place surrounded by rich lush vegetation (of bananas and coconuts).

The Chengannoor Mahadevar temple with a shrine to Bhagavati is of great significance in this town.

In its good days, this temple's annual festival in the malayalam month of Meenam witnessed elaborate celebrations with performances of Chakkiyar koothy, Koodiyattam etc.

Legend has it that Dharmaputra (Yuddhishtra) offered worship to Vishnu, seeking pardon for his act on the battlefield, where he uttered the words 'Ashwattaama hatah kunjaraha' in an attempt to deceive Drona and lead him to a defenceless state where Arjuna brought his (Drona's) life to an end.

TIRUPPULIYUR

Tirupuliyur is one of the five ancient shrines in the Chengannur area of Kerala, connected with the Mahabharatam. (Chengannur - Yuddhishtra, Tiruppuliyur - Bheema, Aranmula - Arjuna, Tiruvamundur - Nakula and Tirukkadittaanam - Sahadeva). It has been glorified by the tamil hymns of Nammalwar of the 1st millennium CE. Another of the Alwars, Tirumangaialwar has mentioned Tirupuliyur in one of his verses in his Siriya Tirumadal.

Legend has it that Bhima the Pandava prince built this temple and worshipped Vishnu here. A colorful legend regarding the saptarishis and a great famine that occurred in this area is associated with this temple. Other local legends associated with feudal warfare amongst the local rulers and the priests are also associated with this temple. It is believed that this temple lay without worship for a 200 year period after which it was consecrated and reopened.

At Malanad near Kollam there is a temple dedicated to Duryodhana of the Kauravas of Mahabharata. A local community known as Kuravas offers worship at the Duryodhana temple. It is widely believed by the Kuravas that harm would befall them if they spent a night at Tiruppuliyur housing the temple established by Bheema.

The food offerings made at the Tiruppuliyur temple are vast in magnitude. At least 400 measures of rice are used in the preparation of special offerings, acknowledging the hearty appetite associated with Bheema the builder of the temple.

ARANMULA

Aranmula is a beautiful village located further inland from Chengannur, (9 km west) on the Ernakulam Quilon railroad. It is on the left bank of the Pampa river; it is from here that the sacred jewels of Ayyappan are taken in procession to Sabarimalai each year. Aranmula is also known for the watersports involving a spectacular procession of snake boats. It is also linked with legends from the Mahabharata.

Among the Krishna temples in Kerala, the most important ones are at Guruvayur, Trichambaram, Tiruvarppu, Ambalappuzha and Aranmula.

Aranmula is one of the five ancient shrines in the Chengannur area of Kerala, connected with the Mahabharatam. (Chengannur - Yuddhishtra, Tiruppuliyur - Bheema, Aranmula - Arjuna, Tiruvamundur - Nakula and Tirukkadittaanam - Sahadeva). It has been glorified by the tamil hymns of Nammalwar of the 1st millennium CE.

The temple has four towers over its entrances on its outer wall. The eastern tower is accessed through a flight of 18 steps. Descending 57 steps through the northern tower, one can reach the Pampa river. Legend has it that the Pandava princes, after crowning Parikshit left on a pilgrimage of India, and in Kerala, each of these brothers installed Vishnu on the banks of the Pampa and nearby places and offered worship. (Chengannur - Yuddhishtra, Tiruppuliyur - Bheema, Aranmula - Arjuna, Tiruvamundur - Nakula and Tirukkadittaanam - Sahadeva). It is said that Arjuna built this temple at Nilackal near Sabarimalai. and the image was brought here in a raft made of six pieces of bamboo to this site, and hence the name Aranmula (six pieces of bamboo).

Legend has it that Arjuna built this temple, to expiate for the sin of having killed Karna on the battlefield, against the dharma of killing an unarmed enemy. It is also believed that Vishnu (here) revealed the knowledge of creation to Bhrama, from whom the Madhukaitapa demons stole the Vedas.

There is yet another legend associated with Parthasarathy here. On the ninth day of the battle of Kurukshetra, the Kauravas reigned supreme under the leadership of Bheeshma, when krishna motivated Arjuna to take initative and vanquish his foe. Upon his hesitating to do so, Krishna jumped down in rage, and took up his discus; seeing this sight Bheeshma surrendered to him and Arjuna beseeched him not to kill Bheeshma, as it would bave been against Krishna's vow to take up arms in his battle. It is believed that it is this image of Krishna that is enshrined here, with a discus.

The Water Carnival: This temple is located on the banks of the river Pampa. This temple is associated with water carnivals - boat race during the Onam season. A tradition of sending an offering of rice and other material required for a feast from a nearby village, on a waterboat relates to the origin of this festival and this tradition is continued even today (this is related to a legend in which a devotee fed a hungry pilgrim, who directed him to send food to Aranmula and disappeared, revealing that he was none other than Vishnu).

Snake boats accompany the sacred boat. The boat race: Snake boats from 39 Karas from Chennithala in the west to Ranni in the east participate in the watersport Vellamkali. These boats assemble since dawn and sail in pairs for about 2 hours. A snake boat is about 103 feet in length. Each boat has about 4 helmsmen 100 rowers and 25 singers. After the watersport there is an elaborate feast in the Aranmula temple.

Another festival celebrated here is the Khandavanadahanam celebrated in the malayalam month of Dhanus. For this festival, a replica of a forest is created in front of the temple with dried plants, leaves and twigs. This bonfire is lit, symbolic of the Khandavana forest fire of the Mahabharata.

The malayala month of Meenam witnesses a festival where Aranmula Parthasarathy is taken in a grand procession on the garuda mount to the Pampa river bank, where an image of the Bhagawati from the nearby Punnamthode temple is brought in procession for the arattu festival.

TIRUVANVANDUR

Tiruvamundur is one of the five ancient shrines in the Chengannur area of Kerala, connected with the Mahabharatam. (Chengannur - Yuddhishtra, Tiruppuliyur - Bheema, Aranmula - Arjuna, Tiruvamundur - Nakula and Tirukkadittaanam - Sahadeva). It has been glorified by the tamil hymns of Nammalwar of the 1st millennium CE. It is located 6 km north of Chengannur on the Ernakulam Trivandrum railroad.

The temple: This temple has a circular vimanam - a namaskaramandapam and a gopuradwaram. Much of the present structure dates back to the 14th century CE.

The deity Kamalanathan is portrayed in a standing posture; the name Pambaniyappan which also refers to Kamalanathan arises from the fact the river Pampa circles the town (Pampa nadi appan). There is also a shrine to Gopalakrishnan here.

This temple dates back to the period of Kulasekhara Perumaal and was renovated by the Travancore kings (Moolam Tirunaal) in early 20th century. The image of Gopalakrishna was lost many years ago and was rediscovered in the 1960s and reconsecrated.

Legend has it that Nakula the Pandava prince built this temple. Narada is believed to have been blessed here with the duty of preaching the truth to humanity. Vishnu is said to have created a text describing the protocol to be adopted for worshipping him, at this shrine.

TIRUVANANDAPURAM

Tiruvanandapuram (Trivandrum) gets its name from the grand Anantapadmanabhaswamy temple, enshrining the tutelary deity - Anantapadmanabha of the Travancore kingdom. It is one of the grandest temples of Kerala, exhibiting an amalgamation of Dravidian and Kerala temple architectural styles. It is a temple vibrant with tradition, having been associated for years with the arts and music. The rulers of Travancore have held this temple in the highest regard. Even today, an elaborate worship protocol is followed in the strictest sense and this is one of the best maintained temples in India.

This is an ancient temple and has been revered by the tamil hymns of the Alwar Saint Nammalwar of the 1st millennium CE. Eight shrines in Kerala Tirunaavai, Trikakkara, Moozhikkalam, Tiruvalla, Tirukkodittanam, Chengannur, Tirupuliyur, Aranmula, Tiruvanvandur and Tiruvanantapuram and two in Kanyakumari district (formerly in Travancore) Tiruvaattar and Tirupatisaram have been revered by the tamil hymns of Nammalwar. Tirumangaialwar has sung of Tiruvalla, and has mentioned Tirupuliyur in one of his hymns.

Deities: This temple enshrines an imposing image of Vishnu, in the Anantasayanam posture; an image viewed through three doors in front of the shrine. The original image was of wood; the current image was fashioned out of 1200 saalagramams which were specially brought down for this purpose and moulded into shape with a special paste kadusarkara - a mixture of lime, granite, molasses and mustard. Vishnu is viewed through three doors in a row - the face on the southern side, the feet on the northern side and the nabhi (navel) in the middle. Padmanabhan is enshrined in the yoganidhra posture, reclining on Aadiseshan - (making offerings of vilvam to a small Shivalingam, to his right).

The sanctum of this temple is fashioned in the style of the temples of Kerala, while the surrounding walls and the towers resemble that of the Tamil (Dravidian architecture) temples. Interesting murals adorn the outer walls of the sanctum. There are shrines to Narasimha, Hanuman and Krishna near the sanctum.

An interesting legend surrounds the origin of the imposing image. A rishi by name Divakara Yogi, who was engaged in the worship of Vishnu, was enraged by the sight of a two year old toddler swallowing his Salagramam, the object of his worship. The toddler, upon being chased by the yogi, entered a tree; the tree split, and Vishnu revealed himself in all his splendour to the Rishi, who then requested him to assume a form that could be held in worship, upon which Vishnu assumed the form of the image, now held in worship in this temple.

History: Martanda Varma of the Travancore Kingdom, in a spectacular ceremony in 1750 surrendered the kingdom to the presiding deity of the temple, and received it back as a fiefdom and ruled Travancore as a servant of Padmanabhan; all of his successors adopted this custom. Much of the present structure dates back to the period of Martanda Varma, who made several renovations and built the eastern gopuram, which got completed by 1798.

The flagstaff is enclosed in a casing of gold. The Kulasekhara mandapam near the flagstaff has fine sculptures dating back to the 17th century. The long prakaram, with a terraced roof with 324 columns, mesaures 540 feet by 325 feet, and is about 24 feet wide. It has two rows of granite pillars, and every pillar bears an image of a Deepalakshmi. Also here are images of yalis (mythological animal), with non removable stone balls in their mouths.

TEMPLES OF KARNATAKA

Karnataka has innumerable sites in the Temple Map of India, with its some of its still surviving monuments going back to the 7th century CE. The Badami Chalukyas were the builders of rock cut caves and ancient temple complexes. At Pattadakal, there are Temples in the Dravidian style along with Temples in styles that were later adopted in Eastern and Central India. The sculptural quality in these temples is outstanding.

The subordinate rulers of the Chalukyas were the Gangas and the Kadambas. The colossal monolithic statue of Gomateswara was built by the Gangas in the 10th century CE.

The Badami Chalukyas were succeeded by the Rashtrakutas and the Kalyani Chalukyas. In Southern Karnataka, the Hoysalas reigned supreme. The Hoysalas (12th century CE) were great builders and they built great temples at Halebidu, Belur and Somanathapura.

The Hoysalas built temples on raised complex star shaped platforms. This star shaped plan is carried all the way from the platform to the shikhara. Horizontal bands of sculptural motifs and monolithic pillars adorn these temples. There is a profusion of sculptural work in the Hoysala style of temple building. Also in Southern Karnataka, are temples which benefited from the patronage of the Chola rulers of Tamilnadu. A notable example is the Kolaramma temple at Kolar.

Next, the Vijayanagar Empire founded in the 14th century CE marks the period of great Temple building activity in Karnataka and these temples are characterized by the building of pillared mandapas and lofty entrance towers. Vijayanagar temples have several of the features exhibited by the temples of Tamilnadu, such as a covered pradakshinapatha (circumambulatory path) around the sanctum, and a mahamandapam in front. The ornate pillars are a distinctive mark of the Vijayanagar style.

Several of the monuments in the capital Vijayanagar - now in ruins at Hampi are attributed to Harihara II, Sadasiva and Krishna Deva Raya. The Vijayanagar Empire was destroyed by the Deccan Sultanates in the 16th century and the ruins can be seen at Hampi.

The Mysore Maharajas (Wodeyars) who ruled from around 1400 CE through the British period, with the brief lapse during Tipu Sultans rule, have also made contributions to temples in this State, the Chamundeswari temple near Mysore being a point in illustration. The temples of the southern coastal/ghat region of Karnataka (such as Kollur) are markedly different in architectural styles and they resemble the Keralite temples to a larger extent.

PROMINENT TEMPLES

The State of Karnataka is known for its multitude of tourist attractions and temples. Pilgrimage centers such as Mookambika and Udupi cradled in the western ghats offer a contrast to the ruins of the once grand Vijayanagar edifices at Hampi. The Hoysala temples marked with a profusion of intricate sculpture, and the ancient temples built by the Cholas, and the Chalukyan temples add to the variation in style across this state.

MOOKAMBIKA (KOLLUR)

The Mookambika shrine at Kollur is one of the most revered pilgrimage centers in Karnataka (and in Kerala). It is located at a distance of 147 km from Mangalore. The nearest railhead is Udupi, and it is well connected with tourist centers such as Mangalore and Shimoga in Karnataka and Kannanur in Kerala.

Kollur is regarded as one of the Seven Muktistala pilgrimage sites in Karnataka which are (Kollur), Udupi, Subrahmanya, Kumbasi, Kodeshwara, Sankaranarayana and Gokarna.

Kollur is known for its association with Aadi Sankara. Mookambika is said to have appeared before Aadi Sankara here, and he is said to have installed her image at this shrine. There is a room near the sanctum - enshrining the Sankara Simhasanam which is regarded as the very spot where he meditated and had a vision of Mookambika. Mookambika is regarded as a manifestation of Shakti, Saraswathi and Mahalakshmi. The Kudashadri hill houses sites such as Ambavanam and Chitramoolam where Adi Sankara is believed to have meditated.

Deities: The swayambhu lingam in front of the image installed by Adi Sankara, has a golden rekha (line) approximately at the center, and is considered to be a Shiva-Shakti manifestation. The image of Mookambika is in a seated posture, bearing the conch and the discus. Also enshrined near this image are those of Mahakali and Saraswathi. There are also shrines to Veerabhadra, Subramanya, Naga, Vinayaka and Anjaneya. Veerabhadra is worshipped first by devotees before entering the shrine to Mookambika.

The Temple: Located in very picturesque surroundings, Kollur is on the banks of the river Sauparnika (said to possess medicinal properties) at the foot of the hill Kudashadri. The temple is located in a spacious courtyard, and is entered through the easternt gopuradwara. The western entrance, is opened only on special occasions. It is believed that Aadi Sankara entered the temple through the western entrance.

Legends: Kollur is referred to in the Skanda Purana. It was originally known by the name Maharanyapura. It is said to have been home to several sages and yogis. A sage by name Kola was advised to worship Shakti at Kollur. A lingam appeared on its own accord then at Kollur, and Shiva requested Kola rishi to worship it and that in due course Shakti would manifest herself as Mahalakshmi there. The name Kolapura eventually changed to Kollur.

Further, the ravages of the demon Kamha bothered the ascetics of Kollur. Upon being requested by Kola and other sages of Kollur, Shakti cursed the demon to become mooka or dumb. Undaunted, the demon continued his attrocities, and an enraged Devi vanquished him. Upon vanquishing Mookasura, Devi is believed to have merged into this self manifested Lingam in this temple. 24 km from Kollur is Maarana Ghat where it is believed that the demon Mookasura was destroyed. In the temple at Maarana Ghat, there is a Sri Chakra symbolizing Devi.

GOMATESWARA – SRAVANABELAGOLA

This is one of the most popular Jain pilgrimage center in South India, and is known for its collossal monolithic statue of Gomateswara, on top of a hill. Sravanbelagola is at a distance of 93 km from Mysore. The nearest railhead is Hassan (49 km). Belur is at a distance of 86 km from here. The Karnataka State Tourism Office, organizes day trips which cover Sravanabelagola, Halebidu and Belur in a single day.

The temple to Gomateswara is built on top of a hill, in between two hills - at a height of 3000 feet above sea level. A flight of 500 steps provides access to this temple. Views of the neighborhood from the top of the hill are spectacular.

The image of Gomateswara is an awe inspiring one. Carved out of a single block of granite, this 50 feet high statue, stands majestically on top of the hill. This image was created during the period of Chamundaraya, a minister of the Ganga King Rajamalla. The neighboring area abounds in Jaina bastis and several images of the Jaina Theerthankaras.

Festivals: The Mahamastakabhishekam festival is held once in 12 years, when the image of Gomateswara is bathed in milk, curds, ghee, saffron and gold coins.

VIRUPAKSHA TEMPLE AT HAMPI

Hampi, now in ruins is the site of the ancient city of Vijayanagar, capital of the Vijayanagar empire (founded under the spiritual guidance of Vidyaranya of Sringeri in early 14th century CE) which brought about a renaissance of indigenous art and culture, as it defended the region against the plundering armies from elsewhere.

Much of Vijayanagar is now in ruins, as when the rulers were defeated at the hands of the invaders at the battle of Talikota in the 16th century, most of the marvelous structures and edifices were systematically destroyed.

The Virupaksha or the Pampapathi temple is the main center of pilgrimage at Hampi. It is fully intact, and it incorporates some earlier structures. This temple has three towers, the eastern tower rises to a height of 160 feet and is nine tiered. It dates back to the first half of the fifteenth century and was renovated in the sixteenth century by Krishnadevaraya.

This tower has been built such that an inverted shadow of this huge tower falls on the western wall of the temple through a small hole behind the sanctum. The northern gopuram has five storeys, and the inner eastern gopuram is endowed with three storeys.

The presiding deity here is Virupaksheshwara or Pampapathi. His consort Pampa, is believed to be the daughter of Brahma. There is an ornate shrine to Bhuvaneswari. There is a shrine to Vidyaranya, the spiritual founder of Vijayanagar in this temple. The inner prakaram consists of shrines and pillars dating back to the 12th century.

Krishnadevaraya also built a mandapam in front of the sanctum, and embellished it with Vijayanagar style bas reliefs and murals. Several of Shiva's manifestations, and the ten incarnations of Vishnu are portrayed here, as is the classic scene from

Mahabharata depicting Arjuna's shooting the fish device in order to secure Draupadi's hand in marriage. There is also a mural depicting Vidyaranya the spiritual founder of Vijayanagar in procession.

In the vicinity of the Virupaksha temple are several dilapidated mandapams. In front of the temple was once an ancient shopping center lined with mandapams, the ruins of which stand today.

Festivals: The chariot festival in the month of February is the chief annual festival celebrated here. The divine marriage between Virupaksheshwara and Pampa is celebrated in the month of December.

VITTHALA TEMPLE AT HAMPI

The most splendid of temples at Vijayanagar is the Vitthala temple, near the Tungabhadra river. It is considered to be the most ornate of the Vijayanagar temples. Hampi, now in ruins is the site of the ancient city of Vijayanagar, capital of the Vijayanagar empire (founded under the spiritual guidance of Vidyaranya of Sringeri in early 14th century) which brought about a renaissance of indigenous art and culture, as it defended the region against the plundering armies from elsewhere.

Much of Vijayanagar is now in ruins, as when the rulers were defeated at the hands of the invaders at the battle of Talikota in the 16th century, most of the marvelous structures and edifices were systematically destroyed.

Vitthala - Vishnu is enshrined in this temple. The mahamandapam of this temple, in front of the sanctum - enclosed in the inner courtyard is of great beauty. It's base is chiseled with friezes of the swan, the horse and the warrior. At intervals, there are projections with bas reliefs portraying the deification of the ten avataras of Vishnu.

The steps on the east of the mahamandapam are flanked by an elephant balustrade. The facades are lined with forty pillars, each over 10 feet in height. Each group of pillars has a central pillar with slender shafts around. The center of the Mahamandapam has sixteen pillars decorated with Narasimha and Yali, forming a rectangular court. The ceiling of the Mahamandapam is also covered with sculptural work.

The stone chariot in this temple is of great fame. Its stone wheels, each shaped in the form of a lotus, are capable of revolving. It represents the sprakling creativity of the artists of the fifteenth century. Temple chariots are often mobile reproductions of a temple. The stone chariot here is in turn a static version of the mobile temple chariot.

VIDYASHANKARA TEMPLE – SRINGERI

Sringeri is one of the most celebrated pilgrimage centers in Karnataka, and is home to the Sarada Peetham established by the revered spiritual leader Aadi Sankaracharya.

Sringeri is located amidst the Sahyadri hills in Chikmaglur district of Karnataka on the left bank of the river Tungabhadra. The nearest railhead is Birur on the Bangalore - Pune railroad. The nearest airport is at Mangalore (150 km). Bangalore is at a distance of 336 km from Sringeri. Near Sringeri, are the Sringagiri hills, said to be the birth place of Sage Rishyasringa.

Aadi Sankaracharya established the Sarada Peetham here in the 1st millennium CE, and installed an image of Sarada with a Sri Chakra in front of her, and started the Bharati Sampradaya to propagate the philosophy of non dualism. Sankara's disciple Sureshwaracharya was the first head of the Sringeri Peetham.

Vidyashankara of Vidyathirtha, who was the head of this Peetham for a period of 105 years from 1228 CE to 1333 CE is considered to be one of the greatest Gurus of this Peetham. Vidyaranya who headed the peetham from 1331 CE to 1386 CE was another extraordinary leader, who was instrumental in the establishment of the Vijayanagara Empire, which not only offered stiff resistance to the onslaught of destruction from the invading foreign armies, but also caused the flowering of literary works and great monuments throughout South India and the preservation of the ancient temple traditions.

The Vidyashankara temple at Sringeri was built in memory of Guru Vidyashankara or Vidyathirtha by Vidyaranya, with the aid of the Vijayanagar rulers in the 14th century. The golden image of Sarada was also installed then at the Sarada temple. The temple also houses ruby images of Venugopala and Srinivasa and a Nandi made out of a large pearl. Several inscriptions are seen in the temple, describing contributions made by the Vijayanagar emperors.

This temple combines the Hoysala and Dravida architectural features. It stands on a richly sculptured basement. There are six doorways leading into the temple. The twelve pillars in the mandapam are named the Raasi pillars, and are so arranged that the sun's rays fall on each of them, in the order of the solar months.

Each column also has a large rearing lion, with non removable rolling stone balls in its mouth. A circular shikhara crowns the sanctum. This temple also features 61 images carved in bas relief, of various scenes from the puranas. Buddha is depicted as one of the incarnations of Vishnu here. From across the river, this temple looks seated like a majestic swan.

The Saradamba Temple: Sarada Devi is enshrined seated on the Sri Chakra Peetham, holding a Japa Mala, with a parrot perched on the top of her hand. The original image of sandalwood was installed by Adi Sankaracharya, and it was replaced with a golden image, in the 14th century. The processional image of Saradamba is enshrined in the sourhern prakaram. There are also shrines to Shakti Ganapati and Bhuvaneswari here. There is also a shrine to Aadi Sankara here. Each Friday witnesses the procession of

Saradamba in a silver chariot around the temple. The Navaratri festival season also witnesses processions of the processional image of Saradamba. Also in this temple are shrines to Shakti, Ganapati, Mahishasuramardini and Rajarajeswari.

Also in Sringeri is the Janardhana temple, where carved in one of the niches of the sanctum is an image of Aadi Sankaracharya. Near this temple is the brindavanam of Sureshwaracharya. At Rishyasringapuram on the banks of the Nandini river, enshrines Sringeswara. Legend has it that the sage Rishyasringa attained salvation here.

Tippu Sultan of Srirangapatna is believed to have made gifts to Sringeri for the conduct of the Sahasra Chandi Japa for the welfare of the country.

SUBRAHMANYA

This ancient pilgrimage shrine enshrining Subramanya on the Kumara Parvata is located at a distance of 103 km from Mangalore, and 97 km from Hassan. Also nearby is the famous pilgrimage center of Dharmastala.

Subrahmanya is regarded as one of the Seven Muktistala pilgrimage sites in Karnataka which are Kollur, Udupi, (Subrahmanya), Kumbasi, Kodeshwara, Sankaranarayana and Gokarna.

Deities: Subramanya is enshrined seated on a peacock in the sanctum of this temple. Also enshrined here are images of Vasuki and Adi Sesha. The sanctum is full of ant hills, and the sand from the ant hills believed to possess medicinal properties, is distributed as prasada here. The Garuda stambha in front of the sanctum is believed to ward off the poisonous breath of snakes here.

There are also shrines to Uma Maheswara, Kukke Lingam (celebrating the legend that a basket - Kukke full of Shivalingams were discovered here) and Narasimha here. Also worshipped here is a box of saligramams, said to have been given by Sage Vyasa to Madhvacharya.

Legend has it that Garuda, the mount of Vishnu was once chasing Vasuki, the king of snakes. Vasuki took refuge in Subramanya who offered protection to the snake from Garuda. There is another shrine to Aadi Subramanya where Subramanya is worshipped in an ant hill with offerings of mirrors and images of Naga.

UDUPI

Udupi is one of the most revered pilgrimage sites in Karnataka and is known for its association with Madhvacharya, the founder of the dualistic - Dvaita school of philosophy. Seven Muktistala pilgrimage sites in Karnataka are Kollur, Udupi, Subrahmanya, Kumbasi, Kodeshwara, Sankaranarayana and Gokarna. Udupi is located at a distance of 36 km from Mangalore, the nearest airport.

The name Udupi arises from the legend that Chandra - the king of the stars (Udu-star, pa-king) performed penances towards Shiva (Chandramouleeswara) here to relieve himself of the curse that had been inflicted upon him by Daksha Prajapati.

Udupi is also known as Shivali - or Shiva belli. Legend has it that Parasurama upon reclaiming land from the sea, crowned his devotee Ramabhoja as a ruler. Ramabhoja killed a snake accidentally and to redeem himself from sarpa dosha, he created a silver peetham with a snake carved on it, installed Parasurama in the linga swaroopam and worshipped him as Ananteswara. The Balakrishna temple at Udupi enshrines an image of Krishna believed to have been made by the divine architect Viswakarma.

Legend has it that Krishna's mother Devaki and his wife Rukmini wished to enjoy his childhood pranks, at the end of the Dwapara yuga. The divine architect Viswakarma then created this image of Krishna bearing a churn in his right hand and a string in his left. Rukmini worshipped this image every day.

After Krishna's departure from this world, Arjuna is believed to have hidden it, and the image is believed to have gotten covered with gopi chandanam - a substance similar to sandal paste. A ship proceding from Dwarka is beleived to have carried this 'lump' bearing the image of Krishna and as it proceded through the stormy seas, Madhvacharya sensed the divine cargo, and calmed the storm and saved the ship. In return, he accepted this lump of a cargo, and discovered the image of Krishna. Madhva then installed and worshipped this image at Udupi.

The Balakrishna temple founded by Madhvacharya dates back to the 13th century CE. It is a modest structure enshrining the image of Balakrishna in a sanctum viewed through a grating referred to as the Navagraha kindi, which has nine square holes. The Navagraha window is covered with silver sheets embossed with 24 different images of Krishna.

To the west of this is the Kanakadasa mandapa. Legend has it that Krishna's image turned towards the western wall, which had collapsed to reveal a full darshan of Krishna to Kanakadasa who had earlier been denied entry into the temple. There is also a shrine to Chenna Kesava behind the sanctum. Behind this shrine is the eastern entrance of the sanctum, which is open only on Vijayadasami. Also in the temple are shrines to Garuda and Hanuman. Madhva's shrine is situated right next to the sanctum. There are also shrines to Subramanya and Vaadiraaja in this temple.

Worship: Worship services here begin at 4 AM. The worship services carried out here are the Nirmalya Darshana, Ushatkaala pooja, Panchamrita pooja, Udvardana pooja, Kalas Pooja, Go Pooja, Alankar Pooja, Maha Pooja, Brindavana Pooja, Samara Seva, Ranga Seva, Seeveli Seva and the Ekanta Seva.

Festivals: Makara Sankranti in the month of Makara (January 15) when the sun transits to the zodiac sign of Capricorn, a grand chariot festival is celebrated - carrying images of Krishna, Chandamouleeswara and Ananteshwara in procession. This seven day festival involves a float festival, and another chariot festival the Bhramma Rathotsavam is celebrated on the 7th day, when the Aaraattu is carried out in the Madhva Sarovar tank. Krishna Janmashtami is also celebrated with great splendour here.

Other temples at and near Udupi include the Ananteshwara and Chandramouleeswara temples mentioned above, Shakti temples at Puttur, Kannarpadi, Bailur and Kadiyali, and Subramanya temples at Tangodu, Mangodu, Aritodu and Muchilkodu and the Balarama temple at Vada Pandeshwara.

The Mutts around Udupi: Udupi as mentioned before is the seat of Madhva's dvaita philosophy. Eight of Madhva's successors headed mutts established by him in this area. These mutts are located at Palimar (Sri Rama), Admar (Kaliyamardana Krishna), Krishnapura (Kaliyamardana Krishna), Sode (Bhu Varaaha), Puthige (Vitthala), Sirur (Vitthala), Kaniyur (Narasimha), and Pejawar (Vitthala). The spectacular Paryaya festival, when the leadership of the mutts changes, is celebrated once in two years.

GOKARNA

Gokarna is a celebrated pilgrimage center on the coast of Karnataka, enshrining the Aatma Lingam Mahabaleshwar. It is regarded as one of the 7 Mukti Stalas of Karnataka, and it has been revered by the hymns of the Tamil Saints (Nayanmars) of the 1st millennium CE. Gokarna is located at a distance of 170 km from Mangalore, the nearest airport. The seven muktistalas of Karnataka are Udupi, Kollur, Subramanya, Kumbasi, Kodeshwara, Sankaranarayana and Gokarna. All these shrines are also known as Parasurama Kshetras, created on the land reclaimed from the sea by Parasurama. This is the only Tevara Stalam in Karnataka (Tulu Nadu) hailed by the Tamil songs of the Bhakti movement.

Legends: Vinayakar (Dwibhuja Vinayakar shrine) is said to have tricked the demon Ravana into leaving behind a Shivalingam here in a legend similar to that at Tiruchirappalli. In spite of the might exerted by Ravana (Maha Bala), the Shivalingam stayed fixed, hence the name Mahabaleshwar. The pull exerted by Ravana, is said to have caused the Shivalingam to resemble the shape of a cow's ear and hence the name Gokarnam. A very similar legend holds at the Vaidyanath - Jyotirlingam temple at Deogarh in Bihar.

The Temple: This west facing temple enshrines Mahabaleshwar, in a square Saligrama Peetham. A golden rekha on the peetham, and a small hole in its middle permits devotees to have a glimpse of the top of the Aatma Lingam. The six foot tall Shivalingam is encolsed inside the peetham, and it can be seen only once in 40 years, when the Ashta bandana Kumbhahishekam is performed. There are also shrines to Vinayaka, Chandikeswara, Aadi Gokarneswara and Dattatreya. Gokarnanayaki is also known as Taamragowri, and her shrine is behind the sanctum.

The sacred thirtham here is the Koti theertham. The image of Vinayaka bears a dent, said to have been caused when Ravana, enraged at the loss of the Atma Lingam had hit him.

Festivals: It is customary here to have a dip in the sea and then worship a Shivalingam made out of sand, before worshipping at the temple. Maha Sivaratri is of great significance in this shrine located in idyllic surroundings. Also located around Gokarna are Sejjeshwara, Gunavanteshwara, Murudeshwara and Dhareshwara. These four temples along with Mahabaleshwara are known as the Pancha Maha Kshetras.

NANJANGUD

Nanjangud located near Mysore houses an ancient temple dedicated to Shiva - Nanjundeswara or Srikanteswara that is rich in legend, historical and artistic significance. This temple celebrates the legend of Shiva consuming the poison that emanated when the milky ocean was churned by the devas and the asuras in their joint quest for the nectar of immortality; hence the name Nanjundeswara. Legend has it that Parvati arrested the spread of the venom by placing a firm grip on Shiva's neck, causing it to turn blue, and hence the name Neelakanta.

Legend also has it that Parasurama worshipped at this shrine. There is a shrine for Parasurama nearby. The temple: This temple has an imposing Rajagopuram and an array of sculptural work depicting mythological scenes. There is a shrine to Adi Kesava in between the Shiva and Parvati shrines. The 63 Nayanmar saints of the Tamil region are portrayed as life sized images. The temple is located by the side of the Kapila river. The Wodeyars of Mysore have made many endowments to this temple.

Tipu Sultan of Mysore was a patron of this temple. It is said that the sultan believed that his elephant was cured of diseases by the grace of the presiding deity of this temple and hence he made endowments to this temple.

KESAVA TEMPLE

Somnathapura near Mysore houses the Kesava temple - the last great temple built by the Hoysala dynasty. The village of Somanathapura is named after a minister by name Soma in the court of the Hoysala king Narasimha III (13th century CE), who founded it.

The Kesava temple is a fantastic piece of art. It consists of three identical shrines built on a raised platform - with a common entrance chamber in an enclosed courtyard.

The main shrine is dedicated to Kesava; however there is no image of worship now. The other shrines are dedicated to Janardhana and Venugopala.

These shrines are only about 30 feet in height. Yet they are covered profusely with ornate sculpture of the highest order, as seen in the Hoysala temples of Belur and Halebidu, with themes from the Indian epics, nature and so on.

An open corridor runs around the circumambulatory path and it has sixty four cells, meant for housing images of divinities (as in the kailasanatha temple at Kanchipuram).

MELKOTE

Melkote located near Mysore in Karnataka houses an ancient shrine to Vishnu, worshipped as Tiru Narayana. This shrine is known for its long standing association with the spiritual leader Ramanujacharya. Melkote is also known as Yadavagiri, yatistalam, Vedadri and Narayanadri.

The presiding deity here (moolavar) is known by the name Tiru Narayana, while the processional image of Vishnu goes by the name Selva Pillai or Sampath Kumara. Vishnu's consort is known by the name Yadugiri Taayaar. The image of Selvappillai is housed in the Rangamandapa. There are shrines to Yadugiri Taayaar and Kalyani Nachiyaar. The temple tank is known by the name Kalyani theertham.

Legend has it this image of Vishnu was held in worship by Brahma. It is believed that the festival image Sampat Kumara was worshipped by Rama and his son Kusha; hence the name Ramapriya. Legend has it that Krishna installed this image here at Melkote.

Melkote has two distinct temples. The Tiru Narayana temple at the foothills and the hill temple to Yoga Narasimha. Legend has it that the Yoga Narasimha temple image was installed here by Prahlada.

King Bittideva of Karnataka who embraced the Sri Vaishnava way of life and patronized the saint Ramanujacharya, assumed the name of Vishnuvardhana and built five shrines known as the Panchanarayana temples. It is believed that at that time the Narayanapura shrine was in ruins and that both the images of Tiru Narayana and Sampath Kumara were missing and that Ramanujacharya discovered the image of Tiru Narayana in the midst of Tulasi shrubs on the Yadavagiri hill and installed it back in the temple.

Legend has it that during the Muslim raids of South India, the festival image of Melkote was stolen and taken away and that Ramanujacharya restored it from the court of the ruler. It is said that it a muslim princess had gotten attached to the image of Selvappillai and that being unable to part with it, she followed the Acharya to Melkote and then merged into the shrine there. In honor of this, there is an image of Bibi Nachiyar here.

This temple is known for its Vairamudi Sevai in the month of March-April, when the image of Selvappillai is adorned with a diamond crown and taken out in procession. It is traditional belief that this crown is not to be looked at when it is not worn by the festival image; hence each year, during the occasion, the officiating priest picks up the crown from its chest with his eyes blindfolded and then places it upon the head of the image of Selvappillai. Thousands congregate to celebrate this occasion each year.

NANDI HILLS

Nandi hills are a resort at a distance of about 60 km north of Bangalore. Here, are wo ancient temples, the Bhoganandeeswara temple at the foothills and the Yoganandeeswara hill temple.

The ancient rulers of this region - the Banas built the Bhoganandeeswara temple in the 9th century. The Chola rulers of Tamil Nadu built the hill temple.

The Bhoganandeeswara temple in the foothills shows an assimilation of architectural styles of several dyanasties that ruled the area. The Banas, the Cholas, the Hoysalas and the Vijayanagar rulers made contributions to this temple.

The original shrine is attributed to the Bana queen Ratnavali. Later on, the Arunachaleswara shrine was added to the temple complex. The Cholas of the eleventh century added Nandi mandapas to the temple. The Hoysalas who came in later built an ornate Kalyana mandapam. The Vijayanagar rulers added shrines to Uma Maheswara, Girijaamba and Apita Kuchaambal. Local chieftans added two more prakarams to the existing temples. Thus the temple now consists of three prakarams and a tank.

The Yoganandeeswara hill temple is attributed to the Cholas of Tamil Nadu. The Vijayanagar rulers added a shrine to Ambal and connected the two shrines with a corridor. The temple's carvings on pillars and doorways are noteworthy.

CHAMUNDESWARI HILL TEMPLE – MYSORE

Chamundi Hill is one of the landmark tourist attractions of Mysore, and it never fails to fall on the itenerary of those visiting Mysore. Other historic temples in the vicinity of Mysore are Srirangapatna, Talakkad and Somnathpur.

The Chamundeswari temple is located on a hill in the vicinity of Mysore and is accessed through a motorable road. Chamundeswari the tutelary deity of the Mysore

Maharajas has been held in reverence for centuries, and the Wodeyars of Mysore have made extensive contributions to this shrine.

A flight of one thousand steps built by the Maharaja Dodda Devaraja in 1659 also leads up to the summit of the hill which is at a height of about 3000 feet. Chamraja Wodeyar IV is said to have worshipped here in 1573 and was miraculously saved from a lightning hit. Krishnaraja III (late 18th century) built the temple tower and presented the Nakshatramalika jewel with sanskrit verses inscribed on it.

Thus much of the current temple is the result of renovation efforts carried out in early nineteenth century, although the original shrine is much older. Chamundi Hill has been associated with the Hoysala ruler Vishnu Vardhana (12th century) and with the Vijayanagar rulers of the 17th century.

Chamundeswari, or Durga is the fierce form of Shakti who vanquished the demon Mahishasuran. A colorful image of the demon greets visitors as they reach the summit of the hill.

Also on this temple are several images of Nandi (the bull mount of Shiva). The best known of these is the collossal Nandi on the 800th step on the hill. This Nandi is over 15 feet high, and 24 feet long. It was created during the reign of Dodda Devaraja, who also built the steps leading up the hill.

There are also shrines dedicated to Shiva - Mahabaleshwar (attributed to Vishnu Vardhana the Hoysala ruler of the 12th century CE) and Lakshmi Narayana - Vishnu on this hill.

BADAMI

Aihole, Badami and Pattadakal near Bijapur in Karnataka are centers of Early Chalukyan art. Badami is located at a distance of about 500 km from Bangalore, the capital of Karnataka and is well connected by road.

Badami or Vatapi was the center of ancient Chalukyan glory. It was home to several rock-cut temples and structural temples. Historically, Vatapi suffered defeat at the hands of the Pallava king Narasimhavarma Pallavan (Mamalla after whom Mamallapuram is named) and his general Sirutonda Naayanaar in the year 642 CE. Twelve years later, the Chalukyas recaptured Vatapi and led a successful attack on Kanchipuram the capital of Pallavas.

Legend has it there were two demon siblings Vatapi and Ilvala, who had a trick by which they could kill and make a meal of mendicants passing by. Their tricks worked until Agastya muni came by and counter-tricked them and brought an end to Vatapi's life. Two of the hills in Badami are supposed to represent the demons Ilvalan and Vatapi.

There are several temples dating from the Chalukyan period in Badami. The first set of temples is a group of four on a hill adjacent to the Bhutanata tank, connected through flights of stairs.

The first temple dating back to the 5th century CE has gigantic carvings of Ardhanareeswara and Harira manifestations of Shiva in bas relief. It enshrines a Shivalingam. In the adjacent wall there is a carving of the cosmic dance of Shiva Nataraja depicted with eighteen arms. There are also reliefs of Ganapati, Shanmukha and Mahishasuramardhini.

The second temple bears images of Vishnu in his Varaha and Trivikrama incarnations. It is reached through a flight of 64 stairs from the first one. On its ceiling, are carvings of Vishnu on Garuda and several other scenes from the puranas.

The third rock cut temple is reached from the 2nd temple through a flight of 60 steps. It is a 100 feet deep cave, with inscriptions dating this Vishnu temple to 578 CE during, the period of Kiritivarma Chalukya. Here there are carved images of the Narasimha and Trivikrama avataras of Vishnu. There are also murals depicting the divine marriage of Shiva and Parvati.

Further up, is a Jain rock cut temple dedicated to the Tirtankara Adinatha with inscriptions dating back to the 12th century.

Of the structural temples in Badami, the Dattatreya temple and the Mallikarjuna are noteworthy. The Mallikarjuna temple dating back to the 11th century is built on a star shaped plan. There are also temples with the Dravidian style of vimanas.

Badami is noted for two early inscriptions dating events in history in the 6th century. The earlier one in sanskrit dates back to 543 CE, from the period of Pulakesi I (Vallabheswara), on a hillock. Near the Bhutanata temple, on a rock, there is an inscription testifying Mamalla Pallava's victory over the Chalukyas in the year 642 CE.

TALAKKAD - PANCHALINGA TEMPLES

Talakkad is a town known for its sand dunes, located near Mysore in Karnataka. A historic site, Talakkad once had over 30 temples. It stands at a sharp bend of the Kaveri river eastwards from a southerly course. Sand dunes are formed here persistently, extending over a mile, burying a large number of monuments. Talakkad houses the imposing temple to Vaidyeshwara - Shiva.

Talakkad was patronized by the Western Gangas in the first millennium CE, and then by the Tamil Cholas from the 11th through the 12th centuries. Talakkad came under the Hoysalas in the 12th century. It was then patronized by the Vijayanagar rulers and the Maharajas of Mysore.

The Vaidyeshwara temple is built in the Dravidian style of granite. Much of the structure is here is attributed to the Vijayanagar period (14th century), although several Hoysala features are seen in this temple. The eastern doorway of the Navaranga is beautifylly sculptured. Collossal dwarapalakas adorn the entrances.

The Vaidyeshsara temple along with four others - Arkeshwara, Vasukishwara or Pataleshwara, Saikateshwara or Maraleshwara and Mallikarjuna constitue the Panchalingams here. These five Lingams are said to represent the five faces of Shiva. The Pataleshwara Shivalingam is said to change colors during the day (red in the morning, black in the afternoon and white in the evening).

Panchalinga darshana is a rare pilgrimage occasion, occuring once in every few years. Tradition has it that pilgrims should first bathe in the Gokarna theertham, worship Gokarneswara and Chandikadevi, and then worship Vaidyeshwara, and then bathe in the northern eastern southern and western stretches of the Kaveri and then worship Arkeshwara, Pataleshwara, Maraleshwara and Mallikarjuna, returning to Vaidyeshwara after each worship, finally worship Kirtinarayana and conclude the pilgrimage in one day.

Several interesting legends surround this shrine. It is believed that an ascetic Somadatta headed out to Siddharanya Kshetra Talakkad to worship Shiva. Having been killed by wild elephants enroute, he and his disciples re-incarnated as wild elephants and worshipped Shiva in the form of a tree at Talakkad.

Two hunters Tala and Kada, are believed to have struck the tree with an axe to find blood gushing forth, and upon the bidding of a heavenly voice, dressed the wound of the tree with thre tree's leaves and fruits. The tree healed, and the hunters became immortal. Since Shiva is believed to have healed himself through this incident, he is referred to as Vaidyeshwara. The Panchalingams here are all associated with this legend.

Also located at Talakkad is the Kirtinarayana temple constructed by the Hoysala ruler Vishnuvardhana.

DHARMASTALA

Dharmastala is a revered pilgrimage center in Karnataka enshrining Manjunatha - Shiva, under the trusteeship of a Jain family, with worship services being performed by Madhva priests. Dharmastala is at a distance of about 75 km from Mangalore located in a picturesque settings, it is one of the well visited pilgrimage centers in Karnataka.

Local disputes are settled out of court here in the name of God, and the temple trustee Veerendra Heggade serves as the representative of the presiding deity in settling disputes.

Dharmastala is regarded as the home of Dharma or righteousness. The temple complex houses a shrine to Manjunatha and the Dharma Devatas. Thousands of pilgrims are offered food in the temple everyday. Dharmastala also houses a huge monolithic statue of Gomateshwara.

KOLAR

The Kolar district in Karnataka is bounded by Tamilnadu and Andhra Pradesh and has been at the center of history, with several dynasties ruling the region.

Historically The Banas and the Gangas ruled this region until the 9th and the centuries respectively. The Cholas took over this region around 1000 CE, and later on the Hoysalas and the Vijayanagara rulers ruled this area. They were followed by the Deccan rulers of Bijapur and then the Mysore Wodeyars.

This region is home to legends from the Ramayana and Mahabharata.

It is believed that Rama so journed in this region during his victorious return from Lanka to Ayodhya.

The village of Kaivara is associated with the legend that the Pandavas spent their exile at this site. The demon Bakasura is said to have been killed here. There are temples to Bhimeshwara and Amaranarayana here.

On the Bangalore Hindupur railroad is Gauribidenur where Vidura, the uncle of the Pandavas and Kauravas is said to have lived. A tree believed to have been planted by him is held in reverence and is surrounded by stone images of snake gods.

The ancient Kolaramma temple was renovated during the period of the Chola monarch Rajendra Chola I and is a center of Shakti worship. In Kolar district are Kurudumale and Mulbagal housing temples to Someshwara dating back to the Vijayanagar period. Virupakshapura near Mulbagal bears the Virupaksha temple again in the Vijayanagar style.

Avani near Mulbagal is known as the Gaya of the south and it bears a cluster of temples known as the Rameshwara, Lakshmaneshwara, Bharateshwara and Shatrugneshwara, dating back to the period of the Nolamba dynasty.

The Bethamangala village at a distance of about 30 km from Kolar is home to the Vijayendra temple. It dates back to the period of the Gangas, and has been renovated by the Hoysalas and the Vijayanagar rulers.

Nearby is the town of Malur, with the Shankaranarayana and the Markandeswhwara temples. The village of Tekal between Malur and Bangarpet is said to have been a city of temples in the past. There are several temple ruins here.

5

BUDDHIST ART AND ARCHITECTURE
IN INDIA

LATE BUDDHIST ART IN BENGAL: THE PÂLA-SENA PERIOD

By the seventh century A.D., Buddhism had largely disappeared from northern India, following the invasion of the White Huns. In the south the rise of Hinduism had gradually supplanted the religion of Sâkyamuni. Only in Bengal does Buddhism survive as an important force until the final annihilation of its establishments by the Mohammedan invasions of the twelfth century. Buddhist art in this last phase of its development in India was produced under the patronage of the Pâla and Sena Dynasties (730-1197) that were the heirs of Harsha's Empire in the Ganges Valley.

The Buddhism of the Pâla Period represents that outgrowth of Mahâyâna described as Tantrism, a syncretic assimilation into Buddhism of many elements of Hindu origin, such as the concept of the shakti or female energy of the Bodhisattva and the reliance on magic spells and ritual. The worship of the mystical *Dhyâni* Buddhas of the Four Directions and the creator, Âdi-Buddha, a kind of Buddhist Brahma, completely replaces any devotion to the person of the mortal Buddha. It is this phase of Buddhism, usually described as the Vajrayâna, that, together with the paraphernalia of its art, finds its way to Tibet and Nepal in the eighth and ninth centuries. Progressively until its extinction in the twelfth century, Buddhism takes on the aspects of Saivism and Vaishnavism. The principal site of this last centre of Indian Buddhism and its art was the great university city of Nalanda.

Among the inscriptions found at Nalanda is one recording a dedication by a certain Baladeva, ruler of Sumatra and Java, in 860, a clear indication of the intimate relations existing between this last stronghold of Indian Buddhism and the Sailendra Empire in Indonesia. The description of the monasteries of Nalanda by Hsüan-tsang, who saw them at the height of their splendour in the seventh century, is worth quoting *in extenso*:

The whole establishment is surrounded by a brick wall, which encloses the entire convent from without. One gate opens into the great college, from which are separated eight other halls, standing in the middle of the Sangharama. The richly adorned towers, and the fairy-like turrets, like pointed hill-tops, are congregated together. The observatories seem to be lost in the vapours of the morning, and the upper rooms tower above the clouds.... All the outside courts, in which are the priests' chambers, are of four stages. The stages have dragon-projections and coloured eaves, the pearl-red pillars, carved and ornamented, the richly adorned balustrades, and the roofs covered with tiles that reflect the light in a thousand shades, these things add to the beauty of the scene.

The actual monasteries or vihâras are ranged one next to another like so many adjacent colleges in a university complex. The plan of the individual vihâras is nearly identical in the structures excavated, and consists of many small cells grouped around the four sides of an open courtyard, an arrangement already found in earlier examples of the type. In another place Hsüan-tsang observed: 'To the north... is a great vihâra, in height about three hundred feet.... With respect to its magnificence, its dimensions, and the statue of Buddha placed in it, it resembles the great vihâra built under the Bodhi tree.'

The actual excavations at Nalanda have revealed little of the magnificence described by Hsüan-tsang. Certain buildings are sufficiently preserved to give an idea of the architectural character of this last stronghold of Indian Buddhism. A stupa that was disengaged from the masonry of a larger structure built around it at a later period reveals a style that is a continuation of Gupta architectural forms. The building rests on a podium. The elevation of the base consists of two storeys, the first filled with Buddhas and Bodhisattvas in niches separated by columns derived from the Gupta order; the second zone is decorated with chaitya arches framing smaller images. Above this is an attic storey separated into two levels by projecting roll cornices. The drum of the stupa is octagonal, with its faces alternately plain and decorated with Buddha statues in niches. The whole is surmounted by a saucer-like dome.

The treatment of the façade is not unlike that of the Mahâbodhi temple as we see it today. As the view of the ground storey reveals, the revetment of the Mahâbodhi shrine dating from the Pâla Period consists mainly of multiple niches separated by square engaged pillars ringed by garland collars and surmounted by lotiform capitals. This arrangement was repeated on every successive level of the shrine proper and the pyramidal tower. Originally these recesses contained Dhyâni Buddha images, probably placed with reference to the Four Directions; at present, the niches are filled with a haphazard collection of sculpture recovered in the course of the nineteenth-century restoration. The wall space, as in the stupa at Nâlandâ, is repeatedly divided into horizontal zones by projecting string courses; and above the band of niches is a massive frieze of lion heads supporting a continuous ribbon-like garland.

If the reader will turn to the plate of the temple as a whole, he will note that just as on the œikharas of the late Gupta temples at Aihole, the storeys of the tower are marked by lotiform quoins at the corners of each level, and the finial of the spire comprises a complete âmalaka that is repeated at the lower stages. The style of the figure sculpture in stucco at Nâlan#d#â is a dry repetition of the Gupta statuary of Sârnâth, as may be seen by comparing the statue in the topmost niche with the famous preaching Buddha. Since these statues are so much in the style of early Mahâyâna imagery before the development of Tantric forms, this structure and its decoration may be dated as early as the seventh century. It seems highly likely that the original form of the great vihâra described by Hsüan-tsang was only a larger version of this same type of monument.

What must have been one of the greatest religious establishments of the Pâla Period is to be seen in the ruins at Paharpur in Bengal. The remains consist of a vast square court nearly a thousand feet on a side, surrounded by an enclosing peristyle consisting of more than one hundred and seventy-five individual cells. In the centre is a shrine in the form of a Maltese cross with a number of recessed projecting corners between the arms. In elevation this sanctuary consisted of a pyramid of three superimposed terraces and at the summit a square cella with projecting porticoes on all four sides. The shrine can be described as a prâsâda. or Meru type of temple, in which the diminishing terraces magically symbolize the steps and peak of the world mountain. The decoration consisted of multiple terra-cotta relief plaques attached to the brick façades, as in the Gupta temple at Bhîtârgâon.

Since there is no mention of this imposing monument by Hsüan-tsang, it has been conjectured that it must be dated in the late seventh or eighth century. The indications are that it was originally a Brahmanic installation which at some later period was taken over by the Buddhists. As may be seen by a glance at the ground plan, the arrangement is unique among Indian temples, although its general disposition is reminiscent of the shrine at Parihâsapura in Kashmir. Actually the closest approximations to the temple at Paharpur, both in plan and in the elevation in successive levels for circumambulation, are to be found in Java in such temples as Loro Jongrang and Canadai Sewu at Prambanam and, ultimately, the vast temple-mountain at Barabudur. It furnishes the clearest possible evidence for the close relations between Bengal and Java already suggested by the Nalanda inscription.

Characteristic of the sculpture of the Pâla and Sena Periods are the numerous examples of images carved in hard, black stone found at Nalanda and many other sites in Bengal. All of them are characterized by a great finesse and precision of execution. Many of these icons give the impression of being stone imitations of metal-work, and in almost every case the sense of plastic conception is lost under the intricacy of surface detail.

A typical example is the seated Buddha in the collection of the Museum of Fine Arts, Boston. The Buddha is represented in the yoga pose and earth-touching gesture of the Enlightenment. A feature that might at first strike the observer as a rather strange anachronism is that the Buddha wears the crown and jewels of a royal personage, the very worldly attributes discarded at the time of the renunciation. This can best be explained as part of the process of the Buddha's deification in Mahâyâna Buddhism; the crown and jewels not only proclaim his power as Cakravartin or universal sovereign, but are intended to suggest that state of radiant splendour or transfiguration attained at the supreme moment of Enlightenment. The actual style of the carving is a kind of desiccated perpetuation of the Gupta school of the fifth and sixth centuries; in it one is much more conscious of the precise and sharp definition of the detail of jewelled ornaments than of the plastic significance of the bodily form that seems to exist as a framework for these attributes.

A very famous example of Indian sculpture, generally accepted as of Gupta date, is more likely an exceptional masterpiece of the Pâla Period; this is the so-called Sâñchî torso in the Indian Museum in London. From both the stylistic and iconographic points of view it seems to correspond closely to the sculptural technique of Bengal in the centuries of Pâla domination. The fragment serves as an illustration of a technical method practised in all periods of Indian sculpture: the suggestion of the nature of flesh in stone by the contrast between the hard, cold definition of the metal accessories with the rounded smooth planes that interlock to give the structure of the body; the softness of the flesh is suggested again by the device of the constricting belt raising a welt of flesh below the navel. In addition to the exquisite refinement in the carving of details, the torso has a certain athletic litheness imparted by the breaking of the body on its axis, a pose already familiar to us in many earlier examples.

Not only the similarity of the technique to other examples of Pâla sculpture, but the attribute of the antelope skin worn as a scarf across the body point to the Pâla. Period; since this emblem was used to identify the esoteric deity Khasarpana

Avalokitesvara, whose worship, related to Saivite concepts, does not begin before the rise of Tantric Buddhism. The Sânchî torso, probably datable between the seventh and ninth centuries, is a masterpiece of its kind, in which emphasis on technical finish and virtuosity of carving and plastic modelling are maintained in perfect equilibrium; whereas in the vast majority of Pâla sculptures the elaboration of surface detail militates against the properly sculptural conception of the whole.

Of greater aesthetic as well as iconographical interest than the stone sculpture of Bengal in the last centuries of Buddhist power are the large numbers of bronze images found at Nalanda and elsewhere. Like the stone images, they reveal a development reflecting changes in the character of Buddhism from Mahâyâna types to purely Tantric forms of Saivite and Vaishnavite derivation. Many of these images were exported for dedication all over south-eastern Asia in the centuries when Nalanda was in close touch with the Srîvijaya and Sailendra Dynasties in Malaya and Java. Indeed, at one time it was uncertain whether these metal statuettes were made in India or in Java, so exact was the correspondence and so large the numbers of examples found in the two regions.

Some examples of Nalanda bronze images appear to be close imitations of earlier types of the Gandhâra and Gupta Periods, and it may well be that some of these were specifically intended as more or less faithful replicas of famous images venerated at the holy sites of Buddhism. The vast majority of them, like their stone counterparts, perpetuate the Gupta style of Sârnâth. They are characterized by the same kind of stylized elegance and fondness for precise definition of detail that characterize the stone figures. This finicky and often 'rococo' manner is, of course, more suited to malleable metal than stone. It is on the basis of the Pâla style of metal imagery that the whole of later Nepalese and Tibetan sculpture is founded; and there are indications that this manner was also translated to Kashmir.

DEVELOPMENT OF BUDDHIST ART AND ARCHITECTURE

Buddhist art originated on the Indian subcontinent following the historical life of Gautama Buddha, 6th to 5th century BCE, and thereafter evolved by contact with other cultures as it spread throughout Asia and the world.

Early Buddhist art followed the Indian aniconic tradition, which avoids direct representation of the human figure. Around the 1st century CE an iconic period emerged lasting to this day which represents the Buddha in human form.

Buddhist art followed believers as the dharma spread, adapted, and evolved in each new host country. It developed to the north through Central Asia and into Eastern Asia to form the Northern branch of Buddhist art, and to the east as far as Southeast Asia to form the Southern branch of Buddhist art. In India, Buddhist art flourished and even influenced the development of Hindu art, until Buddhism nearly disappeared in India around the 10th century due in part to the vigorous expansion of Islam alongside Hinduism.

ANICONIC PHASE (5TH CENTURY - 1ST CENTURY BCE)

During the 2nd to 1st century BCE, sculptures became more explicit, representing episodes of the Buddha's life and teachings. These took the form of votive tablets or friezes, usually in relation to the decoration of stupas. Although India had a long sculptural tradition and a mastery of rich iconography, the Buddha was never represented in human form, but only through some of his symbols.

This reluctance towards anthropomorphic representations of the Buddha, and the sophisticated development of aniconic symbols to avoid it (even in narrative scene where other human figures would appear), seems to be connected to 70 of the Buddha's sayings, reported in the Dighanikaya, that disfavored representations of himself after the extinction of his body. This tendency remained as late as the 2nd century CE in the southern parts of India, in the art of the Amaravati school. It has been argued that earlier anthropomorphic representations of the Buddha may have been made of wood and may have perished since then. However, no related archaeological evidence has been found.

ICONIC PHASE (1ST CENTURY CE – PRESENT)

Anthropomorphic representations of the Buddha started to emerge from the 1st century CE in northern India. The two main centers of creation have been identified as Gandhara in today's Punjab, in Pakistan, and the region of Mathura, in central northern India.

The art of Gandhara benefited from centuries of interaction with Greek culture since the conquests of Alexander the Great in 332 BCE and the subsequent establishment of the Greco-Bactrian and Indo-Greek Kingdoms, leading to the development of Greco-Buddhist art. Gandharan Buddhist sculpture displays Greek artistic influence, and it has been suggested that the concept of the "man-god" was essentially inspired by Greek mythological culture. Artistically, the Gandharan school of sculpture is said to have contributed wavy hair, drapery covering both shoulders, shoes and sandals, acanthus leaf decorations, etc.

The art of Mathura tends to be based on a strong Indian tradition, exemplified by the anthropomorphic representation of divinities such as the Yaksas, although in a style rather archaic compared to the later representations of the Buddha. The Mathuran school contributed clothes covering the left shoulder of thin muslin, the wheel on the palm, the lotus seat, etc.

Mathura and Gandhara also strongly influenced each other. During their artistic florescence, the two regions were even united politically under the Kushans, both being capitals of the empire. It is still a matter of debate whether the anthropomorphic representations of Buddha was essentially a result of a local evolution of Buddhist art at Mathura, or a consequence of Greek cultural influence in Gandhara through the Greco-Buddhist syncretism.

This iconic art was characterized from the start by a realistic idealism, combining realistic human features, proportions, attitudes and attributes, together with a sense of perfection and serenity reaching to the divine. This expression of the Buddha as a both a man and a god became the iconographic canon for subsequent Buddhist art.

Buddhist art continued to develop in India for a few more centuries. The pink sandstone sculptures of Mathura evolved during the Gupta period (4th to 6th century) to reach a very high fineness of execution and delicacy in the modeling. The art of the Gupta school was extremely influential almost everywhere in the rest of Asia. By the 10th century, Buddhist art creation was dying out in India, as Hinduism and Islam ultimately prevailed.

As Buddhism expanded outside of India from the 1st century CE, its original artistic package blended with other artistic influences, leading to a progressive differentiation among the countries adopting the faith.

- A Northern route was established from the 1st century CE through Central Asia, Tibet, Bhutan, China, Korea, and Japan, in which Mahayana Buddhism prevailed.
- A Southern route, where Theravada Buddhism dominated, went through Myanmar, Thailand, Cambodia, and Vietnam.

NORTHERN BUDDHIST ART

The Silk Road transmission of Buddhism to Central Asia, China and ultimately Korea and Japan started in the 1st century CE with a semi-legendary account of an embassy sent to the West by the Chinese Emperor Ming (58-75 CE). However, extensive contacts started in the 2nd century CE, probably as a consequence of the expansion of the Kushan Empire into the Chinese territory of the Tarim Basin, with the missionary efforts of a great number of Central Asian Buddhist monks to Chinese lands. The first missionaries and translators of Buddhists scriptures into Chinese, such as Lokaksema, were either Parthian, Kushan, Sogdian or Kuchean.

Central Asian missionary efforts along the Silk Road were accompanied by a flux of artistic influences, visible in the development of Serindian art from the 2nd through the 11th century CE in the Tarim Basin, modern Xinjiang. Serindian art often derives from the Greco-Buddhist art of the Gandhara district of what is now Pakistan, combining Indian, Greek and Roman influences. Silk Road Greco-Buddhist artistic influences can be found as far as Japan to this day, in architectural motifs, Buddhist imagery, and a select few representations of Japanese gods.

The art of the northern route was also highly influenced by the development of Mahayana Buddhism, an inclusive faith characterized by the adoption of new texts, in addition to the traditional Pali canon, and a shift in the understanding of Buddhism. Mahayana goes beyond the traditional Theravada ideal of the release from suffering (dukkha) and personal enlightenment of the arhats, to elevate the Buddha to a god-like status, and to create a pantheon of quasi-divine Bodhisattvas devoting themselves to personal excellence, ultimate knowledge and the salvation of humanity. Northern Buddhist art thus tends to be characterized by a very rich and syncretic Buddhist pantheon, with a multitude of images of the various Buddhas, Bodhisattvas and lesser deities.

AFGHANISTAN

Buddhist art in Afghanistan (old Bactria) persisted for several centuries until the spread of Islam in the 7th century. It is exemplified by the Buddhas of Bamyan. Other sculptures, in stucco, schist or clay, display very strong blending of Indian post-Gupta mannerism and Classical influence, Hellenistic or possibly even Greco-Roman.

Although Islamic rule was rather tolerant of other religions "of the Book", it showed little tolerance for Buddhism, which was perceived as a religion depending on idolatry. Human figurative art forms also being prohibited under Islam, Buddhist art suffered numerous attacks, which culminated with the systematic destructions by the Taliban regime. The Buddhas of Bamyan, the sculptures of Hadda, and many of the remaining artifacts at the Afghanistan museum have been destroyed.

The multiple conflicts since the 1980s also have led to a systematic pillage of archaeological sites apparently in the hope of reselling in the international market what artifacts could be found.

CENTRAL ASIA

Central Asia long played the role of a meeting place between China, India and Persia. During the 2nd century BCE, the expansion of the Former Han to the West led to increased contact with the Hellenistic civilizations of Asia, especially the Greco-Bactrian Kingdom.

Thereafter, the expansion of Buddhism to the North led to the formation of Buddhist communities and even Buddhist kingdoms in the oases of Central Asia. Some Silk Road cities consisted almost entirely of Buddhist stupas and monasteries, and it seems that one of their main objectives was to welcome and service travelers between East and West.

The eastern part of Central Asia Chinese Turkestan (Tarim Basin, Xinjiang) in particular has revealed an extremely rich Serindian art (wall paintings and reliefs in numerous caves, portable paintings on canvas, sculpture, ritual objects), displaying multiple influences from Indian and Hellenistic cultures. Works of art reminiscent of the Gandharan style, as well as scriptures in the Gandhari script Kharoshti have been found. These influences were rapidly absorbed however by the vigorous Chinese culture, and a strongly Chinese particularism develops from that point.

CHINA

Buddhism arrived in China around the 1st century CE, and introduced new types of art into China, particularly in the area of statuary. Receiving this distant religion, strong Chinese traits were incorporated into Buddhist art.

NORTHERN DYNASTIES

In the 5th to 6th centuries, the Northern Dynasties, developed rather symbolic and abstract modes of representation, with schematic lines. Their style is also said to be solemn and majestic. The lack of corporeality of this art, and its distance from the original Buddhist objective of expressing the pure ideal of enlightenment in an accessible and realistic manner, progressively led to a change towards more naturalism and realism, leading to the expression of Tang Buddhist art.

Sites preserving Northern Wei Dynasty Buddhist sculpture:

- Longmen Grottoes, Henan
- Bingling Temple, Gansu

TANG DYNASTY

Following a transition under the Sui Dynasty, Buddhist sculpture of the Tang evolved towards a markedly life-like expression. Because of the dynasty's openness to foreign influences, and renewed exchanges with Indian culture due to the numerous travels of Chinese Buddhist monks to India, Tang dynasty Buddhist sculpture assumed a rather classical form, inspired by the Indian art of the Gupta period. During that time, the Tang capital of Chang'an (today's Xi'an) became an important center for Buddhism. From there Buddhism spread to Korea, and Japanese embassies of Kentoshi helped it gain a foothold in Japan.

However, foreign influences came to be negatively perceived in China towards the end of the Tang dynasty. In the year 845, the Tang emperor Wuzong outlawed all "foreign" religions (including Christian Nestorianism, Zoroastrianism and Buddhism) in order to support the indigenous religion, Taoism. He confiscated Buddhist possessions, and forced the faith to go underground, therefore affecting the development of the religion and its arts in China. Chán Buddhism however, at the origin of Japanese Zen, continued to prosper for some centuries, especially under the Song Dynasty (960-1279), when Chan monasteries were great centers of culture and learning.

The popularization of Buddhism in China has made the country home to one of the richest collections of Buddhist arts in the world. The Mogao Caves near Dunhuang and the Bingling Temple caves near Yongjing in Gansu province, the Longmen Grottoes near Luoyang in Henan province, the Yungang Grottoes near Datong in Shanxi province, and the Dazu Rock Carvings near Chongqing municipality are among the most important and renowned Buddhist sculptural sites. The Leshan Giant Buddha, carved out of a hillside in the 8th century during the Tang Dynasty and looking down on the confluence of three rivers, is still the largest stone Buddha statue in the world.

KOREA

Korean Buddhist art generally reflects an interaction between Chinese Buddhist influence and a strongly original Korean culture. Additionally, the art of the steppes, particularly Siberian and Scythian influences, are evident in early Korean Buddhist art based on the excavation of artifacts and burial goods such as Silla royal crowns, belt buckles, daggers, and comma-shaped gogok. The style of this indigenous art was geometric, abstract and richly adorned with a characteristic "barbarian" luxury. Although Chinese influence was strong, Korean Buddhist art "bespeaks a sobriety, taste for the right tone, a sense of abstraction but also of colours that curiously enough are in line with contemporary taste".

THREE KINGDOMS OF KOREA

The first of the Three Kingdoms of Korea to officially receive Buddhism was Goguryeo in 372. However, Chinese records and the use of Buddhist motifs in Goguryeo murals indicate the introduction of Buddhism earlier than the official date. The Baekje Kingdom officially recognized Buddhism in 384. The Silla Kingdom, isolated and with no easy sea or land access to China, officially adopted Buddhism in 535 although the foreign religion was known in the kingdom due to the work of Goguryeo monks since the early fifth century.

The introduction of Buddhism stimulated the need for artisans to create images for veneration, architects for temples, and the literate for the Buddhist sutras and transformed Korean civilization. Particularly important in the transmission of sophisticated art styles to the Korean kingdoms was the art of the "barbarian" Tuoba, a clan of non-Han Chinese Xianbei people who established the Northern Wei Dynasty in China in 386. The Northern Wei style was particularly influential in the art of the Goguryeo and Baekje. Baekje artisans later transmitted this style along with Southern Dynasty elements and distinct Korean elements to Japan. Korean artisans were highly selective of the styles they incorporated and combined different regional styles together to create a specific Korean Buddhist art style.

While Goguryeo Buddhist art exhibited vitality and mobility akin with Northern Wei prototypes, the Baekje Kingdom was also in close contact with the Southern Dynasties of China and this close diplomatic contact is exemplified in the gentle and proportional sculpture of the Baekje, epitomized by Baekje sculpture exhibiting the fathomless smile known to art historians as the Baekje smile. The Silla Kingdom also developed a distinctive Buddhist art tradition epitomized by the Bangasayusang, a half-seated contemplative maitreya whose Korean-made twin, the Miroku Bosatsu, was sent to Japan as a proselytizing gift and now resides in the Koryu-ji Temple in Japan. Buddhism in the Three Kingdoms period stimulated massive temple-building projects, such as the Mireuksa Temple in the Baekje Kingdom and the Hwangnyongsa Temple in Silla.

Baekje architects were famed for their skill and were instrumental in building the massive nine-story pagoda at Hwangnyongsa and early Buddhist temples in Yamato Japan such as Hoko-ji (Asuka-dera) and Hôryû-ji. Sixth century Korean Buddhist art exhibited the cultural influences of China and India but began to show distinctive indigenous characteristics. These indigenous characteristics can be seen in early Buddhist art in Japan and some early Japanese Buddhist sculpture is now believed to have originated in Korea, particularly from Baekje, or Korean artisans who immigrated to Yamato Japan. Particularly, the semi-seated Maitreya form was adapted into a highly developed Korean style which was transmitted to Japan as evidenced by the Koryu-ji Miroku Bosatsu and the Chugu-ji Siddhartha statues. Although many historians portray Korea as a mere transmitter of Buddhism, the Three Kingdoms, and particularly Baekje, were instrumental as active agents in the introduction and formation of a Buddhist tradition in Japan in 538 or 552.

UNIFIED SILLA

During the Unified Silla period, East Asia was particularly stable with China and Korea both enjoying unified governments. Early Unified Silla art combined Silla styles and Baekje styles. Korean Buddhist art was also influenced by new Tang Dynasty styles as evidenced by a new popular Buddhist motif with full-faced Buddha sculptures. Tang China was the cross roads of East, Central, and South Asia and so the Buddhist art of this time period exhibit the so-called international style. State-sponsored Buddhist art flourished during this period, the epitome of which is the Seokguram Grotto.

GORYEO DYNASTY

The fall of the Unified Silla Dynasty and the establishment of the Goryeo Dynasty in 918 indicates a new period of Korean Buddhist art. The Goryeo kings also lavishly sponsored Buddhism and Buddhist art flourished, especially Buddhist paintings and illuminated sutras written in gold and silver ink. The crowning achievement of this period is the carving of approximately 80,000 woodblocks of the Tripitaka Koreana which was done twice.

JOSEON DYNASTY

The Joseon Dynasty actively suppressed Buddhism beginning in 1406 and Buddhist temples and art production subsequently decline in quality in quantity although beginning in 1549, Buddhist art does continue to be produced.

JAPAN

Before the introduction of Buddhism, Japan had already been the seat of various cultural (and artistic) influences, from the abstract linear decorative art of the indigenous Neolithic Jômon from around 10500 BCE to 300 BCE, to the art during the Yayoi and Kofun periods, with developments such as Haniwa art.

Japan, the largest Buddhist country today, discovered Buddhism in the 6th century when missionary monks travelled to the islands together with numerous scriptures and works of art. The Buddhist religion was adopted by the state in the following century. Being geographically at the end of the Silk Road, Japan was able to preserve many aspects of Buddhism at the very time it was disappearing in India, and being suppressed in Central Asia and China.

From 711, numerous temples and monasteries were built in the capital city of Nara, including a five-story pagoda, the Golden Hall of the Horyuji, and the Kôfuku-ji temple. Countless paintings and sculpture were made, often under governmental sponsorship. Indian, Hellenistic, Chinese and Korean artistic influences blended into an original style characterized by realism and gracefulness. The creation of Japanese Buddhist art was especially rich between the 8th and 13th centuries during the periods of Nara, Heian and Kamakura. Japan developed an extremely rich figurative art for the pantheon of Buddhist deities, sometimes combined with Hindu and Shinto influences. This art can be very varied, creative and bold.

From the 12th and 13th, a further development was Zen art, following the introduction of the faith by Dogen and Eisai upon their return from China. Zen art is mainly characterized by original paintings (such as sumi-e) and poetry (especially haikus), striving to express the true essence of the world through impressionistic and unadorned "non-dualistic" representations. The search for enlightenment "in the moment" also led to the development of other important derivative arts such as the Chanoyu tea ceremony or the Ikebana art of flower arrangement. This evolution went as far as considering almost any human activity as an art with a strong spiritual and aesthetic content, first and foremost in those activities related to combat techniques (martial arts). Buddhism remains very active in Japan to this day. Still around 80,000 Buddhist temples are preserved. Many of them are in wood and are regularly restored.

TIBET AND BHUTAN

Tantric Buddhism started as a movement in eastern India around the 5th or the 6th century. Many of the practices of Tantric Buddhism are derived from Brahmanism (the usage of mantras, yoga, or the burning of sacrificial offerings). Tantrism became the dominant form of Buddhism in Tibet from the 8th century. Due to its geographical centrality in Asia, Tibetan Buddhist art received influence from Indian, Nepali, Greco-Buddhist and Chinese art.

One of the most characteristic creations of Tibetan Buddhist art are the mandalas, diagrams of a "divine temple" made of a circle enclosing a square, the purpose of which is to help Buddhist devotees focus their attention through meditation and follow the path to the central image of the Buddha. Artistically, Buddhist Gupta art and Hindu art tend to be the two strongest inspirations of Tibetan art.

VIETNAM

Chinese influence was predominant in the north of Vietnam (Tonkin) between the 1st and 9th centuries, and Confucianism and Mahayana Buddhism were prevalent. Overall, the art of Vietnam has been strongly influenced by Chinese Buddhist art.

In the south, the kingdom of Champa has a strongly Indianized art, just as neighboring Cambodia. Many of its statues were characterized by rich body adornments. The capital of the kingdom of Champa was annexed by Vietnam in 1471, and it totally collapsed in the 1720s.

SOUTHERN BUDDHIST ART

During the 1st century CE, the trade on the overland Silk Road tended to be restricted by the rise of the Parthian empire in the Middle East, an unvanquished enemy of Rome, just as Romans were becoming extremely wealthy and their demand for Asian luxury was rising. This demand revived the sea connections between the Mediterranean Sea and China, with India as the intermediary of choice. From that time, through trade connections, commercial settlements, and even political interventions, India started to strongly influence Southeast Asian countries. Trade routes linked India with southern Burma, central and southern Siam, lower Cambodia and southern Vietnam, and numerous urbanized coastal settlements were established there.

For more than a thousand years, Indian influence was therefore the major factor that brought a certain level of cultural unity to the various countries of the region. The Pali and Sanskrit languages and the Indian script, together with Mahayana and Theravada Buddhism, Brahmanism and Hinduism, were transmitted from direct contact and through sacred texts and Indian literature such as the Ramayana and the Mahabharata. This expansion provided the artistic context for the development of Buddhist art in these countries, which then developed characteristics of their own.

Between the 1st and 8th centuries, several kingdoms competed for influence in the region (particularly the Cambodian Funan then the Burmese Mon kingdoms) contributing various artistic characteristics, mainly derived from the Indian Gupta style. Combined with a pervading Hindu influence, Buddhist images, votive tablets and Sanskrit inscriptions are found throughout the area.

From the 9th to the 13th centuries, Southeast Asia had very powerful empires and became extremely active in Buddhist architectural and artistic creation. The Sri Vijaya Empire to the south and the Khmer Empire to the north competed for influence, but both were adherents of Mahayana Buddhism, and their art expressed the rich Mahayana pantheon of the Bodhisattvas. The Theravada Buddhism of the Pali canon was introduced to the region around the 13th century from Sri Lanka, and was adopted by the newly founded ethnic Thai kingdom of Sukhothai. Since in Theravada Buddhism only monks can reach Nirvana, the construction of temple complexes plays a particularly important role in the artistic expression of Southeast Asia from that time.

From the 14th century, the main factor was the spread of Islam to the maritime areas of Southeast Asia, overrunning Malaysia, Indonesia, and most of the islands as far as the Philippines. In the continental areas, Theravada Buddhism continued to expand into Burma, Laos and Cambodia.

MYANMAR

A neighbor of India, Myanmar was naturally strongly influenced by the eastern part of Indian territory. The Mon of southern Burma are said to have been converted to Buddhism around 200 BCE under the proselytizing of the Indian king Ashoka, before the schism between Mahayana and Hinayana Buddhism.

Early Buddhist temples are found, such as Beikthano in central Myanmar, with dates between the 1st and the 5th centuries. The Buddhist art of the Mons was especially influenced by the Indian art of the Gupta and post-Gupta periods, and their mannerist style spread widely in Southeast Asia following the expansion of the Mon Empire between the 5th and 8th centuries.

Later, thousands of Buddhist temples were built at Bagan, the capital, between the 11th and 13th centuries, and around 2,000 of them are still standing. Beautiful jeweled statues of the Buddha are remaining from that period. Creation managed to continue despite the seizure of the city by the Mongols in 1287.

CAMBODIA

Cambodia was the center of the Funan kingdom, which expanded into Burma and as far south as Malaysia between the 3rd and 6th centuries CE. Its influence seems to have been essentially political, most of the cultural influence coming directly from India.

Later, from the 9th to 13th centuries, the Mahayana Buddhist and Hindu Khmer Empire dominated vast parts of the Southeast Asian peninsula, and its influence was foremost in the development of Buddhist art in the region. Under the Khmer, more than 900 temples were built in Cambodia and in neighboring Thailand.

Angkor was at the center of this development, with a Buddhist temple complex and urban organization able to support around 1 million urban dwellers. A great deal of Cambodian Buddhist sculpture is preserved at Angkor; however, organized looting has had a heavy impact on many sites around the country.

Often, Khmer art manages to express intense spirituality through divinely beaming expressions, in spite of spare features and slender lines.

THAILAND

From the 1st to the 7th centuries, Buddhist art in Thailand was first influenced by direct contact with Indian traders and the expansion of the Mon kingdom, leading to the creation of Hindu and Buddhist art inspired from the Gupta tradition, with numerous monumental statues of great virtuosity.

From the 9th century, the various schools of Thai art then became strongly influenced by Cambodian Khmer art in the north and Sri Vijaya art in the south, both of Mahayana faith. Up to the end of that period, Buddhist art is characterized by a clear fluidness in the expression, and the subject matter is characteristic of the Mahayana pantheon with multiple creations of Bodhisattvas.

From the 13th century, Theravada Buddhism was introduced from Sri Lanka around the same time as the ethnic Thai kingdom of Sukhothai was established. The new faith inspired highly stylized images in Thai Buddhism, with sometimes very geometrical and almost abstract figures.

During the Ayutthaya period (14th-18th centuries), the Buddha came to be represented in a more stylistic manner with sumptuous garments and jeweled ornamentations. Many Thai sculptures or temples tended to be gilded, and on occasion enriched with inlays.

INDONESIA

Like the rest of Southeast Asia, Indonesia seems to have been most strongly influenced by India from the 1st century CE. The islands of Sumatra and Java in western Indonesia were the seat of the empire of Sri Vijaya (8th-13th century CE), which came to dominate most of the area around the Southeast Asian peninsula through maritime power. The Sri Vijayan Empire had adopted Mahayana and Vajrayana Buddhism, under a line of rulers named the Sailendras. Sri Vijaya spread Mahayana Buddhist art during its expansion into the Southeast Asian peninsula. Numerous statues of Mahayana Bodhisattvas from this period are characterized by a very strong refinement and technical sophistication, and are found throughout the region.

Extremely rich and refined architectural remains can be found in Java and Sumatra. The most magnificence is the temple of Borobudur (the largest Buddhist structure in the world, built from around 780-850 AD). This temple modeled after Buddhist concept of universe, the Mandala which counts 505 images of the seated Buddha and unique bell-shaped stupa that contains the statue of Buddha. Borobudur is adorned with long series of bas-reliefs narrated the holy Buddhist scriptures. The oldest Buddhist structure in Indonesia probably is the Batu Jaya stupas at Karawang, West Java, dated from around 4th century AD. This temple is some plastered brick stupas. However, Buddhist art in Indonesia reach the golden era during the Sailendra dynasty rule in Java. The bas-reliefs and statues of Boddhisatva, Tara, and Kinnara found in Kalasan, Sewu, Sari, and Plaosan temple is very graceful with serene expression, While Mendut temple near Borobudur, houses the giant statue of Buddha, Avalokitesvara, and Vajrapani.

In Sumatra Sri Vijaya probably built the temple of Muara Takus, and Muaro Jambi. The most beautiful classical Javanese art is the serene and delicate statue of Prajnaparamita (the collection of National Museum Jakarta) the goddess of transcendental wisdom from Singhasari. The Indonesian Buddhist Empire of Sri Vijaya declined due to conflicts with the Chola rulers of India, then followed by Majapahit empire, before being destabilized by the Islamic expansion from the 13th century.

BUDDHIST ART IN INDIA

Indian art is an expression of Indian life and thought attuned to its vast natural background and its socio-religious traditions. It is not exclusive or sectarian in the narrow sense of the term. Its style, technique or general tenor has nothing to do with any particular religious outlook. It is fed and fostered upon a vast store-house of Indian traditions, symbols and designs. The term Hindu, Jaina or Buddhist art is but a popular nomenclature to distinguish one group of monuments, including painting, cave-temples and architecture, etc., from another stand point of the predominance of one or the other religious theme. Hence, by Buddhist art is meant popularly those monuments and paintings which have for the main purpose the edification or popularization of Buddhism. Fortunately enough in India and outside where Buddhism did exist, or still exists, there are innumerable monuments representing different phases of Buddhism and these help us to visualize the trend of Buddhist art through the ages.

In Buddhist legends and Mythology, Gautama Buddha has been represented as superior not only to the popular cult divinities of the soil, such as the Yakshas, Nagas, etc. but also to Indra, Brahma and others of the earlier Brahmanical pantheon. Everything with him has been described as transcendental. This is amply represented in Buddhist art.

THE EARLY SYMBOLS AND THEIR EVOLUTION

Buddhist art reflects very faithfully all the important aspects of Buddhism. In primitive Buddhism, Gautama Sakyamuni has been regarded as an ideal human being and quite naturally we find that the early Buddhist art of Bharhut, Sanchi, Bodh-Gaya and Amaravati and other places shows no anthropomorphic representation of the Master. His presence is indicated by means of an empty throne, or a Bodhi tree or a pair of foot-prints, or a dharma-chakra, symbolizing one or the other event of his life. As the time passed, Buddhism acquired greater popularity and drew adherents from all sections of the people.

The discipline and austerities of the early Buddhism were beyond the comprehension of the ordinary followers of the religion. A religion without a personal god in whom one can repose faith had but little appeal to them. The demand of the popular mind as met by the Mahayanists who defied Buddha and introduced the concept of divine Bodhisattvas and several other deities. With the progress of time, the Buddhist pantheon was enlarged to include several hundred deities. Among the male deities, the Bodhisattva Avalokitesvara became the most popular because of his great compassion for the living creatures.

He is an emanation of the Dhyani Buddha Amitabha and his shakti Pandara (the Sukhavati-Vyuha or the Amitayus Sutra, translated into Chinese between A.D. 148-170, seems to refer for the first time to the name of Amitabha or Amitayus), Avalokitesvara is the personification of universal compassion. As described in the Karanda-vyuha he refused or renounced Nirvana in favour of affected humanity. He is supposed to impart spiritual knowledge to fellow creatures so that all, by a gradual process, may advance on the path of salvation. Different forms of the Avalokitesvara have been mentioned in the Sadhana-mala, of these the important ones are Shadakshari Lokeshvara, Simhanada, Khasharpana. Lokanatha, Halahala, Nilakantha and few others.

THE BHARHUT STUPA

The Sunga-Andhra epoch (2-1 Century B.C.) was one of the most creative periods of Buddhist art. Though the Sunga rulers were followers of the Brahmanical faith and Buddhism was deprived of the State patronage which it enjoyed during the reign of the Mauryan rulers, like Asoka and some of his successors, there was no set-back in the propagation or popularity of the Buddhist faith. Buddhist establishments flourished in Bodh-Gaya, Bharhut, and Sanchi in Northern and Central India, in Amaravati and Jaggayapeta in South India, at Bhaja, Nasik, Karle and Janta and at several other places in Western India.

The art of this period consists mainly in the excavation of the rock-cut temples or viharas (some of which are embellished with paintings) and the erection of railings and toranas (gateways) to the Buddhist Stupas at different places. General Cunningham found remains of the railings and on gateway of the Stupa at Bharhut (Madhya Pradesh) during the years 1872-74 and had them deposited in the Indian Museum in the year following. The Stupa in question was built during the 2 Century B.C. In the absence of the Stupa itself it is difficult to ascertain its shape and size. But it was probably similar to the Stupas represented on its panels and the almost contemporary Stupas of Sanchi. All these Stupas consist of hemispherical dome with a harmika above suppporting the umbrellas.

One of the main interest of the Bharhut sculptures consists in the representation of the birth-stories of the Gautama Budha. These stories (or the Jatakas) are of two main classes, those relating to the previous births of Buddha as a Bodhisattva (a Buddha potentia), and those of his last appearance as Gautama Shakyamuni when he attained Enlightenment of Buddhahood. The Jatakas represented on the Bharhut panels include Mahakapi-Jataka, Latuva-Jataka, Miga-Jataka, Sujata-gahuto-Jataka, Mahajanaka-Jataka and Vidhurapandita-Jataka, Chhadanta Jataka, etc.

The scenes on the Bharhut sculptures, relating to the life of Gautama Shakyamuni include, among others, the dream of Maya (Illustrating the descent of a Bodhisattva in the form of an elephant into the mothers womb), the defeat of Mara, Gautama's Enlightenment under the Bodhi tree, the worship of the Bodhi tree, the worship of Gautama's hair-locks by celestial beings, the visits of king Ajatashatru of Magadha and of Prasenjit of Koshala, etc.

The worship of the Bodhi tree, seems to have been widely prevalent, as there are many representation of it on the sculptured panels of Bharhut, Sanchi and Amaravati.

Again, in the Divyavandana it is related that the Bodhi tree was Asoka's favourite object of worship. The lowest architrave of the Eastern Gateway Stupa I, Sanchi (1 Century B.C.) depicts the ceremonial visits of king Asoka and his queen, Tishyarakshita to the Bodhi Tree. In the centre of the panel are the tree and the temple of Bodh Gaya. On the left is seen a crowd of musicians and devotees carrying water vessels. On the right are the king and the queen descending from the elephant and payment homage to the Bodhi tree.

THE SANCHI STUPA

In addition to Bharhut, the other important centres of Buddhist art and religion in north India during this period were Sanchi (Madhya Pradesh) and Bodh Gaya (Bihar). The main interest of the art at Sanchi centres round the Great Stupa. Originally built of brick, during the reign of Asoka (3 Century B.C.), it was encased in stone and brought to its present dimension about a century later. The other additions, such as the erection of the toranas and the ground balustrade were done still later, probably about 50 B.C. of all the four gateways, the south gateways seems to be the oldest. On one of its architraves, there is an inscription showing that it was the work of one of the artisans of king Sri Satakarni (1 Century B.C.), who was evidently the son of Simuka, the founder of the Satavahana family of the Deccan.

Of all toranas or gateways, the best preserved is the northern gateway which enables the visitor to have a complete idea of the appearance of all the gateways. Each gateway is composed of two square pillars with capitals at the top. These capitals of standing dwarfs or elephants support a superstructure of architraves. Finally, on the summit of the gateway is the dharma-chakra symbol in the middle. The pillars and superstructures are elaborately decorated with representation of Jataka legends (stories of Buddha's past lives). There are also representations of the sacred trees, stupas and other motifs to indicate the presence of Gautam Buddha symbolically. As in Bharhut art, here also, in conformity with the tradition of early Indian art, there is no anthropomorphic representation of Buddha.

About 50 yards north-east of the great stupa of Sanchi is another monument of the same nature but smaller in proportions. Inside this stupa the relics of two very important disciples of Buddha, Sariputta and Maha-Moggalana, were discovered by General Cunnigham.

JAGGAPETTA STUPA

A stylistic equivalent of the panels of Sanchi is to be found in a carving from a Jaggayapeta stupa near Amaravati on the Krishna river. This will show how little differences existed between different regions in the field of art. A monument to be ascribed to the early Sunga period is the old Vihara at Bhaja which is situated in the hills of the Western ghats to the south of Bombay. It is a rectangular chamber with several cells. The decoration of the Bhaja monastery includes among other the representation of Yakshas, a sun god on a four-horse chariot and Indra riding his vehicle, i.e., Airavat. The art of Bharhut and other early contemporaneous sites has a primitive simplicity. (It is permitted by naturalism, enlivened by humour, dance and music. From the standpoint of technique the figures are in low relief, somewhat flattened with angular limbs).

Although there are innumerable references in the Jatakas and other Buddhist literature to the pointed decorations, the earliest surviving examples of Buddhist paintings are met with at the oldest Chaitya Halls at Ajanta in the Deccan, dedicated in the 2 Century B.C. The principal wall painting in cave 10 is devoted to the illustration of the Chaddanta Jataka.

AMARAVATI STUPA

The Buddhist art in South India during this period is best illustrated by the remains of the Maha-Chaitya (or stupa) of Amaravati. As the earliest Buddhist Sculptures found here are primitive in style resembling those of Bharhut, it can be presumed that the Maha-Chaitya was built during the 2 Century B.C. to 250 A.D. Its earliest pieces, show affinities to Bharhut art The images of Buddha were introduced here about the 1–2 Century A.D. The Amaravati art of this period is highly elegant and sensitive.

GANDHARA ART

Buddhist art entered upon a new phase with the rise of Mahayana Buddhism during the 1 Century B.C. to 1 Century A.D. The period is remarkable in that it gave for the first time the figure art or the anthropomorphic representations of the Buddha. Under the patronage of Kushana rulers (1-2 Century A.D.) a new school of art flourished in the Gandhara region, i.e. Peshawar and its neighbouring districts. Because of its strategic geographical position the region became a meeting place of various races and cultures. As a result of this, the art of the region shows mingling of both Indian and foreign ideas and motifs. Gandhara art is a hybrid product; though Buddhist in theme it is Graeco-Roman in style or technique as is evident from the physiognomy and drapery of the images.

The artists of this region have produced a large number of Buddha and Bodhisattva images along with other Buddhist deities. Gandhara art flourished for about four to five hundred years and to a great extent it influenced the indigenous art of Mathura, Amaravati and Nagarjunakonda. It exercised a profound influence upon the art of Afgahnistan and Central Asia The Buddha and Bodhisattva images of many sites in Central Asia show an affiliations to the Gandhara style. The art of the region received a greatblow at the hands of the Huna invaders. Mihirakula, a cruel king of the Huna had destroyed, as Xuanzang was told during his travel to this country, the Buddhist monasteries of the region. The main centres of Gandhara art were the cities of Peshawar and Taxila, and also Afghanistan where a large number of stupas, monasteries and sculptures have been unearthed by the archaeologists.

MATHURA – A GREAT CENTRE OF ART

Mathura also was a great centre of art and culture during this period. Here flourished side by side all the important religions of India, such as Brahmanism, Jainism and Buddhism. It is believed that the first Buddha images were carved at Mathura simultaneously if not earlier, with the Gandhara school. Mathura has produced Buddha images of various dimensions. The Kushana Buddha or Bodhisattva images of Mathura served as the prototypes of the more beautiful specimens of the Gupta period.

The workshop of Mathura exported several Buddhist images to various other places, such as Sarnath and even as far as Rajgir in Bihar. It is well known that Friar-Bala an inhabitant of Mathura had several Bodhisattva images set up at different places. Two of them were found at Sravasti and Sarnath. (The Kushana art of Mathura is somewhat heavy. The style and technique which the Kushana artists were trying to evolve were brought to the Gupta period. But the art of South India during this time is more elegant and sophisticated. The sculptured panels of Amaravati and Nagarjunakonda, Goli, Ghantasals, belonging to the 2 – 3 Century A.D., are characterised by delicasy of forms, and linear grace.

THE GUPTA ART

The Gupta period (4 – 6 Century A.D.) marks the bright period of art in India. Gupta art is marked by restraint combined with a high aesthetic sense and discipline. The main centres of Buddhist art during this period were Mathura, Sarnath and Nalanda in the north. The Buddhist images of Mathura and Sarnath are some of the best specimens of Indian art, never equalled by any art creations of later period. The delicate folds of the transparent garment adorning the Gupta figures were done in a beautiful style. The profusely decorated halo is another special feature of the art of the Gupta figure. The delicate modelling of forms with meditative repose has rendered the Buddha and Bodhisattva figures of the Gupta period most attractive. The Gupta artists showed an equal ingenuity in the carving of metal images also. The bronze Buddha image from Sultanganj and also one from Dhanesar Khera together with a number of specimens found in north-western part of India are some excellent specimens testifying to the skill and ability of the Gupta metal carvers.

This period is also known for excavations of several rock-cut viharas and temples at Ajanta and Ellora, in Maharashtra, under the patronage of the Vakataka King. Caves 16, 17 and 26 at Ajanta are excellent examples of pillared halls with usual cells with shrines in the back containing Budha figures. The beauty and variety of the pillars are remarkable. Caves 16 and 17 were excavated in the last quarter of the 5 Century A.D. by a Minister and feudatory of the Vakataka king Harisena. The mural paintings in the Ajanta caves of the Vakataka period contain representations of scenes from Buddha's life from the conception to enlightenment. Some of them are devoted to the illustrations of Jataka stories, including one of Prince Visvantara, hero of immeasurable bounty. The Ajanta paintings both in composition and technique are characterised by a delicacy and depth of feelings. The artists excel not only in depicting human and animal figures but also in decorative genius. They adorned the ceilings, pedestals of columns, door and window frames, with patterns and motifs of kaleidoscopic variety. Several Buddhist caves are to be found also at Bagh (Madhya Pradesh) and Ellora (Maharashtra), containing numerous Budha and Bodhisattva figures (5 – 6 Century).

POST – GUPTA – DEVELOPMENTS

The Gupta art tradition was followed in later period also. The art of Nalanda, Kurkihar, Sarnath, Orissa and other places during the medieval period is based upon the Gupta art idiom. The north Indian Buddhism of the mediaeval period (8 – 11 Century A.D). is a peculiar synthesis of the Mahayana ideals and tantric elements. The concept of the Adi-Budha, the Dhyani-Buddhas, the divine Bodhisattvas as well as the concept of Shakti or the female energy figures most prominently in the Buddhist art of the period. One anachronism of Buddhist art in medieval period is the introduction of the crowned Buddhas with jewelleries. Though incompatible to the idea of renunciation which Buddha followed and preached, such images were made probably to lay emphasis on the concept of Buddha as a Chakravartin, the supreme universal monarch.

NALANDA

The art of Nalanda shows very high standard of stone carving as well as metal casting. The minute execution of the bronzes specially of the smaller ones, has excited the admiration of all art lovers of the world. Several Nalanda bronzes were exported to Nepal and Tibet and also to Java. Equally interesting are the palm leaf illustrations of the Buddhist manuscripts of the Pala period. Their minature size, colour scheme and linear grace show the skill of the painters of these illustrations. The Pala style of painting, as Pala sculptures and bronzes, very much influenced the art of Nepal, Tibet and the further East. Bodh-Gaya and Nalanda in Magadha drew pilgrims from different parts of the Buddhist world.

NAGAPATTINAM

A flourishing centre of Buddhism in South India during the period was Naga-pattinam, near Madras on east coast. There existed here in the medieval period a colony of the Malaya Buddhists who, patronized by the Cholas erected here two temples in the 11 Century A.D., with the aid granted by the Sailendra kings of Java and Sumatra. One of the temples was called Rajarajaperumpalli and the Rajendracholaperumpalli. Naga-pattinum was a place of piligrimage for the Buddhists of different places in India as well as outside. Since 1856 about 350 bronzes have been found in these vihara sites. Some of them are of the early Chola times while the rest belong to the later Chola period. The Nagapattinam bronzes are some of the finest metal works of South India.

GRECO-BUDDHIST ART

Greco-Buddhist art is the artistic manifestation of Greco-Buddhism, a cultural syncretism between the Classical Greek culture and Buddhism, which developed over a period of close to 1000 years in Central Asia, between the conquests of Alexander the Great in the 4th century BCE, and the Islamic conquests of the 7th century CE. Greco-Buddhist art is characterized by the strong idealistic realism of Hellenistic art and the first representations of the Buddha in human form, which have helped define the artistic (and particularly, sculptural) canon for Buddhist art throughout the Asian continent up to the present. It is also a unique example of cultural syncretism between eastern and western traditions, which has been achieved by no other art to such a degree.

The origins of Greco-Buddhist art are to be found in the Hellenistic Greco-Bactrian kingdom (250 BCE- 130 BCE), located in today's Afghanistan, from which Hellenistic culture radiated into the Indian subcontinent with the establishment of the Indo-Greek kingdom (180 BCE-10 BCE). Under the Indo-Greeks and then the Kushans, the interaction of Greek and Buddhist culture flourished in the area of Gandhara, in today's northern Pakistan, before spreading further into India, influencing the art of Mathura, and then the Hindu art of the Gupta empire, which was to extend to the rest of South-East Asia. The influence of Greco-Buddhist art also spread northward towards Central Asia, strongly affecting the art of the Tarim Basin, and ultimately the arts of China, Korea, and Japan.

HELLENISTIC ART IN SOUTHERN ASIA

Powerful Hellenistic states were established in the areas of Bactria and Sogdiana, and later northern India for three centuries following the conquests of Alexander the Great around 330 BCE: the Seleucid empire until 250 BCE, followed by the Greco-Bactrian kingdom until 130 BCE, and the Indo-Greek kingdom from 180 BCE to around 10 BCE.

The clearest examples of Hellenistic art are found in the coins of the Greco-Bactrian kings of the period, such as Demetrius I of Bactria. Many coins of the Greco-Bactrian kings have been unearthed, including the largest silver and gold coins ever minted in the Hellenistic world, ranking among the best in artistic and technical sophistication: they "show a degree of individuality never matched by the often more bland descriptions of their royal contemporaries further West". ("Greece and the Hellenistic world").

These Hellenistic kingdoms established cities on the Greek model, such as in Ai-Khanoum in Bactria, displaying purely Hellenistic architectural features, Hellenistic statuary, and remains of Aristotelician papyrus prints and coin hoards.

These Greek elements penetrated in northwestern India following the invasion of the Greco-Bactrians in 180 BCE, when they established the Indo-Greek kingdom in India. Fortified Greek cities, such as Sirkap in northern Pakistan, were established. Architectural styles used Hellenistic decorative motifs such as fruit garland and scrolls. Stone palettes for aromatic oils representing purely Hellenistic themes such as a Nereid riding a Ketos sea monster are found.

In Hadda, Hellenistic deities, such as Atlas are found. Wind gods are depicted, which will affect the representation of wind deities as far as Japan. Dyonisiac scenes represent people in Classical style drinking wine from amphoras and playing instruments.

GRECO-BUDDHIST ARTISTIC INTERACTION

As soon as the Greeks invaded India to form the Indo-Greek kingdom, a fusion of Hellenistic and Buddhist elements started to appear, encouraged by the benevolence of the Greek kings towards Buddhism. This artistic trend then developed for several centuries and seemed to flourish further during the Kushan Empire from the first century CE.

Artistic model

Greco-Buddhist art depicts the life of the Buddha in a visual manner, probably by incorporating the real-life models and concepts which were available to the artists of the period.

The Bodhisattvas are depicted as bare-chested and jewelled Indian princes, and the Buddhas as Greek kings wearing the light toga-like himation. The buildings in which they are depicted incorporate Greek style, with the ubiquitous Indo-Corinthian capitals and Greek decorative scrolls. Surrounding deities form a pantheon of Greek (Atlas, Herakles) and Indian gods (Indra).

Stylistic evolution

Stylistically, Greco-Buddhist art started by being extremely fine and realistic, as apparent on the standing Buddhas, with "a realistic treatment of the folds and on some even a hint of modelled volume that characterizes the best Greek work" (Boardman). It then lost this sophisticated realism, becoming progressively more symbolic and decorative over the centuries.

Architecture

The presence of stupas at the Greek city of Sirkap, built by Demetrius around 180 BCE, already indicates a strong syncretism between Hellenism and the Buddhist faith, together with other religions such as Hinduism and Zoroastrianism. The style is Greek, adorned with Corinthian columns in excellent Hellenistic execution.

Later in Hadda, the Greek divinity Atlas is represented holding Buddhist monuments with decorated Greek columns. The motif was adopted extensively throughout the Indian sub-continent, Atlas being substituted for the Indian Yaksa in the monuments of the Sunga around the 2nd century BCE.

The Buddha

Sometime between the 2nd century BCE and the 1st century CE, the first anthropomorphic representations of the Buddha were developed. These were absent from earlier strata of Buddhist art, which preferred to represent the Buddha with symbols such as the stupa, the Bodhi tree, the empty seat, the wheel, or the footprints. But the innovative anthropomorphic Buddha image immediately reached a very high level of sculptural sophistication, naturally inspired by the sculptural styles of Hellenistic Greece.

Many of the stylistic elements in the representations of the Buddha point to Greek influence: the Greek himation (a light toga-like wavy robe covering both shoulders: Buddhist characters are always represented with a dhoti loincloth before this innovation), the halo, the contrapposto stance of the upright figures, the stylized Mediterranean curly hair and top-knot apparently derived from the style of the Belvedere Apollo (330 BCE), and the measured quality of the faces, all rendered with strong artistic realism. Some of the standing Buddhas were sculpted using the specific Greek technique of making the hands and sometimes the feet in marble to increase the realistic effect, and the rest of the body in another material.

Foucher especially considered Hellenistic free-standing Buddhas as "the most beautiful, and probably the most ancient of the Buddhas", assigning them to the 1st century BCE, and making them the starting point of the anthropomorphic representations of the Buddha.

Development

There is some debate regarding the exact date for the development of the anthropomorphic representation of the Buddha, and this has a bearing on whether the innovation came directly from the Indo-Greeks, or was a later development by the

Indo-Scythians, the Indo-Parthians or the Kushans under Hellenistic artistic influence. Most of the early images of the Buddha (especially those of the standing Buddha) are anepigraphic, which makes it difficult to have a definite dating. The earliest known image of the Buddha with approximate indications on date is the Bimaran casket, which has been found buried with coins of the Indo-Scythian king Azes II (or possibly Azes I), indicating a 30-10 BCE date, although this date is not undisputed.

Such datation, as well as the general Hellenistic style and attitude of the Buddha on the Bimaran casket (himation dress, contrapposto attitude, general depiction) would made it a possible Indo-Greek work, used in dedications by Indo-Scythians soon after the end of Indo-Greek rule in the area of Gandhara. Since it already displays quite a sophisticated iconography (Brahma and Œakra as attendants, Bodhisattvas) in an advanced style, it would suggest much earlier representations of the Buddha were already current by that time, going back to the rule of the Indo-Greeks (Alfred A. Foucher and others).

The next Greco-Buddhist findings to be strictly datable are rather late, such as the c.120 CE Kanishka casket and Kanishka's Buddhist coins. These works at least indicate though that the anthropomorphic representation of the Buddha was already extant in the 1st century CE. From another direction, Chinese historical sources and mural paintings in the Tarim Basin city of Dunhuang accurately describe the travels of the explorer and ambassador Zhang Qian to Central Asia as far as Bactria around 130 BCE, and the same murals describe the Emperor Han Wudi (156-87 BCE) worshipping Buddhist statues, explaining them as *"golden men brought in 120 BCE by a great Han general in his campaigns against the nomads."* Although there is no other mention of Han Wudi worshipping the Buddha in Chinese historical literature, the murals would suggest that statues of the Buddha were already in existence during the 2nd century BCE, connecting them directly to the time of the Indo-Greeks.

Later, the Chinese historical chronicle Hou Hanshu describes the enquiry about Buddhism made around 67 CE by the emperor Emperor Ming (58-75 CE). He sent an envoy to the Yuezhi in northwestern India, who brought back paintings and statues of the Buddha, confirming their existence before that date:

"The Emperor, to discover the true doctrine, sent an envoy to Tianzhu (Northwestern India) to inquire about the Buddha's doctrine, after which paintings and statues [of the Buddha] appeared in the Middle Kingdom." (Hou Hanshu, trans. John Hill)

An Indo-Chinese tradition also explains that Nagasena, also known as Menander's Buddhist teacher, created in 43 BCE in the city of Pataliputra a statue of the Buddha, the Emerald Buddha, which was later brought to Thailand.

Artistic Model

The Greco-Bactrian king Demetrius I (205-171 BCE) himself may have been the prototype for the image of the Buddha. He was king and saviour of India, as confirmed by his successors King Apollodotus I and Menander I, who were officially described as "saviour king" in the bilingual Greek and Kharoshthi legends of their coins. Demetrius was named *Dharmamita* ("Friend of the Dharma") in the Indian text of the Yuga Purana. Buddhism flourished under his reign and that of his successors, precisely as it was being oppressed by the Indian dynasty of the Sunga in the East.

The earliest Hellenistic statues of the Buddha portray him in a style reminiscent of a king, where the traditional Buddhist symbols (the Dharma wheel, the empty throne, the Bodhi tree, the lions) are absent. Demetrius may have been deified, and the first Hellenistic statues of the Buddha we know may be representations of the idealized Greek king, princely, yet friendly, protective and open to Indian culture. As they progressively incorporated more Buddhist elements, they became central to the Buddhist movement, and influenced the representations of the Buddha in Greco-Buddhist art and later.

Another characteristic of Demetrius is associated to the Buddha: they share the same protector deity. In Gandharan art, the Buddha is often shown under the protection of the Greek god Herakles, standing with his club (and later a diamond rod) resting over his arm. This unusual representation of Herakles is the same as the one on the back of Demetrius' coins, and it is exclusively associated to him (and his son Euthydemus II), seen only on the back of his coins.

Soon, the figure of the Buddha was incorporated within architectural designs, such as Corinthian pillars and friezes. Scenes of the life of the Buddha are typically depicted in a Greek architectural environment, with protagonist wearing Greek clothes.

Gods and Bodhisattvas

Deities from the Greek mythological pantheon also tend to be incorporated in Buddhist representations, displaying a strong syncretism. In particular, Herakles (of the type of the Demetrius coins, with club resting on the arm) has been used abundantly as the representation of Vajrapani, the protector of the Buddha. Other Greek deities abundantly used in Greco-Buddhist art are representation of Atlas, and the Greek wind god. Atlas in particular tends to be involved as a sustaining elements in Buddhist architectural elements. The Greek wind god Boreas became the Japanese wind god Fujin through the Greco-Buddhist Wardo. The mother deity Hariti was inspired by Tyche.

Particularly under the Kushans, there are also numerous representations of richly adorned, princely Bodhisattvas all in a very realistic Greco-Buddhist style. The Bodhisattvas, characteristic of the Mahayana form of Buddhism, are represented under the traits of Kushan princes, completed with their canonical accessories.

Cupids

Winged cupids are another popular motif in Greco-Buddhist art. They usually fly in pair, holding a wreath, the Greek symbol of victory and kingship, over the Buddha. These figures, also known as "apsarases" were extensively adopted in Buddhist art, especially throughout Eastern Asia, in forms derivative to the Greco-Buddhist representation. The progressive evolution of the style can be seen in the art of Qizil and Dunhuang. It is unclear however if the concept of the flying cupids was brought to India from the West, of if it had an independent Indian origin, although Boardman considers it a Classical contribution: "Another Classical motif we found in India is the pair of hovering winged figures, generally called apsaras." (Boardman)

Scenes of cupids holding rich garlands, sometimes adorned with fruits, is another very popular Gandharan motif, directly inspired from Greek art. It is sometimes argued that the only concession to Indian art appears in the anklets worn by the cupids. These scenes had a very broad influence, as far as Amaravati on the eastern coast of India, where the cupids are replaced by yakcas.

Devotees

Some Greco-Buddhist friezes represent groups of donors or devotees, giving interesting insights into the cultural identity of those who participated in the Buddhist cult. Some groups, often described as the "Buner reliefs," usually dated to the 1st century CE, depict Greeks in perfect Hellenistic style, either in posture, rendering, or clothing (wearing the Greek chiton and himation). It is sometimes even difficult to perceive an actual religious message behind the scenes. (The devotee scene on the right might, with doubt, depict of the presentation of Prince Siddharta to his bride. It may also just be a festive scene.) About a century later, friezes also depict Kushan devotees, usually with the Buddha as the central figure.

Fantastic Animals

Various fantastic animal deities of Hellenic origin were used as decorative elements in Buddhist temples, often triangular friezes in staircases or in front of Buddhist altars. The origin of these motifs can be found in Greece in the 5th century BCE, and later in the designs of Greco-Bactrian perfume trays as those discovered in Sirkap. Among the most popular fantastic animals are tritons, ichthyo-centaurs and ketos sea-monsters. It should be noted that similar fantastic animals are found in ancient Egyptian reliefs, and might therefore have been passed on to Bactria and India independently of Greek imperialism.

As fantastic animals of the sea, they were, in early Buddhism, supposed to safely bring the souls of dead people to Paradise beyond the waters. These motifs were later adopted in Indian art, where they influenced the depiction of the Indian monster makara, Varuna's mount.

THE KUSHAN CONTRIBUTION

The later part of Greco-Buddhist art in northwestern India is usually associated with the Kushan Empire. The Kushans were nomadic people who started migrating from the Tarim Basin in Central Asia from around 170 BCE and ended up founding an empire in northwestern India from the 2nd century BCE, after having been rather Hellenized through their contacts with the Greco-Bactrians, and later the Indo-Greeks (they adopted the Greek script for writing).

The Kushans, at the center of the Silk Road enthusiastically gathered works of art from all the quarters of the ancient world, as suggested by the hoards found in their northern capital in the archeological site of Begram, Afghanistan.

The Kushans sponsored Buddhism together with other Iranian and Hindu faiths, and probably contributed to the flourishing of Greco-Buddhist art. Their coins, however, suggest a lack of artistic sophistication: the representations of their kings, such as Kanishka, tend to be crude (lack of proportion, rough drawing), and the image of the Buddha is an assemblage of a Hellenistic Buddha statue with feet grossly represented and spread apart in the same fashion as the Kushan king. This tends to indicate the anteriority of the Hellenistic Greco-Buddhist statues, used as models, and a subsequent corruption by Kushan artists.

SOUTHERN INFLUENCES OF GRECO-BUDDHIST ART

The Art of the Sunga

Examples of the influence of Hellenistic or Greco-Buddhist art on the art of the Sunga empire (183-73 BCE) are usually faint. The main religion, at least at the beginning, seems to have been Brahmanic Hinduism, although some late Buddhist realizations in Madhya Pradesh as also known, such as some architectural expansions that were done at the stupas of Sanchi and Bharhut, originally started under King Ashoka.

This Sunga-period balustrate-holding Atalante Yaksa from the Sunga period (left), adopts the Atalante theme, usually fulfilled by Atlas, and elements of Corinthian capital and architecture typical of Greco-Buddhist friezes from the Northwest, although the content does not seem to be related to Buddhism. This work suggests that some of the

Gandharan friezes, influential to this work, may have existed as early as the 2nd century or 1st century BCE.

Other Sunga works show the influence of floral scroll patterns, and Hellenistic elements in the rendering of the fold of dresses. The 2nd century BCE depiction of an armed foreigner (right), probably a Greek king, with Buddhist symbolism (triratana symbol of the sword), also indicates some kind of cultural, religious, and artistic exchange at that point of time.

The Art of Mathura

The representations of the Buddha in Mathura, in central northern India, are generally dated slightly later than those of Gandhara, although not without debate, and are also much less numerous. Up to that point, Indian Buddhist art had essentially been aniconic, avoiding representation of the Buddha, except for his symbols, such as the wheel or the Bodhi tree, although some archaic Mathuran sculptural representation of Yaksas (earth divinities) have been dated to the first century BCE. Even these Yaksas indicate some Hellenistic influence, possibly dating back to the occupation of Mathura by the Indo-Greeks during the 2nd century BCE.

In terms of artistic predispositions for the first representations of the Buddha, Greek art provided a very natural and centuries-old background for an anthropomorphic representation of a divinity, whether on the contrary "there was nothing in earlier Indian statuary to suggest such a treatment of form or dress, and the Hindu pantheon provided no adequate model for an aristocratic and wholly human deity" (Boardman).

The Mathura sculptures incorporate many Hellenistic elements, such as the general idealistic realism, and key design elements such as the curly hair, and folded garment. Specific Mathuran adaptations tend to reflect warmer climatic conditions, as they consist in a higher fluidity of the clothing, which progressively tend to cover only one shoulder instead of both. Also, facial types also tend to become more Indianized. Banerjee in "Hellenism in India" describes "the mixed character of the Mathura School in which we find on the one hand, a direct continuation of the old Indian art of Bharut and Sanchi and on the other hand, the classical influence derived from Gandhara".

The influence of Greek art can be felt beyond Mathura, as far as Amaravati on the East coast of India, as shown by the usage of Greek scrolls in combination with Indian deities. Other motifs such as Greek chariots pulled by four horses can also be found in the same area.

Incidentally, Hindu art started to develop from the 1st to the 2nd century CE and found its first inspiration in the Buddhist art of Mathura. It progressively incorporated a profusion of original Hindu stylistic and symbolic elements however, in contrast with the general balance and simplicity of Buddhist art.

Gupta Art

The art of Mathura acquired progressively more Indian elements and reached a very high sophistication during the Gupta Empire, between the 4th and the 6th century CE. The art of the Gupta is considered as the pinnacle of Indian Buddhist art.

Hellenistic elements are still clearly visible in the purity of the statuary and the folds of the clothing, but are improved upon with a very delicate rendering of the draping and a sort of radiance reinforced by the usage of pink sandstone. Artistic details tend to be less realistic, as seen in the symbolic shell-like curls used to render the hairstyle of the Buddha.

GRECO-BUDDHIST ART EXPANSION IN CENTRAL ASIA

Greco-Buddhist artistic influences naturally followed Buddhism in its expansion to Central and Eastern Asia from the 1st century BCE.

Bactria

Bactria was under direct Greek control for more than two centuries from the conquests of Alexander the Great in 332 BCE to the end of the Greco-Bactrian kingdom around 125 BCE. The art of Bactria was almost perfectly Hellenistic as shown by the archaeological remains of Greco-Bactrian cities such as Alexandria on the Oxus (Ai-Khanoum), or the numismatic art of the Greco-Bactrian kings, often considered as the best of the Hellenistic world, and including the largest silver and gold coins ever minted by the Greeks.

When Buddhism expanded in Central Asia from the 1st century CE, Bactria saw the results of the Greco-Buddhist syncretism arrive on its territory from India, and a new blend of sculptural remained until the Islamic invasions.

The most striking of these realizations are the Buddhas of Bamyan. They tend to vary between the 5th and the 9th century CE. Their style is strongly inspired by Hellenistic culture. In another area of Bactria called Fondukistan, some Greco-Buddhist art survived until the 7th century in Buddhist monasteries, displaying a strong Hellenistic influence combined with Indian decorativeness and mannerism, and some influence by the Sasanid Persians.

Most of the remaining art of Bactria was destroyed from the 5th century onward: the Buddhist were often blamed for idolatry and tended to be persecuted by the iconoclastic Muslims. Destructions continued during the Afghanistan War, and especially by the Taliban regime in 2001. The most famous case is that of the destruction of the Buddhas of Bamyan. Ironically, most of the remaining art from Afghanistan still extant was removed from the country during the Colonial period. In particular, a rich collection exists at the Musee Guimet in France.

Tarim Basin

The art of the Tarim Basin, also called Serindian art, is the art that developed from the 2nd through the 11th century CE in Serindia or Xinjiang, the western region of China that forms part of Central Asia. It derives from the art of the Gandhara and clearly combines Indian traditions with Greek and Roman influences.

Buddhist missionaries travelling on the Silk Road introduced this art, along with Buddhism itself, into Serindia, where it mixed with Chinese and Persian influences.

GRECO-BUDDHIST INFLUENCES IN EASTERN ASIA

The arts of China, Korea and Japan adopted Greco-Buddhist artistic influences, but tended to add many local elements as well. What remains most readily identifiable from Greco-Buddhist art are:

- The general idealistic realism of the figures reminiscent of Greek art.
- Clothing elements with elaborate Greek-style folds.
- The curly hairstyle characteristic of the Mediterranean.
- In some Buddhist representations, hovering winged figures holding a wreath.
- Greek sculptural elements such as vines and floral scrolls.

China

Greco-Buddhist artistic elements can be traced in Chinese Buddhist art, with several local and temporal variations depending on the character of the various dynasties that adopted the Buddhist faith. Some of the earliest known Buddhist artifacts found in China are small statues on "money trees", dated circa 200 CE, in typical Gandharan style (drawing): "That the imported images accompanying the newly arrived doctrine came from Gandhara is strongly suggested by such early Gandhara characteristics on this "money tree" Buddha as the high ushnisha, vertical arrangement of the hair, moustache, symmetrically looped robe and parallel incisions for the folds of the arms." Some Northern Wei statues can be quite reminiscent of Gandharan standing Buddha, although in a slightly more symbolic style. The general attitude and rendering of the dress however remain. Other, like Northern Qi Dynasty statues also maintain the general Greco-Buddhist style, but with less realism and stronger symbolic elements. Some Eastern Wei statues display Buddhas with elaborate Greek-style robe foldings, and surmounted by flying figures holding a wreath.

Japan

In Japan, Buddhist art started to develop as the country converted to Buddhism in 548 CE. Some tiles from the Asuka period, the first period following the conversion of the country to Buddhism, display a strikingly classical style, with ample Hellenistic dress and realistically-rendered body shape characteristic of Greco-Buddhist art.

Other works of art incorporated a variety of Chinese and Korean influences, so that Japanese Buddhist became extremely varied in its expression. Many elements of Greco-Buddhist art remain to this day however, such as the Hercules inspiration behind the Nio guardian deities in front of Japanese Buddhist temples, or representations of the Buddha reminiscent of Greek art such as the Buddha in Kamakura.

Various other Greco-Buddhist artistic influences can be found in the Japanese Buddhist pantheon, the most striking of which being that of the Japanese wind god Fujin. In consistency with Greek iconography for the wind god Boreas, the Japanese wind god holds above his head with his two hands a draping or "wind bag" in the same general attitude. The abundance of hair have been kept in the Japanese rendering, as well as exaggerated facial features.

Another Buddhist deity, named Shukongoshin, one of the wrath-filled protector deities of Buddhist temples in Japan, is also an interesting case of transmission of the image of the famous Greek god Herakles to the Far-East along the Silk Road. Herakles was used in Greco-Buddhist art to represent Vajrapani, the protector of the Buddha, and his representation was then used in China and Japan to depict the protector gods of Buddhist temples.

Finally, the artistic inspiration from Greek floral scrolls is found quite literally in the decoration of Japanese roof tiles, one of the only remaining element of wooden architecture throughout centuries. The clearest one are from 7th century Nara temple building tiles, some of them exactly depicting vines and grapes. These motifs have evolved towards more symbolic representations, but essentially remain to this day in many Japanese traditional buildings.

INFLUENCES ON SOUTH-EAST ASIAN ART

The Indian civilization proved very influential on the cultures of South-East Asia. Most countries adopted Indian writing and culture, together with Hinduism and Mahayana and Theravada Buddhism.

The influence of Greco-Buddhist art is still visible in most of the representation of the Buddha in South-East Asia, through their idealism, realism and details of dress, although they tend to intermix with Indian Hindu art, and they progressively acquire more local elements.

CULTURAL SIGNIFICANCE OF GRECO-BUDDHIST ART

Beyond stylistic elements which spread throughout Asia for close to a millennium, the main contribution of Greco-Buddhist art to the Buddhist faith may be in the Greek-inspired idealistic realism which helped describe in a visual and immediately understandable manner the state of personal bliss and enlightenment proposed by Buddhism. The communication of deeply human approach of the Buddhist faith, and its accessibility to all have probably benefited from the Greco-Buddhist artistic syncretism.

MUSEUMS FOR GRECO-BUDDHIST ART

Major Collections

- Peshawar Museum, Peshawar, Pakistan (largest collection in the world).
- Lahore Museum, Lahore, Pakistan.
- Taxila Museum, Taxila, Pakistan.
- National Museum of Pakistan, Karachi, Pakistan.
- Mathura Museum, Mathura, India.
- Musée Guimet, Paris, France (about 150 artifacts, largest collection outside of Asia.)
- British Museum, London, Great Britain (about 100 artifacts).
- Tokyo National Museum, Tokyo, Japan (about 50 artifacts).
- National Museum of Oriental Art, Rome, Italy (about 80 artifacts).
- Museum of Indian Art, Dahlem, Berlin, Germany.

Small Collections

- Metropolitan Museum of Art, New York, USA
- Ancient Orient Museum, Tokyo, Japan (About 20 artifacts)
- Victoria and Albert Museum, London, Great Britain (About 30 artifacts)
- City Museum of Ancient Art in Palazzo Madama, Turin, Italy.
- Rubin Museum of Art in New York City, NY, United States.

Private Collections

- Collection de Marteau, Bruxelles, Belgium.

BUDDHIST ARCHITECTURE

Buddhist religious architecture developed in the South Asia in the third century BC. Two types of structures are associated with the religious architecture of early Buddhism: viharas and stupas.

Viharas initially were only temporary shelters used by wandering monks during the rainy season, but later were developed to accommodate the growing and increasingly formalised Buddhist monasticism. An existing example is at Nalanda (Bihar). A distinctive type of fortress architecture found in the former and present Buddhist kingdoms of the Himalayas are dzongs.

The initial function of a stupa was the veneration and safe-guarding of the relics of the Buddha. The earliest existing example of a stupa is in Sanchi (Madhya Pradesh). In accordance with changes in religious practice, stupas were gradually incorporated into chaitya-grihas (stupa halls). These reached their highpoint in the first century BC, exemplified by the cave complexes of Ajanta and Ellora (Maharashtra). The Pagoda is an evolution of the Indian stupa.

Buddhist temples were developed rather later and outside South Asia, where Buddhism gradually declined from the 6th/7th century AD onwards, though an early example is that of the Mahabodhi Temple at Bodh Gaya in Bihar.

EARLY DEVELOPMENT

Buddhist architecture emerged slowly in the period following the Buddha's life, building on Hindu models, but incorporating a specifically Buddhist symbols. Hindu temples at this time followed a simple plan – a square inner space, the sacrificial arena, often with a surrounding ambulatory route separated by lines of columns, with a conical or rectangular sloping roof, behind a porch or entrance area, generally framed by freestanding columns or a colonnade. The external profile represents Mount Meru, the abode of the gods and centre of the universe. The dimensions and proportions were dictated by sacred mathematical formulae. This simple plan was adopted by early Buddhists, sometimes adapted with additional cells for monks at the periphery (especially in the early cave temples such as at Ajanta, India).

In essence the basic plan survives to this day in Buddhist temples throughout the world. The profile became elaborated and the characteristic mountain shape seen today in many Hindu temples was used in early Buddhist sites and continued in similar fashion in some cultures (such as the Khmer). In others, such as Japan and Thailand, local influences and differing religious practices led to different architecture.

Early temples were often timber, and little trace remains, although stone was increasingly used. Cave temples such as those at Ajanta have survived better and preserve the plan form, porch and interior arrangements from this early period. As the functions of the monastery-temple expanded, the plan form started to diverge from the Hindu tradition and became more elaborate, providing sleeping, eating and study accommodation.

A characteristic new development at religious sites was the stupa. Stupas were originally more sculpture than building, essentially markers of some holy site or commemorating a holy man who lived there. Later forms are more elaborate and also in many cases refer back to the Mount Meru model. The layered, multi-roofed 'pagoda' form emerged in Nepal, and spread east to Japan and China.

One of the earliest Buddhist sites still in existence is at Sanchi, India, and this is centred on a stupa said to have been built by Ashoka the Great (273-236 BCE). The original simple structure is encased in a later, more decorative one, and over two centuries the whole site was elaborated upon. The four cardinal points are marked by elaborate stone gateways.

As with Buddhist art, architecture followed the spread of Buddhism throughout south and east Asia and it was the early Indian models that served as a first reference point, even though Buddhism virtually disappeared from India itself in the 10th century.

Decoration of Buddhist sites became steadily more elaborate through the last two centuries BCE, with the introduction of tablets and friezes, including human figures, particularly on stupas. However, the Buddha was not represented in human form until the first century CE. Instead, aniconic symbols were used. This is treated in more detail in Buddhist art, Aniconic phase. It influenced the development of temples, which eventually became a backdrop for Buddha images in most cases.

As Buddhism spread, Buddhist architecture diverged in style, reflecting the similar trends in Buddhist art. Building form was also influenced to some extent by the different forms of Buddhism in the northern countries, practising Mahayana Buddhism in the main and in the south where Theravada Buddhism prevailed.

VIHARA

Vihara is Sanskrit or Pali for (Buddhist) monastery. It originally meant "dwelling" or "refuge", such as those used by wandering monks during the rainy season.

In the early decades of Buddhism the wandering monks of the Sangha had no fixed abode, but during the rainy season they stayed in temporary shelters. These dwellings were simple wooden constructions or thatched bamboo huts. However, as it was considered an act of merit not only to feed a monk but also to shelter him, sumptuous monasteries were created by rich lay devotees (Mitra 1971). They were located near settlements, close enough for begging alms from the population but with enough seclusion to not disturb meditation.

Trade-routes were therefore ideal locations for a vihara and donations from wealthy traders increased their economic strength. From the first century CE onwards viharas also developed into educational institutions, due to the increasing demands for teaching in Mahayana Buddhism. In the second century BCE a standard plan for a vihara was established. It could be either structural, which was more common in the south of India, or rock-cut like the chaitya-grihas of the Deccan. It consisted of a walled quadrangular court, flanked by small cells. The front wall was pierced by a door, the side facing it in later periods often incorporated a shrine for the image of the Buddha. The cells were fitted with rock-cut platforms for beds and pillows. This basic layout was still similar to that of the communal space of an ashrama ringed with huts in the early decades of Buddhism.

As permanent monasteries became established, the name "Vihara" was kept. Some Viharas became extremely important institutions, some of them evolving into major Buddhist Universities with thousands of students, such as Nalanda.

Life in "Viharas" was codified early on. It is the object of a part of the Pali canon, the Vinaya Pitaka or "basket of monastic discipline".

The northern Indian state of Bihar derives its name from the word "Vihara", probably due to the abundance of Buddhist monasteries in that area. The Uzbek city of Bukhara also probably takes it name from "Vihara".

In Thailand and China, "Vihara" has a narrower meaning, and designates a shrine hall. Buddhist Vihara or monastery is an important form of institution associated with Buddhism. It may be defined as a residence for monks, a centre for religious work and meditation and a centre of Buddhist learning. Reference to five kinds of dwellings (Pancha Lenani) namely, Vihara, Addayoga, Pasada, Hammiya and Guha is found in the Buddhist canonical texts as fit for monks. Of these only the Vihara (monastery) and Guha (Cave) have survived.

Epigraphic, literary and archaeological evidence testify to the existence of many Buddhist Viharas in Bengal (West Bengal and Bangladesh) and Bihar from the 5th century AD to the end of the 12th century. These monasteries were generally designed in the old traditional Kushana pattern, a square block formed by four rows of cells along the four sides of an inner courtyard. They were usually built of stone or brick. As the monastic organization developed, they became elaborate brick structures with many adjuncts. Often they consisted of several stories and along the inner courtyard there usually ran a veranda supported on pillars. In some of them a stupa or shrine with a dais appeared. Within the shrine stood the icon of Buddha, Bodhisattva or Buddhist female deities. More or less the same plan was followed in building monastic establishments in Bengal and Bihar during the Gupta and Pala period. In course of time monasteries became important centres of learning.

An idea of the plan and structure of some of the flourishing monasteries may be found from the account of Hsuan-Tsang, who referred to the grand monastery of po-sipo, situated about 6.5 km west of the capital city of Pundravardhana (Mahasthan). The monastery was famous for its spacious halls and tall chambers. General Cunningham identified this vihara with bhasu vihara. Huen-tsang also noticed the famous Lo-to-mo-chi vihara (Raktamrittika Mahavihara) near Karnasuvarna (Rangamati, Murshidabad, West Bengal). The site of the monastery has been identified at Rangamati (modern Chiruti, Murshidabad, West Bengal). A number of smaller monastic blocks arranged on a regular plan, with other adjuncts, like shrines, stupas, pavilions etc have been excavated from the site.

One of the earliest viharas in Bengal was located at Biharail (Rajshahi district, Bangladesh). The plan of the monastery was designed on an ancient pattern, i.e. rows of cells round a central courtyard. The date of the monastery may be ascribed to the Gupta period. A number of monasteries grew up during the Pala period in ancient Bengal. One of them was Somapura Mahavihara at Paharpur, 46.5 km to the northwest of Mahasthana. The available data suggests that the Pala ruler Dharmapala founded the vihara. It followed the traditional cruciform plan for the central shrine. There were 177 individual cells around the central courtyard. There were central blocks in the middle of the eastern, southern and western sides. These might have been subsidiary chapels. It was the premier vihara of its kind and its fame lingered till the 11th century AD.

The famous Nalanda Mahavihara was founded a few centuries earlier; Huen-tsang speaks about its magnificence and grandeur. Reference to this monastery is found in Tibetan and Chinese sources. The fame of this monastery lingered even after the Pala period.

Reference to a monastery known as Vikramashila is found in Tibetan records. The Pala ruler Dharmapala was its founder. The exact site of this vihara is at Antichak, a small village in Bhagalpur district (Bihar). The monastery had 107 temples and 50 other institutions providing room for 108 monks. It attracted scholars from neighboring countries.

The name of the Odantapuri monastery is traceable in Pagsam jon zang (a Tibetan text), but no full-length description is available in the Tibetan source. Gopala I built it near Nalanda. This was the monastery invaded by Bakhtiyar Khalji.

Very interesting and important structural complexes have been discovered at Mainamati (Comilla district, Bangladesh). Remains of quite a few viharas have been unearthed here and the most elaborate is the Shalvan Vihara. The complex consists of a fairly large vihara of the usual plan of four ranges of monastic cells round a central court, with a temple in cruciform plan situated in the centre. According to a legend on a seal (discovered at the site) the founder of the monastery was Bhavadeva, a ruler of the Deva dynasty.

Other notable monasteries of Pala period were Traikuta, Devikota (identified with ancient kotivarsa, 'modern Bangarh'), Pandita vihara and Jagaddala (situated near Ramavati). Excavations conducted in 1972 to 1974 yielded a Buddhist monastic complex at Bharatpur in the Burdwan district of West Bengal. The date of the monastery may be ascribed to the early medieval period. Recent excavations at Jagjivanpur (Malda district, West Bengal) revealed another Buddhist monastery of the ninth century AD. Unfortunately, nothing of the superstructure has survived. However, a number of monastic cells facing a rectangular courtyard have been found. An interesting feature is the presence of circular corner cells. It is believed that the general layout of the monastic complex at Jagjivanpur is by and large similar to that of Nalanda.

Beside these, scattered references to some monasteries are found in epigraphic and other sources. They were no less important. Among them Pullahari (in western Magadha), Halud vihara (45 km south of Paharpur), Parikramana vihara and Yashovarmapura vihara (in Bihar) deserve mention.

STUPA

A stupa (from the Pâli) is a type of Buddhist mound-like structure found across the Indian subcontinent, other parts of Asia, and increasingly in the Western World. Stupas are known in many Southeast Asian countries as chedi; in some countries (particularly Sri Lanka) as dagoba (from Sanskrit *dhatu,* an element, component, or relic; and *garbha,* a storehouse or repository); or as tope (from Hindi *top,* derived from Sanskrit *stûpa,* a heap). Stupas are an ancient form of mandalas.

The stupa is the latest Buddhist religious monument and was originally only a simple mound of mud or clay to cover supposed relics of the Buddha. After the "passing away" of the Buddha, his remains were cremated and the ashes divided and buried under eight stupas with two further stupas encasing the urn and the embers. Little is known about these early stupas, particularly since it has not been possible to identify the original ten monuments. However, some later stupas, such as at Sarnath and Sanchi, seem to be embellishments of earlier mounds.

In the third century BCE, after his conversion to Buddhism, the emperor Ashoka had the original stupas opened and the remains distributed among the several thousand stupas he had built. Nevertheless, the stupas at the eight places associated with the life of the Buddha continued to be of particular importance. Accordingly, the importance of a stupa changed from being a funerary monument to being an object of veneration. As a consequence their appearance changed also. Stupas were built in Sri Lanka soon after King Devanampiyatissa converted to Buddhism, the first stupa to be built was the Thuparamaya. Later on Sri Lanka went on to build many stupas over the years, some like the Jetavanarama in Anuradhapura being one of the tallest ancient structures in the world.

They evolved into large hemispherical mounds with features such as the torana (gateway), the *vedica* (fence-like enclosure evolved from the vedic villages), the *harmika* (a square platform with railings on top of the stupa), *chattrayashti* (the parasol or canopy) and a circumambulatory around the stupa. From the first century BCE onwards, stupas were incorporated into the hall of the chaitya-griha.

One such stupa is discovered at Sopara an ancient port near Mumbai and is supposed to one of most ancient stupas in the world. The oldest known stupa is the Dhamek Stupa at Sanchi, India, while the tallest is the Phra Pathom Chedi in Nakhon Pathom, Thailand, with a height of 127 metres. The most elaborate stupa is the 8th century Borobudur monument in Java, Indonesia. The upper rounded terrace with rows of bell shaped stupas contained buddha images symbolize Arupadhatu, the sphere of formlesness. The main stupa itself is empty, symbolizing complete perfection of enlightenment. The main stupa is only the crown part of the monument, while the base is pyramidal structure elaborate with galleries adorned with bas relief of scenes derived from Buddhist text depicted the life of Siddharta Gautama. Borobudur unique and significant architecture has been acknowledge by UNESCO as the largest buddhist monument in the world.

The stupa evolved into the pagoda as Buddhism spread to other Asian countries. The pagoda has varied forms that also include bellshaped and pyramidal ones. Today, in the Western context, there is no clear distinction between the stupa and the pagoda. But in general *stupa* is used for a Buddhist structure of India or south-east Asia, while *pagoda* refers to a building in east Asia which can be entered and which may be secular in purpose.

Fundamentally, a stupa is essentially made up of the following five constituent parts:

- a square base
- a hemispherical dome
- a conical spire
- a crescent moon
- a circular disc

Each component is rich in metaphoric content. For example, "the shape of the stupa represents the Buddha, crowned and sitting in meditation posture on a lion throne. His crown is the top of the spire; his head is the square at the spire's base; his body is the vase shape; his legs are the four steps of the lower terrace; and the base is his throne." The components of the stupa are also identified with the five elements — earth, water, fire, air, and space — held to constitute the fabric of manifest existence.

Regional names for stupa include:

- Chaitya - Nepal
- Candi - Indonesia and Malaysia
- Chedi - Thailand
- Chorten - Tibet and Bhutan
- Dagoba/Chaitiya - Sri Lanka
- Chedey - Cambodia
- Sübürgen - Mongol

INTERESTING FACTS ABOUT BUDDHIST ARCHITECTURE

GANDHARA ARCHITECTURE GAVE RISE TO BUDDHIST ARCHITECTURE

Pass to the river Indus which Alexander the Great used to invade India in 326 BC. Gandhara architecture, the merger of Indian and Greek art, took the form of Buddhist cult objects, Buddhas and ornaments for Buddhist monasteries. Hindu icons were few. Monasteries were invariably made of stone, and most of the sculpture (like friezes) was used to decorate the lower levels of buildings.

The genesis of the first Buddhist stupa came about during this period. The more decorative art was in the form of small votive stupas illustrated with clay images of birds, dragons, sea serpents and humans.

The most characteristic trait of Gandhara sculpture is the standing or seated Buddha in the few hundreds of temples which have survived out of thousands. The seated Buddha is always cross legged in the traditional Indian way.

MAGNIFICENT BUDDHIST SCULPTORS

The teachings of the Buddhism were adopted by Mauryan emperor Ashoka in 255 BC as the religion that he as well as most of his subjects would follow. Towards this the king undertook steps to awaken and enlighten his people about the teachings of the Buddha, and to make sure that they would not forget how important it was for them to be Buddhists Ashoka took certain measures. These are the most early Buddhist sculptors, and were mainly of six types: stone pillars with inscriptions on them called edicts; stupas; monolithic pillars; shrines; a vast palace and a group of rock cut chambers. Out of these the most important ones were the edicts and the stupas and can still be seen today.

ASHOKA EDIFICES

The Construction of Pillars

Ashoka's edicts were nothing but circular free standing pillars rising upto to great heights so that they could be seen from a distance, topped off with a stone lion. Made of bricks, they carried declarations from the king regarding Buddhism. There were probably thirty in all, but now only two still stand. The pillars did not stand in isolation, and were usually found near stupas in a spot either unknowingly marked by the Buddha himself or along the royal route to Magadha, the capital.

The pillars were about forty feet in height, circular and rising straight out of the ground without evidence of a base to hold it up. At the top space was left for a Buddhist symbol to be placed, normally a lion. The pillar itself would bear inscriptions from the king, or teachings of the Buddha, upto a readable height and in large letters.

The Stupas

The stupas were large halls capped with a dome and bore symbols of the Buddha. Their purpose was to instill awe into the minds of the common people who, at that time, lived in small wooden houses. But the stupa wasn't the only awe-inspiring monuments; it was associated with a number of additional smaller structures such as pillared gates, decorated railings, umbrellas and lion thrones. All these were first made with brick, but when Ashoka realized that they wouldn't stand the vigours of time and weather, he switched to stone.

The most famous of the stupas, the one at Sanchi, was originally built by Ashoka. In 150 BC, renovation work was undertaken and massive additions were made to it. The stupa was made higher and broader, 120 feet in diameter and 54 feet high, as it is today. The timber railings were replaced by stone ones, standing 11 feet high with entrances at five cardinal point, forming a barricade. The emblem of protection, this stone railing encompassed the entire area around the stupa and the sacred tree (actually a branch from the holy tree in Bodh Gaya in Bihar was planted here) under which the Buddha is said to have attained enlightenment. The entrance to a stupa is through a stone gate, intricately carved with images of daily Buddhist life and stone lions guarding the images and the gate.

Palace of Ashoka- A 'Magnum opus'

Ashoka's palace near Patna was a masterpiece. Made mostly of wood, it seems to have been destroyed by fire. Enclosed by a high brick wall, the highlight of the palace was an immense pillared hall three storey and 250 feet high. Pillars were arranged at intervals of fifteen feet, and the ceiling was adorned with stone images and horizontally supported by wooden beams.

Construction of Monastries

The other all important Buddhist building is the shrine or the monastery. Here the Gandhara style of architecture comes into play, following a similar pattern for all buildings. Definitely religious in nature, the construction of a monastery followed a somewhat irregular design.

Built on the patterns of a fort and defended by a stone wall, the monastery evolved from the site of an ancient stupa. Living quarters for monks were separated from that of prayer, with the former consisting of houses, small votive stupas, solitary pillars and tiny cells for low rank monks. The principle buildings were housed within a rectangular courtyard with a stupa in the south and the monastery in the north. The court was the most important building, surrounded on three sides by a range of small chapels. A flight of stairs connected the stupa with the monastery whose rooms were small and functional. Called the sanghrama, these cells were located around the central courtyard.

BUDDHIST TEMPLES

While the stupas were places of religious learning, Buddhist temples were used for dual purposes; prayers and teachings. Brick was rarely used, and stone formed the base of most temple building. The Hinayana sect concentrated in the southern and western sides of India and excavated halls out of mountains, creating temples out of them in secluded regions. The Mahayanas were more adventurous, as can be seen from the Buddhist temples in Ajanta and Ellora. The Ajanta carvings consist of viharas or halls, supported by pillars, all cut out from one solid piece of mountain.

BUDDHIST CAVE TEMPLES

The task of making a cave temple was a simple one. Wooden pegs were driven into the mountainside and then watered so that they expanded, breaking the rock face into manageable blocks. Huge sections of stone were either moved or left where they were depending on the requirement. The split rock face would then be dug into, carving entire halls from it. After that, all that was left to be done was to carve out intricate details into pillars, walls, ceilings and doorways, which usually took years to complete.

Rock art of the Buddhists was not constricted to temples and stupas. The Buddha himself was the inspiration behind massive statues of his likeness made out of stone, brass and copper. Buddha statues know no boundaries – they can be larger than life, going upto great heights (over 14 metres), reaching up into the sky or showing him reclining. However, in stupas and places of worship, the Buddha is almost never shown and is represented indirectly through foot impressions, empty thrones and the chakra (wheel).

STUPAS

Stupas were built of stones or bricks to commemorate important events or mark important places associated with Buddhism or to house important relics of Buddha. Ashok Maurya who laid the foundation of this group of monuments is said to have built 84,000 stupas, most of which have perished.

The best examples of stupas are those constructed at Amaravati, Sanchi, Barhut and Gaya. "One of the most striking architectural remains of ancient India" and the earliest and largest of the three stupas found in Sanchi was built by Ashoka (273-236 B.C.).

Sanchi in Raisen district of Madhya Pradesh is famous for its magnificent Buddhist monuments and edifices. Situated on a hill, these beautiful and well-preserved stupas depict the various stages of development of Buddhist art and architecture over a period of thirteen hundred years from the third century B.C. to the twelfth century A.D. Inscriptions show that these monuments were maintained by the rich merchants of that region.

The stupa built by Ashoka was damaged during the break-up of the Maurya Empire. In the 2nd century B.C., during the rule of the Sungas it was completely reconstructed. Religious activity led to the improvement and enlargement of the stupa and a stone railing was built around it. It was also embellished with the construction of heavily carved gateways. The Great stupa has a large hemispherical dome which is flat at the top, and crowned by a triple umbrella or Chattra on a pedestal surrounded by a square railing or Karmika. Buddha's relics were placed in a casket chamber in the centre of the Dome. At the base of the dome is a high circular terrace probably meant for parikrama or circumambulation and an encircling balustrade. At the ground level is a stone-paved procession path and another stone Balustrade and two flights of steps leading to the circular terrace. Access to it is through four exquisitely carved gateways or Toranas in the North, South, East and West. The diameter of the stupa is 36.60 metres and its height is 16.46 metres. It is built of large burnt bricks and mud mortar. It is presumed that the elaborately carved Toranas were built by ivory or metal workers in the 1st Century BC during the reign of King Satakarni of the Satavahana Dynasty. The last addition to the stupa was made during the early 4th Century AD in the Gupta period when four images of Buddha sitting in the dhyana mudra or meditation were installed at the four entrances.

The first Torana gateway to be built is the one at the principal entrance on the South. Each gateway has two square pillars. Crowning each pillar on all four sides are four elephants, four lions and four dwarfs. The four dwarfs support a superstructure of three architraves or carved panels one above the other. Between these are intricately carved elephants and riders on horseback. The lowest architrave is supported on exquisitely carved bracket figures. The panels are decorated with finely carved figures of men, women, yakshas, lions and elephants. The entire panel of the gateways is covered with sculptured scenes from the life of Buddha, the Jataka Tales, events of the Buddhist times and rows of floral or lotus motifs. The scenes from Buddha's life show Buddha represented by symbols - the lotus, wheel a riderless caparisoned horse, an umbrella held above a throne, foot prints and the triratnas which are symbolic of Buddha, Dharma and Sangha. The top panel has a Dharma chakra with two Yakshas on either side holding chamaras. South of the Scenes depicted from Buddha's life are the Enlightenment of Buddha (a throne beneath a peepul tree); the First Sermon (a Dharma chakra placed on a throne); The Great Departure (a riderless horse and an empty chariot with an umbrella above); Sujata's offering and the temptation and assault by Mara.

The big Stupa at Bharhut also in Madhya Pradesh was constructed in the 2nd century BC in the Sunga Period. It is a hemispherical dome built of brick and is surmounted by a shaft and an umbrella to represent the spiritual sovereignty of Buddhism. The railing surrounding it is of red sandstone. Scenes from the life of Buddha and the Jataka Tales are sculptured on the gateways, pillars, uprights and cross-bars of the railings.

During the same period, a number of stupas, chaityas, viharas and pillars were constructed in Sanchi, Bodh-Gaya, Mathura, Gandhara, Amaravati and Nagarjunakonda. Though most of these have not remained in their entirety, the ruins are of architectural interest. The Stupas of Nagajunakonda and Amaravati, both in the Guntur District of Andhra Pradesh show that the Stupas of the Southern region differ in structure from those of the North. The architecture here is a shift from the usual Buddhist style, which reflected the two main divisions in Buddhism - Hinayana and Mahayana. Different trends and styles were incorporated here giving rise to new architectural forms, i.e. a quadrangular monastery, square and rectangular image shrine, pillared hall and a small stupa on a square platform.

The stupas of Nagarjunakonda are in the form of a hemispherical dome resting on a low drum encased in panels sculptured with scenes of events depicting the life of Buddha. A notable feature of the stupas here is ayaka platforms in the four directions with five inscribed pillars on each of them. The five pillars symbolise the five important events in the life of Buddha - his Birth, Renunciation, Enlightenment, First Sermon and Parinirvana.

Some of the stupas are built on a square platform having an apsidal shrine on either side and a pillared hall within a quadrangular monastery. Some stupas were wheel-shaped having four to ten spokes and a two or three winged vihara.

The earliest of the Nagarjunkonda stupas is the Maha Chaitya which contains the tooth relic of Buddha. The stupa is wheel-shaped with ayaka platforms surmounted by pillars. The smallest stupa here has only two cells and the Chaitya griha enshrines the image of Buddha.

Ruins of stupas have been found in Rajgriha or Rajgir (Bihar) where the First Buddhist Council was held; at Vaisali (Bihar) where the Second Buddhist Council was held and at Sravasti (U.P.) one of the eight places of Buddhist pilgrimage where Buddha is said to have performed the Great Miracle. To show his spiritual powers, he made a mango tree to sprout in a day and created numerous images of himself, sitting and standing on lotuses with fire and water emanating from his body. The conversion of King Prasenajit and the dacoit Angulimala is also said to have taken place here.

Ruins of the main stupa in Kusinagara where Buddha passed away and was cremated, is believed to contain the bodily remains of Buddha. Both Fa-hien and Hiuen-Tsang have recorded their visits to these places.

The Dhamekh Stupa and the Dharmarajika stupa at Sarnath are believed to have been built by Ashoka and later rebuilt in the Gupta period. These stupas contain the relics of Buddha and are therefore important places of Buddhist pilgrimage. Buddha gave his First Sermon in Sarnath and also founded the Sangha or Order of Monks here. The original Dhamekh Stupa built with mud or brick is a cylindrical structure 43.5 m. high. The stone basement has eight projecting faces with niches in them. Delicately carved with beautiful floral and geometrical patterns, it is believed to have been put up in the Gupta period.

VIHARAS

Viharas or monasteries constructed with brick or excavated from rocks are found in different parts of India. Usually built to a set plan, they have a hall meant for congregational prayer with a running verandah on three sides or an open courtyard surrounded by a row of cells and a pillared verandah in front. These cells served as dwelling places for the monks. These monastic buildings built of bricks were self-contained units and had a Chaitya hall or Chaitya mandir attached to a stupa - the chief object of worship.

Some of the important Buddhist viharas are those at Ajanta, Ellora, Nasik, Karle, Kanheri, Bagh and Badami. The Hinayana viharas found in these places have many interesting features which differentiate them from the Mahayana type in the same regions. Though plain from the point of view of architecture, they are large halls with cells excavated in the walls on three sides. The hall has one or more entrances. The small cells, each with a door have one or two stone platforms to serve as beds.

The excavations of viharas at Nagarjunakonda show large rectangular courtyards with stone-paved central halls. Around the courtyard, the row of cells, small and big, suggest residences and dining halls for monks. Twenty-five of the rock-cut caves of Ajanta are viharas and are the finest of monasteries. Four of the viharas belong to the 2nd century BC. Later, other caves were excavated during the reign of the Vakataka rulers who were the contemporaries of the Gupta Rulers. Some of the most beautiful viharas belong to this period. The finest of them Cave 1, of the Mahayana type consists of a verandah, a hall, groups of cells and a sanctuary. It has a decorated facade. The portico is supported by exquisitely carved pillars. The columns have a square base with figures of dwarfs and elaborately carved brackets and capitals. Below the capital is a square abacus with finely carved makara motifs. The walls and the ceilings of the cave contain the most exquisite paintings.

The viharas of Ellora dated 400 AD to 7th century AD are of one, two, and three storeys and are the largest of the type. They contain sculptured figures and belong to both Hinayana and Mahayana Buddhism.

CHAITYAS

Chaitya grihas or halls of worship were built all over the country either of brick or excavated from rocks. Ruins of a large number of structural Buddhist chaity grihas are found in the eastern districts of Andhra Pradesh, in valleys, near rivers and lakes. The ruins located in the districts of Srikakulam at Salihundam, of Visahkapatnam at Kotturu, of West Godavari at Guntapalli of Krishna at Vijayawada, of Guntur at Nagajunakonda and Amaravati belong to the 3rd century BC and later. The largest brick chaitya hall was excavated at Guntapalli.

Some of the most beautiful rock-cut caves are those at Ajanta, Ellora, Bhaja, Karle, Bagh, Nasik and Kanheri. Some of the chunar sand-stone rock-cut chaityas of Bhaja, Kondane, Karle and Ajanta, all in Maharashtra state are earlier excavations and belong to the first phase or Hinayana creed of Buddhism and are similar to the brick and wooden structures of Ashokan times. Some of the chaityas show that wood had been used in the roofing and entrance arches. The chaitya at Bhaja is a long hall 16.75 metres long and 8 metres broad with an apse at the end. The hall is divided into a central nave and an aisle on either side flanked by two rows of pillars. The roof is vaulted. The rock-cut stupa in the apse is crowned by a wooden harmika. The chaitya has a large arched torana or entrance with an arched portico.

Hinayana rock architecture reaches the peak of excellence in the splendid chaitya at Karle. An inscription in Karle mentions Bhutapala, a banker to be the founder of the chaitya hall but later scholars identify him with Devabhuti, the last of the Sunga rulers.

The chaitya has a double-storeyed facade and has three doorways in the lower part. It has an upper gallery over which there is the usual arch. The walls of the vestibule to the chaitya hall are decorated with sculptured figures of couples. The pillars separating the central nave from the aisles have a pot base, an octagonal shaft, inverted lotus capital with an abacus. The abacus has exquisitely carved pairs of elephants kneeling down, each with a couple in front and caparisoned horses with riders on them. The stupa at the apse end is tall and cylindrical with two tiers of railings around the drum. It is crowned by the original wooden chhatra. This is the most beautiful of the chaityas.

The second phase of Buddhist architecture is marked by the Mahayana creed of Buddhism seen in some of the excellent rock-cut chaityas at Ajanta in Aurangabad district of Maharashtra excavated between 5th AD and 9th century AD during the rule of the Vakatakas, the Guptas and the Rashtrakutas.

The caves were first discovered in the beginning of the 19th century. The caves are excavated from a semi-circular steep rock with a stream flowing below, and were meant for the use of the monks who spent the rainy season there in meditation. The caves are at different levels and have stairs leading down to the stream. Five of the thirty caves arc chaityas or sanctuaries. The earlier group of two caved dated 2nd century BC belong to the style of Kondan and Nasik caves.

The chaityas have a vaulted ceiling with a huge horse-shoe shaped window or chaitya window over the doorway. They are large halls divided into three, parts - the central nave, apse and aisles on either side separated by a row of columns. The side aisles continue behind the apse for circumambulation. At the centre of the apse is a rock stupa with large figure of Buddha, sitting or standing. A remarkable feature of these Chaityas is the imitation of woodwork on rock. Beams and rafters were carved in the rock though they serve no purpose. From the unfinished caves, we get an idea of the method of excavation. Starting from the ceiling, they worked downwards. Solid blocks were left to be carved into pillars. After finishing the verandah, they excavated the interior. Tools used were the pick-axe, chisel and hammer.

The most perfect of this group of chaitya grihas is cave 19. Excavated at the end of the 5th century AD it is similar to the other chaityas in its plan and ribbed vaulted ceiling except for its single doorway and elaborate ornamentation. It has a pillared portico in front leading into a courtyard with the walls on either side heavily sculptured with figures. The interior pillars are well decorated with cushion shaped capitals. The corbel brackets are richly sculptured. The drum of the central stupa is elongated and carved. Projecting from the drum is an arched nasika or niche with the figure of a standing Buddha carved in it. The rounded dome of the stupa is surmounted by a harmika and three tiers of chhatras, diminishing in size and supported by figures on four sides. On top of the chhatras and touching the ceiling is another small stupa with a miniature harmika. The facade of the cave is exquisitely carved. The chaitya-window has figures of yakshas and richly carved, friezes on either side. Two figures of standing Buddha flank the entrance. The walls of the hall and the ceiling of the aisles is richly painted with figures of Buddha, floral motifs, animals and birds.

PAINTINGS

Paintings which has been an accepted art since early times attained heights of excellence in Gupta period. These exquisite paintings or frescos are to be seen in the caves of Ajanta. The entire surface of the caves is exquisitely painted and shows the high standard reached in mural painting. The theme of the painting on the walls is mostly the life of Buddha and Bodhisattvas and the Jataka stories. These topics cover a continuous narration of events on all aspects of human-life from birth to death. Every kind of human emotion is depicted. The paintings reflect the contemporary life of the times, dress, ornaments, culture, weapons used, even their beliefs are portrayed with life-like reality. The paintings include gods, yakshas, kinneras, gandharvas, apsaras and human beings.

The paintings show their intense feeling for nature and an understanding of the various aspects of all living beings. The ceilings are covered with intricate designs, flowers, plants, birds, animals, fruit and people. The ground for painting was prepared by paving it with a rough layer of earth and sand mixed with vegetable fibres, husk and grass. A second coat of mud mixed with fine sand and fibrous vegetable material was applied. A final finish was given with a thin coat of lime-wash, glue was used as a binder. On this prepared surface, the outlines were drawn and the spaces were filled with the required colours; with much attention given to shades and tones. Red, yellow, black, ochre, blue and gypsum were mostly used. Some of the renowned paintings are that of the Bodhisattva holding a lily, the painting of Padmapani, the Apsaras with a turban headgear the painting on the ceiling and the toilet scheme considered to be a masterpiece of the painter.

STHAMBAS

Sthambas or Pillars with religious emblems were put up by pious Buddhists in honour of Buddha or other great Buddhists. Fragments of sthambas belonging to Mauryan times and later were found at Sanchi, Sarnath, Amaravati and Nagarjunkonda.

A portion of the Ashoka Pillar, 15.25 metres high, surmounted by the famous lion-capital and a dharma chakra above the heads of the four lions stands embedded near the Dharmarajika stupa at Sarnath. The pillar bears the edict of Ashoka warning the monks and nuns against creating a schism in the monastic order. The broken fragments of the Pillar are now in the Museum at Sarnath. The lion-capital - the most magnificent piece of Mauryan sculpture is 2.31 metres high. It consists of four parts –

(i) a bell-shaped vase covered with inverted lotus petals,

(ii) a round abacus,

(iii) four seated lions and

(iv) a crowning dharmachakra with thirty two spokes.

The four lions are beautifully sculptured. On the abacus are four running animals - an elephant, a bull, a horse and a lion with a small dharmachakra between them. The dharmachakra symbolises the dharma or law; the four lions facing the four directions are the form of Buddha or Sakyasimha, the four galloping animals are the four quarters according to Buddhist books and the four smaller dharmachakras stand for the intermediate regions and the lotus is the symbol of creative activity. The surface of these pillars has a mirror like finish.

Another Ashokan Pillar of note is the one at Lauriya Nandangarh in Bihar. Erected in the 3rd century BC it is made of highly polished Chunar sand-stone. Standing 9.8 metres high it rises from the ground and has no base structure. It is surmounted by a bell-shaped inverted lotus. The abacus on it is decorated with flying geese and crowning it is a sitting lion. The pillar is an example of the engineering skill of the craftsmen of Mauryan times.

HILL OF SANCHI

The Hill of Sanchi is situated about 9 kilometres south-west of Vidisha in Madhaya Pradesh, India. Crowning the hilltop of Sanchi nearly 91 metres in height, a group of Buddhist monuments commands a grand view even from a distance. It is unique not only in its having the most perfect and well-preserved stupas but also in its offering a wide and educative field for the study of the genesis, efflorescence and decay of Buddhist art and architecture for a period of about thirteen hundred years, from the third century B.C. to the twelfth century, A.D., almost covering the whole range of Indian Buddhism. This is rather surprising, for Sanchi was not hallowed by any incident in Buddha's life; not is it known to have been the focus of any significant event in the history of Buddhist monachism. Hiuen Tsang, who so meticulously recorded the details connected with Buddhist monuments, is silent about it. The only possible reference to it is contained in the chronicles of Sri Lanka, according to which Mahendra, son of Asoka and his queen Devi, daughter of a merchant of Vidisa, (modern Besnagar near Bhilsa or Vidisha) whom Asoka had married during his halt there on his way to

Ujjayani as a viceroy, is said to have visited his mother at Vidisa, and the latter took him up to the beautiful monastery of Vedisagiri built by herself. Mahendra had stayed there for a month before he set out for Sri Lanka.

The foundation of the great religious establishment at Sanchi destined to have a glorious career as an important centre of Buddhism for many centuries to come, was probably laid by the great Maurya emperor Asoka (circa 273-236 B.C.), when he built a stupa and erected a monolithic pillar here. In addition to his marriage with a lady of Vidisa, the reason for his selection of this particular spot may be due to the fact that the hilltop served as an ideal place for giving a concrete shape to the newly aroused zeal for Buddhism in the emperor, who is said to have opened up seven out of the eight original stupas erected over the body relics of Buddha and to have distributed the relics among innumerable stupas built by himself all over his empire. By its quietude and seclusion ensuring a proper atmosphere for meditation, combined with its proximity to the rich and populous city of Vidisa, Sanchi fulfilled all the conditions required for an ideal Buddhist monastic life. The dedicatory inscriptions at Sanchi unmistakably show that the prosperity of the Buddhist establishment here was, to a great extent, due to the piety of the rich mercantile community of Vidisa. The nearness of the city, the strategic situation of which - at the confluence of two rivers, the Betwa and the Bes, as well as on two important trade routes resulted in a great overflow of wealth, was in no small measure responsible for the flourishing condition of Sanchi even when the empire of the Mauryas was a thing of the past.

After a temporary setback following the break-up of the Maurya empire, when the stupa of Asoka was damaged, the cause of the Buddhist establishment of Kakanaya was taken up with a feverish zeal by the monks and the laity alike, not a negligible percentage of the latter being formed by visitors of Vidisa for trade and other purposes. The religious fervour found its expression in vigorous building activity about the middle of the second century B.C., during which the Sungas were ruling and which saw the stone encasing and enlargement of the stupa of Asoka, the erection of balustrades round its ground, berm, stairway and harmika, the reconstruction of Temple 40 and the building of Stupas 2 and 3. The same intense religious aspiration and creative forces continued unabated in the next century as well, when, during the supremacy of the Satavahanas, new embellishments, in the form of elaborately-carved gateways, were added to Stupas 1 and 3.

The political vicissitude which northern India went through immediately before and after the Christian era, when the Scytho-Parthians and Kushans invaded and annexed a large part of the land, had perhaps its repercussions at Sanchi as well, resulting in a slackening of structural activities. The establishment of a foreign power in the Malwa region under the Kshatrapas, engaged in chronic warfare, hardly provided any incentive for the dormant workshop. However, like the contemporary Buddhist centres of north and south-east India, Sanchi freed itself, during the period, from the earlier aniconic tradition, but its contribution to the evolution of the image of Buddha was nil, and it depended for such images on imports from Mathura.

After a prolonged period of stagnation and lassitude under the Kashtrapas, there was a revival of sculptural activity at Sanchi during the reign of the Guptas who, after conquering the Kshatrapas (circa A.D. 400), provided peace and prosperity essential for the growth of artistic pursuits. The discovery a few images in Mathura, sandstone executed in the early Gupta tradition, proves that Mathura continued, even in the fourth century A.D., to meet the demand of the clientele of Sanchi. But soon afterwards the local art of Sanchi once more came to the fore, and to this period belong the four images of Buddha seated under canopies against the berm of Stupa 1 facing the four entrances. But even in the best days of the Guptas the figures of Buddha from the ateliers of Sanchi fell short, in standard and number of their counterparts at such Buddhist centres as Sarnath.

The Gupta period, which ushered in a new epoch in the history of Indian temple-architecture, saw at Sanchi as well as resuscitation of structural activity. In Temple 17 which has withstood the ravages of time, we find one of the earliest Gupta temples noted for their well-balanced proportion, restraint in ornamentation and elegance.

After the glorious days of the Guptas centrifugal forces became once more rampant. And then came the shock of the Hana invasions, which resulted in the seizure of a large part of western and central India by that tribe. But that occupation was short lived, to be shattered by Yasodharman's victory over their chief Mihirakula in the first half of the sixth century.

On the ashes of the Gupta empire rose a number of small kingdoms, none of which was powerful enough to bring any large part of India under its aegis, till Harshavardhana (A.D. 606-647) achieved some sort of political unity in northern India. His espousal of the cause of Buddhism brought a fresh lease of life to that religion. The vestiges of the seventh and eighth centuries, which saw at Sanchi the building of several monasteries and temples, reveal a prosperous condition of the Buddhist community at the place. The number of the images of Buddha made during the period was fairly considerable; executed in late Gupta tradition, they, however, lack the charm and grace of their prototypes and are almost lifeless and mechanical.

After the death of Harsha, northern India once, more became a prey to the ambitions of different dynasties. The Pratiharas, who had established themselves in the Malwa region by the eighth century, were followed by the Paramaras in the next century. But Sanchi seems to have been hardly affected by these political changes, as the existence of a number of medieval monasteries and temples testifies to a period of continued prosperity. Temple 45, for example, which is now a mere shell bereft of its original splendour, has the same architectural pompousness and exuberance of decoration as would characterise the contemporaneous north Indian architecture. From the find of such images like Vajrasattva and Marichi, it is abundantly clear that Vajrayana did extend its roots here as well.

It is not known how end came to the Buddhist establishment at Sanchi. No Buddhist monument can be assigned to the thirteenth century A.D. on the other hand, to this period belong a number of Brahmanical plaques containing representations of Vishnu, Ganega, Mahishasuramardini, etc. We do not know if the Buddhists deserted the place or gradually lost their vital forces to maintain their individuality thus succumbing to the all absorbing force of Brahmanism, which was one of the potent causes of the extinction of Buddhism in the land of its birth.

EXPLORATION AND PRESERVATION

The relics of Sariputra and Maha Moggalana, the two foremost disciples of the Buddha, were found by Colonel Cunningham in 1851 in this stupa, enshrined at the centre of at the centre of the dome on the level of the terrace.

From the fourteenth century onwards, Sanchi was left deserted and unnoticed, till in the year 1818 General Taylor brought it to public attention by discovering its ruins, of which he found Stupas 1, 2 and 3 intact. The great interest which this discovery created accounts to a large extent for the immense damages suffered by the monuments at the hands of amateur archaeologists and treasure-hunters. In 1822, Captain Johnson, Assistant Political Agent in Bhopal, opened up Stupa 1 from top to bottom on one side, thus leaving a great breach which resulted in the collapse of the West Gateway and a part of the enclosing balustrade. Stupa 2 was also partially destroyed. Alexander Cunningham, together with Captain F. C. Maisey, excavated Stupas 2 and 3 in 1851 and found relic caskets within. They also sank a shaft at the centre of Stupa 1, which, however, failed to yield any relies. These operations coupled with the depredations of villagers and the growth of vegetation, wrought havoc to the stupas. The pillar of Asoka was broken into pieces by a local zemindar to be utilized as a sugarcane press.

The question of repairs and preservation was not, at all considered till 1881, when Major Cole took up the work in right earnest and succeeded, in the course of the next three years, in clearing off vegetation, filling in the breach in the dome of Stupa 1, setting up its fallen West and South Gateways and a part of its railing and restoring the gateway in front of Stupa V. The other monuments, however, were left uncared for and no attempt was made to expose the structures lying buried under debris. This work was later on undertaken creditably by Sir John Marshall, Director General of

Archaeology in India, who, between the years 1912 and 1919, brought the monuments to their present condition. His work entailed a large-scale clearance of jungle, excavation and thorough conservation of the edifices, which included the complete dismantling and rebuilding of the south-west quadrant of Stupa 1, setting up of its balustrades and erection of the crowning members, reconstruction of the dome, balustrade and crowning members of Stupa 3, resetting of the out-of-plumb pillars of Temple 18 repairs to the perilously decayed Temple 45, rebuilding of the retaining wall between the Main Terrace and Eastern Area, re-roofing and repairs of Temples 17, 31 and 32 and provision of an effective drainage. The site was next turfed and Planted with trees and flowering creepers. A small museum was also built to house the loose antiquities found in the course of these operations.

BUDDHIST STUPS IN AMARAVATI

THE DISCOVERY OF THE AMARÂVATÎ STÛPA

The modern town of Amarâvatî, largely a creation of the end of the 18th century, is situated in Guntûr district on the right or south bank of the river Krishnâ. About half a mile to the west of Amarâvatî lies the small town of Dharanikota, of which nothing remains, except the massive earthen embankments which surround its four sides, to show that it was once, under its ancient name of Dhânyakataka, the provincial capital of the Sâtavâhanas. A little to the south of Amarâvatî lies the site of the Great Stûpa, which in the 2nd century A.D. was by far the freest monument in the Buddhist world. It is now a circle of debris enclosing a few broken pillars and the course of a small stream.

The history of the Stûpa from its days of splendour to its re-discovery at the end of the 18th century is soon told. Though Buddhism ceased to be the dominant religion in the Andhradeœa after the 4th century A.D., it found no lack of support, even from some of the kings of the ephemeral dynasties which succeeded the Ikshvâkus. When the Chinese pilgrim, Hsüan Tsang, travelled through the country in the first half of the 7th century A.D., he found that, though many Buddhist monasteries were deserted, twenty were still in use with a thousand brethren, adherents for the most part of the Mahâsanghika sect. It is difficult to recognize Dhânyakataka from the pilgrim's description of T'ê-na-ka-che-ka: in any case he does not mention the Stûpa. That Dhânyakataka remained a Buddhist centre of considerable vitality is evident from the finds of two groups of bronze figures of the Buddha and of several stone figures of the Buddha and Bodhisattvas of 6th to 11th century date.

Amarâvatî mentions gifts 'to the lofty stûpa of the Buddha, which is finely decorated with various sculptures.' A second inscription, dated A.D. 1234, on the same pillar speaks of another grant to the Buddha, 'who is pleased to reside at Srî Dhânyakataka.'

The latest reference to the Buddhist shrines at Dhânyakataka is in the rock-inscription, dated A.D. 1344, at Gadalâdeniya, Kandy District, of the famous Sinhalese divine, Dharmmakîrtti, who repaired a two-storied image-house at the site, thus maintaining that intimate connexion between Ceylon and the Andhradeúa which had begun at Nâgârjunikonda in the 3rd century A.D. From the 14th to the end of the 18th century, though the place is frequently mentioned in local inscriptions, nothing more is heard of the Buddhist monuments at Dhânayakataka.

In 1796 a local Zemindar decided to change his residence to Amarâvatî and to found a new city about the Amareúvara temple. The many mounds in the area proved admirable quarries for building material. The Zemindar began to attack the Hill of Lamps, the local name of the Great Stûpa, which after centuries of neglect the jungle had partially reclaimed. By good fortune, the discovery of sculptured slabs came to the ears of Colonel Colin Mackenzie, later to be Surveyor General of India. Mackenzie, a passionate collector and student of antiquity, paid a brief visit to Amarâvatî in 1797. He perceived immediately that the great, low mound, crowned by a smaller one some ninety feet in diameter and twenty feet high, and cased with bricks and slabs of stone, was the remains of a great monument. Campaigning and survey duties occupied Mackenzie until March 1816, when he returned to Amarâvatî with his draughtsmen and assistants.

He himself left in August, but his men stayed on until March, 1818, making careful drawings and plans of the monument, which had further disintegrated since his first visit, for the Zemindar had started to construct a tank in the top of the mound. Mackenzie published the results of his investigations in two important papers. His manuscript volume of plans and drawings is now preserved in the Library of the Commonwealth Relations Office. In a note pasted into the volume, Mackenzie writes: 'Including the inscription eleven stones of Depauldina (the Hill of Lamps) were delivered into the charge of Major Cotgrave at Masulipatam, of which number seven have been sent round to Calcutta. The remaining four; two of which consist of pillars with lions and figures numbered in my sketch 3 and 4, of loose stones a circular stone with beautiful sculptures No 55, and the large inscription stone, a facsimile of which was sent some time during last year.' The sentence ends abruptly. A letter to Cotgrave dated 6 September 1819, and now in the British Museum, acknowledges receipt of the remaining four at Calcutta. Of the eleven sculptures, Mackenzie presented two to the Asiatic Society of Bengal, whence they were later transferred to the Indian Museum, Calcutta.

The remaining nine pieces were sent to London, probably soon after Mackenzie's death in 1821, to the East India Company's Museum at East India House, Leadenhall Street. Mackenzie also had a number of sculptures removed to Masulipatam. These were added to in 1830 by a Mr Robertson and used to decorate the square of a new market-place. Thirty three slabs, set up in a circle, were seen by Dr Benza in 1835. They soon found their way into the garden of a Mr Alexander, who had a taste for such things.

In 1845 the site was visited by Sir Walter Elliot. It had now become simply 'a rounded mound or hillock, with a hollow or depression at the summit, but without a vestige or indication of an architectural structure, or even a fragment of wrought stone, to show that a building had once stood there, every fragment of former excavations having been carried away and burnt into lime.' Elliot dug into the south-west part of the mound 12 and recovered a large number of fragments which he had sent down to Madras, where they lay neglected and exposed until 1856, when Edward Balfour, the officer-in-charge of the newly created Government Museum, requested the Rev William Taylor to publish a description of them. Taylor lists seventy-nine pieces, of which two had already gone astray, and adds thirty-seven pieces, which arrived from Masulipatam in April/ May 1856. Seven more pieces had been added to the collection, when it was photographed at Madras by Captain Tripe, the Government photographer. Elliot himself was largely responsible for getting the additional forty-four pieces, comprising those extracted - with difficulty - from Mr Alexander and a number recently dug out from the mound by the Head Assistant Collector of Guntûr, sent down to Madras.

In 1859 these sculptures, one hundred and twenty-one in number, which it was decided should be called the Elliot Marbles in recognition of that gentleman's efforts on their behalf, were sent to London. They arrived in 1860 and remained for twelve months at Beale *Wharf*, Southwark. It was the period of the dissolution of the East India Company and the creation of the India Office. East India House was being demolished and there was no place for the reception of the sculptures. In 1861 they were moved to the coach-house of Fife House, Whitehall, which was now used to house the India Museum. Two or three of the finest pieces were attached to the outer wall of Fife House, and suffered disastrously in consequence.

The collection remained unnoticed until, in January 1867, it was 'discovered' by James Fergusson, one of the first to appreciate the intention and qualities of Indian art. In 1867 he wrote a brief account of the Amarâvatî Stûpa, utilizing Mackenzie's drawings and papers, and in the following year published his *Tree and Serpent Worship*, which contained photographs of most of the Amarâvatî sculptures in England and an attempted reconstruction of the monument. In 1869 the India Museum was moved to the newly erected India Office; the sculptures were probably held at the India Stores, Belvedere Road, Lambeth. In December of 1874 the Commissioners of the 1851 Exhibition leased the Eastern Galleries in South Kensington to the India Office to house the India Museum.

It was opened in 1875 and the Amarâvatî sculptures were arranged in the Sculpture Court at the South Entrance, probably by Fergusson. This was the first time the sculptures, apart from the Mackenzie Collection and the few pieces exposed at Fife House, had been displayed to the English public. They remained at South Kensington until, in November 1879, the decision was taken to dissolve the India Museum and to distribute its contents between the British Museum and a newly formed Indian Section of the Victoria and Albert Museum. In 1880 the Amarâvatî sculptures came to the British Museum, where Sir Wollaston Franks, an admirer and collector of Indian, as of all Oriental art, arranged them, with the help of Fergusson, on the Main Staircase. The Museum already possessed one important fragment, purchased by one of its officers from his barber in 1860. In 1882 Franks acquired from Elliot a further piece in beautiful condition.

In 1885, again at the instigation of Franks, who was keenly interested in the Stûpa, the Government of Madras presented the Museum with two further pieces, both in fine condition. These last three pieces, compared with the remainder of the collection, show how lamentably the sculptures had suffered before they reached the Museum, having endured successively exposure in Madras, damp at Fife House and frost at South Kensington. This, however, was the end of their adventures; removed for safety during the Second World War, they have now (1951-52) been erected in the Front Hall of the Museum, in such a manner as to suggest the actual monument.

The fate of the site was no happier. In 1877 Robert Sewell carefully dug the northwest part of the mound, discovered many fragments, and published an invaluable report. But three years later the Duke of Buckingham, then Governor of Madras, arbitrarily ordered the complete 'excavation' of the site. The whole of the centre area was cleared of earth, and the final destruction of the Stûpa completed. When James Burgess, the officer in charge of the Archaeological Survey of Madras, visited the site in 1881, it had been converted into a large pit.

The fragments from Sewell's excavations and the Duke of Buckingham's drastic clearance numbered about three hundred; Burgess discovered some ninety more. Most of these, together with a number from the Bezwâda Library, were despatched to the Government Museum, Madras, in batches, in the years 1883, 1890 and 1891. Burgess published a preliminary report on the finds, and later, the volume which he intended to be complementary to Fergusson's book. The area surrounding the site was examined by Alexander Rea in 1888-9, and again in 1905-6 and 1908-9. Some of the finds were sent to Madras; a large and important group remains in the sculpture shed at Amarâvatî. Finally, in 1942, Sivaramamurti published his great catalogue of the Madras collection.

The most important of the other early Buddhist sites, in which the Andhradeœa is so rich, may be mentioned. Jaggayyapeta was explored by Burgess in 1882; Bhattiprolu, *Gudivâda and Ghantaúâla* by Rea in 1892; *Goli* by Jouveau-Dubreuil in 1926; *Alluru and Gummadidurru* by Kuraishi in 1926-7; and *Nâgârjunikonda*, the richest site of all, by Longhurst in 1927-31, and again by Ramachandran in 1938.

THE FORM OF THE STÛPA

The form of the Great Stûpa at Amarâvatî, called in the inscriptions 'the Mahâcaitya, or Great Caitya, of the Buddha, belonging to the Caityika sect', has exercised scholars since Mackenzie made his discovery. It will be obvious from the history of the site that the reconstruction of the Stûpa is no easy matter. Mackenzie had to be content to watch the demolition of what was probably no more than a great mound of earth and brick. We now know that he missed surprisingly little, especially as he did not know what sort of monument to expect. Nevertheless, it was possible for Fergusson, himself a student of architecture, to speculate in 1868 that the monument consisted of two sculptured stone rails surrounding a complex of wooden buildings and a small stûpa thirty feet in diameter. Sewell, from his own observations and a careful study of Mackenzie's papers, was the first to point out that the two rails surrounded a vast, solid dome some one hundred and forty-eight feet in diameter. Later he, Elliot and Franks agreed that the inner 'rail' was, in fact, the decoration of the drum of the dome.

This was accepted by Burgess in 1910; he had formerly been a partisan of Fergusson's theory, but had now had the opportunity to study other stûpas in the Andhradeúa, which had received less violent treatment. The manner in which the dome itself was decorated seemed to be the one remaining problem. An answer, which had already been indicated by Fergusson, was given by the French savant Jouveau-Dubreuil in 1932, and later accepted by Sivaramamurti, Ramachandran and Gravely. However, in 1942, Brown produced a reconstruction of the Stûpa which, apart from the rail, differed entireiy from that of Jouveau-Dubreuil. Since Brown's solution seems to have been accepted by the two most recent writers on the subject, it is necessary to argue the question again in detail.

Though there are small problems which even now admit of no definite solution, there is little doubt that the general plan of the Stûpa and its decoration can be established. Evidence for the reconstruction of the Stûpa comes from three sources; the reports of those who saw the site before its complete destruction, the remains of several other stûpas in the Andhradeúa which have been more carefully dug, and the representations of the Stûpa which are found on many of the sculptured slabs which have survived. Of the reports, Mackenzie's and Sewell's are the most valuable; Elliot published nothing and Burgess arrived too late. The remains of similar stûpas prove most useful in the reconstruction of the dome, for no one, not even Mackenzie, saw how it was decorated. The slabs representing the Stûpa should provide the best evidence for its original appearance. The interpretations of the sculptor's intention are however various. The questions to be answered are: firstly, from what position, in his mind's eye, did the sculptor view the Stûpa, and consequently what are the true proportions of the separate parts of the structure; and secondly, did the sculptor show the decoration of the Stûpa as it actually was, or did he indulge his craftsmanship and knowledge of Buddhist legend to depict an 'ideal' stûpa.

It will be best to deal first with the stone rail, called vetikâ in the inscriptions, about the dimensions and form of which there is least controversy, and then to discuss the Stâpa it encircled. The rail is the most elaborate and richly decorated of any that surrounded a Buddhist stûpa, and more of it has survived than of any other part of the monument, since it was covered, and so protected, by the debris thrown down from the central mound. It measured one hundred and ninety-two feet in diameter and was pierced by gates at the four cardinal points of the compass. It consisted of upright pillars, some nine feet high and two feet ten inches wide, with long, roughly worked stumps set in a foundation of brick and mortar. Between each pair of uprights were three circular cross-bars, about two feet nine inches in diameter, from which projected tenons, lenticular in section, which were let into corresponding mortises cut into the edges of the uprights.

The whole was crowned by a coping, about two feet eight inches high and a foot thick, rounded at the top and fixed by tenon and mortise to the pillars. At each of the four cardinal points the arms of the rail, leaving an opening of twenty-six feet, turned out radially for a distance of sixteen feet, then, having turned inwards at right-angles for a distance of six and a half feet, projected, again at right-angles, a further eight feet. The complete rail would have required about eight hundred feet of coping resting on one hundred and thirty-six pillars and three hundred and forty-eight cross-bars.

The coping, called the unisa in the inscriptions, was in sections of varying length, the largest being about eleven feet. It was carved on both faces throughout. The decoration of the outer face consisted of a continuous garland carried on the shoulders of young men, sometimes accompanied by women. The loops of the garland were filled with various motifs, the most common being the Tree, the Wheel, and the Stûpa, symbolizing the Enlightenment, First Sermon and Death of the Buddha. At the ends of the quadrants the garland is shown as drawn from the mouths of dwarfs (*ganas*) or grotesque monsters, half-animal and half-fish (makaras).

The inner face was reserved for scenes from the life of the Buddha and from the stories of his previous existences (*Jâtakas*). Thus as the devout circumambulated the

Stûpa within the rail, the texts of their faith were unfolded in stone. Fragments of two other types of coping have survived. They are smaller than the main coping, being about twenty-three to twenty-six inches high. The first type is also decorated with a continuous garland, drawn from the mouths of dwarfs and monsters. The garland is however carried by dwarfs and the loops are filled with half-lotuses.

Moreover, one face of the coping is left plain. The second type, rather smaller than the first, has generally been accepted as forming the outer decoration of the plinth of the rail. Whatever the use to which it might subsequently have been put, it was certainly in the first instance a coping. Most of the pieces have been split vertically, but a complete piece in the Museum14 shows not only mortise holes, but a bevelled edge to the plain face, for this type too is carved on one face only. The sculptured face depicts young men fighting or taming bulls, elephants and winged animals. The fragments of these two types of coping were found almost exclusively in the north-west quadrant of the rail, a few in the south-west quadrant. It is evident that the unsculptured face almost certainly faced outwards, thus adhering to the principle that the inner surface was the more important. It is interesting to note that on the slabs representing the Stûpa, the sculptor usually employs on the coping two motifs: men carrying the garland, and men fighting animals; dwarfs carrying the garland are found but rarely. The men fighting animals motif has, however, little in common with the coping just described except the subject.

The decoration of the pillars, sometimes called *pendaka* in the inscriptions, consisted of a full and two half-lotuses separated by three wide and shallow flutes. Some of the freest pieces have the whole surface gently curved. Though there is infinite variety in the detail - it is here that the sculptor lavished all his skill as a decorator - the principle of design is fairly uniform. On the outer face the flutes above the full lotus usually show men and women adoring a Tree, Wheel or Stûpa, while those below depict dancing dwarfs. The inner face is again much more elaborate. The centre lotus, the flutes and sometimes the half-lotuses are given over to Jâtakas and the main events of the Buddha's life, complementary to the inner face of the coping.

One type of pillar - the simplest - is smaller than the main series, a little over eight feet high and two feet six inches or less wide. The flutes are plain, there are no figure subjects, and the decoration is on one face only. This type is again largely found in the north-west quadrant, closely associated with the two simpler varieties of coping. Fortunately, Sewell found fragments of three of these pillars *in situ*; few important pieces were so discovered. Here again the unsculptured side faced outward. The inner face of the pillars was plain for six inches above the foundations, thus gaining a little extra height.

The cross-bars, called *sûci* in the inscriptions, were carved on both faces with full lotuses, except for the inner face of the middle piece. This contained some great event from Buddhist legend. These magnificent *tondi* are perhaps the most satisfying, as they are the most ambitious, of the sculptor's achievements. There is also a less elaborate form of the cross-bar, an example of which Sewell found in position between two of the pillars already mentioned. It was two feet four inches or less in diameter, with one face plain but curved, following the line of the lenticular mortise. The plain side faced outward. This type seems also to be concentrated in the southwest and north-west quadrants, with a larger group in the latter. It seems then that the simpler varieties of coping, pillar and cross-bar were brought into the scheme of the rail with pieces of larger dimension and greater elaboration. This lack of uniformity seemed perhaps no more incongruous to the 'Officer of Works' of the Stûpa than to his medieval counterpart in Europe. In his representations of the Stûpa the sculptor seems to have indulged his imagination. He depicts four cross-bars, separated by a narrow pillar decorated with two full and two half-lotuses.

The gates may be reconstructed from Mackenzie's plan, which is supported by Burgess' discovery of the outline of the brick foundations which secured the pillars at the south gate. It would not however have been possible to infer the double vestibule from the sculptor's representations of the Stûpa. At the gates the coping was crowned with four seated lions, two facing each other across the wider opening and two facing outward at the final projections of the rail. The coping stopped short before it reached the ends of the projecting arms, thus leaving room for a platform for the lions, which was supported by slender, round columns. Since the ground level outside the rail was three to five feet below that within, a semicircular stone threshold and steps decorated with flutes and lotuses were provided. The foundations of the rail seem to have been buttressed on the outer side by another plain, granite rail.

Within the rail lay the processional path (*pradakshinâpatha*) thirteen feet wide and paved with slabs of a grey limestone, which was also used at Nâgârjunikonda for plain work, such as the facing of walls. Pillars, usually topped by a small stûpa or wheel, were erected in the path, though it was presumably left fairly clear. Burgess found at various points portions of a circle of brickwork, one hundred and sixty-two feet seven inches in diameter, which had supported what used to be called 'the inner rail'. The south-east quadrant of this circle was almost complete in Mackenzie's day, and in the earlier of his two plans he shows a band of masonry four feet wide against which stones were placed. He describes them thus: 'The slabs composing the inner circle are remarkable for the beauty of the sculptures upon them, which are small, and consist of figures, festoons, and a variety of ornaments very neatly executed.

On the side are pillars, which are finished either with figures of lions and horses, or of men and women; and over the top is an entablature replete with figures in various acts of devotion or amusement. These inner slabs have been cemented to each other with strong mortar, and supported by a wall of masonry rising to a moderate height in the rear; the adjustment has been very happily executed. Some of these slabs are six inches in thickness, and others nearly nine inches, their shape is chiefly rectangular.' Though most of the slabs representing the Stûpa are in the Museum, the finest is in Madras. It shows, cut from one slab of stone, the Stûpa, flanked on each side by a narrow upright, and crowned by a frieze. Mackenzie's description of the side 'pillars' and 'entablature' will immediately be recognized. Also, in his drawings, these three types of slab are frequently noted as coming from 'the inner circle'. Moreover, where this type of slab is found *in situ* at other stûpas in the Andhradesa, it always decorated the base or drum of the stûpa. Brown objects that these slabs are never so represented on the reproductions of the Stûpa. This is not so.

The tops of such slabs may be seen above the rail coping on several fragments in the Museum. In any case, we have already learned not to interpret the sculptor's statements too literally. The Madras slab stood about six feet above the processional path, so the detail of the frieze could be 'read' at eye level. This, called 'moderate' by Mackenzie, may be taken to be the height of the drum of the Stûpa. Roughly the same height of drum is found on other stûpas in the Andhradesa which have survived. Brown prefers a height of twenty feet. There is no evidence for this. Brown errs because he has not appreciated that in representing the Stûpa the sculptor took up an 'ideal' position from which he could show as much of the Stûpa as possible. He thus looked down into the space between the Stûpa and the rail, making the frieze of the drum, which is clearly represented though larger than life, to appear higher than the coping of the rail. Once this is accepted everything falls into place.

The drum of the Stûpa then was one hundred and sixty-two feet seven inches in diameter and about six feet in height. Against the four foot thick supporting wall were placed the slabs already mentioned. These show considerable variety in detail. Many types of stûpa are represented, more or less ornate. The narrow uprights which separate them are also various; the most frequent subjects are the wheel-crowned pillar above the empty throne of the Buddha, and the Four Great Miracles. Upwards of a hundred of the large slabs would be required to face the drum. They were probably interspersed with other slabs roughly the same size. A slab was said to have been erected at the foot of the Stûpa. The frieze, also called *unisa* in the inscriptions, was like the inner face of the rail, designed to edify, and the Jâtakas and Events of the Buddha's life here predominate. The pieces differ in detail, chiefly in the way the scenes are divided, whether by a pilaster or by three or four small lotus roundels set vertically. There are also several types of smaller frieze. Some belong to a different type of drum slab. Others belong almost certainly to small stûpas set outside the rail, especially those to the north of the West Gate, where a number of small friezes were found.

At the four cardinal points and facing the gates were projections to the drum about thirty-two feet long and six feet wide. On these projecting platforms stood five pillars, about ten to fourteen feet in height, which had rectangular bases, some four feet in height, and octagonal shafts. The drum slabs show them as crowned with four small arched windows, often with a model of a stûpa on the centre pillar. The crowns of complete pillars found at Nâgârjunikonda, however, are slightly domed, having gores or facets which follow the eight sides. On the drum slabs the bases of the pillars are shown decorated with Tree, Wheel, Stûpa, Wheel, Tree or with five stûpas or five standing Buddhas. These five pillars, peculiar to the stûpas of the Andhradesa, are called *âyaka* or *âyaka-khamba*, a term whose significance is as obscure as the function of the objects it describes.

It is not possible to say whether any emphasis was given to the *âyaka*-platforms at Amarâvatî by special treatment or subjects on the drum slabs. For Brown the *âyaka*-platforms were twenty feet in height, enclosed a staircase leading to the 'upper processional path', and on the exterior were elaborated into a recessed shrine or altarpiece. It is sufficient to say that there is no evidence for such a feature in any stûpa in the Andhradeúa, nor do the representations of the Stûpa allow one to infer it. Brown does not indicate what slabs, in two registers each presumably ten feet high, decorated his drum.

We must return again to Mackenzie's first plan. On it, in the south-west quadrant, is shown a band of masonry eight feet thick and forty feet long, standing twelve feet within the circle ot the drum and concentric with it. Mackenzie observes: 'On the south side, within the circles, a strong work of masonry is discernible, which may probably be the remains of an interior wall, as the people of the village informed me that a similar work had been observed all round, which has since been cleared away in removing the earth.' There can be little doubt that it was this eight foot wall which supported the dome itself. This feature is found in many stûpas in the Andhradesa, for example, at Nâgârjunikonda, Alluru, and Ghantasâla. The wall is frequently strengthened by radial walls, often laid, as at Nâgârjunikonda and Ghantasâla, in an elaborate wheel pattern, which may have had some symbolic intention. Whether this was the case at Amarâvatî, there is no means of knowing.

The stûpa at Bhattiprolu, almost as large as that at Amarâvatî, seems to have been constructed of solid brickwork. We may believe that the Amarâvatî Stûpa, the largest and most elaborate in the Andhradesa, was of similar internal construction to that at Ghantasâla, the spaces between the system of walls being filled with earth or alternate layers of earth and concrete. The dome of the Stûpa was then one hundred and thirty-eight feet in diameter, resting on a drum, whose diameter was an additional twenty-four feet. There is no indication that the top of the drum, which formed a platform twelve feet wide, was ever used as a processional path, or, indeed, that it was the vestigial remains of such a path. It was probably used for offerings, possibly for free-standing sculptures, and certainly as a gutter during the rains.

The height and shape of the dome must be inferred, since this feature has survived, and that but fragmentarily, in only one stûpa in the Andhradesa. At Bhattiprolu, Rea found five foot six inches of the dome still standing. It showed a batter of one foot two inches, so the height of the dome would probably have been less than half its diameter, say sixty feet. The height of the Amarâvatî dome may have been roughly the same. Its shape however was probably quite different from that of the Bhattiprolu stûpa. Here again Mackenzie is helpful. He says: 'The upper part (of the mound) rose in a turreted shape to a height of 20 feet, which was cased round with bricks of unusual dimensions; the diameter at top measured 30 yards.' When Mackenzie first visited Amarâvatî in 1797 he found that the Zemindar's men had cut a trench into the drum platform between the wall supporting the drum slabs and that supporting the dome. He notes: 'It is probable that this body of masonry did not extend to a greater depth.' The dome wall then rose vertically to a height of twenty feet, or roughly fourteen feet above the drum.

Some of the elaborate drum slabs show this vertical spring of the dome quite clearly. Practically all show it cased with large sculptured slabs surmounted by two friezes, the lower of running animals and the upper of *trisûlas*. If the sculptor has rendered the relative heights of the friezes and the *âyaka*-pillars correctly, the former stood rather less than twelve feet above the drum level. At Nâgârjunikonda the slabs which decorated the spring of the dome are divided horizontally into three fields with a pilaster down the right-hand side and the same two friezes at the top. Their general design is that of many slabs found at Amarâvatî, which show in three registers the Tree (occasionally the Buddha), the Wheel and the Stûpa, and at the top narrow friezes of running animals and of the trident device (*trisûlas*). The observant Mackenzie notes: 'A great many slabs, of a large size, are seen lying on the surface of the reservoir, but it is difficult to say where they were originally placed.

On these are chiefly represented a few large figures of men and women, in divisions of two or three, one above another, each three feet high.' Now the height of these slabs, usually called *udhapata* in the inscriptions, is about ten feet six inches, thus casing most of the fourteen foot vertical section of the dome. There is another type of slab divided horizontally into three fields. Though no piece has survived entire, the Mackenzie drawings include one almost complete. This type seems to have been about eleven feet high. The base of the slabs is always carved with a rail pattern, above which is frequently represented a Cakravarti or Universal Monarch, and the scene of the First Sermon.

One piece in the Museum shows the Cakravarti above adoring Nâgas. The piece drawn by Mackenzie's draughtsmen shows the Departure, the Enlightenment and - an unusual theme - Asoka's attempt to open the Râmagrâma stûpa. It is here suggested that these pieces formed the decoration of the dome behind the *âyaka*-pillars, their greater scale giving emphasis and dignity to that part of the structure. The small difference in height as between the two types of slab is not likely to have disturbed the mason. In his reconstruction, Brown retains the large slabs shown on the representations of the Stûpa. He does not indicate by which of the surviving fragments they are represented. It may be added that slabs in three registers are not shown on the drum slabs at Nâgârjunikonda, yet it is known that they were used there, and on the dome of the stûpas.

Above the dome slabs began the curve of the dome. At the summit of the dome stood the *harmikâ*, which consisted of a rail, similar in construction to the great rail, forming a square with sides some twenty-four feet long. From the centre of the *harmikâ* projected an octagonal pillar sturdier than an *âyaka*-pillar but of the same form; it was probably set deep in the body of the dome. Small pillars, to which were attached streamers and stone umbrellas, were also erected. The curve of the dome was plastered. It was decorated with friezes of lotus-filled vases (*punnaghatas*), dwarfs carrying the garland, and intricate swags and garlands framing elaborate roundels. All this work was in stucco, and must have been of fine quality, but next to nothing has survived. It was probably painted and gilded, and must have made a splendid show against the dazzling whiteness of the plastered dome.

Nothing is known of the position of the relic-chamber in the Stûpa. A stone box and crystal casket, now in Madras, is said to have been obtained by Elliot from the successors of the Zemindar who first dug the mound. They may well have come from the Stûpa. There remains to be mentioned a type of slab which was carved with the footprints of the Buddha (*Buddhapâda*). This type was found almost exclusively at the east and west gates, and may have been set in the processional path.

In the precincts of the Stûpa stood numerous small stûpas of brick. Some probably resembled the simpler examples on the drum slabs. Others were richly decorated. Indeed, size had little to do with elaboration; the Mahâchaitya at Nâgârjunikonda was severely plain. The monastic buildings which must have surrounded the Stûpa have not yet been investigated. The pillared hall (*mandapam*) of such an establishment would have been raised on columns similar to many pieces in the Museum.

THE DATE AND STYLE OF THE SCULPTURES

Hitherto all accounts of the development of the style of the Amarâvatî sculptures have reflected with minor variations what has here been called the long chronology. While there is general agreement that the mature style covered the 2nd, and first half of the 3rd centuries A.D., developing consistently in the 3rd century A.D. at Nâgârjunikonda and other sites in the Andhradesa, a number of pieces, though not always the same ones, are generally relegated to the 2nd or early 1st century B.C. This large gap is an embarrassment to those who hold that from their rise to power in the late 3rd century B.C. the Sâtavâhanas were in continuous possession of the Andhradesa.

The implications of the short chronology will be obvious. It will be possible to argue that before the 1st century A.D. there was neither the social organization nor the economic wealth to erect a series of monuments in the Andhradesa. It is not even certain that its inhabitants professed the Buddhist religion. Again, the dating of the 'early' Amarâvatî style is largely based on comparison with that of other monuments, especially the cavetemples of the north-west Deccan and the stûpas of North India. The dating of many of the latter, however, may have to be reconsidered in the light of the short chronology.

Since it is the 'early' period which provides the difficulties, it will be best to work from fairly secure to less certain ground, and to deal first with the mature Amarâvatî style, as generally accepted, which is reflected in most of the sculptures which have survived. Once the main constructional work was completed, the erection of the rail and the decoration of the Stûpa - the drum and the dome - were probably carried forward contemporaneously; the speed of the work being conditioned only by the number of masons and amount of money available. The changes in style as the work proceeded are best seen in the rail, especially in its pillars, which fall easily into the following formal series.

1. The simplest type, of which there are two examples in the Museum, is carved on the inner face only. It is smaller than the general run - about eight feet high and two feet six inches wide - and is found almost exclusively in the north-west quadrant of the rail. The narrow friezes at top and bottom and the bands which surround the lotuses are filled either with a geometrical ornament or with a *makara* vomiting a regularly curving flowered scroll. The lotuses are formed of three rows of petals. The corners of the fluted areas, which are otherwise left plain, are filled with lotus buds.

2. This type is generally similar to the preceding, but is larger - about two feet ten inches wide and probably up to nine feet high. Again most pieces were found in the north-west quadrant. A piece in the Museum differs from all other pillars in

that the corners of the fluted area are filled not with lotus buds, but with small jars of lotuses.

3. This type is sculptured on both faces. Into the fluted area, which is otherwise left plain, is introduced the peculiar foliate-wave motif, which on a Museum piece appears on one face only. There is a greater complexity in the scrolls. The lotuses are formed of four rows of petals and the surrounding band is usually filled with scrolls vomited by addorsed *makaras*.

4. Here the fluted areas of the outer face are left plain, except for the foliate-waves. The flutes of the inner face are filled with figure subjects. The Museum piece shows the Elevation of the Headdress and Bowl of the Buddha. The lotuses are formed of four or five rows of petals, the centre row or rows being occasionally incurved.

5. This may be called the fully developed type. The outer face has at the top a frieze of elephants or winged animals adoring the Stûpa, and at the base an elaborate scroll vomited by *makaras*. The upper fluted area is usually filled with men and women adoring the Tree, Wheel, Stûpa or Nâga, the lower with foliate-waves and dwarfs, dancing or making music. The centre lotus occasionally bears a triple-bodied beaked lion. On the inner face, the centre lotus, in addition to the fluted areas, is now filled with a scene, thus illustrating either three separate stories or episodes of the same story. Occasionally even the centre of the top half-lotus is so filled. The decoration at once highly naturalistic and disciplined within its strictly curving scrolls, represents the high-water mark of imaginative ornament at Amarâvatî, indeed in India.

6. The general design of the previous type remains; the style undergoes an important change. Though the friezes, especially at the base of the pillars, retain their interest, the beautifully controlled scrolls lose definition, and may, in a series of Museum pieces, be seen to disintegrate into a shallow-cut, *mouvementé* surface. This manner leads towards the even coarser decorative carving of Nâgârjunikonda. Indeed, the latest in the Museum series shows on its outer face the 'rosette and leaf' ornament ubiquitous at Nâgârjunikonda.

Though there is a real decline in decorative carving, the treatment and composition of the human figures show a remarkable development. There is in the previous style, even in violent subjects, a quality of stillness, of dignity, which we call classical. Now the figures, elongated into a spidery elegance, are stirred by an agitated and nervous movement. The sophistication and sensuous *morbidezza* of Amarâvatî culminated in the hurried cutting and violent diagonals of Nâgârjunikonda design, a style coarser but no less impressive. The latest pillar in the Museum stands at the very beginning of the

Nâgârjunikonda style. It would not perhaps be entirely without meaning to apply here the categories into which the history of European art is made to fall, and to speak of archaic, classical and mannerist phases at Amarâvatî and baroque at Nîgîrjunikonda.

The cross-bars of the rail show a similar development.

1. This type is small - about two feet four inches in diameter - and is carved on the inner face only with a lotus with three rows of petals. It is almost exclusively confreed to the north-west quadrant.

2. This type is similar to the preceding, but is carved with a lotus on both faces, which is often surrounded by a scrolled band. There is no example in the Museum, but a number was found by Burgess in the south-west quadrant.

3. This again is the fully developed type. It is roughly two feet nine inches in diameter, and is carved on both faces with lotuses or, if it occupied the middle position, with a figure subject on the inner face. The lotuses have up to five rows of petals, often surrounded by a scrolled band. The most beautiful use of the lotus is when the centre one or two rows of petals are incurved. Here is found the same treatment and composition of the scrolls and the human figure as in the fully developed type of pillar.

4. The general design of the cross-bar remains the same, but the scrolls show the same deterioration and the style the same development as in the last type of pillar. The band surrounding a lotus roundel in the Museum nicely illustrates the moment at which the regular scrolls began to disintegrate. Another, drawn by one of Mackenzie's draughtsmen, shows the 'rosette and leaf' ornament of Nâgârjunikonda. The latest piece in the Museum again foreshadows the Nâgârjunikonda style.

For convenience the following terms will now be used to describe the mature Amarâvatî style. Pieces which exhibit the characteristics of style of pillar types 1-4 or cross-bar types 1-2 will be considered as belonging to the Early Phase; those of pillar type 5 or cross-bar type 3 as belonging to the Middle Phase; and those of pillar type 6 or cross-bar type 4 as belonging to the Late Phase.

At first sight the coping does not seem to show such a neat progression as the other members of the rail. Having established that two groups at least share the characteristics of the Middle and Late Phases, it will be best to fix some absolute dates before discussing the two remaining types. The Middle Phase is represented by numerous fragments the Late Phase by relatively few. One fragment stands at the beginning, another at the end, of the Late Phase.

There are two historical inscriptions on the fragments of the Stûpa. The first mentions the gift of a 'Wheel of the Law' at the west gate of the Great Stûpa in an unspecified year of the king, Srî Pulumâvi, who has here been dated about A.D. 130 to 159. Unfortunately, none of the sculptured surface of this wheel-crowned pillar has survived, but the inscription does make it clear that by this period the Stûpa and at least the west gate of the rail were already standing. It does not of course follow that the decoration of the Stûpa was already complete.

The second inscription is the most important front the site. It mentions the gift of an official of King Siri Sivamaka Sada, who has been here identified with Úivaskanda Sâtakarni and dated about A.D. 167 to 174. This inscription is carved on a fragment of the rail-coping which belongs to what is here called the Middle Phase. This phase of the mature style was then already established in the third quarter of the 2nd century A.D. As has already been indicated, the Late Phase in its final development comes very close in decorative and figure carving to the style of Nâgârjunikonda.

Unfortunately the stûpas at Nâgârjunikonda which are fairly securely dated, i.e., the Mahâcaitya and possibly stûpa 5, are plain; while those which are richly decorated - 2, 3, 6 and 9 - are undated. However, the inscriptions show that the great period of building activity was during the reigns of Mâtharîputra Vîrapurushadatta and, to a lesser extent, of his successor Ehuvula Sântamûla II. Vîrapurushadatta's reign occupies roughly the third quarter of the 3rd century A.D., and this or a little earlier may reasonably be accepted as the date of the decorated stûpas. It is therefore assumed that at Amarâvatî creative work on any scale did not long survive the fall of the Sâtavâhanas. Indeed, so closely is the Nâgârjunikonda style related to the latest work at Amarâvatî, that it is possible that the masons themselves moved to the capital of the succeeding dynasty, the Ikshvâkus. The transition from the Middle to the Late Phase may be placed about the end of the 2nd century A.D.

To determine the beginning of the mature style it is necessary to go to the northwest Deccan. At Nâsik, on the end walls of the verandah of Cave III, the famous Gautamîputra Cave, are carved pilasters identical in general design, though simpler in detail, with Types 1 and 2 of the pillars at Amarâvatî. Also on the frieze above the verandah is a representation in little of an Amarâvatî rail, with similar pillars, three lotus cross-bars and a coping of looped garlands without supporters. The exact date of the Gautamîputra Cave is a vexed question, but it was certainly dedicated by Queen Balasrî in the nineteenth year of her grandson, Srî Pulumâvi, which according to the chronology adopted here is about A.D. 149.

Whether the more elaborate detail of the Amarâvatî pillars makes them later than the Nâsik pilasters, it is difficult to say, for there are no other examples in the north-west Deccan. That a progression from simple to more elaborate represents a chronological sequence is a dangerous principle, except where there is a large body of material and that from the same locality. Nor is it possible to say whether this type of pillar was a creation of the Amarâvatî sculptor - it was certainly brought to a higher pitch of elaboration in the Andhradesa than elsewhere in India - or adopted by him in its simplest form from the north-west Deccan. It is however possible to say that the Nâsik pilasters and Types 1 and 2 of the Amarâvatî pillars are roughly contemporary, and that the latter may be dated to the second quarter of the 2nd century A.D.

This is the period when the Andhradesa became a part of the Sâtavâhana empire, and we may believe that this was, if not the cause of, at least an important factor in the tremendous outburst of creative activity which filled the Andhradesa with religious monuments. Four generations, roughly from A.D. 125 to A.D. 240, seem quite sufficient to cover the development of the style of those parts of the rail already discussed, once it is appreciated how closely the several manners tread upon each other's heels. Indeed, the decorative elements of one are so closely interwoven with those of the rest, that it would be possible to accept the types leading up to the Middle Phase as contemporary products of different workshops. Though the formal series made here does seem to have a chronological validity, there can be little doubt that the inception, growth and flowering of the mature style was, as often in periods of great creative energy, of brief duration.

We may now return to the remaining fragments of the rail and the rest of the Stûpa and see how they fit into this chronological scheme. The fragments of coping which show the garland supported by dwarfs have been variously dated; as early as 2000 to 100 B.C. and as late as A.D. 200. They are about two feet two inches high and are carved on one side only. Bachhofer has compared the frieze of connected flower disks drawn from the mouths of *makaras* at the bottom of some of the fragments with identical ornament on pillars of Type 2. On certain fragments this ornament is replaced by the square rosette common in all phases of the mature style. The type of lotus is that found on the cross-bars of Type 1. The 'early' appearance of these pieces is due simply to their shallow cutting; otherwise the style is assured. They are found, as has already been indicated, exclusively in the south-west and north-west quadrants, mostly in the latter, closely associated with pillars and cross-bars of Type I. It is difficult to avoid the conclusion that they belong together, forming one unit plain on the outer face, and were an integral part of the rail in its final form. This type of coping may therefore be dated to the second quarter of the 2nd century A.D.

Finally, there is the coping with young men and animals. This type is about two feet high and is again plain on one face. There has been general agreement that it dates before 50 B.C. The frieze at the top of the slabs is filled with a scroll vomited by a dwarf; in its even curves are birds and carefully observed flowers and foliage. The treatment may be compared with that on a pillar in the Museum, which also shares with the coping the egg and dart ornament and the strange semi-circular and oval forms which protrude into the field of the main design.

The style of the decorative carving on the pillar and the coping is that of Type 2 of the rail pillars. Now, Sivaramamurti considered the men and animals coping and the dwarf coping to be contemporary, and when the style of the figures on the former is compared with those on the latter, and both with the dwarf on the pillar, there can be little doubt that this is so. These two types of coping, then, represent the figure carving, as the rail pillars of Types 1 to 3 represent the decorative carving, of the Early Phase of the mature style. The fragments of the men and animals coping are again found in the north-west and south-west quadrants and may have formed a part of the rail in its final form. The shallow cutting and clearly outlined forms of the Early Phase may be seen on several free pieces in the Museum.

The slabs which cased the dome present few problems. They consist of two friezes, of *trisûlas* and running animals, above three panels framing a Stûpa, Wheel and Tree. The decorative elements found on the narrow horizontal friezes which divide the panels belong to the Early and Middle Phases; the figures represent the style of the latter. On a few pieces the scene of the Enlightenment is represented by the Buddha seated under the Tree.

It has here been suggested that the slightly larger slabs, in three registers, also cased the dome behind the *aûyaka*-platforms. The lower group is always shown as standing on a rail, which is a replica of the outer face of what has here been called the early rail, that is, with plain coping and cross-bars and early pillars. The style is of the Middle Phase, and is particularly interesting because the Amarâvatî sculptor is seen so rarely working on this more monumental scale. A frieze of seated Buddha figures appears on one piece and a standing Buddha figure appeared in Mackenzie's day on a slab now in the Museum.

On the surviving fragments two types of stûpa are represented. The first, which has neither rail nor *ayaka*-platform, will be dealt with later. The second, which is found on the slabs which cased the drum, is similar in construction to the Amarâvatî Stûpa itself. It is shown in various forms, and with increasing degrees of elaboration. The simplest has an undecorated dome, except for a stucco collar, a rail pattern for the drum frieze, and the drum left plain, except for the coiled Nâga on the *âyaka*-platform. The cross-bars of the rail are of a type which seems not to have survived. The stûpa is usually flanked by dwarfs and young men.

The second form has the usual type of rail, a more elaborate dome collar and drum frieze, and the drum itself decorated with pilasters at intervals. The third form is similar to the second but with carved slabs on the curve of the dome. In the final form the drum also is cased with carved slabs. It is commonly said that the most elaborate forms of drum slab are rather later in date than the rail. If the stylistic sequence proposed here is accepted, it would be more accurate to say that the most elaborate slabs are contemporary with the last phase of the rail, giving an excellent impression, though by no means accurate in detail, of the Stûpa in its final grandeur in the years immediately following A.D. 200.

The third form may also be considered to belong to the Late Phase. An example of the second form, on a drum slab in three registers, has a flowered scroll which although late still retains the regularity and careful cutting of the Middle Phase. Another example is carved on the back of a Type 2 rail pillar. Of two slabs of this type drawn by Mackenzie's draughtsmen, one however seems to belong to the Late Phase, while the Buddha Image appears on the other. We may assume that the second form belongs to the end of the Middle and beginning of the Late Phases. The first form, judging from the style of the figures which flank the Stûpa, belongs to the Middle Phase. It has been already suggested that other types of slab were interspersed with the representations of the Stûpa; certain of them were perhaps used to give emphasis to the *âyaka*-platforms. They belong to the Middle Phase.

Several of the many types of pilaster which divided the drum slabs are here illustrated. They are contemporary with the most ornate drum slabs, those which show the Four Great Miracles being somewhat later than those carved with the Wheel above the empty Throne; the former come very close to the Nâgârjunikonda style. One important type of spacer, which shows a woman standing under a *torana*, has unfortunately not survived.

The drum friezes also are contemporary with the latest drum slabs. The examples in which the scenes are divided by pilasters come, however, at the very end of the Amarâvatî style. It is interesting to note that on the narrow moulding above the row of lion protomes, appears the young men and animals motif rendered with detail and vivacity on a miniature scale.

So far we have been dealing with the mature Amarâvatî style and with pieces which are generally accepted as belonging to it, though not perhaps as showing the progression of style as suggested here. The only candidates for an early, that is a 2nd or early 1st century B.C. dating, have been the two forms of rail-coping which are plain on one face. The remainder of the 'early' fragments may now be examined.

In discussing the drum slabs, it has been shown that generally only the most ornate show the drum of the Stûpa fully cased with sculptured slabs; on the simpler versions the drum is usually decorated with pilasters at intervals, the *âyaka*-platforms alone being fully carved. This latter method, of decorating the *âyaka*-platforms only, persisted to the end of the style, and is found in the 3rd century A.D. and later at Nâgarjunikonda and Goli. Indeed, apart from Amarâvatî, it is not certain that the drums of any of the great stûpas were completely cased with sculptured slabs. Moreover, it seems probable that the drum of the Amarâvatî Stûpa itself was in the first instance decorated in the simpler manner; and that it was not until the Middle and Late Phases that the earlier slabs were replaced, or reversed and recarved with the representations of the Stûpa and the other scenes already mentioned. Perhaps the most important evidence for this is a slab in the Museum, which bears on its other face one of the finest and most elaborate representations of the Stupa.

It shows the Enlightenment of the Buddha - a Tree, under which is set the Throne and Footprints, with adoring figures and *kinnaras*, half-man, half-bird, bearing offerings. On the shaft of the pilaster is carved a female figure standing on a *makara*, and above the bell capital stand addorsed lions. It may safely be assumed that this piece faced an *âyaka*-platform. There are several other fragments in the same style at Madras and at the sculpture shed at Amarâvatî, though none seem to be palimpsests. There are also several examples of slabs left plain, except for a pilaster up one side; here the shaft of the pilaster is similar in design to the earliest type of rail pillar. The most famous of these is the free drum slab in Madras, on the back surface of which, according to Dr Benza, 'was sculptured a reversed column, the pedestal turned upwards, and the capital downwards.' The most important is the great slab, thirteen feet long, which was discovered by Sewell. It is divided by two pilasters into three plain panels. There are also fragments of similar slabs crowned by a frieze, which consists of scenes of the adoration of the Tree, Wheel and Stûpa, separated by a rail pattern. Separate friezes of identical form are also found.

It is often assumed that these slabs and friezes decorated the Stûpa, when its form was different from, and its dimensions smaller than, the Great Stûpa, as we know it. That there can be no evidence for this will be obvious from the history of the discovery of the site. That it was not so is supported by the fact that the stûpa at Bhattiprolu, though but little smaller than the Amarâvatî Stûpa, retained its original simple decoration in 'early' style, and may therefore be considered to have retained also its original dimensions and form. This does not of course prevent certain of the 'early' slabs from having cased other stûpas at Amarâvatî. Now there was another type or stûpa in the Andhradeúa. It is small, and may be rock-cut or structural, and simply of elaborately decorated. Its proportions are frequently different from those of the Great Stûpa and it had no *âyaka*-platforms. It is commonly found in the northwest Deccan, but there is no evidence that in the Andhradeœa it preceded the other form; they seem to have existed alongside each other into the 3rd century A.D.

This second type of stûpa is frequently represented on the fragments. There are two good examples in the Museum. The first, a drum slab, is of a fairly common type, which by comparison with similar slabs with figures may be dated to the Middle Phase. The second is presumably earlier than the companion piece. A close parallel is the stûpa on a *caitya-khamba* set up at the southern gate of the Stûpa 69. On the left edge of the Museum's slab is cut part of a circular pavilion almost identical with another face of the same *caitya-khamba*. Sivaramamurti has accepted the date of the *caitya-khamba* as about A.D. 100. According to the chronology proposed here, it would belong to the Early Phase and would be some three or four decades later. This dating is perhaps supported by a comparison of the Museum's piece with the representation of a similar *stûpa* on the back of Gautamîputra's Cave at Nâsik, which has here been dated to the 2nd quarter of the 2nd century A.D.

It seems reasonable to place the Museum's slab with its more elaborate arrangement of the umbrellas, its dome collar, pilasters and representations of Tree, Nâga and Wheel, somewhat later than the Nâsik relief. If this is found acceptable, the Museum's slab will help to date the plain 'early' slabs, for the pilasters on both are, except for certain variations in detail, identical. Moreover, a separate frieze in the Museum, of exactly the same type as those which are carved in one piece with the plain slabs, is cut on a split and re-used pillar of the Early Phase, and is not therefore likely to be earlier than the very end of that Phase. Indeed, when these friezes are set beside other small friezes, which are generally accepted as belonging to the mature Amarâvatî style, and which are here attributed to the Middle Phase, there can be no doubt that they are separated by a small interval of time.

It may be asked whether the plain slabs with friezes and pilasters necessarily carry with them the sculptured slabs, on the pilasters of which at Amarâvatî at least, a female figure is carved. It is however acknowledged by every authority that the two form one stylistic group, and there seems to be no reason to separate them from each other, or from the early rail-copings. Unfortunately, though the Museum piece is the most complete example of the style, its surface has gone, and the sharpness of cutting and accurate delineation of forms now appear soft and uncertain. The true feel of the style is best obtained from the Madras fragments, where it appears young and vigorous, the confident beginning of the mature Amarâvatî style.

There are other sites in the Andhradesa which share this early style. The *stûpas* at Bhattiprolu and Garikapâd are not helpful to our enquiry, though sufficient has survived to make it certain that both were decorated in the simple manner and early style. The large *stûpa* at Ghantasâla is however important. It probably exhibited much the same development of style as Amarâvatî, for fragments of several phases have been discovered, including a plain slab with a pilaster up one edge. A fine piece from Ghantasâla in the Musée Guimet shows a three-storied building with adorers. The most important slab however is in the Museum of Fine Arts, Boston. It is carved on both faces. The palimpsest shows an elaborate *stûpa* similar to those on the late drum slabs at Amarâvatî. On the other face is the scene of the Buddha at the Nairanjanâ river; there is a fragmentary pilaster up the left-hand edge. Coomararswamy does not indicate the provenance, but when the figures on the original face are compared with those on the slab in the Musée Guimet, there can be no doubt that it came from Ghantaúâla. Coomaraswamy gave the original face a date not earlier than the Kushân period.

When it is placed alongside the slabs in the Museum which show the same scene, there can be little doubt that it either antedates a little the Middle Phase at Amarâvatî or was directly inspired by it to a somewhat harsher imitation. Finally there is the comparatively small stûpa at Jaggayyapeta. This *stûpa* also seems to have retained its early decoration, and it was not thought necessary to bring it up to date with the then prevailing style, when in the twentieth year of the Ikshvâku King Vîrapurushadatta (third quarter of the 3rd century A.D.), five *âyaka*-pillars were dedicated to the *stûpa*. The sculptured slabs reflect the Early Phase at Amarâvatî, but with a difference. Coomaraswamy has emphasized their assured beauty; they seem already to pre-figure the svelte forms and elegant mannerism of the Late Phase at Amarâvatî.

Such then is the history of the Amarâvatî style. The style which prevailed in the Andhradeœa during the 2nd and 3rd centuries A.D. has rightly been given the modern name of this ancient town, for no other site shows with such continuity and detail its inception and growth; and until we have evidence to the contrary, Amarâvatî may be considered the centre of original experiment and creation in the eastern Deccan, a position which she yielded to Nâgârjunikonda some time in the second quarter of the 3rd century A.D. To summarize our argument we may return to the great monument itself. Once the constructional work was completed, the masons commenced the decoration of the *âyaka*-platforms and the erection of the rail. The dome was plastered, but otherwise left plain except perhaps for a stucco collar, making its effect, as do the Sinhalese domes, by sheer bulk.

In the rail, the chief glory of the Stûpa, can be seen the swift transition from the Early to the Middle Phase as the work proceeded. The decoration of the drum in the simple manner must also have gone on into the Middle Phase. Towards the end of the Middle Phase, the spring of the dome was cased with the slabs in three registers, a task which may not have been completed until the beginning of the Late Phase. The Middle Phase also saw the beginning of the new decoration of the drum. The old slabs were replaced, or reversed and re-carved. Most of this work took place in the Late Phase; possibly it was never completed. Such in broad outline, if our analysis of style is correct, was the growth of the monument, the design of which, continually under revision, embodied the shifting aspirations and taste of little more than four generations of craftsmen.

It remains to enquire the source of the style. A deliberate attempt has here been made to explain its development, as far as possible, with reference only to itself. Stylistic comparison with the other early schools of Indian sculpture can be very misleading. We do not yet know enough to be able to distinguish the metropolitan centres from the provincial, or the primitive from the archaistic or the incompetent. At Amarâvatî, and in the Andhradesa generally, there is at least a large body of material, which, whatever is thought of the absolute chronology accepted here, seems to show within itself a swift and consistent development. The few external comparisons which have been suggested, have been made with the art of the northwest Deccan.

The reason is obvious. The beginning of the Amarâvatî style coincided with the period - the second quarter of the 2nd century A.D. — when, under Pulumâvi, the Andhradesa seems first to have been included in the Sâtavâhana empire. We may believe that it was this factor which gave tremendous impetus to that economic prosperity on which the vast building schemes of the Andhradeúa were undoubtedly founded. The economic, and, indeed, the religious background, if we knew in detail what it was, would however merely explain how the creation of the Amarâvatî Stûpa was made possible; they would not explain the source of the style.

If the latter lay in the north-west Deccan, the present state of our knowledge will not allow us to trace the stages by which it reached Amarâvatî, though paradoxically we can trace to some extent the influence of Amarâvatî, or rather actual examples of its sculpture, moving westwards. Also, the art of the north-west Deccan in the Sâtavâhana period is notable rather for the magnificence and originality of its rock-cut architecture, than for its sculpture, which is as meagre in quantity as it is unequal in quality. The sculptor of the north-west Deccan seems not to have been impelled either to illustrate the Life or *Jâtakas* of the Buddha, or to embellish his magnificent *caityas* and *vihâras* with the splendid decorative carving of the Andhradesa or north India.

The *caitya*-hall at Kârle, the finest monument of the period, contains a fair amount of sculpture. It is unequal in quality, but is very close, especially in the externals of style, such as headdress, ornaments and the treatment of drapery, to the Early Phase at Amarâvatî. The sculpture on the *caitya*-halls at Bedsâ and Kondâne is similar in style, less monumental perhaps, but more assured in the handling. Rightly has Yazdani remarked that the style of Amarâvatî evolved from this earlier phase of Andhra art. Kârle is however usually dated to the early 1st century B.C. On the upper frieze to the right of the central door is an inscription recording a grant of Ushavadâta, the son-in-law of Nahapâna, to the ascetics in the Kârle caves. Also the seventh pillar on the left of the nave was the gift of one Mitadevanaka, son of Ushavadâta.

If this latter Ushavadâta was also the son-in-law of Nahapâna, Kârle might be dated to the first quarter of the 2nd century A.D. or somewhat later. If this is not acceptable, the cave must be dated by style. This will, however, lead to the same conclusion. It has frequently been observed that the large *mithuna* groups at Kârle show the same development of style as the Kushân art of Mathurâ. Again, Kârle is always - and rightly - compared in purity of architectural style with Cave X at Nâsik, Nahapâna's Cave, dedicated according to the chronology accepted here in A.D. 120. We may consider then the *caitya*-hall at Kârle as just preceding the beginning of the Early Phase at Amarâvatî, to which it contributed in the treatment of the human figure.

Though poor in sculpture, the north-west Deccan was rich in painting, and sufficient has survived in Caves IX and X at Ajantâ to indicate its quality and style. The dates given to these paintings, largely on epigraphic grounds, seem at once too early and too late. The left wall of Cave X is dated about 100 B.C. the left and end walls of Cave IX to about the second half of the first century B.C., and the Shad—danta Jâtaka on the right wall of Cave X probably not earlier than the 3rd century A.D. If, however, we are impressed less by epigraphy than by the impact of the style, there can be little doubt that the Shad—danta Jâtaka painting in Cave X is the pictorial equivalent of the sculpture of the Middle Phase at Amarâvatî. It is inconceivable that the painting on the left wall of Cave X is three hundred years earlier than the Shad-danta Jâtaka. Surely not more than a generation separated them from each other, or both from the early paintings of Cave IX. Yazdani rightly compares the paintings on the left wall of Cave X with the sculptures of Kârle and Kondâne. That both should be a century earlier than the mature art of Sânchi would make it impossible to interpret the development of the early art of India.

However, even if it is admitted that the style of the small body of sculpture from the north-west Deccan is reflected in that of the Early Phase at Amarâvatî, and that the elaborate composition and development in the treatment of the human figure seen in the early Ajantâ paintings is paralleled by the sculpture of the Middle Phase, the source of Sâtavâhana art of the 2nd century A.D. still remains a problem. The answer surely is the mature style of Sânchî; that is, the sculpture of the *toranas* of Stûpas I and III and the 'late' pillars of the railing of Stûpa II. Nor is it unreasonable to look in this direction. Sânchî lay close to Vidiúâ, the capital of Avanti, which once certainly, under Gautamîputra, formed part of the Sâtavâhana Empire, and may have done so earlier under a King Sâtakarni, the foreman of whose artisans donated the top cross-bar of the south *torana* of Stûpa I. It is not too much to say that the Early Phase at Amarâvatî, so far as we can judge it from the relatively few surviving fragments, derives all the elements of its style from Sânchî.

If the chronology proposed here for the Amarâvatî style were unacceptable, it would still be impossible to put the Early Phase before Sânchî. The mature art of

Sânchî is usually placed in the second half of the 1st century B.C. There are two dissident opinions. Bachhofer held that the late pillars of Stûpa II belonged to the first half of the 2nd century A.D., and Madame Bénisti believes that the *torana* of Stûpa III belongs to the last quarter of the 1st century or later. The sole evidence for the dating of the mature art of Sânchî, apart from the style of the sculptures, is the inscription already mentioned. If this Sâtakarni were Sâtakarni I, he would, according to our chronology, have reigned during the first quarter or first half of the 1st century A.D., according as we accept eighteen or fifty-six as the years of his reign. If there were a second King of that name who reigned for fifty-six years, the end of his reign would have to be placed about A.D. 80 or later.

It is sufficient to say that the inscription itself does not prevent us from dating what is generally considered to be the earliest of the anywhere in the first three quarters of the 1st century A.D. The style demands a date as close as is compatible with other evidence to the Early Phase at Amarâvatî, and, indeed, to the earlier paintings in Caves IX and X at Ajantâ. If the Early Phase at Amarâvatî is dated to the second quarter of the 2nd century A.D., then Bachhofer's date for the late pillars of Stûpa II, generally accepted as the latest examples of the mature Sânchî style, is not unreasonable. It is not likely that the earliest example of that style, the south *torana* of Stûpa I, is much more than fifty years earlier. Thus Sânchî, though not perhaps a Sâtavâhana monument in the strictest sense, may be considered to be the example which made possible the rapid growth of the art of the Andhradesa in the 2nd century A.D.

6

ISLAMIC ART AND ARCHITECTURE IN INDIA

The fine arts, especially architecture, made tremendous progress during the Islamic rule in India. The architecture of this period can be divided into four categories. They are the Delhi or the Imperial Style, the Provincial Style, the Hindu Architecture and the Mughal Architecture. The Imperial Style developed under the patronage of the Sultans of Delhi. The Provincial Rulers who were mostly Muslims patronized the Provincial Style. Though the Imperial Style influenced this style yet it had its own individuality. The Hindu Architecture evolved under the Hindu kings of Rajasthan and Vijayanagara Empire with an influence of the Imperial style. The Mughal Architecture was a blend of the Islamic Architecture of Central Asia and the Hindu Architecture of India.

The development of the Muslim Style of Architecture of this period can be called the Indo-Islamic Architecture or the Indian Architecture influenced by Islamic Art. This style was neither strictly Islamic nor strictly Hindu. The Muslims provided spaciousness, massiveness and breadth to the Hindu architecture. They added mere or arch, dome and minar to the indigenous architecture. The Muslims borrowed the design of kalash on the top of the Hindu temple by placing a dome on the top of their buildings. The Hindu style of decoration was applied by the Muslims to decorate their arches.

The Provincial Rulers could not provide the grandeur similar to the Imperial or the Mughal buildings to their own buildings because of limited economic resources at their disposal. The local circumstances also influenced the Provincial Style therefore making them different not only from the Imperial Style but also from each other. The Mughal Architecture occupies a most significant place in the history of Indian Architecture. Akbar was responsible for its origin and development.

The Mughal Architecture was basically Indian though it recognized and incorporated foreign influences with in it. Some of the basic features of the Mughal Architecture are the round domes, high minarets, mehrabs, pillars, open courtyards etc. Red sandstone was used for construction of the buildings during the initial period while white marble replaced it during the later period when the stress was more on beautifying of the buildings with the use of colored designs, precious and semi-precious stones, gold and silver waters and minute carvings.

The Muslims mostly constructed tombs, minarets, mosques, palaces and forts while the Hindus mostly constructed temples, forts, palaces, stambhas (victory towers), gopurams, and mandapas in the temples. Though there was no positive effort for the fusion of the Hindu and Muslim architecture yet the synthesis took place and gave birth to the Ind-Islamic style of architecture. The Mughals constructed many mausoleums, mosques places etc. it was influenced by the provincial architectures of the times. The outstanding examples of this period are the Qutub Minar, Alai Darwaza, Quwwat-ul-Islam mosque, Tughlaqabad Fort, Vithala temple, Kirti Stambha, Fatehpur Sikri, Agra Fort, Taj Mahal, Red Fort etc.

AN INTRODUCTION TO ISLAMIC ART

Art is the mirror of a culture and its world view. There is no case to which this statement more directly applies than to the art of the Islamic world. Not only does its art reflect its cultural values, but even more importantly, the way in which its adherents, the Muslims, view the spiritual realm, the universe, life, and the relationship of the parts to the whole.

For the Muslim, reality begins with and centers around God ("Allah" in Arabic), the One, the Unique, the Sovereign, the Holy, the Almighty, the All-Knowing, the Loving, the Most Merciful. All existence is subject to His will and His laws. He is the center of conscious Muslims' worship and aspirations, the focus of their lives.

Since the command and authority are one, all things are bound together under God's Lordship as parts of an all-encompassing divine scheme, which includes all aspects of being and life — whatever is both inside and outside of time and space, and embracing both the macrocosm in its most awesome manifestations and the microcosm in its most minute forms. God creates and sustains His creation how and as He wills, and all affairs return to Him for ultimate decision and judgment.

With such a belief system, the Muslim is convinced of the balance and harmony of all things in existence, even when there appear to be confusing contradictions and imbalances, regarding these as the reflection of man's limited understanding and knowledge. Nothing is looked upon as occurring randomly or by chance, for all is part of the Plan of the All-Wise, Most Merciful Planner. One of the vital beliefs of the

Muslim is that the totality of things, all good and evil, proceed from the Lord of all being.

Because of the strict injunctions against such depictions of humans or animals which might result in idol-worship, Islamic art developed a unique character, utilizing a number of primary forms: geometric, arabesque, floral, and calligraphic, which are often interwoven. From early times, Muslim art has reflected this balanced, harmonious world-view.

THE ISLAMIC VIEW OF THE COSMOS

In the Islamic view, God is the Ultimate Reality. All things in the visible creation emanate from Him and are manifestations of His divine Names or Attributes (Sifat). He created the cosmos, both what is known to man and what is unknown, and He is the Sustainer of all things, with everything turning to Him and centered upon Him. This is evident in the very structure of atoms.

The early Muslim artists and artisans who derived the intricate systems of interconnected geometric forms which constitute the bases of Islamic geometric art of course had no idea of such realities. Nonetheless, the graphic manner in which they conceived God's supreme central place in the cosmos, and the connection of the parts of creation to Him and to the whole, reflects a very significant approximation of what can now be documented by science.

THE TRADITION OF FINE CRAFTSMANSHIP

Throughout the history of Islam, its art has taken a great variety of forms in the different parts of the Muslim world, which stretches from North Africa to Southeast Asia, according to local customs and conditions, ranging from unsophisticated folk art to that of the most skilled artist or artisan. In the works of the latter, whether it be a master calligrapher, a renowned ceramists or potter, a skilled embroiderer or miniature-maker, the legacy of fine craftsmanship, involving the mastery of an art or craft along traditional lines complete with meticulous attention to fine detail, is characteristic.

These traditions persist today, and Islamic architecture and decorative arts are still very much alive and valued in many parts of the Muslim world. While Western-style art forms and machine work have to an extent eroded the traditional forms, nonetheless, handwork is respected and loved, an important aspect of the decoration of mosques and Muslim homes. In particular, decoration featuring Qur'anic calligraphy is an important aspect of Islamic art.

THE AGELESS LEGACY OF ARABIC CALLIGRAPHY

Arabic is the language of Islam. It is the language of its prophet, Muhammad; the language in which the Holy Qur'an, Islam's sacred scripture, was revealed to him by God; the language of Muslims' worship; and the language which binds Muslims of all times and places together in a single cohesive brotherhood.

Because of Muslims' profound respect and love for the Qur'an, the art of calligraphy was developed among them from early times to a very high degree. Throughout the Muslim world, Qur'anic verses embellish mosques, palaces and homes, businesses, and, in some places, public areas. Often the calligraphy is done in conjunction with decorative motifs, lovingly embellishing what is most sacred and precious.

Due to its peculiar character, the Arabic script lends itself wonderfully to decorative use. Over the centuries, many different scripts have evolved in various regions of the Muslim world. Arabic is read from right to left, with an alphabet of twenty-six letters, of which three are long vowels. Short vowels are indicated by small symbols above or under the letters themselves.

"GOD IS BEAUTIFUL AND LOVES BEAUTY"

So said the Prophet of Islam some 1400 years ago. He also said, "God likes that when you do anything, you do it excellently." Such prophetic sayings (hadiths) have provided the impetus for Muslims' embellishment and beautification of their places of worship, homes, and even of articles in common use in everyday life. The emphasis in Islamic art is on ornamentation rather than on art for art's sake; while the names of the producers of the finest works of Islamic art may not have survived, their works have become prototypes and models on which other artists and craftsmen patterned their works, or from which they derived the impetus for related work.

An example of this is a small pouch embellished with cross-stitch embroidery and ornamented with coins. The pouch holds a small unseen bottle, which Jordanian Bedouin women used to hold kohl, a natural eyeliner. But in keeping with the Muslim tradition of ornamenting utilitarian articles, a very ordinary brown glass bottle has been given a place of honor in a beautifully embroidered work of decorative art.

Such arts as embroidery and fine crocheting were commonplace skills among Muslim women in the past — and still are in some places in the Muslim world — as each growing girl and her mother worked in periods of spare time during the years before the girl's marriage to produce a set of finely hand-worked bed linens, towels, prayer rugs, quilt, tablecloths, and the like for the bride to take to her new home.

Today, the finest arts, including rugs, are to be found in Turkey, Iran, Syria, Pakistan, India, Egypt and Morocco, where the legacy of Islamic arts remains alive and strong.

ISLAMIC ARCHITECTURE

Islamic architecture has encompassed a wide range of both secular and religious styles from the foundation of Islam to the present day, influencing the design and construction of buildings and structures within the sphere of Islamic culture. The principle architectural types of Islamic architecture are; the Mosque, the Tomb, the Palace and the Fort. From these four types, the vocabulary of Islamic architecture is derived and used for buildings of lesser importance such as public baths, fountains and domestic architecture.

In 630 C.E. the Islamic prophet Muhammad's army reconquered the city of Mecca from the Banu Quraish tribe. The Kaaba sanctuary was rebuilt and re-dedicated to Islam, the reconstruction being carried out before the prophet Muhammad's death in 632 C.E. by a shipwrecked Abyssinian carpenter in his native style. This sanctuary was amongst the first major works of Islamic architecture. Later doctrines of Islam dating from the eighth century and originating from the Hadith, forbade the use of humans and animals. in architectural design,in order to obey God's command (and thou shalt not make for thyself an image or idol of God) and also (thou shalt have no god before me) from ten commandments and similar Islamic teachings. For Jews and muslims veneration violates these commandments.They read these commandments as prohibiting the use of idols and images during worship in any way.

In the 7th century, Muslim armies conquered a huge expanse of land. Once the Muslims had taken control of a region, their first need was for somewhere to worship - a mosque. The simple layout provided elements that were to be incorporated into all mosques and the early Muslims put up simple buildings based on the model of the Prophet's house or adapted existing buildings for their own use.

Recently discoveries have shown that quasicrystal patterns were first employed in the girih tiles found in medieval Islamic architecture dating back over five centuries ago. In 2007, Professor Peter Lu of Harvard University and Professor Paul Steinhardt of Princeton University published a paper in the journal *Science* suggesting that girih tilings possessed properties consistent with self-similar fractal quasicrystalline tilings such as the Penrose tilings, predating them by five centuries.

INFLUENCES AND STYLES

A specifically recognisable Islamic architectural style developed soon after the time of the Prophet Muhammad, developing from localized adaptations of Roman, Egyptian,

Byzantine, and Persian/Sassanid models. An early example may be identified as early as 691 AD with the completion of the Dome of the Rock (*Qubbat al-Sakhrah*) in Jerusalem. It featured interior vaulted spaces, a circular dome, and the use of stylized repeating decorative patterns (arabesque).

The Great Mosque of Samarra in Iraq, completed in 847 AD, combined the hypostyle architecture of rows of columns supporting a flat base above which a huge spiraling minaret was constructed. The Hagia Sophia in Istanbul also influenced Islamic architecture. When the Ottomans captured the city from the Byzantines, they converted the basilica to a mosque (now a museum) and incorporated Byzantine architectural elements into their own work (e.g. *domes*). The Hagia Sophia also served as model for many of the Ottoman mosques such as the Shehzade Mosque, the Suleiman Mosque, and the Rüstem Pasha Mosque.

Distinguishing motifs of Islamic architecture have always been ordered repetition, radiating structures, and rhythmic, metric patterns. In this respect, fractal geometry has been a key utility, especially for mosques and palaces. Other significant features employed as motifs include columns, piers and arches, organized and interwoven with alternating sequences of niches and colonnettes. The role of domes in Islamic architecture has been considerable. Its usage spans centuries, first appearing in 691 with the construction of the Dome of the Rock mosque, and recurring even up until the 17th century with the Taj Mahal. And as late as the 19th century, Islamic domes had been incorporated into Western architecture.

PERSIAN ARCHITECTURE

One of the first civilizations that Islam came into contact with during and after its birth was that of Persia. The eastern banks of the Tigris and Euphrates was where the capital of the Persian empire lay during the 7th century. Hence the proximity often led early Islamic architects to not just borrow, but adopt the traditions and ways of the fallen Persian empire. Islamic architecture borrows heavily from Persian architecture and in many ways can be called an extension and further evolution of Persian architecture.

Many cities such as Baghdad, for example, were based on precedents such as Firouzabad in Persia. In fact, it is now known that the two designers hired by al-Mansur to plan the city's design were Naubakht, a former Persian Zoroastrian, and Mashallah, a former Jew from Khorasan, Iran.

Persian-style mosques are characterized by their tapered brick pillars, large arcades, and arches each supported by several pillars. In South Asia, elements of Hindu architecture were employed, but were later superseded by Persian designs.

MOORISH ARCHITECTURE

Construction of the Great Mosque at Cordoba (now a Christian Cathedral) beginning in 785 AD marks the beginning of Islamic architecture in the Iberian peninsula and North Africa. The mosque is noted for its striking interior arches. Moorish architecture reached its peak with the construction of the Alhambra, the magnificent palace/fortress of Granada, with its open and breezy interior spaces adorned in red, blue, and gold. The walls are decorated with stylize foliage motifs, Arabic inscriptions, and arabesque design work, with walls covered in glazed tile. Moorish architecture has its roots deeply established in the Arab tradition of architecture and design established during the era of the first Caliphate of the Ummayyads in the Levant circa 660AD with its capital Damascus having very well preserved examples of fine Arab Islamic design and geometrics, including the carmen, which is the typical Damascene house, opening on the inside with a fountain as the house's centre piece.

Even after the completion of the Reconquista, Islamic influence had a lasting impact on the architecture of Spain. In particular, medieval Spaniards used the Mudéjar style, highly influenced by Islamic design. One of the best examples of the Moors' lasting impact on Spanish architecture is the Alcázar of Seville.

TURKISTAN (TIMURID) ARCHITECTURE

Timurid architecture is the pinnacle of Islamic art in Central Asia. Spectacular and stately edifices erected by Timur and his successors in Samarkand and Herat helped to disseminate the influence of the Ilkhanid school of art in India, thus giving rise to the celebrated Mughal school of architecture. Timurid architecture started with the sanctuary of Ahmed Yasawi in present-day Kazakhstan and culminated in Timur's mausoleum Gur-e Amir in Samarkand. The style is largely derived from Persian architecture. Axial symmetry is a characteristic of all major Timurid structures, notably the Shah-e Zendah in Samarkand and the mosque of Gowhar Shad in Meshed. Double domes of various shapes abound, and the outsides are perfused with brilliant colors.

OTTOMAN TURKISH ARCHITECTURE

The most numerous and largest of mosques exist in Turkey, which obtained influence from Byzantine, Persian and Syrian-Arab designs. Turkish architects implemented their own style of cupola domes. The architecture of the Turkish Ottoman Empire forms a distinctive whole, especially the great mosques by and in the style of Sinan, like the mid-16th century Suleiman Mosque. For almost 500 years Byzantine architecture such as the church of Hagia Sophia served as models for many of the Ottoman mosques such as the Shehzade Mosque, the Suleiman Mosque, and the Rüstem Pasha Mosque.

The Ottomans mastered the technique of building vast inner spaces confined by seemingly weightless yet massive domes, and achieving perfect harmony between inner and outer spaces, as well as light and shadow. Islamic religious architecture which until then consisted of simple buildings with extensive decorations, was transformed by the Ottomans through a dynamic architectural vocabulary of vaults, domes, semidomes and columns. The mosque was transformed from being a cramped and dark chamber with arabesque-covered walls into a sanctuary of esthetic and technical balance, refined elegance and a hint of heavenly transcendence.

FATIMID ARCHITECTURE

In architecture, the Fatimids followed Tulunid techniques and used similar materials, but also developed those of their own. In Cairo, their first congregational mosque was al-Azhar mosque ("the splendid") founded along with the city (969–973), which, together with its adjacent institution of higher learning (al-Azhar University), became the spiritual center for Ismaili Shia. The Mosque of al-Hakim (r. 996–1013), an important example of Fatimid architecture and architectural decoration, played a critical role in Fatimid ceremonial and procession, which emphasized the religious and political role of the Fatimid caliph. Besides elaborate funerary monuments, other surviving Fatimid structures include the Mosque of al-Aqmar (1125) as well as the monumental gates for Cairo's city walls commissioned by the powerful Fatimid emir and vizier Badr al-Jamali (r. 1073–1094). Al-Hakim Mosque (990-1012) was renovated by Dr. Syedna Mohammed Burhanuddin (head of Dawoodi Bohra community) and Al-Jame-al-Aqmar built in 1125 in Cairo, Egypt features with its Fatimi philosophy and symbolism and bring its architecture vividly to life.

The reign of the Mamluks (1250-1517 AD) marked a breathtaking flowering of Islamic art which is most visible in old Cairo. Religious zeal made them generous patrons of architecture and art. Trade and agriculture flourished under Mamluk rule, and Cairo, their capital, became one of the wealthiest cities in the Near East and the center of artistic and intellectual activity. This made Cairo, in the words of Ibn Khaldun, "the center of the universe and the garden of the world", with majestic domes, courtyards, and soaring minarets spread across the city. The Mamluk utilized chiaroscuro and dappled light effects in their buildings. Mamluk history is divided into two periods based on different dynastic lines: the Bahri Mamluks (1250–1382) of Qipchaq Turkic origin from southern Russia, named after the location of their barracks on the Nile and the Burji Mamluks (1382–1517) of Caucasian Circassian origin, who were quartered in the citadel. The Bahri reign defined the art and architecture of the entire Mamluk period. Mamluk decorative arts—especially enameled and gilded glass, inlaid metalwork, woodwork, and textiles—were prized around the Mediterranean as well as in Europe, where they had a profound impact on local production. The influence of Mamluk glassware on the Venetian glass industry is only one such example.

The reign of Baybars's ally and successor, Qala'un (r. 1280–90), initiated the patronage of public and pious foundations that included madrasas, mausolea, minarets, and hospitals. Such endowed complexes not only ensured the survival of the patron's wealth but also perpetuated his name, both of which were endangered by legal problems relating to inheritance and confiscation of family fortunes. Besides Qala'un's complex, other important commissions by Bahri Mamluk sultans include those of al-Nasir Muhammad (1295–1304) as well as the immense and splendid complex of Hasan (begun 1356).

The Burji Mamluk sultans followed the artistic traditions established by their Bahri predecessors. Mamluk textiles and carpets were prized in international trade. In architecture, endowed public and pious foundations continued to be favored. Major commissions in the early Burji period in Egypt included the complexes built by Barquq (r. 1382–99), Faraj (r. 1399–1412), Mu'ayyad Shaykh (r. 1412–21), and Barsbay (r. 1422–38).

In the eastern Mediterranean provinces, the lucrative trade in textiles between Iran and Europe helped revive the economy. Also significant was the commercial activity of pilgrims en route to Mecca and Medina. Large warehouses, such as the Khan al-Qadi (1441), were erected to satisfy the surge in trade. Other public foundations in the region included the mosques of Aqbugha al-Utrush (Aleppo, 1399–1410) and Sabun (Damascus, 1464) as well as the Madrasa Jaqmaqiyya (Damascus, 1421).

In the second half of the fifteenth century, the arts thrived under the patronage of Qa'itbay (r. 1468–96), the greatest of the later Mamluk sultans. During his reign, the shrines of Mecca and Medina were extensively restored. Major cities were endowed with commercial buildings, religious foundations, and bridges. In Cairo, the complex of Qa'itbay in the Northern Cemetery (1472–74) is the best known and admired structure of this period. Building continued under the last Mamluk sultan, Qansuh al-Ghawri (r. 1501–17), who commissioned his own complex (1503–5); however, construction methods reflected the finances of the state. Though the Mamluk realm was soon incorporated into the Ottoman empire (1517), Mamluk visual culture continued to inspire Ottoman and other Islamic artistic traditions.

CONTEMPORARY ARCHITECTURE

Modern Islamic architecture has recently been taken on to a whole new level with such buildings being erected such as the Burj Dubai, which is soon to be the world's tallest building. The Burj Dubai's design is derived from the patterning systems embodied in Islamic architecture, with the triple-lobed footprint of the building based on an abstracted version of the desert flower hymenocallis which is native to the Dubai region. Nature and flowers have often been the focal point in most traditional Islamic designs. Many modern interpretations of Islamic architecture can be found in Dubai due to the architectural boom of the Arab World. Yet to be built is Madinat al-Hareer in Kuwait which also has modern versions of Islamic architecture in its super tall tower.

INTERPRETATION

Common interpretations of Islamic architecture include the following: The concept of Allah's infinite power is evoked by designs with repeating themes which suggest infinity. Human and animal forms are rarely depicted in decorative art as Allah's work is considered to be matchless. Foliage is a frequent motif but typically stylized or simplified for the same reason. Arabic Calligraphy is used to enhance the interior of a building by providing quotations from the Qur'an. Islamic architecture has been called the "architecture of the veil" because the beauty lies in the inner spaces (courtyards and rooms) which are not visible from the outside (street view). Furthermore, the use of grandiose forms such as large domes, towering minarets, and large courtyards are intended to convey power.

ARCHITECTURE FORMS AND STYLES OF MOSQUES AND BUILDINGS IN MUSLIM COUNTRIES

Many forms of Islamic architecture have evolved in different regions of the Islamic world. Notable Islamic architectural types include the early Abbasid buildings, T-type mosques, and the central-dome mosques of Anatolia. The oil-wealth of the 20th century drove a great deal of mosque construction using designs from leading modern architects.

Arab-plan or *hypostyle* mosques are the earliest type of mosques, pioneered under the Umayyad Dynasty. These mosques are square or rectangular in plan with an enclosed courtyard and a covered prayer hall. Historically, because of the warm Mediterranean and Middle Eastern climates, the courtyard served to accommodate the large number of worshipers during Friday prayers. Most early hypostyle mosques have flat roofs on top of prayer halls, necessitating the use of numerous columns and supports. One of the most notable hypostyle mosques is the Mezquita in Córdoba, Spain, as the building is supported by over 850 columns. Frequently, hypostyle mosques have outer arcades so that visitors can enjoy some shade. Arab-plan mosques were constructed mostly under the Umayyad and Abbasid dynasties; subsequently, however, the simplicity of the Arab plan limited the opportunities for further development, and as a result, these mosques gradually fell out of popularity.

The Ottomans introduced *central dome mosques* in the 15th century and have a large dome centered over the prayer hall. In addition to having one large dome at the center, there are often smaller domes that exist off-center over the prayer hall or throughout the rest of the mosque, where prayer is not performed. This style was heavily influenced by the Byzantine religious architecture with its use of large central domes.

Iwan

An iwan (derived from Pahlavi word Bân meaning house) is defined as a vaulted hall or space, walled on three sides, with one end entirely open. Iwans were a trademark of the Sassanid architecture of Persia, later finding their way into Islamic architecture. This transition reached its peak during the Seljuki era when iwans became established as a fundamental design unit in Islamic architecture. Typically, iwans open on to a central courtyard, and have been used in both public and residential architecture.

Iwan mosques are most notable for their domed chambers and *iwans*, which are vaulted spaces open out on one end. In *iwan* mosques, one or more iwans face a central courtyard that serves as the prayer hall. The style represents a borrowing from pre-Islamic Iranian architecture and has been used almost exclusively for mosques in Iran. Many *iwan* mosques are converted Zoroastrian fire temples where the courtyard was used to house the sacred fire. Today, iwan mosques are seldom built. A notable example of a more recent four iwan design is the King Saud Mosque in Jeddah, Saudi Arabia, finished in 1987.

Sahn

Almost every mosque and traditionally all houses and buildings in areas of the Arab World contain a courtyard known as a sahn, which are surrounded on all sides by rooms and sometimes an arcade. Sahns usually feature a centrally positioned pool known as a howz. If a sahn is in a mosque, it is used for performing ablutions. If a sahn is in a traditional house or private courtyard, it is used for aesthetics and to cool the summer heat.

Gardens

The Qur'an uses the garden as an analogy for paradise and Islam came to have a significant influence on garden design.

Arabesque

An element of Islamic art usually found decorating the walls of mosques and Muslim homes and buildings, the arabesque is an elaborate application of repeating geometric forms that often echo the forms of plants, shapes and sometimes animals (specifically birds). The choice of which geometric forms are to be used and how they are to be formatted is based upon the Islamic view of the world. To Muslims, these forms, taken together, constitute an infinite pattern that extends beyond the visible material world. To many in the Islamic world, they in fact symbolize the infinite, and therefore uncentralized, nature of the creation of the one God ("Allah" in Arabic). Furthermore, the Islamic Arabesque artist conveys a definite spirituality without the iconography of Christian art. Arabesque is used in mosques and building around the Muslim world, and it is a way of decorating using beautiful, embellishing and repetitive Islamic art instead of using pictures of humans and animals (which is forbidden *Haram* in Islam).

Calligraphy

Arabic calligraphy is associated with geometric Islamic art (the Arabesque) on the walls and ceilings of mosques as well as on the page. Contemporary artists in the Islamic world draw on the heritage of calligraphy to use calligraphic inscriptions or abstractions in their work.

Instead of recalling something related to the reality of the spoken word, calligraphy for the Muslim is a visible expression of spiritual concepts. Calligraphy has arguably become the most venerated form of Islamic art because it provides a link between the languages of the Muslims with the religion of Islam. The holy book of Islam, al-Qur'ân, has played a vital role in the development of the Arabic language, and by extension, calligraphy in the Arabic alphabet. Proverbs and complete passages from the Qur'an are still active sources for Islamic calligraphy.

ELEMENTS OF ISLAMIC STYLE

Islamic architecture may be identified with the following design elements, which were inherited from the first mosque built byr hall (originally a feature of the Masjid al-Nabawi).

- Minarets or towers (these were originally used as torch-lit watchtowers, as seen in the Great Mosque of Damascus; hence the derivation of the word from the Arabic *nur*, meaning "light").
- A four-iwan plan, with three subordinate halls and one principal one that faces toward Mecca.
- Mihrab or prayer niche on an inside wall indicating the direction to Mecca. This may have been derived from previous uses of niches for the setting of the torah scrolls in Jewish synagogues or the haikal of Coptic churches.
- Domes and Cupolas.
- Iwans to intermediate between different pavilions.
- The use of geometric shapes and repetitive art (arabesque).

- The use of muqarnas, a unique Arabic/Islamic space-enclosing system, for the decoration of domes, minarets and portals. Used at the Alhambra.(Compare mocárabe.) Modern muqarnas designs
- The use of decorative Islamic calligraphy instead of pictures which were haram (forbidden) in mosque architecture. Note that in secular architecture, human and animal representation was indeed present.
- Central fountains used for ablutions (once used as a wudu area for Muslims).
- The use of bright color, if the style is Persian or Indian (Mughal); paler sandstone and grey stones are preferred among Arab buildings. Compare the Registan complex of Uzbekistan to the Al-Azhar University of Cairo.
- Focus both on the interior space of a building and the exterior

DIFFERENCES BETWEEN ISLAMIC ARCHITECTURE AND PERSIAN ARCHITECTURE

Like this of other nations that became part of the Islamic realm, Persian Architecture is not to be confused with *Islamic Architecture* and refers broadly to architectural styles across the Islamic world. Islamic architecture, therefore, does not directly include reference to Persian styles prior to the rise of Islam. Persian architecture, like other nations', predates Islamic architecture and can be correctly understood as an important influence on overall Islamic architecture as well as a branch of Islamic architecture since the introduction of Islam in Persia. Islamic architecture can be classified according to chronology, geography, and building typology.

MUGHAL ART AND ARCHITECTURE IN INDIA

Mughal art and architecture, a characteristic Indo-Islamic-Persian style that flourished on the Indian subcontinent during the Mughal empire (1526–1857). This new style combined elements of Islamic art and architecture, which had been introduced to India during the Delhi Sultanate (1192–1398) and had produced great monuments such as the Qutub Minar, with features of Persian art and architecture. Mughal monuments are found chiefly in North India, but there are also many remains in Pakistan. Here we discuss these distinctive forms of art and architecture as they developed under a succession of Mughal emperors.

EARLY MUGHAL ARCHITECTURE

The Mughal dynasty began with the emperor Babur in 1526. Babur erected a mosque at Panipat to celebrate his victory over Ibrahim Lodi. A second mosque, known as the Babri masjid, was built in Ayodhya(on a demolished Hindu Ramjanmabhumi temple), and demolished in 1992 by Hindu fundamentalists. A third mosque also built by Babur during the same period was constructed in Sambhal in Distt Moradabad.

Some of the first and most characteristic examples that remain of early Mughal architecture were built in the short reign (1540–1545) of emperor Sher Shah Suri, who was not a Mughal; they include a mosque known as the Qila i Kuhna (1541) near Delhi, and the military architecture of the Old Fort in Delhi, Lal Bagh (Dhaka) in Bangladesh, and Rohtas Fort, near Jhelum in present-day Pakistan. His mausoleum, octagonal in plan and set upon a plinth in the middle of an artificial lake, is in Sasaram, and was completed by his son and successor Islam Shah Suri (1545-1553).

AKBAR

The emperor Akbar (1556-1605) built largely, and the style developed vigorously during his reign. As in the Gujarat and other styles, there is a combination of Muslim and Hindu features in his works. Akbar constructed the royal city of Fatehpur Sikri, located 26 miles (42 km) west of Agra, in the late 1500s. The numerous structures at Fatehpur Sikri best illustrate the style of his works, and the great mosque there is scarcely matched in elegance and architectural effect; the south gateway is well known, and from its size and structure excels any similar entrance in India. The Mughals built impressive tombs, which include the fine tomb of Akbar's father Humayun, and Akbur's tomb at Sikandra, near Agra, which is a unique structure of the kind and of great merit.

JAHANGIR

Under Jahangir (1605–1627) the Hindu features vanished from the style; his great mosque at Lahore is in the Persian style, covered with enamelled tiles. At Agra, the tomb of Itmad-ud-Daula completed in 1628, built entirely of white marble and covered wholly by pietra dura mosaic, is one of the most splendid examples of that class of ornamentation anywhere to be found. Jahangir also built the Shalimar Gardens and its accompanying pavilions on the shore of Dal Lake in Kashmir. He also built a monument to his pet antelope, Hiran Minar in Sheikhupura, Pakistan and due to his great love for his wife, after his death she went on to build his mausoleum in Lahore.

SHAH JAHAN

The force and originality of the style gave way under Shah Jahan (1627-1658) to a delicate elegance and refinement of detail, illustrated in the magnificent palaces erected in his reign at Agra and Delhi, the latter one the most exquisitely beautiful in India. The most splendid of the Mogul tombs, and the most renowned building in India, is the Taj Mahal at Agra, the tomb of Mumtaz Mahal, the wife of Shah Jahan.The Moti Masjid (Pearl Mosque) in the Agra Fort and The Jama Masjid at Delhi are an imposing building, and their position and architecture have been carefully considered so as to produce a pleasing effect and feeling of spacious elegance and well-balanced proportion of parts. In his works Shah Jahan presents himself as the most magnificent builder of Indian sovereigns. He also built the mausoleum and sections of the huge Lahore Fort that include the impressive Moti Masjid, Sheesh Mahal, and Naulakha pavilion which are all enclosed in the fort. He also built a mosque after himself in Thatta called Shahjahan Mosque. Another mosque was built during his tenture in Lahore called Wazir Khan Mosque, by Shaikh Ilm-ud-din Ansari who was the court physician to the emperor.

ISLAMIC MUSIC IN INDIA

Islamic music is Muslim religious music, as sung or played in public services or private devotions. The classic heartland of Islam is Arabia and the Middle East, North Africa and Egypt, Iran, Central Asia, India, Pakistan, and Afghanistan. Because Islam is a multicultural religion, the musical expression of its adherents is diverse. The indigenous musical styles of these areas have shaped the devotional music enjoyed by contemporary Muslims.

SECULAR AND FOLK MUSICAL STYLES

Middle East

- Arabic classical music

The Seljuk Turks, a nomadic tribe that converted to Islam, conquered Anatolia (now Turkey), and held the Caliphate as the Ottoman Empire, also had a strong influence on Islamic music.

- Turkish classical music

All these regions were connected by trade long before the Islamic conquests of the 600s and later, and it is likely that musical styles traveled the same routes as trade goods. However, lacking recordings, we can only speculate as to the pre-Islamic music of these areas. Islam must have had a great influence on music, as it united vast areas under the first caliphs, and facilitated trade between distant lands. Certainly the Sufis, brotherhoods of Muslim mystics, spread their music far and wide.

South Asia

The music of the Muslim populations of South Asia (Afghanistan, Pakistan, India and Bangladesh, with Nepal and Sri Lanka) had merged the Middle Eastern genres along with indigenous classical musical modes, and is generally distinct in style and orchestration, yet due to the strong links encountered between the Middle-East, Central Asia and South Asia, they are closer to Middle-Eastern styles than those of the peripheric outreaches of the Islamic world, which tend to be purely indigenous.

The Peripheral Islamic World: Sub-Saharan Africa and Southeast Asia/Oceania

Sub-Saharan Africa, the Caucasus, Indonesia, Malaysia, and the southern Philippines also have large Muslim populations, but these areas have incorporated less influences from the heartland than other areas, although in the case of West Africa, a shared trade route between the Berbers and Arabs of North Africa had given a sharing of styles present especially in the Sahelian region, between the Savanna and the Sahara. Of these areas, the music of Mali, the Wolof of Senegal, the Fula, Songhai and Hausa groups had experienced international recognition in the contemporary world.

Many music genres of these areas generally predate the coming of Islam or have very little influence from the Islamic heartland, the exceptions being Taarab music of the Swahili people of East Africa, and the Malay Zapin genres, of which both had taken a lot of influence from the Middle East after Islamization.

TYPES OF MUSLIM DEVOTIONAL RECITATION AND MUSIC

Nasheed

Nasheeds are moral, religious songs sung in various melodies by some Muslims of today without any musical instruments. However some nasheed groups perform by using some percussion instruments. This type of singing of moral songs without Music is considered as permissable (halal) by almost all stern Muslims.

Sufi music

Sufi worship services are often called dhikr or zikr. The dhikr of South Asian Muslims is "quietist". The Sufi services best known in the West are the chanting and rhythmic dancing of the whirling dervishes or Mevlevi Sufis of Turkey. Some Mevlevi music can be heard on the Sufi Music CD recommended below.

However, Sufis may also perform devotional songs in public, for the enjoyment and edification of listeners. The mood is religious, but the gathering is not a worship service.

In Turkey, once the seat of the Ottoman Empire and the Caliphate, concerts of sacred song are called *"Mehfil-e-Sama' "* (or "gathering of *Sama'*"). Song forms include ilahi and nefe.

Qasidah is a form of poetry. In this form of poetry the praise is presented. Qasidah is four types, 1. Hamd (Hymn) 2. Naat (A poem in praise of Prophet Muhammad) 3. Manqabat (A poem in praise of Saints) 4. Madah (A poem in praise of honourables).

In India and Pakistan, these concerts, and the associated style of music, are called qawwali. A traditional qawwali programme would include:

• A hamd — a song in praise of Allah

- A naat — a song in praise of the Prophet Muhammad.
- Manqabats — songs in praise of the illustrious teachers of the Sufi brotherhood to which the musicians belong.
- Ghazals — songs of intoxication and yearning, which use the language of romantic love to express the soul's longing for union with the divine.

Shi'a concerts follow the naat with a song in praise of Ali (also manqabat) and a marsiya, a lamentation over the death of much of Ali's family at the Battle of Karbala.

Qawwali is increasingly popular as a musical genre and performances may attract those who want to hear virtuoso singing rather than contemplate the divine. Some artists may skip the long sequence of praise songs and go straight from the introductory *hamd* to the popular romantic songs, or even dispense with the devotional content completely. This is cause for much consternation for traditional enthusiasts/devotees of the form. The most well known qawwali singer is Nusrat Fateh Ali Khan. The dimension and style of music he brought about no one else is able to produce till this day.

As Sufi music has developed so have the generations. A Pakistani rock band, Junoon, was formed in the 1990s to bring a modern twist to suit the new younger generations. The band was a huge world wide hit that created a lot of popularity for not only Pakistan.

Music for public religious celebrations

- Mawlid music — performed for the birthday of Muhammad, in various regional styles.
- Ta'zieh music — Ta'zieh is a passion play, part musical drama, part religious drama, rarely performed outside Iran. It depicts the martyrdom of Imam Hussein, venerated by Shia Muslims.
- Ashurah music — performed during the Moharram mourning period, commemorating the deaths of Imam Hussein and his followers.
- Sikiri (from the Arabic word "Dhikr" which means remembrance of God — performed by the Qadiriyya Sufi orders of waYao or Yao people in East and Southern Africa (Tanzania, Mozambique, Malawi, Zimbabwe, and South Africa).
- Manzuma — moral songs performed in Ethiopia.
- Madih nabawi — Arabic hymns praising the prophet Muhammad.

FAMOUS ISLAMIC ARCHITECTURE IN INDIA

TAJ MAHAL

The Taj Mahal, is a mausoleum located in Agra, India, that was built under Mughal Emperor Shah Jahan in memory of his favorite wife, Mumtaz Mahal. The Taj Mahal (also "the Taj") is considered the finest example of Mughal architecture, a style that combines elements from Persian, Turkish, Indian, and Islamic architectural styles. In 1983, the Taj Mahal became a UNESCO World Heritage Site and was cited as "the jewel of Muslim art in India and one of the universally admired masterpieces of the world's heritage."

While the white domed marble and tile mausoleum is most familiar, Taj Mahal is an integrated symmetric complex of structures that was completed around 1648. Ustad Ahmad Lahauri is generally considered to be the principal designer of the Taj Mahal.

In 1631, Shah Jahan, emperor during the Mughal empire's period of greatest prosperity, was griefstricken when his third wife, Mumtaz Mahal, died during the birth of their fourteenth child, Gauhara Begum. The court chronicles of Shah Jahan's grief illustrates the love story traditionally held as an inspiration for Taj Mahal. The construction of Taj Mahal begun soon after Mumtaz's death with the principal mausoleum completed in 1648. The surrounding buildings and garden were finished five years later. Empror Shah Jahan himself described the Taj in these words:

"Should guilty seek asylum here, Like one pardoned, he becomes free from sin. Should a sinner make his way to this mansion, All his past sins are to be washed away. The sight of this mansion creates sorrowing sighs; And the sun and the moon shed tears from their eyes. In this world this edifice has been made; To display thereby the creator's glory".

The Taj Mahal incorporates and expands on design traditions of Persian and earlier Mughal architecture. Specific inspiration came from successful Timurid and Mughal buildings including the Gur-e Amir (the tomb of Timur, progenitor of the Mughal dynasty, in Samarkand), Humayun's Tomb, Itmad-Ud-Daulah's Tomb (sometimes called the *Baby Taj*), and Shah Jahan's own Jama Masjid in Delhi. While earlier Mughal buildings were primarily constructed of red sandstone, Shah Jahan promoted the use of white marble inlaid with semi-precious stones, and buildings under his patronage reached new levels of refinement.

ARCHITECTURE OF TAJ MAHAL

The Taj Mahal represents the finest and most sophisticated example of Mughal architecture. Its origins lie in the moving circumstances of its commission and the culture and history of an Islamic Mughal empire's rule of large parts of India.

The distraught Mughal Emperor Shah Jahan commissioned the mausoleum upon the death of his favourite wife, Mumtaz Mahal. Today it is one of the most famous and recognisable buildings in the world and while the white domed marble mausoleum is the most familiar part of the monument, the Taj Mahal is an extensive complex of buildings and gardens that extends over 22.44 Hectares and includes subsidiary tombs, waterworks infrastructure, the small town of 'Taj Ganji' and a 'moonlight garden' to the north of the river. Construction began in 1632 CE, (1041 AH), on the south bank of the River Yamuna in Agra, India and was completed in 1648 CE (1058 AH). The design was conceived as both an earthly replica of the house of Mumtaz in paradise and an instrument of propaganda for the emperor.

Who designed the Taj Mahal is unclear; although it is known that a large team of designers and craftsmen were responsible with Jahan himself taking an active role. Ustad Ahmad Lahauri is considered the most likely candidate as the principal designer.

The erection of Mughal tombs to honour the dead was the subject of a theological dialogue exemplified by the varied ways in which the Mughals their funerary monuments. For the majority of Muslims, the spiritual power (barakat) of visiting the resting places (ziyarat) of those venerated in Islam was a force by which greater personal sanctity could be achieved. However, orthodox Islam found tombs problematic because a number of Hadith forbade the construction of tombs as irreligious. As a culture also attempting to accommodate and assimilate the Hindu populace, opposition also came from the local tradition which held dead bodies as impure, and by extension, the structures over them similarly impure. So for many Muslims, tombs could be considered legitimate providing they did not strive for pomp and were seen as a means to provide a reflection of paradise (Jannah) here on earth. The ebb and flow of this debate can be seen in the Mughul's dynastic mausoleums stretching back to the Tomb of Timur in Samarkand. Here Timur is buried under a fluted dome and a traditional Persian Iwan is employed as an entrance. The Tomb of Babur in Kabul is a much more modest affair where a simple cenotaph, exposed to the sky, is laid out in the centre of a walled garden.

Humayun's tomb is seen as one of the most direct influences on the Taj Mahal's design and was a direct response to the Tomb of Timur, featuring a central dome of white marble, red sandstone facings, a plinth, geometric symmetrical planning, chatris, iwans and a charbagh. Designed by Humayun's son Akbar it set the precedent for Mughal emperor's children constructing the mausoleums of their fathers.

Akbar's tomb at Sikandra, Agra, retains many of the elements of his father's tomb but possesses no dome and reverts to a cenotaph open to the sky. A theme which was carried forward in the Itmad-Ud-Daulah's Tomb also at Agra, built between 1622 and 1628, commissioned by his daughter Nur Jahan.

The Tomb of Jahangir at Shahdara (Lahore), begun in 1628 CE (1037 AH), only 4 years before the construction of the Taj and again without a dome, takes the form of a simple plinth with a minaret at each corner.

Paradise Gardens

The concept of the paradise garden was one the Mughals brought from Persian Timurid gardens. It was the first architectural expression they made in the Indian sub-continent, fulfilling diverse functions with strong symbolic meanings. Known as the charbagh, in its ideal form it was laid out as a square subdivided into four equal parts. The symbolism of the garden and its divisions are noted in mystic Islamic texts which describe paradise as a garden filled with abundant trees flowers and plants. Water also plays a key role in these descriptions: In Paradise four rivers source at a central spring or mountain, and separate the garden by flowing towards the cardinal points. They represent the promised rivers of water, milk, wine and honey. The centre of the garden, at the intersection of the divisions is highly symbolically charged and is where, in the ideal form, a pavilion, pool or tomb would be situated. The tombs of Humayun, Akbar and Jahangir, the previous Mughal emperors, follow this pattern. The cross axial garden also finds independent precedents within South Asia dating from the 5th century with the royal gardens of Sigiriya in Sri Lanka which were laid out in a similar way.

For the tomb of Jahan's late wife though, where the mausoleum is sited at the edge of the garden, a variant of the charbagh is suggested by Ebba Koch; that of the waterfront garden. Developed by the Mughuls for the specific conditions of the Indian plains where slow flowing rivers provide the water source, the water is raised from the river by animal driven devices known as purs and stored in cisterns. A linear terrace is set close to the riverbank with low-level rooms set below the main building opening on to the river. Both ends of the terrace were emphasised with towers. This form was brought to Agra by Babur and by the time of Shah Jahan, gardens of this type as well as the more traditional charbagh lined both sides of the Jumna river. The riverside terrace was designed to enhance the views of Agra for the imperial elite who would travel in and around the city by river. Other scholars suggest another explanation for the eccentric siting of the mausoleum at the Taj Mahal complex. If the Midnight Garden to the north of the river Jumna is considered an integral part of the complex, then the mausoleum can be interpreted as being in the centre of a garden divided by a real river and thus is more in the tradition of the pure charbagh.

Mausolea

The favourite form for both Mughal garden pavilions and mausolea (seen as a funerary form of pavilion) was the hasht bihisht which translates from Persian as 'eight paradises'. These were square or rectangular planned buildings divided into nine sections such that a central domed chamber is surrounded by eight elements. Later developments of the hasht bihisht divided the square at 45 degree angles to create a more radial plan which often also includes chamfered corners; examples of which can be found in

Todar Mal's Baradari at Fatehpur Sikri and Humayun's Tomb. Each element of the plan is reflected in the elevations with iwans with the corner rooms finding expression through smaller arched niches. Often such structures are topped with chattris, small pillared pavilions at each corner. The eight divisions and frequent octagonal forms of such structures represent the eight levels of paradise for Muslims. The paradigm was not confined solely to Islamic antecedents. The Chinese magic square was employed for numerous purposes including crop rotation and also finds a Muslim expression in the wafq of their mathematicians. Ninefold schemes find particular resonance in the Indian mandalas, the cosmic maps of Hinduism and Buddhism.

In addition to Humayun's tomb, the more closely contemporary Tomb of Itmad-Ud-Daulah provided many influences on the Taj Mahal and marked a new era of Mughal architecture. It was built by the empress Nur Jehan for her father from 1622–1625 CE (1031–1034 AH). It is small in comparison to many other Mughal-era tombs, but so exquisite is the execution of its surface treatments, it has been described as a jewel box. The garden layout, hierarchal use of white marble and sandstone, Parchin kari inlay designs and latticework presage many elements of the Taj Mahal. It is also interesting to note that the cenotaph of Nur Jehan's father is laid, off centre, to the west of her mother. These close similarities with the tomb of Mumtaz have earned it the sobriquet - *The Baby Taj*.

Minarets

Minarets did not become a common feature of Mughal architecture until the 17th century, particularly under the patronage of Shah Jahan. A few precedents exist in the 20 years before the construction of the Taj in the Tomb of Akbar and the Tomb of Jahangir. Their increasing use was influenced by developments elsewhere in the Islamic world, particularly in Ottoman and Timurid architecture. This development has been seen as evidence of an increasing religious orthodoxy of the Mughal dynasty.

CONCEPTS, SYMBOLISM AND INTERPRETATIONS

Under the reign of Shah Jahan the symbolic content of mughal architecture reached its peak. Inspired by a verse by Bibadal Khan, the imperial goldsmith and poet, and in common with most Mughal funerary architecture, the Taj Mahal complex was conceived as a replica on earth of the house of Mumtaz in paradise. This theme permeates the entire complex and informs the design of all its elements. A number of secondary principles inform the design and appearance of the complex, of which hiearachy is the most dominant. A deliberate interplay was established between the building's elements, its surface decoration, materials, geometric planning and its acoustics. This interplay extends from what can be seen with the senses, into religious, intellectual, mathematical and poetic ideas. The constantly changing sunlight that illuminates the building reflected from its translucent marble is not a happy accident, it had a metaphoric role associated with the presence of god.

Symmetry and geometric planning played an important role in ordering the complex and reflected a trend towards formal systematization that was apparent in all of the arts emanating from Jahan's imperial patronage. Bilateral symmetry expressed simultaneous ideas of pairing, counterparts and integration, reflecting intellectual and spiritual notions of universal harmony. A strict and complex set of implied grids based on the Mughul Gaz unit of measurement provided a flexible means of bringing proportional order to all the elements of the Taj Mahal.

Hierarchical ordering of architecture is used by most cultures to emphasise particular elements of a design and to create drama. In the Taj Mahal, the hierarchical use of red sandstone and white marble contributes manifold *symbolic* significance. The Mughals were elaborating on a concept which traced its roots to earlier Hindu practices, set out in the Vishnudharmottara Purana, which recommended white stone for buildings for the Brahmins (priestly caste) and red stone for members of the Kshatriyas (warrior caste). By building structures that employed such colour coding, the Mughals identified themselves with the two leading classes of Indian social structure and thus defined themselves as rulers in Indian terms. Red sandstone also had significance in the Persian origins of the Mughal empire where red was the exclusive colour of imperial tents. In the Taj Mahal the relative importance of each building in the complex is denoted by the amount of white marble (or sometimes white polished plaster) that is used.

The use of naturalist ornament demonstrates a similar hierarchy. Wholly absent from the Jilaukhana and caravanserai areas, it is used with increasing frequency as the processionary path approaches the mausoleum. Its symbolism is multifaceted, on the one hand evoking a more perfect, stylised and permanent garden of paradise than could be found growing in the earthly garden; on the other, an instrument of propaganda for Jahan's chroniclers who portrayed him as an 'erect cypress of the garden of the caliphate' and frequently used plant metaphors to praise his good governance, person, family and court. Plant metaphors also find a commonality with Hindu traditions where such symbols as the 'vase of plenty' (Kalasha) can be found and were borrowed by the mughal architects.

Sound was also used to express ideas of paradise. The interior of the mausoleum has a reverberation time (the time taken from when a noise is made until all of its echoes have died away) of 28 seconds providing an atmosphere where the words of the Hafiz, as they prayed for the soul of Mumtaz, would linger in the air.

Interpretation

The popular view of the Taj as one of the world's monuments to a great "love story" is born out by the contemporary accounts and most scholars accept this has a strong basis in fact. The building was also used to assert Jahani propaganda concerning the 'perfection' of the Mughal leadership. The extent to which the Taj uses propaganda is the subject of some debate amongst contemporary scholars. Wayne Begley put forward an interpretation in 1979 that exploits the Islamic idea that the 'Garden of paradise' is also the location of the 'throne of god' on the day of judgement. In his reading the Taj Mahal is seen as a monument where Shah Jahan has appropriated the authority of the 'throne of god' symbolism for the glorification of his own reign. Koch disagrees, finding this an overly elaborate explanation and pointing out that the 'Throne' sura from the Qu'ran (sura 2 verse 255) is missing from the calligraphic inscriptions.

This period of Mughal architecture best exemplifies the maturity of a style that had synthesised Islamic architecture with its indigenous counterparts. By the time the Mughals built the Taj, though proud of their Persian and Timurid roots, they had come to see themselves as Indian. Copplestone writes "Although it is certainly a native Indian production, its architectural success rests on its fundamentally Persian sense of intelligible and undisturbed proportions, applied to clean, uncomplicated surfaces."

ARCHITECTS AND CRAFTSMEN

History obscures precisely who designed the Taj Mahal. In the Islamic world at the time, the credit for a building's design was usually given to its patron rather than its architects. From the evidence of contemporary sources, it is clear that a team of architects were responsible for the design and supervision of the works, but they are mentioned infrequently. Shah Jahan's court histories emphasise his personal involvement in the construction and it is true that, more than any other Mughal emperor, he showed the greatest interest in building, holding daily meetings with his architects and supervisors. The court chronicler Lahouri, writes that Jahan would make "appropriate alterations to whatever the skilful architects designed after many thoughts, and asked competent questions." Two architects *are* mentioned by name, Ustad Ahmad Lahauri and Mir Abd-ul Karim in writings by Lahauri's son Lutfullah Muhandis. Ustad Ahmad Lahauri had laid the foundations of the Red Fort at Delhi. Mir Abd-ul Karim had been the favourite architect of the previous emperor Jahangir and is mentioned as a supervisor, together with Makramat Khan, of the construction of the Taj Mahal.

- Expand and add craftsmen
- Bebadal Khan, the poet and goldsmith
- Hindu craftsmen

The exquisite and highly skilled parchin kari work was developed by Mughal lapidarists from techniques taught to them by Italian craftsmen employed at court. The look of European herbals, books illustrating botanical species, was adapted and refined in Mughal parchin kari work.

SITE

16th–17th Century Agra

Babur, the founder of the Mughal dynasty, created the first Mughal garden known as Ram Bagh in Agra in 1526 CE. Thereafter, gardens became important Mughal symbols of power, changing the emphasis from pre-Mughal symbols such as forts. The shift can be explained in terms of the intoduction of a new ordered aesthetic, an artistic expression with religious and funery aspects and as a metaphor for Babur's ability to control the arid Indian planes and hence the country at large. Babur rejected much of the indigenous and Lodhi built forms on the opposite bank and attempted to create new ones inspired by Persian gardens and royal encampments. Ram Bagh was followed by an extensive, regular and integrated complex of gardens and palaces stretching for more than a kilometer along the river. A high continuous stone plinth bounded the transition between gardens and river and established the framework for future development in the city.

In the following century, a thriving riverfront garden city developed on both sides of the Yamuna. Subsequent Mughal emperors developed both sides of the river including the rebuiding of Agra Fort, by Akbar, completed in 1573. By the time Jahan ascended to the throne, Agra's population had grown to approximately 700,000 and was, as Abdul Aziz writes, "a wonder of the age - as much a centre of the arteries of trade both by land and water as a meeting-place of saints, sages and scholars from all Asia.....a veritable lodestar for artistic workmanship, literary talent and spiritual worth".

Agra became a city centred on its waterfront and developed partly eastwards but mostly westwards from the rich estates that lined the banks. The prime sites remained those that had access to the river and the Taj Mahal was built in this context, but uniquely, on both sides of the river.

The Taj Mahal complex can be conveniently divided into 5 sections. 1. The riverfront terrace, containing the Mausoleum, Mosque and Jawab 2. the Charbagh garden containing pavilions. 3. the jilaukhana containing accommodation for the tomb attendants and two subsidiary tombs 4. The Taj Ganji, originally a bazaar and caravansarai only traces of which are still preserved, and finally, to the north of the river Yamuna, 5. the 'moonlight garden'. The great gate lies between the Jilaukhana and the garden. Levels gradually decend in steps from the Taj Ganji towards the river. Contemporary descriptions of the complex list the elements in order from the river terrace towards the Taj Ganji.

Dimensional Organisation

That the Taj comlex is ordered by grids is self evident from examination of any plan. However, it was not until 1989 that Begley and Desai attempted the first detailed scholastic examination of how the various elements of the Taj might fit into a coordinating grid. Numerous 17th century accounts detail the precise measurements of the complex in terms of the Gaz or *zira*, the Mughal linear yard, equivalent to approximately 80-92 cm. Begley and Desai concluded a 400 gaz grid was used and then subdivided and that the various descrepancies they discovered were due to errors in the contemporary descriptions.

More recent research and measurement by Koch and Richard André Barraud suggests a more complex method of ordering that relates better to the 17th century records. Whereas Begley and Desai had used a simple fixed grid on which the buildings are superimposed, Koch and Barraud found the layout's proportions were better explained by the use of a *generated* grid system in which specific lengths may be divided in a number of ways such as halving, dividing by three or using decimal systems. They suggest the 374 gaz width of the complex given by the contemporary historians was correct and the Taj is planned as a tripartite rectangle of three 374 gaz squares. Different modular divisions are then used to proportion the rest of the complex. A 17 gaz module is used in the jilaukhana, bazaar and caravanserais areas whereas a more detailed 23 gaz module is used in the garden and terrace areas (since their width is 368 gaz, a multiple of 23). The buildings were in turn proportioned using yet smaller grids superimposed on the larger organisational ones. The smaller grids were also used to establish elevational proportion throughout the complex.

Such apparently peculiar numbers make more sense when seen as part of Mughal geometric understanding. Octagons and triangles, which feature extensively in the Taj, have particular properties in terms of the relationships of their sides. A right handed triangle with two sides of 12 will have a hypotenuse of 17, similarly if it has two sides of 17 it's hypotenuse will be 24. An octagon with a width of 17 will have sides of exactly 7, which is the basic grid upon which the mausoleum, mosque and Mihman Khana are planned.

MAUSOLEUM (RAUZA-I MUNAUWARA)

The focus and climax of the Taj Mahal complex is the symmetrical white marble tomb; a cubic building with chamfered corners, with arched recesses known as pishtaqs. It is topped by a large dome and several pillared, roofed chhatris. In plan, it has a near perfect symmetry about 4 axes and is arranged in the 'hasht bihisht' form found in the tomb of Humayun. It comprises 4 floors; the lower basement storey containing the tombs of Jahan and Mumtaz, the entrance storey containing identical cenotaphs of the tombs below in a much more elaborate chamber, an ambulatory storey and a roof terrace.

The hierarchical ordering of the entire complex reaches its crescendo in the main chamber housing the cenotaphs of Shah Jahan and Mumtaz. Mumtaz's cenotaph sits at the geometric centre of the building; Jahan was buried at a later date by her side to the west - an arrangement seen in other Mughal tombs of the period such as Itmad-Ud-Daulah. Marble is used exclusively as the base material for increasingly dense, expensive and complex parchin kari floral decoration as one approaches the screen and cenotpahs which are inlaid with semi-precious stones. The use of such inlay work is often reserved in Shah Jahani architecture for spaces associated with the emperor or his immediate family. The ordering of this decoration simultaneously emphasises the cardinal points and the centre of the chamber with dissipating concentric octagons. Such hierarchies appear in both Muslim and Indian culture as important spiritual and atrological themes. The chamber is an abundant evocation of the garden of paradise with representations of flowers, plants and arabesques and the calligraphic inscriptions in both the thuluth and the less formal naskh script.

Muslim tradition forbids elaborate decoration of graves, so the bodies of Mumtaz and Shah Jahan are laid in a relatively plain chamber beneath the inner chamber of the Taj. They are buried on a north-south access, with faces turned right (west) toward Mecca. The Taj has been raised over their cenotaphs (from Greek *keno taphas,* empty tomb). The cenotaphs mirror precisely the placement of the two graves, and are exact duplicates of the grave stones in the basement below. Mumtaz's cenotaph is placed at the precise center of the inner chamber. On a rectangular marble base about 1.5 by 2.5 m is a smaller marble casket. Both base and casket are elaborately inlaid with precious and semiprecious gems. Calligraphic inscriptions on the casket identify and praise Mumtaz. On the lid of the casket is a raised rectangular lozenge meant to suggest a writing tablet.

Shah Jahan's cenotaph is beside Mumtaz's to the western side. It is the only asymmetric element in the entire complex. His cenotaph is bigger than his wife's, but reflects the same elements: A larger casket on slightly taller base, again decorated with astonishing precision with lapidary and calligraphy which identifies Shah Jahan. On the lid of this casket is a sculpture of a a small pen box. (The pen box and writing tablet were traditional Mughal funerary icons decorating men's and women's caskets respectively.)

An octagonal marble screen or *jali* borders the cenotaphs and is made from eight marble panels. Each panel has been carved through with intricate piercework. The remaining surfaces have been inlaid with semiprecious stones in extremely delicate detail, forming twining vines, fruits and flowers.

RIVERFRONT TERRACE (CHAMELI FARSH)

Plinth and terrace

- Tahkhana
- Towers

Minarets

At the corners of the plinth stand minarets — four large towers each more than 40 meters tall. The towers are designed as working minarets, a traditional element of mosques, a place for a muezzin to call the Islamic faithful to prayer. Each minaret is effectively divided into three equal parts by two working balconies that ring the tower. At the top of the tower is a final balcony surmounted by a chattri that mirrors the design of those on the tomb. Each of the minarets was constructed slightly out of plumb to the outside of the plinth, so that in the event of collapse (a typical occurrence with many such tall constructions of the period) the material would tend to fall away from the tomb.

Jawab and Mosque

The mausoleum is flanked by two almost identical buildings on either side of the platform. To the west is the Mosque, to the east is Jawab. The Jawab, meaning 'answer' balances the bilateral symmetry of the composition and was originally used as a place for entertaining and accommodation for important visitors. It differs from the mosque in that it lacks a *mihrab*, a niche in a mosque's wall facing Mecca, and the floors have a geometric design, while the mosque floor was laid out with the outlines of 569 prayer rugs in black marble.

The mosque's basic tripartite design is similar to others built by Shah Jahan, particularly the Masjid-i-Jahan Numa in Delhi — a long hall surmounted by three domes. Mughal mosques of this period divide the sanctuary hall into three areas: a main sanctuary with slightly smaller sanctuaries to either side. At the Taj Mahal, each sanctuary opens onto an enormous vaulting dome.

Garden (Charbagh)

The large *charbagh* (a formal Mughal garden divided into four parts) provides the foreground for the classic view of the Taj Mahal. The garden's strict and formal planning employs raised pathways which divide each quarter of the garden into 16 sunken parterres or flowerbeds. A raised marble water tank at the center of the garden, halfway between the tomb and the gateway, and a linear reflecting pool on the North-South axis reflect the Taj Mahal. Elsewhere the garden is laid out with avenues of trees and fountains.The *charbagh* garden is meant to symbolize the four flowing Rivers of Paradise. The raised marble water tank (hauz) is called *al Hawd al-Kawthar*, literally meaning and named after the "Tank of Abundance" promised to Muhammad in paradise where the faithful may quench their thirst upon arrival.

Two pavilions occupy the east and west ends of the cross axis, one the mirror of the other. In the classic charbargh design, gates would have been located in this location. In the Taj they provide punctuation and access to the long enclosing wall with its decorative crenellations. Built of sandstone, they are given a tripartite form and over two storeys and are capped with a white marble chhatris supported from 8 columns.

The original planting of the garden is one of the Taj Mahal's remaining mysteries. The contemporary accounts mostly deal just with the architecture and only mention 'various kinds of fruit-bearing trees and rare aromatic herbs' in relation to the garden. Cypress trees are almost certainly to have been planted being popular similes in Persian poetry for the slender elegant stature of the beloved. By the end of the 18th century, Thomas Twining noted orange trees and a large plan of the complex suggests beds of various other fruits such as pineapples, pomegranates, bananas, limes and apples. The British, at the end of the 19th century thinned out a lot of the increasingly forested trees, replanted the cypresses and laid the gardens to lawns in their own taste.

The layout of the garden, and its architectural features such as its fountains, brick and marble walkways, and geometric brick-lined flowerbeds are similar to Shalimar's, and suggest that the garden may have been designed by the same engineer, Ali Mardan.

Early accounts of the garden describe its profusion of vegetation, including roses, daffodils, and fruit trees in abundance. As the Mughal Empire declined, the tending of the garden declined as well. When the British took over management of the Taj Mahal, they changed the landscaping to resemble the formal lawns of London.

Great Gate (Darwaza-i rauza)

The great gate stands at the north of entrance forecourt (Jilaukhana) and provides a transition between the worldly realm of bazaars and caravanserai and the spiritual realm of the paradise garden, mosque and the mausoleum. Its rectangular plan is a variation of the 9-part hasht bihisht plan found in the mausoleum. The corners are articulated with octagonal towers giving the structure a defensive appearance. External domes were reserved for tombs and mosques of the time and so the large central space does not receive any outward expression of its internal dome. From the space the

Mausoleum is framed along its major axis by the pointed arch of the portal. Inscriptions from the Qu'ran are inlaid around the two northern and southern pishtaqs, the southern one 'Daybreak' invites believers to enter the garden of paradise.

Southern Galleries (Iwan Dar Iwan)

Running the length of the northern side of the southern garden wall to the east and west of the great gate are galleried arcades. A raised platform with geometric paving provides their base and between the columns are cusped arches typical of the Mughul architecture of the period. The galleries were used during the rainy season to admit the poor and distribute alms. The galleries terminate at each end with a transversely placed room with tripartite divisions.

Forecourt (Jilaukhana)

The Jilaukhana (literally meaning 'in front of house') was a courtyard feature introduced to mughal architecture by Shah Jahan. It provided an area where visitors would dismount from their horses or elephants and assemble in style before entering the main tomb complex. The rectangular area divides north-south and east-west with an entry to the tomb complex through the main gate to the north and entrance gates leading to the outside provided in the eastern, western and southern walls. The southern gate leads to the Taj Ganji quarter.

Bazaar Streets

Two identical streets lead from the east and west gates to the centre of the courtyard. They are lined by verandahed colonnades articulated with cusped arches behind which cellular rooms were used to sell goods from when the Taj was built until 1996. The tax revenue from this trade was used for the upkeep of the Taj complex. The eastern bazaar streets were essentially ruined by the end of the 19th century and were restored by Lord Curzon restored 1900 and 1908.

Inner Subsidiary Tombs (Saheli Burj)

Two mirror image tombs are located at the southern corners of the Jilaukhana. They are conceived as miniature replicas of the main complex and stand on raised platforms accessed by steps. Each octagonal tomb is constructed on a rectangular platform flanked by smaller rectangular buildings in front of which is laid a charbargh garden. Some uncertainty exists as to whom the tombs might memorialise. Their descriptions are absent from the contemporary accounts either because they were unbuilt or because they were ignored, being the tombs of women. On the first written document to mention them, the plan drawn up by Thomas and William Daniel in 1789, the eastern tomb is marked as that belonging to Akbarabadi Mahal and the western as Fatehpuri Mahal.

Northern Courtyards (Khawasspuras)

A pair of courtyards is found in the northern corners of the Jilaukhana which provided quarters (Khawasspuras) for the tombs attendants and the Hafiz. This residential element provided a transition between the outside world and the other-worldy delights of the tomb complex. The Khawasspurs had fallen into a state of disrepair by the late 18th century but the institution of the Khadim continued into the 20th century. The Khawasspuras were restored by Lord Curzon as part of his repairs between 1900 and 1908, after which the western courtyard was used as a nursery for the garden and the western courtyard was used as a cattle stable until 2003.

Bazaar and Caravanserai (Taj Ganji)

The Bazaar and caravanserai were constructed as an integral part of the complex, initially to provide the construction workers with accommodation and facilities for their wellbeing, and later as a place for trade, the revenue of which supplemented the expenses of the complex. The area became a small town in its own right during and after the building of the Taj. Originally known as 'Mumtazabad', today it is called Taj Ganji or 'Taj Market'. Its plan took the characteristic form of a square divided by two cross axial streets with gates to the four cardinal points. Bazaars lined each street and the resultant squares to each corner housed the caravanserais in open courtyards accessed from internal gates from where the streets intersected (Chauk). Contemporary sources pay more attention to the north eastern and western parts of the Taj Ganji (Taj Market) and it is likely that only this half received imperial funding. Thus, the quality of the architecture was finer than the southern half.

The distinction between how the sacred part of the complex and the secular was regarded is most acute in this part of the complex. Whilst the rest of the complex only received maintenance after its construction, the Taj Ganji became a bustling town and the centre of Agra's economic activity where "different kinds of merchandise from every land, varieties of goods from every country, all sorts of luxuries aof the time, and various kinds of necessitities of civilisation and comfortable living brought from all parts of the world" were sold. An idea of what sort of goods might have been traded is found in the names for the caravanserais; the north western one was known as Katra Omar Khan (Market of Omar Khan), the north eastern as Katra Fulel (Perfume Market), the south western as Katra Resham (Silk Market) and the south-eastern as Katra Jogidas. It has been constantly redeveloped ever since its construction, to the extent that by the 19th century it had become unrecognisable as part of the Taj Mahal and no longer featured on contemporary plans and its architecture was largely obliterated. Today, the contrast is stark between the Taj Mahal's elegant, formal geometric layout and the narrow streets with organic, random and un-unified constructions found in the Taj Ganji. Only fragments of the original constructions remain, most notably the gates.

Waterworks

Water for the Taj complex was provided through a complex infrastructure. It was drawn from the river by a series of *purs* - an animal-powered rope and bucket mechanism. The water flowed along an arched aqueduct into a large storage tank, where, by thirteen additional purs, it was raised to large distribution cistern above the Taj ground level located to the west of the complex's wall. From here water passed into three subsidiary tanks and was then piped to the complex. The head of pressure generated by the height of the tanks (9.5m) was sufficient to supply the fountains and irrigate the gardens. A 0.25 m diameter earthenware pipe lies 1.8 m below the surface, in line with the main walkway which filled the main pools of the complex. Some of the earthenware pipes were replaced in 1903 with cast iron. The fountain pipes were not connected directly to the fountain heads, instead a copper pot was provided under each fountain head: water filled the pots ensuring an equal pressure to each fountain. The purs no longer remain, but the other parts of the infrastructure have survived with the arches of the aqueduct now used to accommodate offices for the Archaeological Survey of India's Horticultural Department.

Moonlight Garden (Mahtab Bagh)

To the north of the Taj Mahal complex, across the river is another Charbagh garden. It was designed as an integral part of the complex in the riverfront terrace pattern seen elsewhere in Agra. Its width is identical to that of the rest of the Taj. The garden historian Elizabeth Moynihan suggests the large octagonal pool in the centre of the terrace would reflect the image of the Mausoleum and thus the garden would provide a setting to view the Taj Mahal. The garden has been beset by flooding from the river since Mughal times. As a result, the condition of the remaining structures is quite ruinous. Four sandstone towers marked the corners of the garden, only the south-eastward one remains. The foundations of two structures remain immediately north and south of the large pool which were probably garden pavilions. From the northern structure a stepped waterfall would have fed the pool. The garden to the north has the typical square, cross-axial plan with a square pool in its centre. To the west an aqueduct fed the garden.

Exterior Decoration

The exterior decorations of the Taj Mahal are among the finest to be found in Mughal architecture. As the surface area changes, a large pishtaq has more area than a smaller one, and the decorations are refined proportionally. The decorative elements were created by applying paint or stucco, or by stone inlays or carvings. In line with the Islamic prohibition against the use of anthropomorphic forms, the decorative elements can be grouped into either calligraphy, abstract forms or vegetative motifs.

The calligraphy found in Taj Mahal are of florid thuluth script, created by Persian calligrapher Amanat Khan, who signed several of the panels. The calligraphy is made by jasper inlaid in white marble panels, and the work found on the marble cenotaphs in the tomb is extremely detailed and delicate. Higher panels are written slightly larger to reduce the skewing effect when viewing from below. Throughout the complex, passages from the Qur'an are used as decorative elements. Recent scholarship suggests that Amanat Khan chose the passages as well. The texts refer to themes of judgment and include:

Surah 91 - The Sun

Surah 112 - The Purity of Faith

Surah 89 - Daybreak

Surah 93 - Morning Light

Surah 95 - The Fig

Surah 94 - The Solace

Surah 36 - Ya Sin

Surah 81 - The Folding Up

Surah 82 - The Cleaving Asunder

Surah 84 - The Rending Asunder

Surah 98 - The Evidence

Surah 67 - Dominion

Surah 48 - Victory

Surah 77 - Those Sent Forth

Surah 39 - The Crowds

As one enters through Taj Mahal Gate, the calligraphy reads *"O Soul, thou art at rest. Return to the Lord at peace with Him, and He at peace with you."*

Abstract forms are used especially in the plinth, minarets, gateway, mosque, jawab, and to a lesser extent, on the surfaces of the tomb. The domes and vaults of sandstone buildings are worked with tracery of incised painting to create elaborate geometric forms. On most joining areas, herringbone inlays define the space between adjoining elements. White inlays are used in sandstone buildings and dark or black inlays on the white marbles. Mortared areas of marble buildings have been stained or painted dark and thus creating a geometric patterns of considerable complexity. Floors and walkways use contrasting tiles or blocks in tessellation patterns.

Vegetative motifs are found at the lower walls of the tomb. They are white marble dados that have been sculpted with realistic bas relief depictions of flowers and vines. The marble has been polished to emphasise the exquisite detailing of these carvings. The dado frames and archway spandrels have been decorated with pietra dura inlays of highly stylised, almost geometric vines, flowers and fruits. The inlay stones are yellow marble, jasper and jade, leveled and polished to the surface of the walls.

Interior Decoration

The interior chamber of the Taj Mahal steps far beyond traditional decorative elements. Here the inlay work is not pietra dura, but lapidary of precious and semiprecious gemstones. The inner chamber is an octagon with the design allowing for entry from each face, though only the south garden-facing door is used. The interior walls are about 25 metres high and topped by a "false" interior dome decorated with a sun motif. Eight pishtaq arches define the space at ground level. As with the exterior, each lower pishtaq is crowned by a second pishtaq about midway up the wall. The four central upper arches form balconies or viewing areas and each balcony's exterior window has an intricate screen or *jali* cut from marble. In addition to the light from the balcony screens, light enters through roof openings covered by chattris at the corners. Each chamber wall has been highly decorated with dado bas relief, intricate lapidary inlay and refined calligraphy panels, reflecting in miniature detail the design elements seen throughout the exterior of the complex. The octagonal marble screen or *jali* which borders the cenotaphs is made from eight marble panels. Each panel has been carved through with intricate pierce work. The remaining surfaces have been inlaid with semiprecious stones in extremely delicate detail, forming twining vines, fruits and flowers.

Muslim tradition forbids elaborate decoration of graves and hence Mumtaz and Shah Jahan are laid in a relatively plain crypt beneath the inner chamber with their faces turned right and towards Mecca. Mumtaz Mahal's cenotaph is placed at the precise center of the inner chamber with a rectangular marble base of 1.5 meters by 2.5 meters. Both the base and casket are elaborately inlaid with precious and semiprecious gems. Calligraphic inscriptions on the casket identify and praise Mumtaz. On the lid of the casket is a raised rectangular lozenge meant to suggest a writing tablet. Shah Jahan's cenotaph is beside Mumtaz's to the western side. It is the only visible asymmetric element in the entire complex.

His cenotaph is bigger than his wife's, but reflects the same elements: a larger casket on slightly taller base, again decorated with astonishing precision with lapidary and calligraphy that identifies Shah Jahan. On the lid of this casket is a traditional sculpture of a small pen box. The pen box and writing tablet were traditional Mughal funerary icons decorating men's and women's caskets respectively. Ninety Nine Names of God are to be found as calligraphic inscriptions on the sides of the actual tomb of Mumtaz Mahal, in the crypt including *"O Noble, O Magnificent, O Majestic, O Unique, O Eternal, O Glorious... "*. The tomb of Shah Jahan bears a calligraphic inscription that reads; *"He traveled from this world to the banquet-hall of Eternity on the night of the twenty-sixth of the month of Rajab, in the year 1076 Hijri."*

The Garden

The complex is set around a large 300-meter square *charbagh*, a Mughal garden. The garden uses raised pathways that divide each of the four quarters of the garden into 16 sunken parterres or flowerbeds. A raised marble water tank at the center of the garden, halfway between the tomb and gateway, with a reflecting pool on North-South axis reflects the image of the Taj Mahal. Elsewhere, the garden is laid out with avenues of trees and fountains. The raised marble water tank is called *al Hawd al-Kawthar*, in reference to "Tank of Abundance" promised to Muhammad. The charbagh garden, a design inspired by Persian gardens, was introduced to India by the first Mughal emperor Babur. It symbolizes four flowing rivers of Paradise and reflects the gardens of Paradise derived from the Persian *paridaeza*, meaning 'walled garden'. In mystic Islamic texts of Mughal period, paradise is described as an ideal garden of abundance with four rivers flowing from a central spring or mountain, separating the garden into north, west, south and east.

Most Mughal charbaghs are rectangular with a tomb or pavilion in the center. The Taj Mahal garden is unusual in that the main element, the tomb, instead is located at the end of the garden. With the discovery of Mahtab Bagh or "Moonlight Garden" on the other side of the Yamuna, Archaeological Survey of India interprets that the Yamuna itself was incorporated into the garden's design and was meant to be seen as one of the rivers of Paradise. The similarity in layout of the garden and its architectural features such as fountains, brick and marble walkways, and geometric brick-lined flowerbeds with Shalimar's suggest that the garden may have been designed by the same engineer, Ali Mardan. Early accounts of the garden describe its profusion of vegetation, including roses, daffodils, and fruit trees in abundance. As the Mughal Empire declined, the tending of the garden declined as well. When the British took over the management of Taj Mahal, they changed the landscaping to resemble that of lawns of London.

Outlying Buildings

The Taj Mahal complex is bounded by crenellated red sandstone walls on three sides with river-facing side open. Outside these walls are several additional mausoleums, including those of Shah Jahan's other wives, and a larger tomb for Mumtaz's favorite servant. These structures, composed primarily of red sandstone, are typical of the smaller Mughal tombs of the era. The garden-facing inner sides of the wall are fronted by columned arcades, a feature typical of Hindu temples later incorporated into Mughal mosques. The wall is interspersed with domed kiosks (*chattris*), and small buildings that may have been viewing areas or watch to.vers like the *Music House*, which is now used as a museum.

The main gateway (*darwaza*) is a monumental structure built primarily of marble and is reminiscent of Mughal architecture of earlier emperors. Its archways mirror the shape of tomb's archways, and its *pishtaq* arches incorporate calligraphy that decorates the tomb. It utilizes bas-relief and pietra dura (inlaid) decorations with floral motifs. The vaulted ceilings and walls have elaborate geometric designs, like those found in the other sandstone buildings of the complex.

At the far end of the complex, there are two grand red sandstone buildings that are open to the sides of the tomb. Their backs parallel western and eastern walls, and these two buildings are precise mirror images of each other. The western building is a mosque and its opposite is the *jawab* (answer) whose primary purpose was architectural balance and may have been used as a guesthouse. The distinctions between these two buildings include the lack of *mihrab*, a niche in a mosque's wall facing Mecca, in the *jawab* and that the floors of *jawab* have a geometric design, while the mosque floor was laid with outlines of 569 prayer rugs in black marble. The mosque's basic design is similar to others built by Shah Jahan, particularly to his Masjid-Jahan Numa, or Jama Masjid of Delhi, a long hall surmounted by three domes. The Mughal mosques of this period divide the sanctuary hall into three areas with a main sanctuary and slightly smaller sanctuaries on either side. At the Taj Mahal, each sanctuary opens onto an enormous vaulting dome. These outlying buildings were completed in 1643.

MYTHS

Ever since its construction, the building has been the source of an admiration transcending culture and geography, and so personal and emotional responses to the building have consistently eclipsed scholastic appraisals of the monument.

A longstanding myth holds that Shah Jahan planned a mausoleum to be built in black marble across the Yamuna river. The idea originates from fanciful writings of Jean-Baptiste Tavernier, a European traveller who visited Agra in 1665. It was suggested that Shah Jahan was overthrown by his son Aurangzeb before it could be built. Ruins of blackened marble across the river in *Moonlight Garden*, Mahtab Bagh, seemed to support this legend. However, excavations carried out in the 1990s found that they were discolored white stones that had turned black. A more credible theory for the origins of the black mausoleum was demonstrated in 2006 by archeologists who resconstructed part of the pool in the Moonlight Garden. A dark reflection of the white mausoleum could clearly be seen, befitting Shah Jahan's obsession with symmetry and the positioning of the pool itself.

No evidence exists for claims that describe, often in horrific detail, the deaths, dismemberments and mutilations which Shah Jahan supposedly inflicted on various architects and craftsmen associated with the tomb. Some stories claim that those involved in construction signed contracts committing themselves to have no part in any similar design. Similar claims are made for many famous buildings. No evidence exists for claims that Lord William Bentinck, governor of India in the 1830s, supposedly planned to demolish the Taj Mahal and auction off the marble. Bentinck's biographer John Rosselli says that the story arose from Bentinck's fund-raising sale of discarded marble from Agra Fort.

In 2000, India's Supreme Court dismissed P.N. Oak's petition to declare that a Hindu king built the Taj Mahal. Oak claimed that origins of the Taj, together with other historic structures in the country currently ascribed to Muslim sultans pre-date Muslim occupation of India and thus, have a Hindu origin. A more poetic story relates that once a year, during the rainy season, a single drop of water falls on the cenotaph, as inspired by Rabindranath Tagore's description of the tomb as *"one tear-drop...upon the cheek of time"*. Another myth suggests that beating the silhouette of the finial will cause water to come forth. To this day, officials find broken bangles surrounding the silhouette.

HUMAYUN'S TOMB

Humayun's tomb is a complex of buildings in Mughal architecture built as Mughal Emperor Humayun's tomb. It is located in Nizamuddin east, New Delhi.

In time of Slave Dynasty this land was under the KiloKheri Fort which was capital of Sultan Kequbad son of Nasiruddin (1268-1287). It encompasses the main tomb of the Emperor Humayun as well as numerous others. The complex is a World Heritage Site and the first example of this type of Mughal architecture in India.

The architecture of the mausoleum is similar to Taj Mahal.

History

The tomb of Humayun was built by the orders of Hamida Banu Begum, Humayun's widow starting in 1562. The architect of the edifice was reportedly *Sayyed Muhammad ibn Mirak Ghiyathuddin* and his father *Mirak Ghiyathuddin* who were brought in from

Herat. It took 8 years to build and had a Chahr Bagh Garden style in its design, the first of its kind in the region.

Restoration

Restoration work by the Aga Khan Trust for Culture was completed in March 2003, enabling water to flow through the watercourses in the gardens once more. Funding for this work was a gift from the institutions of His Highness the Aga Khan to India. In addition, AKTC is conducting a more significant restoration at Babur's tomb, the resting place of Humayun's father in Kabul.

QUTUB MINAR

Qutub Minar is the tallest brick minaret in the world, and an important example of Indo-Islamic Architecture. The tower is in the Qutb complex at Mehrauli in South Delhi, India. The Qutub Minar and its monuments are listed as a UNESCO World Heritage Site.

The Qutub Minar is 72 meters high (237.8 ft) with 379 steps leading to the top. The diameter of the base is 14.3 meters wide while the top floor measures 2.75 meters in diameter. Surrounding the building are many fine examples of Indian artwork from the time it was built in 1193. A second tower was in construction and planned to be taller than the Qutub Minar itself. Its construction ended abruptly when it was about 12 meters tall.The name of this tower is given as Alau Minar and construction of the same ended due to the death of the Sultan Alauddin Khilji. Only the core made of random rubble masonry and mortar remain of this unfinished tower which was to have been twice the height of the Qutub Minar of Qutub ud din Aibak.

Inspired by the Minaret of Jam in Afghanistan and wishing to surpass it, Qutub-ud-din Aibak, the first Muslim ruler of Delhi, commenced construction of the Qutub Minar in 1193, but could only complete its base. His successor, Iltutmish, added three more storeys and, in 1368, Firuz Shah Tughluq constructed the fifth and the last storey. The development of architectural styles from Aibak to Tuglak are quite evident in the minaret. Like earlier towers erected by the Ghaznavids and Ghurids in Afghanistan, the Qutub Minar comprises several superposed flanged and cylindrical shafts, separated by balconies carried on Muqarnas corbels. The minaret is made of fluted red sandstone covered with intricate carvings and verses from the Qur'an. The Qutub Minar is itself built on the ruins of Lal Kot, the Red Citadel in the city of Dhillika, the capital of the Tomars and the Chauhans, the last Hindu rulers of Delhi.

The purpose for building this monument has been variously speculated upon. It could take the usual role of a minaret, calling people for prayer in the Quwwat-ul-

Islam mosque, the earliest extant mosque built by the Delhi Sultans. Other possibilities are a tower of victory, a monument signifying the might of Islam, or a watch tower for defense. Controversy also surrounds the origins for the name of the tower. Many historians believe that the Qutub Minar was named after the first Turkish sultan, Qutub-ud-din Aibak but others contend that it was named in honour of Qutubuddin Bakhtiar Kaki, a saint from Baghdad who came to live in India and was greatly venerated by Iltutmish.

According to the inscriptions on its surface it was repaired by Firuz Shah Tughlaq (AD 1351–88) and Sikandar Lodi (AD 1489–1517). Major R. Smith also repaired and restored the minaret in 1829.

The nearby Iron Pillar is one of the world's foremost metallurgical curiosities, standing in the famous Qutub Complex. According to the traditional belief, any one who can encircle the entire column with their arms, with their back towards the pillar, can have their wish granted. Because of the corrosive qualities of sweat, people are no longer allowed to perform this act.

AGRA FORT

Agra Fort is a UNESCO World Heritage site located in Agra, India. The fort is also known as Lal Qila, Fort Rouge and Red Fort of Agra. It is about 2.5 km northwest of its much more famous sister monument, the Taj Mahal. The fort can be more accurately described as a walled palatial city.

It is the most important fort in India. The great Mughals Babur, Humayun, Akbar, Jehangir, Shah Jahan and Aurangzeb lived here, and the country was governed from here. It contained the largest state treasury and mint. It was visited by foreign ambassadors, travellers and the highest dignitaries who participated in the making of history in India.

History

This was originally a brick fort and the Chauhan Rajputs held it. It was mentioned for the first time in 1080 AD when a Ghaznavide force captured it. Sikandar Lodi (1487-1517) was the first Sultan of Delhi who shifted to Agra and lived in the fort. He governed the country from here and Agra assumed the importance of the 2nd capital. He died in the fort in 1517 and his son, Ibrahim Lodi, held it for nine years until he was defeated and killed at Panipat in 1526. Several palaces, wells and a mosque were built by him in the fort during his period.

After Panipat, Mughals captured the fort and a vast treasure - which included a diamond that was later named as the Koh-i-Nor diamond - was seized. Babur stayed in the fort in the palace of Ibrahim. He built a baoli (step well) in it. Humayun was crowned here in 1530. Humayun was defeated in Bilgram in 1530. Sher Shah held the fort for five years. The Mughals defeated the Afghans finally at Panipat in 1556.

Realizing the importance of its central situation, Akbar decided to make it his capital and arrived in Agra in 1558. His historian, Abdul Fazal, recorded that this was a brick fort known as 'Badalgarh'. It was in a ruined condition and Akbar had it rebuilt with red sandstone. Architects laid the foundation and it was built with bricks in the inner core with sandstone on external surfaces. Some 1,444,000 builders worked on it for eight years, completing it in 1573.

It was only during the reign of Akbar's grandson, Shah Jahan, that the site finally took on its current state. The legend is that Shah Jahan built the beautiful Taj Mahal for his wife, Mumtaz Mahal. Unlike his grandfather, Shah Jahan tended to have buildings made from white marble, often inlaid with gold or semi-precious gems. He destroyed some of the earlier buildings inside the fort in order to make his own.

At the end of his life, Shah Jahan was imprisoned by his son, Aurangzeb, in the fort, a punishment which might not seem so harsh, considering the luxury of the fort. It is rumored that Shah Jahan died in Muasamman Burj, a tower with a marble balcony with an excellent view of the Taj Mahal.

This was also a site of one of the battles during the Indian rebellion of 1857, which caused the end of the British East India Company's rule in India, and led to a century of direct rule of India by Britain.

Layout

The Agra Fort has won the Aga Khan Award for Architecture in the year 2004 and India Post has issued a Stamp to commemorate this prestigious award on 28.11.2004.

The fort has a semi-circular plan, its chord lying parallel to the river. Its walls are seventy feet high. Double ramparts have massive circular bastions are regular intervals as also battlements, embrasures, machicolations and string courses. Four gates were provided on its four sides, one Khizri gate" opening on to the river. Two of the gates are called the 'Delhi Gate' and the 'Lahore Gate' (sometimes called Amar Singh Gate).

The Delhi Gate, which faces the city, is considered the grandest of the four gates. It leads to an inner gate called the Hathi Pol (Elephant Gate) where two life sized stone elephants with their riders stand guard. A draw-bridge, the slight ascent and 90 degree turns before each subsequent gate make it impregnable: during a siege, attackers had elephants crush the gates. Without a level, straight run-up to gather speed, which is prevented by this layout, they are not effective, though.

The monumental Delhi gate was built as the king's formal gate. Because the Indian military (the Parachute Brigade in particular) is still using the northern portion of the Agra Fort, the Delhi Gate cannot be used by the public. Tourists enter via the Lahore Gate so named because it faces Lahore, now in Pakistan.

The site is very important in terms of architectural history. Abul Fazal recorded that five hundred buildings in the beautiful designs of Bengal and Gujarat were built in the fort. Some of them were demolished to make way for his white marble palaces. Most of the others were destroyed by the British between 1803 and 1862 for raising barracks. Hardly thirty Mughal buildings have survived on the south-eastern side, facing the river. Of these, the Delhi Gate and Akbar Gate and one palace - "Bengali Mahal" - are representative Akbari buildings.

Akbar Gate Akbar Darwazza was renamed "Amar Singh Gate" by Jahangir. The gate is similar in design to the Delhi gate. Both are built of red sandstone. The Bengali Mahal is also built of red sandstone and is now split into "Akbari Mahal" and "Jehagiri Mahal".

Some of the most historically interesting mixing of Hindu and Islamic architecture are found here. In fact, some of the Islamic decorations feature haraam (forbidden) images of living creatures - dragons, elephants and birds, instead of the usual patterns and calligraphy seen in Islamic surface decoration.

Sites and Structures within Agra Fort

- Anguri Bagh - 85 square, geometrically arranged gardens
- Diwan-i-Aam (Hall of Public Audience) - was used to speak to the people and listen to petitioners and once housed the Peacock Throne
- Diwan-i-Khas (Hall of Private Audience) - was used to receive kings and dignitary, features black throne of Jehangir
- Golden Pavilions - beautiful pavilions with roofs shaped like the roofs of Bengali huts
- Jehangiri Mahal - built by Akbar for his son Jehangir
- Khas Mahal - white marble palace, one of the best examples of painting on marble
- Macchi Bhawan (Fish Enclosure) - grand enclosure for harem functions, once had pools and fountains
- Mina Masjid (Heavenly Mosque)- a tiny mosque; closed to the public
- Moti Masjid (Pearl Mosque) - a private mosque of Shah Jahan
- Musamman Burj - a large, octagonal tower with a balcony facing the Taj Mahal
- Nagina Masjid (Gem Mosque) - mosque designed for the ladies of the court, featuring the Zenana Mina Bazaar (Ladies Bazaar) right next to the balcony, where only female merchants sold wares

- Naubat Khana (Drum House) - a place where the king's musicians played
- Rang Mahal - where the king's wives and mistresses lived
- Shahi Burj - Shah Jahan's private work area
- Shah Jahani Mahal - Shah Jahan's first attempt at modification of the red sandstone palace
- Sheesh Mahal (Glass Palace) or Shish Mahal - royal dressing room featuring tiny mirror-like glass-mosaic decorations on the walls

Other Notable Facts

Agra Fort should not be confused with the much smaller Red Fort at Delhi. The Mughals never referred the Red Fort as a fort; rather, it was referred as the 'Lal Haveli', or the Red Bungalow. The Prime Minister of India addresses the nation from Delhi's Red Fort on August 15, India's Independence Day.

The Agra Fort plays a key role in the Sherlock Holmes mystery, *The Sign of the Four*, by Sir Arthur Conan Doyle. The Agra Fort was featured in the music video for Habibi Da, a hit song of Egyptian pop star Hisham Abbas.

Shivaji came to Agra in 1666 as per the "Purandar Treaty" entered into with Mirza Raje Jaisingh to met Aurangzeb in the Diwan-i-khas. In the audience he was deliberately placed behind men of lower rank, Insulted he stormed out of the imperial audience and was confined to Jai Sing's quarters on 12th May 1666. Fearing the dungeons and execution, in a famously sweet legend, he escaped on the 17th of August 1666. A heroic equestrian statue of Shivaji has been erected outside the fort.

In the second expansion pack for Age of Empires 3, the Asian Dynasties, Agra fort is one of five wonders for the Indian civilization to advance to the next age. Once built, it sends player a shipment of coin. This wonder acts as a Fortress, with an attack (though weaker than European versions) and the ability to train infantry and cavalry units.

In the game "Rise of Nations" the Red Fort can be built by players as a wonder. The Red Fort acts just like a normal castle/fortress/redoubt. But has the ability to heal troops garrisoned inside by 500%, and is also resistant to air attacks. Attack range is also longer, and certain unit upgrades are gained automatically, at no cost.

RED FORT

The Delhi Fort also known as Lal Qil'ah, or Lal Qila, meaning the Red Fort, located in Delhi, India and became a UNESCO World Heritage Site in 2007.

The Red Fort and the city of Shahjahanabad was constructed by the Emperor Shah Jahan in 1639 A.D. The layout of the Red Fort was organised to retain and integrate this site with the Salimgarh Fort. The fortress palace is an important focal point of the medieval city of Shahjahanabad. The planning and aesthetics of the Red Fort represent the zenith of Mughal creativity which prevailed during the reign of Emperor Shahjahan. This Fort has had many developments added on after its construction by Emperor Shahjahan. The significant phases of development were under Aurangzeb and later Mughal rulers. Important physical changes were carried out in the overall settings of the site after the First War of Independence during British Rule in 1857. After Independence, the site experienced a few changes in terms of addition/alteration to the structures. During the British period the Fort was mainly used as a cantonment and even after Independence, a significant part of the Fort remained under the control of the Army until the year 2003.

The Red Fort was the palace for Mughal Emperor Shah Jahan's new capital, Shahjahanabad, the seventh Muslim city in the Delhi site. He moved his capital from Agra in a move designed to bring prestige to his reign, and to provide ample opportunity to apply his ambitious building schemes and interests.

The fort lies along the Yamuna River, which fed the moats that surround most of the wall. The wall at its north-eastern corner is adjacent to an older fort, the Salimgarh Fort, a defense built by Islam Shah Suri in 1546. Construction on the Red Fort began in 1638 and was complete by 1648. However, it is believed that it is the ancient city of Lal Kot which was captured by Shah Jahan since Lal Kot literally means Red (Lal) Fort (Kot). Lal Kot was the capital city of Prithviraj Chauhan in the late 12th century.

On 11 March 1783, Sikhs entered Red Fort in Delhi and occupied the Diwan-i-Aam. The city was essentially surrendered by the Mughal wazir in cahoots with his Sikh Allies. This task was carried out under the command of the Sardar Baghel Singh Dhaliwal of the Karor Singhia misl.

Dimensions

The Red Fort stands at the eastern edge of Shahjahanabad, and gets its name from the massive wall of red sandstone that defines its four sides. The wall is 1.5 miles (2.5 km) long, and varies in height from 60 ft (16 m) on the river side to 110 ft (33 m) towards the city. Measurements have shown that the plan was generated using a square grid of 82 m.

Architectural Design

Red Fort showcases the very high level of art form and ornamental work. The art work in the Fort is a synthesis of Persian, European and Indian art which resulted in the development of unique Shahjahani style which is very rich in form, expression and colour. Red Fort, Delhi is one of the important building complexes of India which encapsulates a long period of Indian history and its arts. Its significance has transcended time and space. It is relevant as a symbol of architectural brilliance and power. Even before its notification as a monument of national importance in the year 1913, efforts were made to preserve and conserve the Red Fort, for posterity.

The walls of the fort are smoothly dressed, articulated by heavy string-courses along the upper section. They open at two major gates, the Delhi and the Lahore gates. The Lahore Gate is the main entrance; it leads to a long covered bazaar street, the Chatta Chowk, whose walls are lined with stalls for shops. The Chatta Chowk leads to a large open space where it crosses the large north-south street that was originally the division between the fort's military functions, to its west, and the palaces, to its east. The southern end of this street is the Delhi Gate.

Important Buildings Inside Fort

Naqqar Khana

On axis with the Lahore gate and the Chatta Chowk, on the eastern side of the open space, is the Naqqar Khana ("drum house"), the main gate for the palace, named for the musicians' gallery above it.

Diwan-i-Aam

Beyond this gate is another, larger open space, which originally served as the courtyard of the Diwan-i-Aam, the large pavilion for public imperial audiences. An ornate throne-balcony for the emperor stands at the center of the eastern wall of the Diwan.

Nahr-i-Behisht

The imperial private apartments lie behind the throne. The apartments consist of a row of pavilions that sits on a raised platform along the eastern edge of the fort, looking out onto the river Yamuna. The pavilions are connected by a continuous water channel, known as the Nahr-i-Behisht, or the "Stream of Paradise", that runs through the center of each pavilion. The water is drawn from the river Yamuna, from a tower, the *Shah Burj*, at the northeastern corner of the fort. The palace is designed as an imitation of paradise as it is described in the Koran; a couplet repeatedly inscribed in the palace reads, "If there be a paradise on earth, it is here, it is here". The planning of the palace is based on Islamic prototypes, but each pavilion reveals in its architectural elements the Hindu influences typical of Mughal building. The palace complex of the Red Fort is counted among the best examples of the Mughal style.

Zenana

The two southernmost pavilions of the palace are *zenana*s, or women's quarters: the Mumtaz Mahal (now a museum), and the larger, lavish Rang Mahal, which has been famous for its gilded, decorated ceiling and marble pool, fed by the *Nahr-i-Behisht*.

Khas Mahal

The third pavilion from the south, the Khas Mahal, contains the imperial chambers. These include a suite of bedrooms, prayer rooms, a veranda, and the *Mussaman Burj*, a tower built against the fortress walls, from which the emperor would show himself to the people in a daily ceremony.

Diwan-i-Khas

The next pavilion is the Diwan-i-Khas, the lavishly decorated hall of private audience, used for ministerial and court gatherings. This finest of the pavilions is ornamented with floral pietra dura patterns on the columns, with precious stones and gilding. A painted wooden ceiling has replaced the original one, of silver inlaid with gold. The next pavilion contains the hammam, or baths, in the Turkish style, with Mughal ornamentation in marble and colored stones.

Moti Masjid

To the west of the hammam is the Moti Masjid, the Pearl Mosque. This was a later addition, built in 1659 as a private mosque for Aurangzeb, Shah Jahan's successor. It is a small, three-domed mosque in carved white marble, with a three-arched screen which steps down to the courtyard.

Hayat Bakhsh Bagh

To its north lies a large formal garden, the Hayat Bakhsh Bagh, or "Life-Bestowing Garden", which is cut through by two bisecting channels of water. A pavilion stands at either end of the north-south channel, and a third, built in 1842 by the last emperor, Bahadur Shah Zafar, stands at the center of the pool where the two channels meet.

The Fort Today

The Red Fort is one of the most popular tourist destinations in Old Delhi, attracting thousands of visitors every year. The fort is also the site from which the Prime Minister of India addresses the nation on August 15, the day India achieved independence from the British. It also happens to be the largest monument in Old Delhi.

At one point in time, more than 3,000 people lived within the premises of the Delhi Fort complex. But after the Sepoy Mutiny of 1857, the fort was captured by Britain and the residential palaces destroyed. It was made the headquarters of the British Indian Army. Immediately after the mutiny, Bahadur Shah Zafar was tried at the Red Fort. It was also here in November 1945, that the most famous courts-martial of three officers of the Indian National Army were held. After India gained independence in 1947, the Indian Army took control over the fort. In December 2003, the Indian Army handed the fort over to the Indian tourist authorities.

The fort was the site of a December 2000 attack by terrorist group Lashkar-e-Toiba which killed two soldiers and one civilian in what was described in the media as an attempt to derail the India-Pakistan peace process in Kashmir.

MUGHAL STYLE IN INDIAN GARDENS

MUGHAL GARDEN

Mughal gardens are amongst the popular gardens in Delhi. Situated within Rashtrapati Bhawan, the official residence of the President of India, these gardens forms a major part of tourist attractions in Delhi.

Designed by Sir Edwin Lutynes for Lady Harding, the garden occupies an area of 13 acres and is divided into three sections (rectangular, long and circular gardens) and is a blend of the formal Mughal style with the design of a British Garden. The garden is beautified with Mughal style canals, fountains and terraces. The garden is retreat to eyes as it is adorned beautifully with hedges and flowers. The garden have variety of trees and flowers like roses, marigold, bougainvillea, sweet william, viscaria etc among many others.

The garden has four waterways with uniquely crafted fountains at their intersections that consists of 3 tiered huge red sandstone discs that resemble lotus leaves. The chequered flowerbeds lend an enchanting look to this wonderfully landscaped garden. With in the campus, there are many small and big lawns, like Pearl garden, butterfly garden and circular garden. The circular garden is the place which is beautified with massed segmental and tiered flower beds and is considered the best place to see butterflies.

Endorsing some of the best varieties of roses in the country, these gardens are beautified worth artificial ponds where you will have the opportunity to watch fishes. The garden also endorses romantically designed fountains with multicolored lights that forms the major attractions.

Two channels running North to South and two running East to West divide this garden into a grid of squares. There are six lotus shaped fountains at the crossings of these channels. Whereas the energetic fountains rising upto a height of 12 feet create soothing murmur that enthralls the visitor, the channels are so tranquil in their movement that they seem frozen. In the channels at appropriate times of day can be seen reflections of the imposing building and the proud flowers. There are wooden trays placed on stands in the centre of the channels where grain is put for the birds to feed upon.

There are two big lawns, the central one is a square with each side being 45 meters and the East lawn adjacent to the building, oblong in shape and about three fourth the size of Central lawn. The lawns are covered by 'Doob' grass which was originally brought from Belvedere Estate, Calcutta when they were initially laid. The entire turf of the lawn is removed once in a year before the monsoons, new top soil is spread and it takes three weeks for the grass to grow again. In the evenings Peacock with their consorts can be seen leisurely moving around. And once in a while a lapwing can be seen meditating oblivious of the surrounding splendour. Then there are Spotbiils (Resident ducks of Delhi Region) who have made a home of the channels and the garden. They are often seen enjoying a family picnic what with gardeneres in attendance with bread rmbs and choicest greens for their repast. And then there are parrots, mynahs, dovesm piegons who bath and bask with an ease of manner that evokes envy and admiration in all onlookers. Few lucky ones have also spotted birds like cormorant, jay or a transiting stork.

This garden derives it's evergreen texture from Moulsri, Putranjiva Roxburgi, Cypress, Thuja Orientalis and China Orange trees, rose shrubs and a variety of climbers.

Moulsri or Bakul is a typically Indian tree. Planted in the square patches of lawns along the channels and on the periphery of the two main lawns, they are pruned to look like mushrooms. They provide character and depth to the garden. They flower in the months of May and June and their mild sweet fragrance saturates the surroundings. This tree has been mentioned in the 'Sangam' literature, in the plays of the great poet Kalidasa and more recently by Abul Fazl in Ain-in-Akbari. There is an interesting details of this tree in a play by Kalidasa. The tree about to bear flowers is compared to a pregnant woman who nurtures desires for unusual things. Thus during the budding period the tree was said to have a desire to be sprinkled with mouthfuls of liquor by a virtuous maiden. This privilege was reserved for the queens and the princesses and celebrated in a royal ceremony.

Cypresses line the pavement and give a touch of formality, by virtue of their unchanging, full, erect shape. Planted axially they provide a perspective of depth. China Oranges alternate with Cypresses, and provide a welcome break from monotony. Whereas Cypress symbolises death and afterlife the China Oranges change their appearance through various stages of growth from season to season, symbolising renewal and celebration of life.

Putranjiva Roxburgi are planted around the two gazebos located at the western ends of the two terrace gardens. Not more than a skeletal structure of stone beams these gazebos are unique by themselves and in combination with the shade of Putrnajiva Roxburgi create an inviting grove of peace and repose.

Thuja Orientalis, a coniferous tree ornately hemmed in squares of well chiselled hedges of Golden Duranta presents a marvellous spectacle. This combination is placed along the periphery of the main garden and marks the various intersections and terminations in the pattern.

The following evergreen fragrant shrubs and creepers are planted along the terrace walls:

1. Raat ki Rani
2. Mogra
3. Motiya
4. Juhi
5. Bignenia Vanista (Golden Showers)
6. Gardenia
7. Rhyncospermum
8. Petrea
9. Harshringar
10. Bougainvillea
11. Adenocalymma (Garlic Creeper)
12. Hedera Helix
13. Climbing Roses
14. Tecoma Grandiflora
15. The Rangoon Creeper.

Roses flower throughout the year. The prime bloom though is after they are pruned in October every year. Along with the evergreens mentioned so far, roses help in achieving the permanence in texture throughout the year.

The garden has more than 250 celebrated varieties of roses, which makes it one of the best Rose Gardens in the world. It has roses like Bonne Nuit, Oklahoma which are neares to being black. In blues it has Paradise, Blue Moon, Lady X. We also have the rare green rose. The Roses have some very interesting names. Few Indians that have found place here are Mother Teresa, Arjun, Bhim, Raja Ram Mohun Roy, Jawahar,

Dr. B. P. Pal. The international celebrities here are John F. Kennedy, Queen Elizabeth, Mr. Lincoln, Montezuma. Others worth mentioning are Christian Diar, Happiness, Century Two, First Prize, Jantar Mantar, Peter Frankenfeld, American Heritage, Bejazzo, Iceberg, Granada, World Rose, Command Performance, Imperator. The list is endless and the spectacle delightful.

Various herbaceous annuals and biannuals are grown in beds and informal borders. The beds are sited at the edge of lawns or along the pavements. Also the floweres are massed irregularly with respect to their height and grouped in colour combinations to produce harmonious, natural and pleasing effect.

The planting of seasonals is done twice a year in preparation for the "At Homes" hosted by the President on the occassion of the Republic Day (26th January) and the Independence Day (15th August) every year, which are hosted in the Central lawn.

For winters the garden is replete with a number of annuals that have to compete with each other to find a place. Dwarf annuals like Calendula, Antirrhinum, Alyssum, Dimorphotheca, Eschscholzia (Californian Poppy), Larkspur, Gaznia, Gerbera, Godetia, Linaria, Mesembryanthemum, Portulaca, Brachycome, Metucharia, Verbena, Viola, Pansy, Stock grow well in flower beds. Other annuals that are grown include Dahlia, Aster, Carnation, Chrysamthemum, Clarkia, Statice, Lupin, Marigold, Nicotinia, Nemesia, Bells of Ireland, Poppy, Stock, Salvia, Cosmos, Linum, Sweet Sultan, Sweet Pea, Cineraria, Sweet William etc. They are used in pure beds and in combinations of varying heights create a pyramid of colours.

Edging and bordering of flower beds is done by Alyssum, Phlox, Petunia, Dasy, Pansy, Mimulus etc. Under the standard roses are grown Daisies, Mesembryanthemum, Pansies, Viola etc.

Naturalizing effect is created by the bulbous flowering plants like Narcissus, Freesia, Zephyranthrus, Gladiola, Tuberos, Oriental Lily, Asiatic Lily, Tulips, Anemone, Ranunculus, Iris, Daffodils etc.

For summers the choice is rather limited. But the dedication of the gardeners and bravery displayed by the plants sees them through. The August bloom would consist of Gaillardia, Vinca, Cosmos, Zinnia, Sunflower, Gomphrena, Portulaca, Balsam, Verbena, Celosia, Canna, Cochia, Rudbeckia etc.

Terrace Garden

There are two longitudinal strips of garden at a higher level on either side of the Main Garden forming the Northern and Southern boundary. The plants grown are the same as in the Main Garden. At the centre of both the strips is a fountain which falls inwards forming a well. On the Western tips are located two gazebos and on the

Eastern tips two ornately designed sentry posts.

Long Garden or the 'Purdha Garden'

This is located to the West of the Main Garden, and runs along on either side of the central pavement which goes to the circular garden. Enclosed in walls about 12 feet high this is predominantly a rose garden. It has 16 square rose beds encased in low hedges. There is a red sandstone pergola in the centre over the central pavement which is covered with Rose creepers, Petrea, Bougainvillea and Grape Vines. The walls are covered with creepers like Jasmine, Rhyncospermum, Tecoma Grandiflora, Bignonia Vanista, Adenoclyma, Echitice, Parana Paniculata. Along the walls are planted the China Orange trees. Atop these walls are often seen vain Peacocks dancing, vying for the attention of the demure peahens

The Circular (Sunken or Butterfly) Garden

This is the westernmost portion of the garden, A jewel, A delight to behold, A terraced bowl planted with fragrant varieties like Stock, Verbena, Mignonette, with tall Dahlias planted along the periphery keenly watching,and Jasmines of all kinds tenderly leaning on to the circular enclosure.

There is a bubble fountain concealed in a pool in the centre. Soft consistent waves keep eddying outwards-transform into the static waves of colours-climb up along the curious Dahlias upto the walls and thereafter disintegrate into the oblivion- the depth of unfathomable skies whereas the fragrance returns to the bedazzled onlooker. Unsuspecting butterflies flutter incessently. Once in a while a naughty Peacock shakes the frozen tranquility by a sharp mating call or a clumsy flight across two meditating trees. Around the circular garden there are rooms for office of the horticulturist, a green house, stores, nursery etc. Here only is housed the collection of Bonsais, one of the best in the country.

7

JAIN ART AND
ARCHITECTURE IN INDIA

In Jain style of architecture, bricks were hardly used, and the system of carving out temples from rock faces was adopted.

THE JAIN TEMPLE CITIES CROWNED ON HILLS

However, in later years when Jains discovered the concept of 'mountains of immortality', they proceeded to deviate from Hindu and Buddhist sites and build on their own. An important aspect to be noted is that Hindus and Buddhists built temples, Jains built temple-cities on hills. To put it in their own words, they "ornamented these holy hills with a crown of eternal Arhat chaityas (tabernacles of saints) shining with the splendor of jewels."

THE TEMPLE STRUCTURE

Compared to the number of Hindu temples in India, Jain ones are few and spaced out. The latter used to tear down their older, decaying temples and build new ones at the same site. On the other hand Jain temples had a certain militant aura around them, probably because of plunderers who may have carried away riches. Surrounded by embattled walls, the Jain temples are divided into wards in a manner similar to fortified cities with parapets and niches to repel armed aggression. Each ward in turn was guarded by massive bastions at its ends, with a fortified gateway as the main entrance. The reason being that Jain temples are the richest temples in the world, surpassing even Mughal buildings in terms of grandeur and material wealth.

These temple-cities were not built on a specific plan; instead they were the results of sporadic construction. Natural levels of the hill on which the 'city' was being built accommodated various levels so that as one goes higher so does the architecture and grandeur increases. Each temple, though, followed a set pattern, styles, designed on principles of architecture in use during the period. The only variation was in the form of frequent chamukhs or four-faced temples. In these the image of a Tirthankar (fordmaker) would face four sides, or four Tirthankars would be placed back to back to face four cardinal points. Entry into this temple would be from four doors. The Chamukh temple of Adinath is a characteristic example of the four-door temple. Built in 1618AD on the site of an older structure, it houses a 23 sq feet cell chamber. One doorway leads out to the assembly hall in front while the other three have porches leading into the main courtyard.

INTERIOR LAYOUT OF TEMPLE

Usually the exits lead into a series of columned chambers into the central halls of the temple. These columns, standing around for no apparent purpose, might make the place seem like a mindless labyrinth, but on closer scrutiny it becomes evident that there is a style and method in it. Simply put, these are temples within a temple, divided into sanctums and surrounded by a range of chapels and shrines, and the maze of columns act as a defense against plunderers. The principle impression gathered from these temples is the variety of their sections but in harmony with each other. The pointed spires above each dome is different, yet it signifies the position of a chapel, hall or any other chamber inside.

THE ARCHITECTURE SPLENDOR OF JAIN TEMPLES

From the architectural perspective, Jain Temple-cities seem to be rather cold compared to Hindu or Buddhist temples. However, in Ranakpur and Mount Abu in Rajasthan are found the most spectacular style of all Jain temples. The Ranakpur temple is built in white marble and the main chamber is supported by finely carved columns, totaling 1,444 in all.

The first principle of all art or architecture is the transformation of ideas into a visible object or symbolic expression. Architecture further serves as a kind of history. It is a standing and living historical record, providing a more vivid and lasting picture of a cultural tradition than conventional written history does.

An understanding of the motivation behind Jain art and architecture is an important prerequisite for the serious student of art. A.N. Upadhye surmises this motivation in the following from Jain Art and Architecture:

"The Jain ethic aims at improving oneself by eradicating one's attachment and aversion, which, in other forms are the four passions of anger, greed, ego and deceit. If these are brought under control, then the eternal soul is on the path of becoming *paramatman, i.e.,* one evolves oneself to the higher spiritual status.... Yearning for wealth and pleasures must be subordinated to *Dharma*, religious attitude, which takes one to salvation, the liberation from all karmas. The worship of the Jina involves the adoption of a number of virtues, to the best of one's ability and honesty, such as *non-violence, truthfulness, non-stealing, celibacy,* and *posessionlessness.*

"Most of these ethical concepts are reflected, in some form or other, in Jain art and architecture.... Jain pieces of art aim at elevating our spirit; they inspire religious values; and they present, in concrete form, the philosophical concepts and rules of conduct laid down in Jainism. They satisfy the yearning spirit to identify itself and evolve into the higher spirit which is characterized by infinite knowlege, perception, strength and bliss."

And as with its philosophy, Jain symbolism, manifested in its arts and architectures, bears awesome peculiarities.

Much has been written in the twentieth century about Indian art and architecture, but the aforementioned depth of philosophical conviction which Jain art and architecture are intended to convey, has generally been overlooked. To a limited extent, however, observations of the bulk of Indian art can be applied to Jain art as well. V.A. Smith in his History of Fine Arts in India and Ceylon writes that "Hindu Art, including Jain and Buddhist in the comprehensive, is the real Indian Art. The special feature of Jain art lies in the fact that it shows the relative position of natural objects with great fineness. It is sometimes called 'conventionalistic', but that is true of all arts devoted to religious subjects." In the opinion of Colonel Tod, "['The Jains'] arts, like their religion, were of a character quite distinct from those of [the Hindus]. The temple of Mahavira, the last of their twenty-four apostles, at Nadole (Rajasthan) is a very fine piece of architecture. Its vaulted roof is a perfect model of the most ancient style of dome in the East, probably invented anterior to the Romans."

On Jain Architecture, a prominent scholar writes, "The earliest Jain architects seem to have used wood as their chief building material." Lack of supporting evidence, however, hinders scholarly consideration of this notion. As far as the existing materials can evince, by the fifth century, B.C., when its primal homeland of modern Bihar and Uttar Pradesh had become Sanskritized, Jainism was widespread among the middle class. Its lay followers, the *Shravakas* and *Shravikas*, were mostly engaged in commerce and academics. Thus, the architects and artisans employed by the lay Jains came primarily from socio-economic classes engaged solely in such trades. In order to allow permanency to their religious sanctuaries and objects of worship, they invariably used stone and metal. More recent discoveries of the remains of many Jain temples, built centuries before the Christian era, further confirms the fact that the earliest Jain architecture was not limited to wood.

As for the antiquity of Jain architecture, the excavations of Kankali Tilla, near Mathura, establish beyond doubt that the erection of Jain *stupas* took place several centuries before the Christian era. According to some Western scholars, these structures are perhaps the oldest standing buildings in the modern land of India.

Modern and medieval Jains have been the most prolific temple builders in Western India. The famous Jain temples atop Mt. Abu (modern Indian state of Rajasthan) are triumphs of architecture. The intricacy and richness of their carvings are truly unsurpassed in the world. The great Jain pilgrimage in the Shatrunjay Hills near Palitana (state of Gujarat), sometimes called the "City of Temples", is an imposing edifice. Its close, systematic grouping of buildings, given dramatic changes in altitude and very limited spaces, is another peculiarity of Jain architecture.

In southern India, there exist several Jain columns which Colonel Tod noted as being "of a remarkably pleasing design. They are a wonder of light, elegant, highly decorated stone-work, and nothing can surpass the stately grace of these beautiful pillars whose proportions and adaptations to surrounding scenery are always perfect and whose richness of decoration never offends. In the whole range of Indian Art, there is nothing perhaps equal to the Kanara Jain pillars in taste."

Numerous cave-temples have been discovered in different parts of the Indian subcontinent, West and South. The Jain caves at Ellora (state of Maharashtra) form a series by themselves and contain elaborate frescoes and other architectural works. Griffiths writes in the introduction of his well-known work Ajanta, "The Jains excavated some five or six extensive works which form a very important group of caves; one of the largest and most elaborate, the Indra Sabha, being about 90 feet deep, 80 feet wide, and 14 feet high. There are a number of ancient Jain caves in Orissa on hills known as Khandgiri, Udaigiri, and Nilgiri, dating as far back as the second century, B.C."

A number of salient ascetic ideals expressed in Jain and Buddhist sculpture are similar, and modern art historians have often mistaken images of the Buddhas and Jain Tirthankaras for one another. The images of Jain Tirthankaras are generally seated in the meditative *padmasana* position (the "lotus posture"), and sometimes in the standing *kayotsarga* posture (the "body abondoning" pose), or in *ardhapadmasana* (the "half lotus"). The Shvetambar laity has created a unique class of metal-cast images known as *panchatirthis*, or "five holies". The central images on these artefacts consist of any of the twenty-four Tirthankaras in the padmasana pose; two standing, kayotsarga figures appear on each side of the middle image; and two more padmasana images are formed on either side, above the same kayotsarga figures.

Other prominent themes within Indian Jain art include celestial beings, or angels, as musicians and votaries: some adoring the omniscient Tirthankaras, some waving *chamaras*, and some in prayer, kneeling or standing with folded hands, etc. One also encounters images of saluting elephants, carrying water-pots in their trunks, pouring at the feet of a kayotsarga Tirthankara figure, on either side.

Among the Digambar Jain temples in southern India, the enormous statues at Shravana Belagola (state of Karnataka), Karkala, Yemur, and Canara are the largest monolithic, free-standing statues in the world. The tallest one, of Lord Bahubali (at Shravana Belagola, completed in 981 A.D.), is over 57 feet high and was carved from a single block of granite.

The place of Jain paintings among the world's treasury of fine arts is also of importance. A special feature of Jain painting lies in the drift and quality of its lines. Line is so finely drawn in the some Jain schools of painting that few other art traditions bear comparison with it. (It has been demonstrated that the Chinese technique for creating powerful lines was borrowed from India; perhaps time will produce evidence that the Chinese may have learned the skill from Jains artisans.) Jain paintings generally depict important historical events, such as the lives and deeds of Tirthankaras, ascetics and monarchs, or pilgrimage centers, or illustrations pertaining to Jain philosophy and cosmology. Since they sustain a sanctity of their own in finished form, such works of art were preserved with great veneration in both temples and homes.

The Jains have also been keen on illustrating religious texts with miniature paintings whose renditions of man and nature also bear a unique style and taste. Coomarswami, in his "Notes on the Jain Art", writes, "The Jain paintings are not only very important for the students of Jain iconography and archaeology, and not only are they significant for their illustrations of costume, manners and customs, but they are of equal or greater interest as being the oldest known Indian paintings on paper." The Nahar family collection of manuscripts of the Kalpa Sutra (a revered text dating back to the fourth century, B.C.), which deals with the lives of the Tirthankaras and ascetic conduct, contains exquisite miniatures which have been gaining the attention of modern art critics. Their interesting changes in drapery, posture and colour, as well as their peculiar stylizations, are quite striking to the average, unacquainted observer.

The Moghul period of miniature painting significantly influenced Jain miniature art. In fact, it was only in that later epoch that paintings of buildings, scenery, and portraits become prevalent throughout the subcontinent.

CONTRIBUTION OF JAINISM TO INDIAN CULTURE

It is evident that Jainism is an ancient religion of India and that right from hoary antiquity to the present day it has continued to flourish, along with other religions, in different parts of India. Jainas, the followers of Jainism, are, therefore, found all over India from ancient times. The Jainas are also known everywhere for the strict observance of their religious practices in their daily lives. That is why Jainism could survive in India for the last so many centuries. The Jainas, in this way, succeeded in continuing to exist as devout followers of a distinct religion in India.

But this is not the only distinguishing feature of Jainas in India. In fact, the most outstanding characteristic of Jainas in India is their very impressive record of contributions to Indian culture. In comparison with the limited and small population of Jainas. the achievements of Jainas in enriching the various aspects of Indian culture are really great.

LANGUAGES AND LITERATURE

Perhaps the most creditable contribution of Jainas is in the field of languages and literature. It is quite evidence that right from the Vedic period two different currents of thought and ways of life known as (a) Brahman culture and (b) Sramana culture are prevalent in India. The Sramana culture is mainly represented by the Jainas and the Buddhists and of them the Jainas were the first to propagate that culture. That is why from ancient times we have the Sramana literature besides the Brahmanic literature. The characteristic features of the Sramana literature are as follows: It disregards the system of castes and *Asramas;* its heroes are, as a rule, not Gods and Rule, but kings or merchants or even Sudras. The subjects of poetry taken up by it are not Brahmanic myths and legends, but popular tales: fairy stories, fables and parables. It likes to insist on the misery and sufferings of *samsara* and it teaches a morality of compassion and *ahimsa,* quite distinct from the ethics of Brahmanism with its ideals of the great sacrificers and generous supporter of the priests, and of strict adherence to the caste system.

The authors of this Sramana literature have contributed enormously to the religious, ethical, poetical, and scientific literature of ancient India. A close examination of the vast religious literature of the Jainas has been made by M. Winternitz in his 'History of Indian Literature'. In this masterly survey of ancient Indian literature, M. Winternitz has asserted that the Jainas were foremost in composing various kinds of narrative literature like *puranas, charitras, kathas, prabandhas,* etc. Besides a very extensive body of poetical narratives, the non canonical literature of the Jainas consists of an immense number of commentaries and independent works on dogma, ethics and monastic discipline. They also composed legends of saints and works on ecclesiastical history. As fond of story telling, the Jainas were good story tellers themselves, and have preserved for us numerous Indian tales that otherwise would have been lost. *Kavyas* and *maha-kavyas* too, of renowned merit have been composed by Jaina poets. Lyrical and didactic poetry are also well represented in the literature of the Jainas.

Apart from these, the most valuable contributions have been made by the Jainas to the Indian scientific and technical literature on various subjects like logic, philosophy, poetics, grammar, lexicography, astronomy, astrology, geography, mathematics and medicine. The Jainas have paid special attention to the *arthasastra* (or politics) which is considered to be "a worldly science" par excellence. Thus there is hardly any branch of science that has not been ably treated by the Jainas.

The literature of the Jainas is also very important from the point of view of the history of Indian languages for the Jainas always took care that their writings were accessible even to the masses of the people. Hence the canonical writings and the earliest commentaries are written in Prakrit dialects and at a later period Sanskrit and various modern Indian languages were used by the Jainas. That is why it is not an exaggeration when the famous Indologist H.H. Wilson says that every province of Hindustan can produce Jaina compositions either in Sanskrit or in its vernacular idioms. It is an established fact that the Jainas have enriched various regional languages and especially Hindi, Gujarati, Kannada, Tamil and Telugu.

Regarding the Jaina contribution to Kannada literature, the great Kannada scholar R. Narasimhacharya has given his considered opinion in the following terms: "The earliest cultivators of the Kannada language were Jainas. The oldest works of any extent and value that have come down to us are all from the pen of the Jainas. The period of the Jainas' predominance in the literary field may justly be called the 'Augustan Age of Kannada Literature'. Jaina authors in Kannada are far more numerous than in Tamil. To name only a few, we have Pampa, Ponna, Ranna, Gunavarman, Nagachandra, Nayasena, Nagavarman, Aggala, Nemichandra, Janna, Andayya, Bandhuvarma and Medhura, whose works are admired as excellent specimens of poetical composition. It is only in Kannada that we have a *Ramayana* and a *Bharata* based on the Jaina tradition in addition to those based on Brahmanical tradition. Besides *kavyas* written by Jaina authors, we have numerous works by them dialing with subjects such as grammar, rhetoric, prosody, mathematics, astrology, medicine, veterinary science, cookery and so forth. In all the number of Jaina authors in Kannada is nearly two hundred".

As the Jainas have produced their vast literature in these languages from very ancient times, they have certainly played a very important part in the development of the different languages of India. The medium of sacred writings and preachings of the Brahmins has all along been Sanskrit and that of the Buddha's Pali. But the Jainas alone utilized the prevailing languages of the different places, besides Sanskrit, Prakrit and Apabhramsha, for their religious propagation as well as for the preservation of knowledge. It is thus quite evident that the Jainas occupy an important position in the history of the literature and civilization of India.

ARTS AND ARCHITECTURE

Along with literature the Jainas have always contributed considerably to the development of the arts in the country The Jainas have taxed their mite to enhance the glory of India in several branches of arts. Compared with their number their contributions appear to be very imposing and distinctive.

ARCHITECTURE

It must be remembered that Jainism did not create a special architecture of its own, for wherever the Jainas went they adopted the local building traditions For example, while in Northern India the Jainas followed the Vaisnava cult in building in southern India they adhered to the Dravidian type. The *stupas* of the Jainas are indistinguishable in form from those of the Buddhists, and a Jaina curvilinear steeple is identical in outline with that of a Brahmanical temple.

Even though the Jainas have not evolved a distinct style of architecture, yet it must be said to their credit that they have produced numerous and finest specimens of architecture in different parts of the country. In this regard it is quite clear that more than any other religion in India the Jainas have displayed their intense love of the picturesque while selecting the sites for the construction of their sacred buildings like temples, temple cities, cave temples, *stupas*, pillars and towers. They have erected their temples either on lonely hill tops or in deep and secluded valleys.

TEMPLES

As the Jaina religion considers construction of temples as a meritorious act, the Jainas have constructed an unusually larger number of temples throughout India. Nearly 90 percent of Jaina temples are the gifts of single wealthy individuals and as such the Jaina temples are distinguished for elaborate details and exquisite finish.

Of these innumerable Jaina temples, the two marble temples at Mount Abu in Rajasthan are considered as the most notable contributions of the Jainas in the domain of architecture. The two temples are famous as unsurpassed models of Western or Gujarati style of architecture which is characterized by a free use of columns carved with all imaginable richness, strut brackets, and exquisite marble ceilings with cusped pendants. The temples are known for the beauty and delicacy of the carving and for the richness of the design. As Cousens remarks:

"The amount of beautiful ornamental detail spread over these temples in the minutely carved decoration of ceilings, pillars, door ways, panels and niches is simply marvelous; the crisp, thin, translucent, shell like treatment of the marble surpasses anything seen elsewhere and some of the designs are veritable dreams of beauty. The work is so delicate that an ordinary chiseling would have been disastrous. It is said that much of it was produced by scrapping the marble away, and that the masons were paid by the amount of marble dust so removed."

Again, the Jaina temple at Ranakpur in Mewar, a part of Rajasthan (which was built in 1440 A.D.), is the most complex and extensive Jaina temple in India and the most complete for the ritual of the sect. The temple covers altogether about 48,000 sq. feet of ground and on the merits of its design, the notable art historian Dr. Fergusson remarks that:

"The immense number of parts in the building, and their general smallness, prevents its laying claim to anything like architectural grandeur: but their variety, their beauty of detail—no two pillars in the whole building being exactly alike—the grace with which they are arranged, the tasteful admixture of domes of different heights with flat ceilings, and mode in which the light is introduced, combine to produce an excellent effect. Indeed I know of no other building in India, of the same class that leaves so pleasing an impression, or affords so many hints for the graceful arrangements of columns in an interior".

The other temples of such superb character are (i) the temple of Parsvanatha at Khajuraho in Bundelkhand in Madhya Pradesh, (ii) the temple at Lakkundi in North Karnataka, (iii) the temple known as Jinanathapura Basadi near Sravana belagola in South Karnataka, (iv) Seth Hathisinghi's temple at Ahmedabad, and (v) The temple known as Hose Vasadi at Mudabidri in South Kanara District of Karnataka.

As regards the spread of beautiful Jaina temples in India it may be noted that the number of such temples in India was considerably reduced during the Muslim period because the structure of Jaina temple was such that it could easily be converted into a mosque. The light columnar style of the Jaina temples not only supplied materials more easily adopted to the purposes of Muslims. but furnished hints of which the Muslim architects were not slow to avail themselves. A mosque obtained in this way was, for convenience and beauty, unsurpassed by anything the Muslims afterwards erected from their own original designs. Thus the great mosques of Ajmer, Delhi, Kanauj and Ahmedabad are merely reconstruction on the temples of Hindus and Jainas.

TEMPLE-CITIES

Further, the grouping together of their temples into what may be called 'Cities of Temples' is a peculiarity which the Jainas have practiced to a greater extent than the followers of any other religion in India. Such notable temple cities are found, among other places, at (i) Satrunjaya or Palitana in Gujarat, (ii) Girnar in Gujarat, (iii) Sammed-Shikhara in Bihar, (iv) Sonagiri in Bundelkhand in Madhya Pradesh, (v) Muktagiri in

Vidarbha, Maharashtra, (vi) Kunthalgiri in Marathwada, Maharashtra, (vii) Sravana belagola in Hassan District, Karnataka and (viii) Mudabidri in South Kanara District, Karnataka.

CAVE TEMPLES

Again, the Jainas also like the Buddhists, built several cave temples cut in rocks from the early times. But in dimensions, the Jaina cave temples were smaller than the Buddhist ones because the Jaina religion gave prominence to individualistic and not to congregational ritual. The most numerous cave temples are in Udayagiri and Khandagiri Hills in Orissa. The picturesqueness of their forms, the character of their sculptures, and the architectural details combined with their great antiquity render them one of the most important groups of caves in India. These and those of Junagadh in Gujarat belong to the second century B.C. while the others are of a later date of which the important ones are found at (i) Aihole and Badami in Bijapur District (Karnataka), (ii) Ankai and Patana in Khandesh District (Maharashtra), (iii) Ellora and Oosmanabad in Marathwada (Maharashtra), (iv) Chamar Lena near Nasik City (Maharashtra), and (v) Kalugumalai in Tinnevelly District (Tamilnadu).

STUPAS

Like the Buddhists, Jainas also erected *stupas* in honor of their saints, with their accessories of stone railings, decorated gateways, stone umbrellas, elaborate carved pillars and abundant statues. Early examples of these have been discovered in the Kankali mound near Mathura in Uttar Pradesh, and they are supposed to belong to the first century B.C.

MANA-STAMBHAS OR PILLARS

Another remarkable contribution of the Jainas in the field of architecture is the creation of many *stambhas or* pillars of pleasing design and singular grace which are found attached to many of their temples. In connection with these *manastambhas*, as they are popularly called, the famous authority on Jaina architecture, Dr. James Fergusson, states that it may be owing to the iconoclastic propensities of the Muslims that these pillars are not found so frequently where they have held sway, as in the remoter parts of India; but, whether for this cause or not, they seem to be more frequent in south India than in any other part of India. Dr. James Fergusson further suggests that there may be some connection between these Jaina *stambhas* and the obelisks of the Egyptians. Regarding these Jaina pillars in the South Kanara District of Karnataka, the research scholar Mr. Walhouse has remarked that "the whole capital and canopy are a wonder of light, elegant, highly decorated stone work, and nothing can surpass the stately grace of these beautiful pillars whose proportions and adaptation to surrounding scenery are always perfect, and whose richness of decoration, never offends." According to another eminent authority on Indian Architecture, Dr. Vincent Smith, in the whole range of Indian Art there is nothing perhaps equal to these pillars in the Kanara District for good taste.

TOWERS

There is evidence to show that apart from pillars the Jainas, especially from northern India, constructed a great number of beautiful towers dedicated to their Tirthankaras. There is such a tower which is still adorning Chittor in Mewar (Rajasthan) and it is considered as one of the best preserved monuments in India. This Jaina Tower at Chittor is a singularly elegant specimen of its class, about 75 feet in height and adorned with sculpture and moldings from the base to the summit. The Tower was constructed in the 12th century and was dedicated to Adinatha, the first of the Jaina Tirthankaras, and nude figures of them are repeated some hundreds of times on the face of the Tower.

SCULPTURE

The innumerable specimens of Jaina sculpture found in practically all parts of India show that the Jainas enlisted the services of sculptors from very ancient times. Their most common form of sculpture up to this day is modeling of images or statues of their Tirthankaras. But in giving shape to these figures no scope at all was given for the free play of imagination of individual sculptors as regular rules regarding the form and pose of statues of Tirthankara had been prescribed by the Jaina religion from the very beginning. Consequently, practically all Jaina images pertain to one class and therefore Jaina images from any part of the country cannot be distinguished from their style even though they belong to different ages altogether.

Further, it is significant to note that the Jaina images have been made of all sizes and substances and are almost always invariable in attitude, whether seated or standing. Small images are made of crystal, alabaster, soapstone, bloodstone, and various other precious and semiprecious materials, while the larger ones are carved from whatever kind of stone happens to be locally available.

Undoubtedly the most remarkable of the Jaina statues are the celebrated colossi of southern India, the largest free standing statues in Asia which are three in number, situated in Karnataka State respectively at Sravana-Belgola in Hassan District (constructed in 981 A.D. and 56.5 feet in height), at Karkala in South Kannada District (constructed in 1432 A.D. and about 41 feet in height) and at Yenura or Venura in South Kanara District (Constructed in 1604 A.D. and 35 feet in height). All these three images of Lord Bahubali, the son of first Tirthankar Adinatha, being set of the top of eminence, are visible for miles around, and inspire of their formalism they command respectful attention by their enormous mass and expression of dignified serenity. That is why these three images are considered by authorities like Dr. James Fergusson and Dr. Vincent Smith as the most remarkable works of native art in south India.

DECORATIVE SCULPTURE

Regarding the unrivaled progress of the Jainas in decorative sculpture, as distinguished from individual statuary, Dr. Vincent Smith remarks that "The Jainas encouraged the work of a high order of excellence and beauty, employed to adorn with the utmost possible magnificence and pillared chambers which were their favorite form of architecture. Nothing in the world can surpass for richness and delicacy of detail the marble columns and ceilings of the Mount Abu temples and it would be easy to fill to large volume with illustrations of more or less similar exquisite work in many localities."

PAINTING

Along with architecture and sculpture, the, Jainas have contributed in a large measure to the development of art of painting in India. The tradition of Jaina painting is as old as Buddhist painting and innumerable Jaina paintings of exquisite quality could be found on walls, palm leaves, paper, cloth, wood, etc. It is significant to note that the Jainas possess a very extensive treasure of manuscript paintings drawn in the early Western Indian Style, sometimes called the 'Gujarat Style' or specifically the 'Jaina Style'.

PHILOSOPHY

As Jainism is an original system, quite distinct and independent from all others, the Jainas have developed a separate philosophy which is regarded as a valuable contribution to Indian philosophy.

In philosophy the Jainas occupy a distinct position between the Brahmanic and Buddhist philosophical systems. This has been shown very clearly by Dr. Hermann Jacobi in his paper on 'The Metaphysics and Ethics of the Jainas'. Regarding the problem of Being the three hold different opinions. The Vadantins consider that underlying and up-holding from within all things there is one absolute permanent Being' without change and with none other like it. On the contrary the Buddhists hold that all things are transitory. The Jainas, however, contend that Being' is joined to production. continuation and destruction and that they call their theory of multiple view points (i.e. *Anekantavada*). in contradistinction to the theory of permanency (i.e. *Nityavada*) of the Vedantins, and to the theory of Transitoriness (i.e. *Ksanika vada*) of the Buddhists.

The Jainas think that the existing things are permanent only as regards their substance, but their accidents or qualities originate and perish. To emphasize once again here the significance of this Jaina theory of 'Being' comes out more clearly when it is regarded in relation to the doctrines of *Syadvada* and of *Nayavada*. According to the doctrine of *Syadvada* any proposition about an existing thing must, somehow, reflect the many-sidedness of Being.' i.e., any metaphysical proposition is right from one point of view, and, the contrary proposition is also right from another point of view. The *Nayas* are ways of expressing the nature of things; all these ways of judgment are, according to the Jainas, one sided, and they contain but a part of truth. The doctrine of the *Nayas is* thus, the logical complement to the *Syadvada* which is the outcome of the theory of the many-sidedness of 'Being' From this Dr. H. Jacobi affirms that the Jaina theory of Being is an indication of the commonsense view.

ETHICAL CODE

As the Jainas have evolved a philosophy of their own, they follow a distinct ethical code based on their philosophy. The Jaina ethics stands as a class by itself in the sense that it is the only system which is founded, on the main principle of *ahimsa. It* has already been noted how the principle of *ahimsa* forms the basis of various rules of conduct prescribed for both the Jaina laymen and ascetics.

Thus one of the significant contributions of the Jainas is the *ahimsa* culture. It the Jainas are known for anything it is for the evolution of *ahimsa* culture and it must be said to the credit of the Jainas that they practiced and propagated that culture from ancient times. In fact the antiquity and continuity of *ahimsa* culture is mainly due to the incessant efforts of the Jaina ascetics and householders. Naturally wherever the Jainas were in great numbers and wielded some influence they tried to spread *ahimsa* culture among the masses. That is why we find that the States of Gujarat and Karnataka, which are the strongholds of Jainas from the beginning, are mainly vegetarian.

In fact it is admitted that as a result of the activities of the Jainas for the last so many centuries, *ahimsa* still forms the substratum of Indian character as a whole.

POLITICAL PROGRESS

The Jainas also distinguished themselves in giving their unstinted support for the improvement of political and economic life in the country. The Jainas, especially in southern and western India, produced a large number of eminent and efficient monarchs, ministers, and generals and thereby contributed to maintain and improve the political importance of the people. Not only the ordinary Jainas but their *acharyas*, i.e., saints, also aided materially to create the proper political environment based on *ahimsa* culture necessary for the resuscitation of the life in the country.

It is considered that due to the keen interest taken by the Jaina Acharyas, i.e., saints. in political affairs of the country, Jainism occupies an important place in the history of India. The Jaina ascetics were never indifferent towards the secular affairs in general. We know from the account of Megasthenes that, in the 4th century B.C., the *Sramanas* of Jaina ascetics who lived in the woods were frequently consulted by the kings through their messengers regarding the cause of things. So far as Karnataka is concerned Jainism, throughout its course of more than one thousand years, was an example of a religion which showed that religious tenets were practiced without sacrificing the political exigencies when the question of rejuvenating life in the country was at stake. That is why in Karnataka we find that the Jaina *acharyas* ceased to be merely exponents of dogmas and turned themselves into creators of kingdoms. It has already been noted that the Jaina saints were virtually responsible for the founding of the Ganga kingdom in the 2nd century A.D. and the Hoyasala kingdom in the 11th century A.D.

8

SIKH ARCHITECTURE IN INDIA

Sikh architecture, is a style of architecture that is characterized with values of progressiveness, exquisite intricacy, austere beauty and logical flowing lines. Due to its progressive style, it is constantly evolving into many newly developing branches with new contemporary styles. Although Sikh architecture was initially developed within Sikhism its style is used in many non-religious building due its beauty. 300 years ago, Sikh architecture was distinguished for its many curves and straight lines, Shri Keshgarh Sahib and the Golden Temple are prime examples and history of a gurdwara.

Further examples of Sikh architecture can be found in India, Pakistan, Afghanistan, Bangladesh, Saudi Arabia, Iraq and Turkey- these examples are mostly memorials of the places the Sikh gurus visited. Modern examples can be found world-wide: America, Australia, United Kingdom, Europe and Asia.

This paper attempts to outline the main elements, principles, and objectives of building design with a view to conjuring up an overall picture of a style of architecture which can be doubtlessly called Sikh architecture. This venture will be extended to touch upon another area of architecture which has come to be known as urban design, and whose existence in Sikh architecture can also be substantiated by apt examples.

TYPES OF BUILDINGS

Apart from buildings of religious order, Sikh architecture has secular types of forts, palaces, bungas (residential places), colleges, etc. The religious structure is the gurdwara, a place where the Guru dwells. A gurdwara is not only the all-important building of the Faith, as masjid or mosque of the Islamic faith and mandir or temple of the Hindu religion, but it is also, like its Islamic and Hindu counterparts, the keynote of Sikh architecture.

The word *gurdwara* is a compound of *guru* (guide or master) and *dwara* (gateway or seat) and therefore has an architectural connotation. Sikh temples are by and large commemorative buildings connected with the ten gurus in some way, or with places and events of historical significance. For example, Gurdwara Dera Sahib (Halting place), in Batala in Gurdaspur district, was erected to commemorate the brief stay here of Guru Nanak along with the party on the occasion of his marriage. Gurdwara Shish Mahal (Hall of Mirrors) in Kiratpur in Ropar district was built where the eighth Guru, Harkishan, was born and so on. Gurdwara Shahid Ganj (Martyr's Memorial) in Muktsar in Faridkot district commemorates the place where the dead bodies of the Sikhs, who were killed in the battle between Guru Gobind Singh and the Mughal forces in 1705, were cremated.

The buildings of the Sikh shrines cover a wide spectrum of structures varying from the simple and the austere to the richly embellished and respondent. There are over five hundred *gurdwaras*, big and small, which have an historical past. They are to be found throughout India, although a majority of them are located in the Punjab and its surrounding provinces. Some important *gurdwaras* also exist in Pakistan, Bangladesh and elsewhere in the world.

The buildings of the Sikh shrines, when classified according to their plan, are of four basic types: the square, the rectangular, the octagonal, and the cruciform. On the basis of the number of storeys, gurdwaras have structures, which may be one, two, three, five or nine storeys high. One comes across several interesting variations of gurdwara designs worked out on the permutations and combinations of the aforesaid basic plan and elevation types.

GOLDEN TEMPLE

A few examples are now given to illustrate the above categories. Darbar Sahib at Dera Baba Nanak in Gurdaspur district is constructed on a square plan and is a single-storeyed structure. Gurdwara Shahid Ganj at Muktsar in Faridkot district has one storey built on a rectangular plan. Examples of this plan shape are extremely rare. Gurdwara Lohgarh in Anandpur Sahib in Ropar district has an octagonal plan and a single-storied elevation. Gurdwara Tamboo (tent) Sahib in Muktsar is a double-storied building constructed on a square plan, on a raised basement. Gurdwara Chobara Sahib (room on terrace) at Goindwal in Amritsar district is a three-storeyed structure elevated on a square plan. Gurdwara Tham Sahib (pillar) at Kartarpur in Jullunder district has a square plan and five storeys.

Gurdwara Shadian (martyrs') in Amritsar is a three-storied octagonal structure. Gurdwara Baba Atal Sahib (immutable) in Amritsar, basically a smadh (cenotaph) raised in the memory of Baba Atal, the revered son of the sixth Guru, Hargobind, is a nine storeyed building standing on an octagonal plan. It reminds one of Firoae Minar in Gaur. Gurdwara Dera Baba Gurditta at Kartarpur in Ropar district is a square structure placed on a high plinth, which has a ten-sided plan. This polygonal plan shape is quite unusual. Baolis (stepped wells) are also not uncommon in Sikh architecture. Gurdwara Baoli Sahib at Goindwal in Amritsar district is representative example of such structures, which, belong to the miscellaneous class. Gurdwara Nanak Jhira in Bidar in Karnataka, stands on a cruciform plan.

There are five historical shrines which have been given the status of *thakats* (thrones) where the *gurmattas* (decisions) of a binding character taken through a consensus of the *sangat* (congregation) have great importance, affecting as they did the social and political life of the Sikh community. These are: Akal Takht, Amritsar; Harmandir Sahib, Patna, Bihar; Keshgarh Sahib, Anandpur; Damdama Sahib, Talwandi Sabo; and Hazur Sahib, Nanded, Maharashtra. Of these five takhats, the Akal Takhat (Indestructible Throne) is the most important by virtue of its location in Amritsar, the Vatican for the Sikhs.

As a rule, a *gumbad* (dome) is the crowning feature of a *gurdwara*. Rarely, a shrine may be flat-roofed, as in the case of Gurdwara Guru-ka-Lahore near Anandpur Sahib in Ropar district. Sometimes, a small single roomed shrine is topped by a *palaki*, a palanquin-like roof, derived from Bengal style of architecture, as can be seen in Gurdwara Tahli Sahib, in the village Tahala in the Bhatinda district. Gurdwara Bahadur Garh in Patiala has a *palaki* instead of a dome as its crowning feature.

More often than not, a dome is fluted or ribbed but a plane dome has also been used in many cases, as in Manji Sahib at Damdama Sahib in Bhatinda district. Several dome shapes are to be found in Sikh shrines — hemispherical, three-quarters of a sphere, etc., although the last mentioned is more frequently used. The shape of the dome of Gurdwara Patal Puri at Kiratpur in Ropar district has a remarkable likeness to the domes seen in Bijapur provincial style of architecture.

The dome is usually white, and sometimes gilded, as in the Golden Temple at Amritsar, Darbar Sahib at Taran Tarn, and Sis Ganj in Delhi. Alternatively, in some cases, domes have been covered with brass, while in others, at least the finial has been given copper-gilt sheathing. Usually domes on Sikh shrines spring from a floral base, and have inverted lotus symbol top from which rises the kalasa, an ornate finial. Based on Mount Kailasa it shoots up in the form of a cylindrical construction, of ten with some concentric discs, spheroids, culminating in a small canopy with pendants hanging at the outer rim.

An interesting point to note is the manner in which the dome is related to the cuboid structure of the shrine. As a rule, the lower part dominates the domical structure and looks somewhat austere in comparison with it. Apart from the larger central dome, there are often four other smaller cupolas, one on each corner of the unusually cuboid structure of the shrine. The parapet may be embellished with several turrets, or small rudimentary domes, or crenellations, or replicas of arcades with domical toppings, or strings of guldastas (bouquets) or similar other embellishments. Minarets - the symbols of royalty - are rarely seen in a Gurdwara. An exception Katal Garh (Place of Execution) at Chamkaur Sahib in Ropar district has several minarets.

A recurrent element of *gurdwara* design is the preferred usage of two storeys to gain sufficient elevation for the shrine. However restrained the design may be, the elevation is usually treated by dividing the facade in accordance with the structural lines of columns, piers and pilasters, with vertical divisions creating areas of well-molded surfaces. The most important division is, of course, the entrance which receives more ornate treatment than other areas. The treatment often creates bas-reliefs of geometrical, floral, and other designs. Where magnificence is the aim, repousse work in brass or copper gilt sheathing is often introduced with a note of extravagance.

Jaratkari or in-lay work, gach or plaster-of-Paris work, tukri work, fresco painting, pinjra or lattice work are the techniques used for embellishment of exterior surfaces as well as for interior decoration.

Jaratkari is both a very extensive and time-consuming technique of studding precious and colored stones into marble slabs. The slabs often have florid or geometrical borders, which enclose painstakingly, executed in-lay work using floral shapes and patterns. Beautiful designs are made on the walls with gach, which is subsequently gilded. Excellent examples of this work can be seen in the Golden Temple at Amritsar. Sometimes, the gach work is rended highly ornamental by means of colored and mirrored cut glass as well as precious stones. This is called tukri (small piece) work. Frescoes depicting popular episodes from the lives of the ten Gurus, are to be found in some shrines. Designs employed are based on vine, plant, flower, bird and animal motifs. The largest numbers of such frescoes have been painted on the first floor of Baba Atal at Amritsar. Pinjras or delicate stone grilles are used for screens, enclosures and parapets.

Brick, lime mortar as well as lime or gypsum plaster, and lime concrete have been the most favored building materials, although stone, such as red stone and white marble, has also been used in a number of shrines. The latter found use more as cladding or decorative material than for meeting structural needs for well over two hundred years. Nanak Shahi (from the times of Nanak) brick was most commonly used for its intrinsic advantages. It was a kind of brick tile of moderate dimensions used for reinforcing lime concretes in the structural walls and other components, which were generally very thick.

The brick-tile made moldings, cornices, plasters, etc., is easy to work into a variety of shapes. More often than not, the structure was a combination of the two systems, viz, trabeated or post-and-lintal, and acerated or based on arches. The surfaces were treated with lime or gypsum plaster which was molded into cornices, pilasters, and other structural as well as non-structural embellishments.

Sikh architecture represents the last flicker of religious architecture in India. The Golden Temple at Amritsar is the most celebrated example, as this is one monument in which all the characteristics of the style are fully represented. With the Golden Temple being the sheet anchor of the stylistic index of Sikh architecture, it may well be to give some details of the revered temple.

Almost leviating above and in the middle of an expansive water-body, the 'Pool of Nectar', the Darbar (Court) Sahib, or Harmandir Sahib (Lord's Temple) as it is called, stirs one deeply with glitters of its golden dome, kiesks, parapets, repousse work, and the enchanting evanescence of its shimmering reflection in the pool. With the temple and tank as the focus, a complex of buildings, most of which repeat in their architectural details the characteristics of the central structure, have come up in the vicinity, in the course of time.

The temple has four entrances and is approached by means of a causeway which connects the entrance gateway, darshani deorhi, with the main shrine. The causeway is a marble paved access bordered by latticed balustrades and lamp-posts with elegant copper gilded lanterns at close intervals, and meets the parkarma or circumambulatory. The outer parkarma or promenade of the Holy Tank had a string of bungas, once rooms or halting places built by villages or misals, the Sikh confederacies, for lodging their people during the visits to the shrine. Some of the bungas have now been demolished to widen the parkarma.

Over the two-storied structure of the shrine rises a low gilt-metal flutted dome. There are kiesks also with fluted-metal cupolas at each corner while several small domes of similar design embellish the parapet. The first floor is designed as a gallery so that the central part of the shrine has unobstructed two-storey height. Sri Guru Granth Sahib, the Holy Book, is placed at the ground floor, facing the entrance off the causeway, while a small area around it is cordoned off by a row railing.

The whole building of Harmandir Sahib is richly ornamented with floral designs, either painted in tempera or embossed in metal. The skillful handling of brass and copper is one of the crafts in which Sikh artisans excel. Golden Temple is the soul-stirring expression of intense religious emotion of the Sikh faith materialized in marble, glass, color and metal. In this respect, it has few equals in the world.

Although Sikh architecture undoubtedly originated with the idea of devotion, it had to undergo rigors of compulsively transforming itself into buildings meant for defense purposes. It assumed the character of military fortification, which was reflected in a number of buildings throughout Punjab. Gurdwara Baba Gurditta, Kiratpur, is a representative example of this type of Sikh architecture. With all the paraphernalia of multiple gateways, series of battlemented enclosures, placement of the structure atop a strategic point of a hill, etc., this shrine was virtually transformed into an architectural rendering of a fortification. As conditions became favorable, however, Sikh religion changed its militant posture and assumed the character of an organized institution, with consequent effect on the nature, character and aesthetic of its architecture.

As a style, Sikh architecture is essentially eclectic [universal] in nature, which is an appropriate expression of the eclectic content of the Sikh faith itself. It shares its essence with imported monotheism and its lush exuberance with indigenous polytheism. Not only has Sikh architecture thrived at this but also flourished to the extent of working out its own stylistic idiosyncrasies.

Pointed, semicircular, elliptical arches, with or without cusps, as well as ogee arches, are the ubiquitous elements of Sikh architecture. Among its typical features are the multiplicity of chattris, kiesks or pevilions, which embellish the parapets, angles, and every prominence and projection; the invariable use of the fluted or ribbed dome generally covered with brass or copper-gilt; the frequent introduction of oriel or embowed windows with shallow elliptical conics and supported on carved brackets; slanting over-hanging eaves also supported on brackets thrown out as an element emphasizing the string-course to decorate the lower structure and the parapet; elliptical eaves with multi-foil seffits a lavish enrichment of all arches by means of numerous foliations; and other structural ornamentation of a similar order.

Sikh architecture is a lively blend of the Mughal and Rajput styles. Onion-shaped domes, multi-foil arches, paired pilasters, in-lay work, frescoes, etc. are of Mughal extraction, more specially of Shah Jahan's period, while oriel windows, bracket supported eaves at the string-course, chattris, richly ornamented friezes, etc., are derived from elements of Rajput architecture such as is seen in Jaipur, Jodhpur, Bikaner and other places in Rajasthan.

Sikh architecture expresses the characteristic resilience of the Sikh spirit and its inviolable freedom to deviate from the artistic exuberance, aesthetic magnificence and creative fullness. The curious mannerist emphasis on creative freedom makes Sikh architecture the Indian Baroque, with its characteristics of sculptured skylines, variegated wall treatments, interesting juxtaposition and or disposition of recesses and projections - at once bold, vigorous, and tastefully sumptuous.

Use of water as an element of design has been frequently exploited in Mughal and Hindu architecture, but nowhere in so lively a manner as in Sikh architecture. Water becomes a sine qua non of Sikh architectural design, as in the Golden Temple at Amritsar or Darbar Sahib at Tarn Taran, and not merely an appendage to the main shrine. The gurdwara is placed lower down than the structures in the vicinity [signifying humility], unlike a masjid (mosque) or a mandir (Hindu temple), which are usually placed on raised platforms.

With the main shrine as the focus, Sikh architecture has tended to develop into a complex of several buildings serving different functions including residences, offices, museums, community kitchens, etc. These characteristics aptly express the three commandments of the Sikh Faith: working, worshipping and sharing.

While sticking to the same basic requirements, different Sikh shrines have developed their own characteristic expression. It may be recalled that most of the Gurdwaras are commemorative buildings, and therefore the sites on which they have been built, had the intrinsic challenges and advantages which were more fortuitous than premeditated. Most situations have been dealt with remarkable imagination and ingenuity. Eventually, no two shrines look exactly alike although there are exceptions such as Dera Sahib, Lahore, and Panja Sahib, both in Pakistan. Also the low metal-gilt fluted dome of the Golden Temple has been copied in these two shrines as well as in the Darbar Sahib at Tarn Taran. Sometimes, the difference in design is so great that it would be difficult to recognize a Gurdwara if the Sikh standard or Nishan Sahib [Sikh flag] were not there to help in its identification.

Some of the Gurdwaras look more like gateways, as is the case with Fatehgarh Sahib (Town of Victory), Sirhind, or like an educational institution, as in the case with Ber (berry) Sahib, Sultanpur Lodhi, or like a Rajput Palace, as in the case of Gurdwara Bahadur Garh (Fort of the Valient) in Patiala district, when one first encounters its enclosing structures. But all this deviation, if somewhat baffling, does not detract one from the essentials of Sikh architecture. On the contrary, it substantiates the very basis of creative freedom on which it is built.

As exemplified by Gurdwaras, Sikh Architecture is a veritable artistic expression of the evergreen ebullience of the Sikh way of life - its intensity, open-mindedness, and exuberance. It imparts a dimension of palpable immanence to the Transcendent Principle of Truth on which the Sikh faith is founded.

The uniqueness of the Sikh religious thought lies in its willing acceptance of the perennial coexistence of paired opposites like good and evil, virtue and vice, health and disease, life and death, riches and poverty, etc. It is grounded in the domain of the Concrete from where it takes off for an ever-extended adventure into the realm of the Abstract. It encompasses the polychronic, polymorphic and polycreative dimension of the world of relativity and transforms them into the colorless, formless, uncreated self-existence of the ever-abiding Absolute. All this is powerfully expressed in a form of urban design, which is an important dimension of Sikh architecture.

The Golden Temple complex at Amritsar is an apt example of excellence in urban design. It performs a variety of functions such as religious, social, cultural and spiritual. It's location is in the heart of the walled city, where it dwells in the midst of the entire civic organism with all its vital organs, veins and arteries. From the narrow lanes, among which are some handshake bazaars, which links it to the various parts of the city, one enters the grand, mystifying openness and splendor of Darbar Sahib complex. The access to the complex (and then to the main shrine) expresses the Sikh faith's willing acceptance of this world as it is, and symbolizes the progressive quest of the human spirit towards communion with God. The whole charm of spiritual experience lies in such exploration and should never be obvious. All such elements of curiosity, surprise, anticipation, encounter, excitement and fulfillment were there in the original city plan.

Unfortunately, all these are being systematically destroyed in the name of urban renewal and redevelopment by widening roads and building the so-called modern structures. Once the Golden Temple becomes visible from various sides, as it seems is now intended, it will lose much of its expressive magnificence. The obvious can never be grand! Must we therefore, not save it from irreparable damage that planning would without doubt cause to it in a big way.

There is a variety of scattered evidence that structures other than Gurdwaras still exists, if in a state of utter neglect, here and there, on this side and across the border, which were/are significant contributions of Sikh architecture to the art and science of building. For instance, it has been reliably learnt that Hari Singh Nalwa built a 14-storeyed structure with additional three in the basement (taikhanas) for use during summer. Only four storeys now survive. It is said that the (taikhanas were cold enough for use of blankets even when there was sweltering heat outside. If it could be established that such a structure did come up in the first quarter of the 19th century, Sikh architecture would have the proud privilege of having put up the first skyscraper of the world. History has recorded that the age of the skyscraper began when Home Insurance building, a ten-storied structure was constructed in Chicago towards the end of the 19th century. It is thus reasonable to surmise that a rich repertoire of buildings, which through their distinctive character belong to Sikh architecture, can be reconstructed through proper search and research in the field, which has hitherto remained neglected for various reasons.

Undoubtedly, there is an urgent need for exhaustive documentation, in-depth study and thorough research in the field of Sikh Architecture (and Art). There is also a need for preserving our tradition, and for extending it through a continued process of modernization. As members of a young and living faith, we owe it to posterity.

SOME FACTS ON SIKH ARCHITECTURE

So little has been written about Sikh architecture that it is difficult for anyone to believe that such a style of architecture exists at all. It is ironic that whereas the Sikhs are known the world over for their characteristic vigor, valor, versatility, above all their distinct physical, moral and spiritual identity, their architecture should have remained so abjectly unidentified.

This paper attempts to outline the main elements, principles, and objectives of building design with a view to conjuring up an overall picture of a style of architecture which can be doubtlessly called Sikh Architecture. This venture will be extended to touch upon another area of architecture which has come to be known as urban design, and whose existence in Sikh architecture can also be substantiated by apt examples.

Apart from buildings of religious order, Sikh architecture has secular types of forts, palaces, *bungas* (residential places), colleges, etc. The religious structure is the *gurdwara*, a place where the Guru dwells. A gurdwara is not only the all-important building of the Faith, as *masjid* or mosque of the Islamic faith and *mandir* or temple of the Hindu religion, but it is also, like its Islamic and Hindu counterparts, the keynote of Sikh architecture.

The word gurdwara is compounded of Guru (Guide or Master) and Dwara (Gateway or Seat) and therefore has an architectural connotation. Sikh temples are by and large commemorative buildings connected with the ten Gurus in some way, or with places and events of historical significance. For example, Gurdwara Dera Sahib (Halting place) in Batala in Gurdaspur district was erected to commemorate the brief stay here of Guru Nanak along with the party on the ocassion of his marriage. Gurdwara Shish Mahal (Hall of Mirrors) in Kiratpur in Ropar district was built where the eighth Guru, Harkishan, was born and so on. Gurdwara Shahid Ganj (Martyr's Memorial) in Muktsar in Faridkot district commemorates the place where the dead bodies of the Sikhs, who were killed in the battle between Guru Gobind Singh and the Mughal forces in 1705, were cremated. Gurdwara Ram Sar (God's Pool) in Amritsar stands on a site where the fifth Guru, Arjan Dev, got the Adi Granth compiled by Bhai Gurdas.

According to the Sikh faith, while prayers to God can be offered any time and at any place, a gurdwara is built particularly for congregational worship. Even a very small group of devotees living anywhere in the world would generally require a gurdwara to be built so as to get together for religious or even social purposes. The building could be as simple as a temporary shack, or a small room in a house, depending upon the resources of the local community. But the Sikhs would not stint in this matter, and they have thus built several beautiful and imposing gurdwaras some of which can accommodate hundreds of devotees.

The main requirement of a gurdwara is that of a room in which the Adi Granth, the Holy Book, can be placed and a small *sangat* or congregation can be seated to listen to the *path* or readings from the Holy Book and to sing and recite its verses. The buildings of the Sikh shrines cover a wide spectrum of structures varying from the simple and the austere to the richly embellished and respondent.

Gurdwaras have entrances on all the sides signifying that they are open to one and all without any distinction whatsoever. This distinguishing feature also symbolizes the essential tenet of the Sikh faith that God is omnipresent. In some cases, however, space shortage does not permit entry from all the sides, as in Gurdwara Sis Ganj in Delhi.

Many Sikh temples have a *deorhi*, an entrance or gateway, through which one has to pass before reaching the shrine. A *deorhi* is often an impressive structure with an imposing gateway, and sometimes provides accommodation for office and other use. The visitors get the first glimpse of the sanctum sanctotum from the *deorhi*.

There are over five hundred gurdwaras, big and small, which have an historical past. They are to be found throughout India, although a majority of them are located in the Punjab and its surrounding provinces. Some important gurdwaras also exist in Pakistan, Bangladesh and elsewhere in the world.

9

COLONIAL ARCHITECTURE IN INDIA

The British followed various architectural styles – Gothic, Imperial, Christian, English Renaissance and Victorian being the essentials. Bombay, a forgotten port because of its weather, was renovated after the Sepoy Mutiny in 1857. The town hall, built from 1820 to 1835 by Colonel Thomas Cowper and St Thomas' Cathedral were already there, but Governor Sir Bartle Frere's aim was to build a city out of fragments. The old town walls were broken down, and the Gateway of India (through which the last British troops left) was built.

The idea was definitely Gothic, to give Bombay a truly Imperial ambience. The Secretariat, University Library, Rajabai Tower, the Law Courts, Public Works office, Telegraph office, Victoria Terminus all followed the Victorian Gothic style, similar to buildings in London. Built during 1878 and 1887, the Victoria Terminus, or VT as it is fondly called, is the finest example of Gothic architecture in India. Its architect was Frederick Willaim Stevens, an unknown in England, who married marble, decorated tiles, stained glass, metal, concrete and bricks in a fusion which never happened again. High above the huge stairway inside a massive dome looms up as statement of Imperial progress in all its glory. The entrance is flanked by symbolic sentinels of the Raj, a tiger and a lion. Stevens was a practitioner of Victorian Gothic architecture and also designed the Churchgate Terminus. But Stevens' Municipal Building opposite the Victoria Terminus with the intermingling of Gothic and Indo-Saracenic architecture stands as the final testament of his brilliance, unsurpassed in British India. Built from 1888 to 1893, the Building is a massive conglomeration of masonry crowned with a true Islamic dome.

BRITISH GOTHIC ARCHITECTURE

Across India Gothic architecture flourished under the British. In Varanasi, one of the true Gothic monuments is Queen's College, built in a perpendicular style by Major Kitoe from 1847 to 1852. In nearby Allahabad, the British went on a rampage, building a series of edifices which include the colossal University, All Saints Cathedral, the High Court and Mayo College (now a sports association called Mayo Hall). In the east in Calcutta a High Court was erected on the Gothic style. All Saints Church in Nagpur was redesigned, the plans being sent to India from England by G F Bodley.

But it is Calcutta that takes the architectural cake. Who can forget the massive Howrah Bridge, finished in 1943 to replace a pontoon bridge built in 1874? The Bridge spans 1,500 feet, leading to Howrah Station whose red brick facade is surrounded by eight square towers in the Oriental and Roman style. 1880's Writer's Building was refaced with terracotta and conceals an earlier structure which were the mercantile headquarters of the East India Company. Fort William, the stronghold of the British in mid 19 century, took 13 years to construct at a cost of more than $3.5 million.

GOTHIC ARCHITECTURE

Gothic architecture is a style of architecture which flourished during the high and late medieval period. It evolved from Romanesque architecture and was succeeded by Renaissance architecture. Originating in 12th-century France and lasting into the 16th century, Gothic architecture was known during the period as "the French Style" (*Opus Francigenum*), with the term *Gothic* first appearing during the latter part of the Renaissance as a stylistic insult. Its characteristic features include the pointed arch, the ribbed vault and the flying buttress.

Gothic architecture is most familiar as the architecture of many of the great cathedrals, abbeys and parish churches of Europe. It is also the architecture of many castles, palaces, town halls, guild halls, universities, and to a less prominent extent, private dwellings.

It is in the great churches and cathedrals and in a number of civic buildings that the Gothic style was expressed most powerfully, its characteristics lending themselves to appeal to the emotions. A great number of ecclesiastical buildings remain from this period, of which even the smallest are often structures of architectural distinction while many of the larger churches are considered priceless works of art and are listed with UNESCO as World Heritage Sites. For this reason a study of Gothic architecture is largely a study of cathedrals and churches.

A series of Gothic revivals began in mid-18th century England, spread through 19th-century Europe and continued, largely for ecclesiastical and university structures, into the 20th century.

The term "Gothic", when applied to architecture, has nothing to do with the historical Goths. It was a pejorative term that came to be used as early as the 1530s by Giorgio Vasari to describe culture that was considered rude and barbaric. At the time in which Vasari was writing, Italy had experienced a century of building in the Classical architectural vocabulary revived in the Renaissance and seen as the finite evidence of a new Golden Age of learning and refinement.

The Renaissance had then overtaken Europe, overturning a system of culture that, prior to the advent of printing, was almost entirely focused on the Church and was perceived, in retrospect, as a period of ignorance and superstition. Hence, François Rabelais, also of the 16th century, imagines an inscription over the door of his Utopian Abbey of Thélème, "Here enter no hypocrites, bigots..." slipping in a slighting reference to "Gotz" and "Ostrogotz."

In English 17th-century usage, "Goth" was an equivalent of "vandal", a savage despoiler with a Germanic heritage and so came to be applied to the architectural styles of northern Europe from before the revival of classical types of architecture.

According to a 19th-century correspondent in the London Journal *Notes and Queries*: There can be no doubt that the term 'Gothic' as applied to pointed styles of ecclesiastical architecture was used at first contemptuously, and in derision, by those who were ambitious to imitate and revive the Grecian orders of architecture, after the revival of classical literature. Authorities such as Christopher Wren lent their aid in deprecating the old mediæval style, which they termed Gothic, as synonymous with every thing that was barbarous and rude.

On 21 July 1710, the Académie d'Architecture met in Paris, and among the subjects they discussed, the assembled company noted the new fashions of bowed and cusped arches on chimneypieces being employed *"to finish the top of their openings. The Company disapproved of several of these new manners, which are defective and which belong for the most part to the Gothic."*

INFLUENCES

Regional

At the end of the 12th century Europe was divided into a multitude of city-states and kingdoms. The area encompassing modern Germany, The Netherlands, Belgium, Luxembourg, Switzerland, Austria, eastern France and much of northern Italy, excluding Venice, was nominally under the authority of the Holy Roman Empire, but local rulers exercised considerable autonomy. France, Scotland, Spain and Sicily were independent kingdoms, as was England, whose Plantagenet kings ruled large domains in France. Norway came under the influence of England, while the other Scandinavian countries and Poland were influenced by Germany.

Throughout Europe at this time there was a rapid growth in trade and an associated growth in towns. Germany and the Lowlands had large flourishing towns that grew in comparative peace, in trade and competition with each other, or united for mutual weal, as in the Hanseatic League. Civic building was of great importance to these towns as a sign of wealth and pride. England and France remained largely feudal and produced grand domestic architecture for their dukes, rather than grand town halls for their burghers.

Materials

A further regional influence was the availability of materials. In France, limestone was readily available in several grades, the very fine white limestone of Caen being favoured for sculptural decoration. England had coarse limestone, red sandstone as well as dark green Purbeck marble which was often used for architectural features.

In Northern Germany, Netherlands, Scandinavia, Baltic countries and northern Poland local building stone was unavailable but there was a strong tradition of building in brick. The resultant style, Brick Gothic, is called "Backsteingotik" in Germany and Scandinavia.

In Italy, stone was used for fortifications, but brick was preferred for other buildings. Because of the extensive and varied deposits of marble, many buildings were faced in marble, or were left with undecorated facades so that this might be achieved at a later date.

The availability of timber also influenced the style of architecture. It is thought that the magnificent hammer-beam roofs of England were devised as a direct response to the lack of long straight seasoned timber by the end of the Medieval period, when forests had been decimated not only for the construction of vast roofs but also for ship building.

Religious

The early Medieval periods had seen a rapid growth in monasticism, with several different orders being prevalent and spreading their influence widely. Foremost were the Benedictines whose great abbey churches vastly outnumbered any others in England. Part of their influence was that they tended to build within towns, unlike the Cistercians whose ruined abbeys are seen in the remote countryside. The Cluniac and Cistercian Orders were prevalent in France, the great monastery at Cluny having established a formula for a well planned monastic site which was then to influence all subsequent monastic building for many centuries.

In the 13th century St. Francis of Assisi established the Franciscans, or so-called "Grey Friars", a mendicant order. Its off-shoot, the Dominicans, founded by St. Dominic in Toulouse and Bologna, were particularly influential in the building of Italy's Gothic churches.

Architectural

Gothic architecture grew out of the previous architectural genre, Romanesque. For the most part, there was not a clean break, as there was later to be in Renaissance Florence with the sudden revival of the Classical style by Brunelleschi in the early 15th century.

ROMANESQUE TRADITION

Romanesque architecture, or Norman architecture as it is generally termed in England because of its association with the Norman invasion, had already established the basic architectural forms and units that were to remain in slow evolution throughout the Medieval period. The basic structure of the cathedral church, the parish church, the monastery, the castle, the palace, the great hall and the gatehouse were all established. Ribbed vaults, buttresses, clustered columns, ambulatories, wheel windows, spires and richly carved door tympanums were already features of ecclesiastical architecture.

The widespread introduction of a single feature was to bring about the stylistic change that separates Gothic from Romanesque, and broke the tradition of massive masonry and solid walls penetrated by small openings, replacing it with a style where light appears to triumph over substance. The feature that brought the change is the pointed arch. With its use came the development of many other architectural devices, previously put to the test in scattered buildings and then called into service to meet the structural, aesthetic and ideological needs of the new style. These include the flying buttresses, pinnacles and traceried windows which typify Gothic ecclesiastical architecture.

ISLAMIC INFLUENCE

The pointed arch had its origins in ancient Assyrian architecture where it occurs in a number of structures as early as 720 BC. It passed into Sassanian-Persian architecture and from the conquest of Persia in 641 AD, became a standard feature of Islamic architecture.

The Norman conquest of Islamic Sicily in 1090, the Crusades which began in 1096 and the Islamic presence in Spain all brought about a knowledge of this significant structural device. It is probable also that decorative carved stone screens and window openings filled with pierced stone also influenced Gothic tracery. In Spain in particular individual decorative motifs occur which are common to both Islamic and Christian architectural mouldings and sculpture.

Concurrent with its introduction and early use as a stylistic feature in French churches, it is believed that the pointed arch evolved naturally in Western Europe as a structural solution to a purely technical problem.

ABBOT SUGER

Abbot Suger, friend and confidante of the French Kings, Louis VI and Louis VII, decided in about 1137, to rebuild the great Church of Saint-Denis, attached to an abbey which was also a royal residence.

Suger began with the *West front*, reconstructing the original Carolingian facade with its single door. He designed the façade of Saint-Denis to be an echo of the Roman Arch of Constantine with its three-part division and three large portals to ease the problem of congestion. The rose window is the earliest-known example above the West portal in France.

At the completion of the west front in 1140, Abbot Suger moved on to the reconstruction of the eastern end, leaving the Carolingian nave in use. He designed a *choir* (chancel) that would be suffused with light. To achieve his aims his architects drew on the several new features which evolved or been introduced to Romanesque architecture, the pointed arch, the ribbed vault, the ambulatory with radiating chapels, the clustered columns supporting ribs springing in different directions and the flying buttresses which enabled the insertion of large *clerestory* windows.

The new structure was finished and dedicated on June 11, 1144, in the presence of the King. The Abbey of Saint-Denis thus became the prototype for further building in the royal domain of northern France. It is often cited as the first building in the Gothic style. A hundred years later, the old nave of Saint-Denis was rebuilt in the Gothic style, gaining, in its transepts, two spectacular rose windows.

Through the rule of the Angevin dynasty, the style was introduced to England and spread throughout France, the Low Countries, Germany, Spain and northern of Italy and Sicily.

CHARACTERISTICS OF GOTHIC CHURCHES AND CATHEDRALS

In Gothic architecture, a unique combination of existing technologies established the emergence of a new building style. Those technologies were the ogival or pointed arch, the ribbed vault, and the flying buttress. The Gothic style, when applied to an ecclesiastical building, emphasizes verticality and light. This appearance was achieved by the development of certain architectural features, which together provided an engineerical solution. The structural parts of the building ceased to be its solid walls, and became a stone skeleton comprised of clustered columns, pointed ribbed vaults and flying buttresses.

A Gothic cathedral or abbey was, prior to the 20th century, generally the landmark building in its town, rising high above all the domestic structures and often surmounted by one or more towers and pinnacles and perhaps tall spires.

PLAN

Most Gothic churches, unless they are entitled chapels, are of the Latin cross (or "cruciform") plan, with a long nave making the body of the church, a transverse arm called the *transept* and beyond it, an extension which may be called the *choir*, chancel or presbytery. There are several regional variations on this plan.

The nave is generally flanked on either side by aisles, usually singly, but sometimes double. The nave is generally considerably taller than the aisles, having *clerestorey* windows which light the central space. Gothic churches of the Germanic tradition, like St. Stephen of Vienna, often have nave and aisles of similar height and are called *Hallenkirche*. In the South of France there is often a single wide nave and no aisles, as at Sainte-Marie in Saint-Bertrand-de-Comminges.

In some churches with double aisles, like Notre Dame, Paris, the transept does not project beyond the aisles. In English cathedrals transepts tend to project boldly and there may be two of them, as at Salisbury Cathedral, though this is not the case with lesser churches.

The eastern arm shows considerable diversity. In England it is generally long and may have two distinct sections, both choir and presbytery. It is often square ended or has a projecting *Lady Chapel*, dedicated to the Virgin Mary. In France the eastern end is often polygonal and surrounded by a walkway called an ambulatory and sometimes a ring of chapels called a *chevette*. While German churches are often similar to those of France, in Italy, the eastern projection beyond the transept is usually just a shallow apsidal chapel containing the *sanctuary*, as at Florence Cathedral.

STRUCTURE: THE POINTED ARCH

Origins

The *defining* characteristic of Gothic architecture is the pointed or ogival arch. Arches of this type were used in Islamic architecture before they were used structurally in European architecture, and are thought to have been the inspiration for their use in France, as at Autun Cathedral, which is otherwise stylistically Romanesque.

However, it appears that there was probably simultaneously a structural evolution towards the pointed arch, for the purpose of vaulting spaces of irregular plan, or to bring transverse vaults to the same height as diagonal vaults. This latter occurs at Durham Cathedral in the nave aisles in 1093. Pointed arches also occur extensively in Romanesque decorative *blind arcading*, where semi-circular arches overlap each other in a simple decorative pattern, and the points are accidental to the design.

Functions

The Gothic vault, unlike the semi-circular vault of Roman and Romanesque buildings, can be used to roof rectangular and irregularly shaped plans such as trapezoids. The other structural advantage is that the pointed arch channels the weight onto the bearing piers or columns at a steep angle. This enabled architects to raise vaults much higher than was possible in Romanesque architecture.

While, structurally, use of the pointed arch gave a greater flexibility to architectural form, it also gave Gothic architecture a very different visual character to Romanesque, the verticality suggesting an aspiration to Heaven.

In Gothic Architecture the pointed arch is used in every location where a vaulted shape is called for, both structural and decorative. Gothic openings such as doorways, windows, arcades and galleries have pointed arches. Gothic vaulting above spaces both large and small is usually supported by richly molded ribs.

Rows of pointed arches upon delicate shafts form a typical wall decoration known as blind arcading. Niches with pointed arches and containing statuary are a major external feature. The pointed arch lent itself to elaborate intersecting shapes which developed within window spaces into complex Gothic tracery forming the structural support of the large windows that are characteristic of the style.

Height

A characteristic of Gothic church architecture is its height, both real and proportional. A section of the main body of a Gothic church usually shows the nave as considerably taller than it is wide. In England the proportion is sometimes greater than 2:1, while the extreme is reached at Cologne Cathedral with a ratio of 3.6:1. The extreme of actual internal height was achieved at Beauvais Cathedral at 157' 6" (48 m).

Externally, towers and spires are characteristic of Gothic churches both great and small, the number and positioning being one of the greatest variables in Gothic architecture. In Italy, the tower, if present, is almost always detached from the building, as at Florence Cathedral, and is often from an earlier structure. In France and Spain, two towers on the front is the norm. In England, Germany and Scandinavia this is often the arrangement, but an English cathedral may also be surmounted by an enormous tower at the crossing. Smaller churches usually have just one tower, but this may also be the case at larger buildings, such as Salisbury cathedral or Ulm Minster, which has the tallest spire in the world, slightly exceeding that of Lincoln Cathedral, the tallest which was actually completed during the medieval period, at 527 feet (160 m).

Vertical emphasis

The pointed arch lends itself to a suggestion of height. This appearance is characteristically further enhanced by both the architectural features and the decoration of the building. On the exterior, the verticality is emphasised in a major way by the towers and spires and in a lesser way by strongly projecting vertical buttresses, by narrow half-columns called *attached shafts* which often pass through several storeys of the building, by long narrow windows, vertical mouldings around doors and figurative sculpture which emphasises the vertical and is often attenuated. The roofline, gable ends, buttresses and other parts of the building are often terminated by small *pinnacles*, Milan Cathedral being an extreme example in the use of this form of decoration.

On the interior of the building *attached shafts* often sweep unbroken from floor to ceiling and meet the ribs of the vault, like a tall tree spreading into branches. The verticals are generally repeated in the treatment of the windows and wall surfaces. In many Gothic churches, particularly in France, and in the *Perpendicular period* of English Gothic architecture, the treatment of vertical elements in gallery and window tracery creates a strongly unifying feature that counteracts the horizontal divisions of the interior structure.

Light

One of the most distinctive characteristics of Gothic architecture is the expansive area of the windows as at Sainte Chapelle and the very large size of many individual windows, as at Gloucester Cathedral and Milan Cathedral. The increase in size between windows of the Romanesque and Gothic periods is related to the use of the ribbed vault, and in particular, the pointed ribbed vault which channeled the weight to a supporting shaft with less outward thrust than a semicircular vault. Walls did not need to be so weighty.

A further development was the flying buttress which arched externally from the springing of the vault across the roof of the aisle to a large buttress pier projecting well beyond the line of the external wall. These piers were often surmounted by a pinnacle or statue, further adding to the downward weight, and counteracting the outward thrust of the vault and buttress arch.

The internal columns of the arcade with their attached shafts, the ribs of the vault and the flying buttresses, with their associated vertical buttresses jutting at right-angles to the building, created a stone skeleton. Between these parts, the walls and the infill of the vaults could be of lighter construction. Between the narrow buttresses, the walls could be opened up into large windows.

Through the Gothic period, due to the versatility of the pointed arch, the structure of Gothic windows developed from simple openings to immensely rich and decorative sculptural designs. The windows were very often filled with stained glass which added a dimension of colour to the light within the building, as well as providing a medium for figurative and narrative art.

Majesty

The facade of a large church or cathedral, often referred to as the *West Front*, is generally designed to create a powerful impression on the approaching worshipper, demonstrating both the might of God, and the might of the institution that it represents. One of the best known and most typical of such facades is that of Notre Dame de Paris.

Central to the facade is the main portal, often flanked by additional doors. In the arch of the door, the tympanum, is often a significant piece of sculpture, most frequently *Christ in Majesty* and *Judgment Day*. If there is a central door jamb or a tremeu, then it frequently bears a statue of the *Madonna and Child*. There may be much other carving, often of figures in niches set into the mouldings around the portals, or in sculptural screens extending across the facade.

In the centre of the middle level of the facade, there is a large window, which in countries other than England and Belgium, is generally a rose window like that at Reims Cathedral. The gable above this is usually richly decorated with arcad ng or sculpture, or in the case of Italy, may be decorated, with the rest of the facade, with polychrome marble and mosaic, as at Orvieto Cathedral.

The West Front of a French cathedral and many English, Spanish and German cathedrals generally has two towers, which, particularly in France, express an enormous diversity of form and decoration. However, some German cathedrals have only one tower located in the middle of the facade (such as Freiburg Münster).

BASIC SHAPES OF GOTHIC ARCHES AND STYLISTIC CHARACTER

The way in which the pointed arch was drafted and utilised developed throughout the Gothic period. There were fairly clear stages of development, which did not, however, progress at the same rate, or in the same way in every country. Moreover, the names used to define various periods or styles within the Gothic differs from country to country.

Lancet Arch

The simplest shape is the long opening with a pointed arch known in England as the *lancet*. Lancet openings are often grouped, usually as a cluster of three or five. Lancet openings may be very narrow and steeply pointed. Salisbury Cathedral is famous for the beauty and simplicity of its Lancet Gothic, known in England as the

Early English Style. York Minster has a group of lancet windows each fifty feet high and still containing ancient glass. They are known as the Five Sisters. These simple undecorated grouped windows are found at Chartres and Laon Cathedrals and are used extensively in Italy.

Equilateral Arch

Many Gothic openings are based upon the equilateral form. In other words, when the arch is drafted, the radius is exactly the width of the opening and the centre of each arch coincides with the point from which the opposite arch springs. This makes the arch higher in relation to its width than a semi-circular arch which is exactly half as high as it is wide.

The Equilateral Arch gives a wide opening of satisfying proportion useful for doorways, decorative arcades and big windows. The structural beauty of the Gothic arch means, however, that no set proportion had to be rigidly maintained. The Equilateral Arch was employed as a useful tool, not as a Principle of Design. This meant that narrower or wider arches were introduced into a building plan wherever necessity dictated. In the architecture of some Italian cities, notably Venice, semi-circular arches are interspersed with pointed ones.

The Equilateral Arch lends itself to filling with tracery of simple equilateral, circular and semi-circular forms. The type of tracery that evolved to fill these spaces is known in England as Geometric Decorated Gothic and can be seen to splendid effect at many English and French Cathedrals, notably Lincoln and Notre Dame in Paris. Windows of complex design and of three or more *lights* or vertical sections, are often designed by overlapping two or more equilateral arches.

Flamboyant Arch

The Flamboyant Arch is one that is drafted from four points, the upper part of each main arc turning upwards into a smaller arc and meeting at a sharp, flame-like point. These arches create a rich and lively effect when used for window tracery and surface decoration. The form is structurally weak and has very rarely been used for large openings except when contained within a larger and more stable arch. It is not employed at all for vaulting.

Some of the most beautiful and famous traceried windows of Europe employ this type of tracery. It can be seen at St Stephen's Vienna, Sainte Chapelle in Paris, at the Cathedrals of Limoges and Rouen in France, and at Milan Cathedral in Italy. In England the most famous examples are the West Window of York Minster with its design based on the Sacred Heart, the extraordinarily rich seven-light East Window at Carlisle Cathedral and the exquisite East window of Selby Abbey.

Doorways surmounted by Flamboyant mouldings are very common in both ecclesiastical and domestic architecture in France. They are much rarer in England. A notable example is the doorway to the Chapter Room at Rochester Cathedral.

The style was much used in England for wall arcading and niches. Prime examples in are in the Lady Chapel at Ely, the Screen at Lincoln and externally on the facade of Exeter Cathedral. In German and Spanish Gothic architecture it often appears as openwork screens on the exterior of buildings. The style was used to rich and sometimes extraordinary effect in both these countries, notably on the famous pulpit in Vienna Cathedral.

Depressed Arch

The Depressed or four-centred arch is much wider than its height and gives the visual effect of having been flattened under pressure. Its structure is achieved by drafting two arcs which rise steeply from each springing point on a small radius and then turn into two arches with a wide radius and much lower springing point.

This type of arch, when employed as a window opening, lends itself to very wide spaces, provided it is adequately supported by many narrow vertical shafts. These are often further braced by horizontal transoms. The overall effect produces a grid-like appearance of regular, delicate, rectangular forms with an emphasis on the perpendicular. It is also employed as a wall decoration in which arcade and window openings form part of the whole decorative surface.

The style, known as Perpendicular, that evolved from this treatment is specific to England, although very similar to contemporary Spanish style in particular, and was employed to great effect through the 15th century and first half of the 16th as Renaissance styles were much slower to arrive in England than in Italy and France.

It can be seen notably at the East End of Gloucester Cathedral where the East Window is said to be as large as a tennis court. There are three very famous royal chapels and one chapel-like Abbey which show the style at its most elaborate- King's College Chapel, Cambridge; St George's Chapel, Windsor; Henry VII's Chapel at Westminster Abbey and Bath Abbey. However very many simpler buildings, especially churches built during the wool boom in East Anglia, are fine examples of the style.

SYMBOLISM AND ORNAMENTATION

The Gothic cathedral represented the universe in microcosm and each architectural concept, including the loftiness and huge dimensions of the structure, were intended to convey a theological message: the great glory of God. The building becomes a microcosm in two ways. Firstly, the mathematical and geometrical nature of the construction is an image of the orderly universe, in which an underlying rationality and logic can be perceived.

Secondly, the statues, sculptural decoration, stained glass and murals incorporate the essence of creation in depictions of the Labours of the Months and the Zodiac and sacred history from the Old and New Testaments and Lives of the Saints, as well as reference to the eternal in the Last Judgment and *Coronation of the Virgin*.

The decorative schemes usually incorporated Biblical stories, emphasizing visual typological allegories between Old Testament prophecy and the New Testament.

Many churches were very richly decorated, both inside and out. Sculpture and architectural details were often bright with coloured paint of which traces remain at the Cathedral of Chartres. Wooden ceilings and panelling were usually brightly coloured. Sometimes the stone columns of the nave were painted, and the panels in decorative wall arcading contained narratives or figures of saints. These have rarely remained intact, but may be seen at the Chapterhouse of Westminster Abbey.

Some important Gothic churches could be severely simple such as the Basilica of Mary Magdalene in Saint-Maximin, Provence where the local traditions of the sober, massive, Romanesque architecture were still strong.

THE MAGNIFICENT VICTORIAL MEMORIAL

The Victoria Memorial (1921) is probably the most imposing of all British structures in India. Located at a short distance from Fort William, it stands as a silent sentinel of the departed Raj, dominating the entire city by its sheer beauty. Dedicated to Queen Victoria, is rises up behind two ornamental tanks leading from a pathway featuring a statue of the Queen. The entire exterior of this massive edifice is in Makrana marble, the same which was used to build the Taj Mahal in Agra. A 16 feet bronze statue of Victory, weighing three tons, revolves in the uppermost section of the building. The domes around the corners resemble those of the Mughals, and the south has a triumphant archway where a statue of Lord Curzon, the architect, is placed. The interior has statues of the young Queen Victoria, representing her accession to the throne along with bronze and marble statues and busts of King George V and Queen Mary. A succession of rooms follow which house paintings, artifacts, sculptors, books and manuscripts.

THE INDO-SARACENIC STYLE OF ARCHITECTURE

Towards the end of the 19th century, the Victorian Indo-Saracenic style came to the forefront. Rising Indian nationalism prompted the revival of this style, and the British began to adapt their image to mingle with that of Indians. Victorian in essence, it borrowed from the Islamic style of Mughal and Afghan rulers, perhaps as a subtle statement that the British were the real powers behind the princely states.

The Indo-Saracenic style was Indian on the outside and British inside; the facade built with an Indian touch while the interior was solely Victorian. Madras (now known as Chennai) is home for some finest masterpieces of this style, like the Law Courts, Presidency College and Senate House. The Law Courts especially stand out for their grandeur in a splendid rendezvous of Muslim domes, canopied balconies, arcaded verandahs all topped off with a minaret at whose pinnacle is a bulbous dome. In Mysore, the Maharaja's palace was designed on the lines of the Madras Courts, with a dome and minarets.

COLONIAL ARCHITECTURE SPLENDOR AT NEW DELHI

New Delhi is a city made by the British, not the Mughals. In 1911 the King Emperor George V passed an order declaring that the capital would be moved from Calcutta to Delhi. The city was planned systematically, combining 20 century architecture with that of two centuries before. Sir Edward Lutyens was responsible for the overall plan of Delhi, and his tour de forte is Rajpath, approached by a 3.2 km long road flanked by the imposing buildings of the two Secretariats, built by Herbert Baker. The Rashtrapati Bhawan, built of brown stone, is truly a befitting home for the President of the second largest democracy in the world.

But it wasn't Lutyens or Bakers who built the rest of Delhi as is commonly believed; most if its structures were designed by an unknown Englishman called Robert Tor Tussell, who built Connaught Place, Eastern and Western Courts, Flagstaff House (where Jawaharlal Nehru lived later) and the thousands of public buildings, post offices, officer's bungalows and public buildings. St Martin's Garrison Church is the final British piece of architecture, one of the most important ones because it represents the end of a search for an definitive style over 200 years. Looming out of the ground and made of three and a half million red bricks, the Church is a huge monolith with a high square tower and deeply sunken window ledges reminiscent of Dutch and German architecture. With India's independence in 1947, British architecture died a gradual death, especially after the new city of Chandigarh was completed by Le Corbusier and his English colleagues.

10

PHILOSOPHICAL CONTENTS OF INDIAN ART AND ARCHITECTURE

Academic appraisals of Indian art and architecture in the Western world have suffered from many of the same biases and prejudices that have infected analyses of Indian philosophy and culture. In the colonially constructed model, India was to be pigeon-holed as a land seeped in incomprehensible mysticism - where religion dominated all aspects of social life, but unlike the "noble" piousness of the Western world, India's religious practices were often seen as bizarre and grotesque.

Although the subcontinent has enjoyed a virtually uninterrupted history of developments in the realm of art and architecture, India has been either studiously ignored in compilations of "world" art - or it has been represented by a very small and limited number of examples. When volumes on Indian art and architecture have been produced, it has not been unusual for the commentaries to begin with generalizations like "all Indian architecture has been religious" and very quickly through the text, one runs into comparative statements suggesting that Indian art and architecture was never quite able to reach the grand heights achieved by Western art and architecture.

The statement that all Indian architecture has been "religious" displays not only a poor understanding of philosophical practices in ancient India, but also a remarkable lack of perspective concerning not only the archeological discoveries in India, but also in the West. Such characterizations of the Indian legacy are especially puzzling because the urban character of the Harappan civilization ought to be quite well-known to all Western academics as should the cosmopolitan and secular character of the Mauryan era.

If one wished to be biased and subjective in summarizing the Western architectural record, one could just as easily claim that all Western art and architecture has been "religious". One could point to Greek and Roman temples, the sculptures in the burial tombs, the numerous synagogues, Byzantine and gothic churches, the monasteries of Eastern Europe and the thousands of paintings of the christ and the cross to bolster ones case.

And while such a description would do great injustice to the Roman period when aqueducts, amphitheatres, palaces and private villas were also built and have survived, churches and religious paintings predominate the surviving historical record of the Christian period before the renaissance.

By and large, throughout the world, religious inspired architecture predominates the planet's archeological record simply because religious monuments were often built from more permanent building materials.

INDIA'S SECULAR ARCHITECTURE

Much of India's oldest secular architecture has not survived because it was built from wood. Stone was a cumbersome and time consuming material for construction, and given the intense heat, it is a particularly unsuitable material for closed construction. That is why stone was used primarily for buildings where much of the activity would take place in an outdoor setting. However, anecdotal accounts of Greek and Chinese travellers, surviving literature and court histories, ancient sculptural finds and cave paintings - all indicate that India was not lacking in secular buildings, many of which were embellished with architectural ornamentation and painted in naturally available colours.

For instance, there is considerable literary evidence to indicate that public gateways known as *Toranas* were constructed by numerous rulers throughout India - some of which were vandalized or destroyed during the early period of Islamic invasions, and some remodelled or adapted, and incorporated into structures utilized by later royal courts.

Nevertheless, some have survived intact and there are enough surviving physical remains to suggest that Indian architecture achieved it's greatest heights in the construction of these *Toranas* that once graced the entries to the major capitals of India's ancient and medieval past.

Gupta period remains from the 5th-6th C in Delhi are particularly impressive, as are the exquisitely carved *Toranas* from Vadnagar in Gujarat (of which only one is left standing), and probably dates from the 9th or 10th C. Dabhoi, the 12th-13th C capital of the Solankis, has four gateways, each of which is richly carved, and four handsome *Toranas* still stand in Warangal, the 13th C capital of the Kakathiyas. Most of Warangal was sacked in the 14th C, but the ruins of the city point to an impressive architectural complex that probably included an amphitheater, royal pavillions and perhaps public meeting halls.

(The tradition of the *Torana* continued with the Bengal Sultans, Sher Shah Suri and the Mughals who converted the rectangular or stylized U and V shaped forms into the classical arch, but in Srirangam (Tamil Nadu), the older style prevailed, but took on a more grand and imposing aura.)

Stones (sometimes brick) were also used in constructing step-wells and sunken swimming pools (or bathing tanks) in the manner of Mohenjodaro, but often became exceedingly elaborate after the 9th C. While some of these were constructed next to temples (as in Modehra, Gujarat) others were part of royal complexes such as the Queen's step-well of Patan with it's stunning sculpture galleries, and Adalaj with it's many terraces and carved ornamental niches. A less elaborate but aesthetically pleasing example is to be found in the old town of Bundi (Rajasthan) and several other interesting examples (mostly attributed to the Chauhans) are to be found in the Ajmer-Delhi region.

(Al Beruni makes special note of these step-wells (i.e.Baolls) in his India chronicles. Step-wells for both royal and public use were constructed in much of the Indian North West, and some may have been part of water management projects as evident in Farrukhnagar in Haryana.)

Also of note are the remains of the universities of ancient India - such as Taxila, Nalanda, Vikramshila or Sarnath - where instruction was provided on a variety of subjects including mathematics, epistemology and logic, the natural sciences and medicine. Nalanda, even today retains the unmistakable air of a college campus with it's many dorms and what appear to be lecture halls. To classify such historical sites as "religious" sites would be clearly misleading.

Although it has been customary to treat India's forts as a largely an Islamic contribution and to treat the Rajput forts as quite apart from the general Indian tradition, India was dotted with hill-top forts that were constructed several centuries before they were conquered and occupied by India's Islamic rulers. (Examples of such forts, some of them long abandoned, can still be found in Kalinjar and Ajaigarh in Central India, for instance.) Over time, India's Rajput, and other rulers learnt to build enormous palaces within these forts and evolved techniques of insulating them from the heat, and palace architects found ways of ensuring optimal ventilation and exposure to light. Most of these palaces were richly decorated and provide tremendous insight into the artistic and decorative choices that were favored by the royalty.

It is therefore quite bizarre how influential Western academics have tried to confine the historic Indian legacy to the sphere of religion. But even when Western art historians have concentrated exclusively on India's temples and stupas, they have seriously erred in their analyses of these monuments and the impulses that led to their creation.

PHILOSOPHICAL CONTENT OF INDIAN ART

Unlike the Western religions, which have little philosophical content and belief in the "One God" is mandatory, many of India's ancient religions were not religions in the narrow sense in which religion is construed today. India's early Buddhists were predominantly atheists, the early Jains were agnostic, and within the broad umbrella of Hinduism, there was space for considerable philosophical variety. In the Upanishads, god is described in an extremely abstract and metaphysical way. The philosophical content is essentially secular and spiritual ideas emerge from debate and speculation - not immortal revelations that cannot be challenged or modified with time. In the Nyaya-Sutras, the overwhelming focus is on rational and scientific thinking and analysis, on human understanding of natural phenomenon and physical processes occurring in nature.

This rich tradition of philosophy - both rational and spiritual - found it's way into Indian art and architecture as well. Stupas and temples incorporated a profound symbolic language based on visual representations of all the important philosophical concepts. These included the *Chakra* - the revolving wheel of time which symbolized the cyclical rhythms of the cosmos; the *Padma* - or the lotus symbol which embodied the prime symbol of creation - of the universal creative force that springs from the bosom of the earth; the *Ananta* (represented as a snake) symbolized water - the most important life-giving force and the infinite ocean from which all life emerged, got differentiated and then got re-merged and redissolved; the *Swastika* - representing the four-fold aspects of creation and motion; the *Purnakalasa* - or the overflowing flower pot - a symbol of creativity and prosperity; the *Kalpalata* and *Kalpavriksha* - *the* wish-fulfillment creeper or tree that were also symbols of imagination and creativity; *Gavaska* - sometimes understood to be the third eye; *Mriga* - or deer - symbolic of erotic desire and beauty; and *lingam* and *yoni* - the male and female fertility symbols.

Rules were also evolved to provide additional symbolic content through hand gestures (*mudra*) of sculptured deities. Deities were sometimes given multiple arms to signify energy or power or to suggest movement and as symbolic of the celestial dance. Different arm positions embodied different virtues such as wisdom, strength, generosity, kindness and caring. Multiple arms could thus be used to signify multiple virtues.

Western analysts have often had difficulty understanding the complex cultural and philosophical systems that gave birth to India's artistic tradition. For many, Indian sculptural panels appeared to be nothing more than a random collection of strange or arbitrary juxtapositions of primitive beliefs and superstitions. This is not to say that Indian spirituality was always free from superstition or arbitrary constructs, but in the best of the sculptural panels, there was a conscious and knowledgeable attempt to convey powerful philosophical ideas.

SECULAR AND SPIRITUAL FUSION

As physical embodiments of philosophical systems that combined the secular with the spiritual, India's stupas and temples were not just religious monuments but also cultural centres that had both spiritual and secular significance. That is why the stupa or the temple could never be completely equated to a synagogue or church. And this is why, when built, they incorporated so many images from secular life.

For instance, take the stupas at Amravati (1st C BC), Sanchi (1st C AD) or Nagarjunakonda (2nd-3rd C AD). Each displays a wealth of carving and the main themes uniting the sculpted panels in all three stupas are scenes from the life of the 'Buddha'. Yet, in the Amravati panels, there is an intense and barely concealed sensuality that pervades throughout, and flowers and creepers are depicted with a loving tenderness. In the Sanchi *toranas* there are also depictions of warriors on horses, royal processions, traders' caravans, merchant families in their multi-storied homes with balconies, farmers with produce and animals, and again, there are beautiful depictions of plants and animals.

In contrast to synagogues, churches or mosques, the Indian temple from the 8th C onwards incorporated sculpted images of musicians, dancers, acrobats and romantic couples, in addition to depictions of a variety of deities. After the 10th C, erotic themes begin to make their mark. Sensuality and sexual interation is displayed without inhibition in the temples of Khajuraho, Konarak and Bhubaneshwar and in the Kakathiya temples of Palampet. (Erotic carvings are also to be found in many of the lesser-known temples of Rajasthan and the Jabalpur-Chhatisgarh region). This may have seemed shocking and scandalous to the puritanically minded Western art critic but it showed that in that period of Indian history, Tantric ideas on the compatibility of human sexuality with human spirituality had entered the mainstream. Erotic desires were not considered to be antagonistic to spiritual liberation but instead an important component of spiritual release. A completely different moral outlook was at work here - religion was not based on sensual starvation but on a healthy and egalitarian acceptance of all activities that contributed to the emotional health and well-being of human society.

In many ways, the temples of Khajuraho and Konarak were a logical culmination of the general trend towards including all things sensual in the temple. Beginning with lyrical depictions of flutists and drummers and expressive depictions of romantic couples and continuing with lively depictions of dancers and acrobats, the Indian temple evolved into breaking the very last taboo. The most intimate and personal of human interactions (normally shrouded behind a veil of secrecy) were now sculpted in stone, in full public view. For some, this represented decadence and a regression from spiritual purity - for others it was a sign of remarkable advance - that society had been able to break down the shackles of hypocritical prudery.

But no matter how this was viewed, it demonstrated in a very powerful way that at that time, Indian religion and it's monumental expression were based not on worldly denial but instead on an unabashed acceptance of essential human urges.

However, Islamic invasions created an enormous challenge for this fusion of the secular - (especially the sensual) with the spiritual to survive. Monuments were vandalized beyond recognition, with monasteries and institutions of learning becoming particular targets. Manuscripts were put to fire while some temples and stupas were rebuilt as mosques or madrasahs. In the Gangetic plain, virtually nothing of the old civilization was left to illuminate the future. Fear of vandalism caused new temples built during the period of Islamic rule to largely eschew sculptural decoration. Although in places like Benaras floral and abstract decorations filled the gap, and in Maharashtra there were successful attempts to enliven the temples with bold use of color and architectural embellishment, the long tradition of sculptural exuberance that characterized the classical Indian temple gradually came to an end in most parts of Northern and Central India.

When the European world began to experience a renaissance in the realm of art and sculpture, exactly the opposite processes were at work in India. After the renaissance, much of the new patronage for European sculpture came from the urban areas, and this is why European sculptors infused their creations with an urbane sophistication. The strong shadow of Islamic prudery prevented such a development from taking place in India. The great wealth of Indian sculpture was created during Europe's Christian era, in a society where the divide between the city and the countryside had not yet sharpened as much. This is why so much of Indian sculpture retains such a strong link to nature and seems less urbane and cosmopolitan, and hence less meritorious to the Western eye.

Another aspect of the Indian tradition that has baffled Western critics is the apparent lack of individualistic expression in traditional India art and sculpture. There are few Indian sculptures of actual personages. There are no sculptures of rulers or rich patrons.

But that should be seen as the strength of Indian art - that it strived for the universal as opposed to the particular. That Indian rulers were not so vain as to think that their portraits would have any meaning for posterity. In this regard, Indian tastes appear to resemble Greek/Mediterranean tastes in that most sculpture celebrates gods and goddesses in their most idealized forms (unlike the Roman elite who were more vain, and displayed a preference for their own portraits).

Finally, it should be noted that it isn't always essential to be knowledgeable about Indian philosophy to enjoy or appreciate Indian sculpture. Because the best of Indian sculpture is imbued with an advanced degree of expressive visual realism comparable to the sculpture of the pre-Christian Mediterranean civilizations, one might think that it might make it easier for an unbiased Western viewer to appreciate Indian sculpture on at least that common basis. But many Western art critics have simply avoided trying to see any commonalities between the two traditions. And when they have noted this aspect, they have immediately rushed to making poorly substantiated claims that the realism in Indian sculpture must have been a Western import forgetting that Indian sculpture from the Harappan period was also realistic or that the rich tradition of realism in Indian philosophy might very naturally have given birth to an aesthetics that favored realistic rendering in sculpture albeit modified by locally prevalent ideas of poise, expression and beauty.

THE INDIAN MINIATURE

Painting in India has a very old tradition, with ancient texts outlining theories of color and aesthetics and anecdotal accounts suggesting that it was not uncommon for households to paint their doorways or facades or even indoor rooms where guests were received. Cave paintings from Ajanta, Bagh and Sittanvasal and temple paintings testify to a love of naturalism - both in the depiction of the human form and in the depiction of nature.

But in Ajanta, we also see the emergence of a style that appears again and again, and many centuries later: the tendency to draw abstractions from nature in a manner that is both aesthetically pleasing and very effective as decorative embellishment. In the illustrated manuscripts of later eras, it is this latter trend that becomes most important and provides the foundation for the Indian miniature in which even the human form can become exceedingly stylized.

When analyzing Indian miniature paintings, art critics have often focused on the absence of perspective as employed by European painters. This has led many art historians to view Indian miniatures as naive or primitive and inferior to the large canvasses in Europe that depicted scenes with photographic accuracy. Indian art critics swayed by the importance given to the single vanishing point perspective scheme used by European painters after the European Renaissance, accept this as a weakness of Indian painting, and some have sought to classify Mughal paintings as superior because they were able to find hints of Western influence in some of the Mughal miniatures.

What these art critics and historians fail to note is that every artist faces an enormous dilemma in deciding what aspects of multi-dimensional reality to portray in two dimensions. When we observe reality, our eyes rarely rest on a single scene absorbing it from one angle alone. Our eyes focus far and near, they move spatially across a wide panorama. A single snapshot-like depiction, no matter how skillfully executed, and no matter how brilliantly accurate, is obviously capable of relaying only one view of that reality.

When the Indian painter employed multiple perspectives, he/she was trying to convey more than what would have been possible had he/she merely imitated the European approach. Often, the Indian painter was interested in conveying the reality that existed behind walls and doors, or on the other side of a hill or a tree. These attempts were not naive or simplistic, they reflected larger goals. They attempted to demonstrate that reality was more than what could be observed from a single focal point or a single perspective - that a reality existed that may be unseen from a certain vantage point - yet required to be conveyed. Since the genesis of the Indian miniature lay in the illustrated book, this approach to painting becomes very easily understandable.

Indian miniatures have also been criticized for their flatness - i.e. lack of body and shading, but here again, we might observe that a different value system may be at work. For instance, reality is never constant. Trees bend with the wind, birds fly around, people shake their heads and shift their body parts - none of this can be conveyed through any standardized rules concerning perspective. Sometimes a painting that appears to lack three-dimensionality may actually better convey a sense of motion than one that seems three-dimensional in appearance. Miniatures depicting dance scenes might float the dancers around curved lines set against a flat background to emphasize the fluidity of motion and to bring out the gaiety of the scene. Flatness also assisted the painter in shifting focus away from individuals to broader groups such as an ensemble of dancers or ensemble of musicians, or a crowd at a festival.

Many of the finest Indian miniatures were based on *Ragmalas* - i.e. moods associated with different musical *ragas*. Here the emphasis was on conveying a particular sentiment or mood, or atmosphere. Through the bold use of color, abstract touches, and deliberate flattening of three-dimensional textures, the artist succeeded in bringing out certain hidden nuances that simply would not be possible any other way.

Painting was also a medium for the expression of visual fantasies. Birds and flowers, trees and creepers have often been depicted with a loving grace by Indian sculptors and painters alike. In the miniature paintings from Mewar or the Kangra Valley, idyllic nature scenes were created to convey a sense of joy and wonder, or a mood of unspoiled romance and eroticism.

In recent years, the sheer decorative brilliance and luminescent color of some Indian miniatures has won over converts amongst Western collectors and critics alike. And they have begun to realize that a different aesthetic principle is at work. The decorative brilliance of the Shah-Nama (commissioned by Mughal emperor Shah Jahan) and the expressiveness of the bird and animal paintings commissioned by Jehangir have won particular international acclaim. But appreciation of Indian miniatures need not be confined to Mughal examples.

Once Indian painting is freed from externally imposed standards, and the motivations of the Indian artist are better understood - a whole new world of visual delight can open up. From the quixotic 15th C illustrations of Jain texts in Gujarat to the deeply expressive miniatures of Malwa, one can move on to the colorful whimsy of 16th C Mewar, the striking elegance of the Kishangarh school, and the refined beauty of later Kangra miniatures. One can appreciate the earnest lyricism of the Orissa palm-leaf miniatures, the decorous elan of the Bundelkhand wall paintings, the bold and dark colors of Lepakshi, and the vivacious renditions in the palaces and temples of Madurai, Thanjavur and Ramanathapuram. In all these varied traditions of Indian painting, an important element that infused Indian painting with charm and vivacity was the folk idiom that unabashedly found it's way in the art of the regional kingdoms who were less infected by formal Mughal tastes.

(Paintings of the Deccan courts, - particularly those illustrating Ragamala themes from Ahmednagar, Aurangabad and Bijapur also reveal folk influences. Ragamala paintings from Hyderabad are particularly evocative and appealing. Although rarely on display in Indian museums, illustrated books with charmingly colorful folk-like renditions were also commissioned during the reign of the Sharqis of Jaunpur.)

ARCHITECTURE OF THE ISLAMIC COURTS

After the Islamic conquest in India - (by the 12th-13th C in the northern plains, and by the 14th C in the Deccan plateau), monumental architecture in India often came to be defined by the tastes of medieval India's Islamic rulers. Construction activity became more geared towards the demands of the elite, and the voluntary participation of the masses in monumental construction became greatly reduced, or even entirely eliminated.

In Sanchi, it is useful to note that the construction of the *Toranas* involved the voluntary labor and contributions of much of the citizenry. Voluntary participation in the construction and maintenance of temples in South India and in the Deccan region has also been recorded and quite likely occurred throughout India.

Yet, it would be an error to think that popular influences on Indian architecture were completely extinguished. In the Gangetic plain, folk influences continued to play a vital role in the decor of Havelis and village homes; traditions like *Rangoli* also continued. In the regional courts, folk influences played an important role not only in the fine arts, but also in royal furniture and architectural decor. Folk influences also found their way in some of the smaller mosques and Sufi shrines which were painted with floral motifs in folkish style.

The change in ethos was reflected most in prominent urban landmarks, in the architecture of city gateways and inns for the nobility, and in the design of royal mosques and tombs. But, it would be incorrect to consider India's Islamic architecture as an entirely foreign implant as some art historians (both in the West and in India) are inclined to do. Traditional Indian tastes and influences played an important role in shaping the most vibrant monuments commissioned by India's Islamic rulers.

Some art historians have routinely treated Indian art and architecture of the Islamic period as a regional derivative of Persian art and architecture - almost a poor cousin of the grand Persian Islamic tradition. Western biases and an admiration of all things Persian amongst sections of the Urdu speaking Indian intelligentsia have combined to spread the myth that all great Islamic art originated in Persia and the quality of art and architecture sponsored by India's Islamic rulers must be judged by how closely it came to meeting Persian ideals. That many of India's Islamic rulers employed Persian artists in their ateliers and Persian poets and writers found favor in the royal courts cannot be denied. But this obsession with connecting all things Islamic in India to Persia has not only led to an extremely selective and distorted analysis of the Islamic legacy in India, it has been based on a rather superficial examination of the Islamic legacy. Not only have art historians often failed to distinguish between what came from Persia from elsewhere, such as Afghanistan, Iraq or Central Asia - it has led to the virtual neglect of those aspects of the Islamic legacy in India where the predominant influences have been almost entirely from within the subcontinent. (Art historians have also failed to investigate the possibility of Indian influences impacting Persian tastes and sensibilities as was quite likely during the reigns of Jehangir and Shah Jehan).

Many art historians who attempt to analyze "Islamic" art in India seem to forget that the Islamic faith was born in a rather barren land without a history or tradition of support for the fine arts. (Although some argue that the Arabian peninsula had a rich tradition of terra-cotta sculpture that vanished with the iconoclastic ascent of Islam.) In any case, in terms of architecture, prior to the ascendance of Islam in the Middle East, one could speak of monumental Egyptian, Persian or Babylonian architecture, but certainly not Meccan architecture. As Islam spread, it was obliged to borrow and adapt from the older traditions that already existed in the lands it conquered. For instance, the Islamic monuments of Syria and Palestine have a remarkable resemblance to Byzantine architecture of earlier centuries with the important exception that all portraiture is avoided. Although vegetal motifs are employed with exuberance in the 7th-8th C Umayyad architecture in Syria and Palestine, later Islamic architecture, especially from Central Asia relied almost exclusively on abstract figuration.

But since sculptural decoration and representation of animals and nature played such a significant role in the architecture of pre-Islamic India - the advent of Islam (at least initially) led to mere imitation of forms borrowed from Central Asia. What seemed fresh and original in Bukhara during the Samanid reign (9-10th C) became dull, laborious and out of place when transplanted into Indian soil. With the exception of a few monuments that make rather effective use of decorative columns and motifs from earlier Jain monuments as in Ajmer or the Qutb area in Delhi - early Islamic architecture in India is singularly bland and uninteresting. Much of it is starkly austere and coldly aloof from the more lively traditions of the subcontinent. It is only after the 13th century when a bit of whimsy and ornamental fancy begins to enliven some of India's Islamic monuments (as in Chanderi). But this influence comes from Turkey, not Persia!

Outside India proper, architecture in the Islamic courts continues to make progress, culminating in the the construction of the overwhelmingly grand monuments of the Timurids in Herat, Samarkand and Bukhara (14th-15th C and onwards). Although the Timurids wreaked considerable havoc on their immediate neighbours and raided and plundered lands as far West as in Eastern Europe, the Timurids were not wedded to Islamic orthodoxy and continued the Samanid tradition of promoting the arts and learning. Samarkand and Bukhara emerged as the most important urban centers of the medieval world where study in astronomy and mathematics was encouraged and poetry and art received royal support. But above all, it was in their sponsorship of monumental architecture where the Timurid rulers excelled. Awe-inspiring monuments with tile work in dazzling green, blue and turquoise rose from the Afghan and Central Asian deserts and these rich urban centers became the models for cities throughout the Middle East. Brilliant regional variants sprang up throughout Afghanistan, Persia and Iraq. However, there were serious obstacles to the import of this new and brilliant architectural style into India.

As self-conscious outsiders, and with a rather tenuous hold on power in a largely non-Islamic land, it was probably difficult for India's Islamic invaders to commission monuments that could have matched the power and grandeur of the monuments in lands where Islam had triumphed completely and concerns of legitimacy had been adequately settled. The Lodhis and the early Mughals could only bring a modest and rather restrained version of the Central Asian style to India.

In Multan, Ucch Sharif, and Dera Ghazi Khan (all in Western Punjab) where a majority of the population had been converted to Islam, tombs built in honour of Sufi saints displayed an expressive originality even as they imbibed influences from Central Asia. But beyond Punjab, the impact was fairly limited, and some of the greatest Islamic monuments of the sub-continent show little if any trace of foreign influence.

The Sultans of Bengal and Gujarat, the Sharqi kings and Sher Shah Suri - all commissioned monuments that were virtually unlike any seen outside the subcontinent. The exquisitely chiseled reliefs in the 14th C Jama Masjid in Pandua (one of the old capitals of the Bengal Sultanate) display a kinship with the carved reliefs of the 13th C Kakathiya monuments of Warangal. Other mosques of the Pandua/Gaur region skilfully recycled material from Hindu and Buddhist temples, creating a uniquely lyrical and expressive Bengali Islamic style. Like the monuments of Bukhara, some of these mosques and gateways were decorated with colored tiles, but the construction techniques and colors were quite original. Many of the tiles were multi-colored and incorporated motifs considered important and auspicious in the Indian tradition.

In Ahmedabad and Champaner, symbolic motifs that had been in use for centuries in Jain and Hindu monuments were employed with abandon and became the very focus of both the internal and external decorative space of the typical mosque or tomb. The *Chakra*, the *Padma*, the *Purnakalasa*, the *Kalpavriksha*, the *Kalpalata* and the Jain 'lamp of knowledge' became vital centerpieces of the monuments of the Gujarat Sultanate.

Although geometrical decoration is a common feature of all Islamic architecture, the Indian *Jaali* developed some original features by combining motifs considered auspicious in the Hindu tradition with arabesques and geometrical designs. Lace like *Jaalis* distinguish the Sharqi monuments of Jaunpur and the Chunar monuments commissioned by Sher Shah Suri.

In the Deccan, architectural forms were sometimes inspired by nature. The Hyderabad monuments stand out for their use of pineapple-like domes and minarets, and columns modelled on palm trees. In many ways, these monuments are more interesting than the more renowned Mughal monuments. While the best of the Mughal monuments stand out for their balance of form, technical virtuosity and the luxuriant use of marble, semi-precious stones and gilt - critics find some Mughal architecture to be excessively formal, and a bit too reliant on architectural clichés.

Nevertheless, the Mughal era monuments of Punjab stand out in some ways. In Nakoddar (near Jullundhur) there are two tombs with brilliant polychrome decorations, unusual not only for their tile-work but also because they were dedicated to a scholar and a court musician, not royal personages. One, (also known as the *Baghdadi* owing to it's imitation of a style popularized in Baghdad) effectively employs geometric arabesques in yellow, green and blue tile set off against a brick background, while the other makes liberal use of the *Purnakalasa* motif, but with an ingenious innovation: the *Purnakalasa* motif appears in a rainbow of colored tiles. To the uninformed this may appear as a Persian transplant since floral motifs were also used in Persian architecture, but the *Purnakalasa* motif had come into frequent use during the reign of Akbar (before floral motifs came to be widely employed in the Persian tombs) and the Nakoddar tomb was more likely a natural evolution of the Mughal style popularized by Akbar. Later tombs in Lahore appear to effectively replicate this style.

However, Mughal architecture took on decisively conservative tone during the reign of Aurangzeb. With the exception of the Qutab Shahis who turned Hyderabad into a grand and glorious city in the 17th C, and the Awadh nawabs who made Lucknow famous in the 18th-19th Century, the last phase of the Islamic chapter in India gradually faded into oblivion.

This was in stark contrast to trends in Persia, where the Safavids continued to build on the achievements of the 16th C until well into the 17th and 18th C when the Safavid capital of Isfahan acquired the reputation of being one of the world's most handsome cities. Whereas Aurangzeb's reign in the subcontinent was marred by tremendous political strife and social upheaval, Safavid Iran enjoyed relative peace and prosperity, causing India's Persian/Urdu-speaking intellectuals and cultural elite to look to Persia for cultural affirmation and inspiration.

THE DECORATIVE ARTS AND CRAFTS

But in the realm of the decorative arts and crafts, India's legacy had few challengers. The Mughals were especially great patrons of the decorative arts, and although initially it appears they may have favored imports from Persia and China, Indian manufactures rapidly perfected and enhanced imported styles and techniques. Indian textiles had always been known for their rich colors and variety of design, and Indian steel products commanded worldwide respect. But very rapidly India also emerged as a preeminent center for a variety of fine arts and crafts, excelling in the manufacture of all manner of objects sought by the royalty including luxuriant carpets, decorated metal-ware, fine jewelry, glass and jade-ware. Although initially, the impetus for some of these crafts may have come from China, Central Asia or Persia - by the late 16th-17th century, rulers in both China and Persia coveted luxury-ware from India, and sought to imitate the perfection of Mughal manufactures in their own ateliers.

But the Mughals were not alone in their encouragement of fine arts and crafts. The Rajput courts were more than equal to the Mughals, and far more amenable to the employment of traditional and folk elements in their furniture, jewelry and other decorative crafts. They also displayed a greater fondness for bold and saturated colors whereas the Mughals (like Shahjahan) showed a distinct preference for formal graces. When the Mughal empire collapsed, it was the Rajput courts that became the models for the regional Sikh kingdoms, the hill kingdoms, the kingdoms of Bundelkhand and Benares, and also the Nawabs of Bengal and Awadh to an extent. The Deccan courts also played a significant part in encouraging the decorative arts and crafts, and they too exerted a strong influence on the courts in Cuttack, as on Lucknow.

ART AND ARCHITECTURE OF THE REGIONAL KINGDOMS

Whereas Mughal architecture went into rapid decline after the ascendance of Aurangzeb, a cultural renaissance of sorts occurred in the regional kingdoms of the North, and the Deccan and Maratha kingdoms of the South. But even during the period of Islamic rule, the Rajputs, the Bundelkhandis, the rulers of Tripura, Manipur and Assam, and the Vijaynagar and Malabar kings retained their independence. In these regions of India, architectural styles emerged that were partially influenced by contacts with the Islamic courts, but retained a large degree of autonomy and continuity with older Indian traditions. In Tripura, Manipur, Assam and the Himachal region, both temple and palace architecture were strongly influenced by vernacular traditions.

In Gwalior, the *Man-Mandir* palace (built in the 15th C) appears to hark back to a much older era. One of it's facades bears striking resemblance to depictions of a palace in the Ajanta wall paintings, and there are also some architectural similarities with the Ajanta caves. A particularly interesting aspect of the indoor designs are the creative transformation of two-dimensional decorative motifs commonly seen in the Indian temple or Stupa into spatially effective three-dimensional architectural features. The resplendant outer facade is in polychrome tiles with a charming frieze of geese, palm and other decorative motifs. All in all, it is one of India's architectural jewels and there are few others quite like it. {The now mostly ruined palace in the Raisen fort (near Bhopal) bears some resemblance to it, as does the much later and considerably more elaborate Nayak palace in Madurai}

In Vijaynagar, there was an eclectic fusion of stylistic inputs derived from previous Southern dynasties. A particularly interesting development was the Srisailam temple (central Andhra 14th-15th C) all of whose carvings are in fascinatingly folkish idiom - a variety of interesting scenes from the popular epics make up the themes of it's sculpted panels. Particularly endearing are the portrayals of yogis, acrobats, folk-dancers, musicians, and queens with their ladies-in-waiting.

A distinctive feature of the Rajput forts was the fanciful use of color, mirror-work, mother-of-pear and gilt in the decoration of their fortress-like palaces. Although not remarkable in architectural terms, the *Jharokhas* and *Aangans,* and richly decorated gateways make these palaces unique and interesting. In Bikaner, the gold lacquer-work is quite exceptional and probably influenced the decoration of the Golden Temple in Amritsar and the Sheesh Mahal in Patiala.

Virtually all of the Rajput Palaces had *Chitra-Shalas* - i.e. painting galleries, and the ones in Jhalawar, Bundi, Nagaur, Karauli, Jaipur, and Kishengarh are especially remarkable as are the galleries in the Bundelkhand palaces of Datia, Orchha and Jhansi. The Himachal palaces also have fine *Chitra-Shalas,* such as in the Sultanpur palace in Kulu and the Rang Mahal of Chamba. In the South, the Ramanathapuram palace is notable for it's engaging wall paintings, while Majuli is a renowned centre of wall paintings in Assam.

THE ROLE OF FOLK ART IN THE INDIAN ARTISTIC TRADITION

As brought out earlier, one of the most endearing aspects of Indian art and architecture prior to colonization has been the strong impact of folk idioms and folk art on courtly art. Although folk art received little encouragement during the period of colonization, independence brought forward a renewed interest in folk paintings. Historically, folk artists not only provided an important recreational service in village and urban communities, they helped preserve cultural traditions through their illustrations of love stories, popular ballads, epics and folk-tales. Along with playwrights and poets, they were instrumental in the spread of social values and ethics, and religious and philosophical ideas that had popular appeal.

But above all, owing to their close contact with the masses, their paintings were often infused with a warmth and attractive simplicity that more than made up for any lack of formal grace or technical brilliance. And in some ways, it is the widespread penetration of the folk idiom into courtly traditions that has been the outstanding hallmark of Indian art, and gives it it's highly characteristic flavor.

11

CONTEMPORARY ARCHITECTURE

Contemporary architecture is the architecture being made at the present time. It also includes that of the last few decades, from the 1980s to the present.

BLOBITECTURE

Blobitecture from blob architecture, blobism or blobismus are terms for a current movement in architecture in which buildings have an organic, amoeba-shaped, bulging form. Though the term 'blob architecture' was in vogue already in the mid-1990s, the word *blobitecture* first appeared in print in 2002, in William Safire's "On Language" column in the *New York Times Magazine* in an article entitled *Defenestration*. Though intended in the article to have a derogatory meaning, the word stuck and is often used to describe buildings with curved and rounded shapes.

ORIGINS OF THE TERM "BLOB ARCHITECTURE"

The term 'blob architecture' was coined by architect Greg Lynn in 1995 in his experiments in digital design with metaball graphical software. Soon a range of architects and furniture designers began to experiment with this "blobby" software to create new and unusual forms. Despite its seeming organicism, blob architecture is unthinkable without this and other similar computer-aided design programs. Architects derive the forms by manipulating the algorithms of the computer modeling platform. Some other computer aided design functions involved in developing this are the nonuniform rational B-spline or NURB, freeform surfaces, and the digitizing of sculpted forms by means akin to computed tomography.

PRECEDENTS

One precedent is Archigram, a group of English architects working in the 1960s, to which Peter Cook belonged. They were interested in inflatable architecture as well as in the shapes that could be generated from plastic. Ron Herron, also member of Archigram created blob-like architecture in his projects from the 1960s, such as *Walking Cities* and *Instant City*, as did Michael Webb with *Sin Centre*. There was a climate of experimental architecture with an air of psychedelia in the 1970s that these were a part of. Frederick Kiesler's unbuilt, *Endless House* is another instance of early blob-like architecture, although it is symmetrical in plan and designed before computers; his design for the Shrine of the Book (construction begun, 1965) which has the characteristic droplet form of fluid also anticipates forms that interest architects today.

Also to be considered, if one views blob architecture from the question of form rather than technology, are the organic designs of Antoni Gaudi in Barcelona and of the Expressionists like Bruno Taut and Hermann Finsterlin.

BUILT EXAMPLES

Despite the narrow interpretation of Blob architecture (i.e. that coming from the computer), the word, especially in popular parlance, has come to be associated quite widely with a range of curved or odd-looking buildings including Frank Gehry's Guggenheim Museum Bilbao (1997) and the Experience Music Project (2000), though these, in the narrower sense are not blob buildings, even though they were designed by advanced computer-aided design tools, CATIA in particular. The reason for this is that they were designed from physical models rather than from computer manipulations. The first full blob building however was build in the Netherlands by Lars Spuybroek (NOX) and Kas Oosterhuis. Called the water pavilion (1993-1997) it does not only have a fully computer-based shape manufactured with computer-aided tools but also has an electronic interactive interior where sound and light can be transformed by the visitor.

A building that also can be considered an example of a blob is Peter Cook and Colin Fournier's Kunsthaus (2003) in Graz, Austria. Other instances are Roy Mason's Xanadu House (1979), and a rare excursion into the field by Herzog & de Meuron in their Allianz Arena (2005). By 2005, Norman Foster had involved himself in blobitecture to some extent as well with his brain-shaped design for the Philological Library at the Free University of Berlin and the Sage Gateshead opened in 2004.

DECONSTRUCTIVISM

Deconstructivism in architecture, also called deconstruction, is a development of postmodern architecture that began in the late 1980s. It is characterized by ideas of fragmentation, an interest in manipulating ideas of a structure's surface or skin, non-rectilinear shapes which serve to distort and dislocate some of the elements of architecture, such as structure and envelope. The finished visual appearance of buildings that exhibit the many deconstructivist "styles" is characterised by a stimulating unpredictability and a controlled chaos.

Important events in the history of the deconstructivist movement include the 1982 Parc de la Villette architectural design competition (especially the entry from Jacques Derrida and Peter Eisenman and Bernard Tschumi's winning entry), the Museum of Modern Art's 1988 *Deconstructivist Architecture* exhibition in New York, organized by Philip Johnson and Mark Wigley, and the 1989 opening of the Wexner Center for the Arts in Columbus, designed by Peter Eisenman. The New York exhibition featured works by Frank Gehry, Daniel Libeskind, Rem Koolhaas, Peter Eisenman, Zaha Hadid, Coop Himmelb(l)au, and Bernard Tschumi. Since the exhibition, many of the architects who were associated with Deconstructivism have distanced themselves from the term. Nonetheless, the term has stuck and has now, in fact, come to embrace a general trend within contemporary architecture.

Originally, some of the architects known as Deconstructivists were influenced by the ideas of the French philosopher Jacques Derrida. Eisenman developed a personal relationship with Derrida, but even so his approach to architectural design was developed long before he became a Deconstructivist. For him Deconstructivism should be considered an extension of his interest in radical formalism. Some practitioners of deconstructivism were also influenced by the formal experimentation and geometric imbalances of Russian constructivism. There are additional references in deconstructivism to 20th-century movements: the modernism/postmodernism interplay, expressionism, cubism, minimalism and contemporary art. The attempt in deconstructivism throughout is to move architecture away from what its practitioners see as the constricting 'rules' of modernism such as "form follows function," "purity of form," and "truth to materials."

HISTORY, CONTEXT AND INFLUENCES

Modernism and postmodernism

Deconstructivism in contemporary architecture stands in opposition to the ordered rationality of Modernism. Its relationship with Postmodernism is also decidedly contrary. Though postmodernist and nascent deconstructivist architects published theories alongside each other in the journal *Oppositions* (published 1973–84), that journal's contents mark the beginning of a decisive break between the two movements. Deconstruction took a confrontational stance toward much of architecture and architectural history, wanting to disjoin and disassemble architecture. While postmodernism returned to embrace— often slyly or ironically—the historical references that modernism had shunned, deconstructivism rejects the postmodern acceptance of such references. It also rejects the idea of ornament as an after-thought or decoration. These principles have meant that deconstructivism aligns itself somewhat with the sensibilities of modernist anti-historicism.

In addition to *Oppositions*, another text that separated deconstructivism from the fray of modernism and postmodernism was the publication of Robert Venturi's *Complexity and Contradiction in architecture* (1966). A defining point for both postmodernism and for deconstructivism, *Complexity and Contradiction* argues against the purity, clarity and simplicity of modernism. With its publication, functionalism and rationalism, the two main branches of modernism, were overturned as paradigms according to postmodernist and deconstructivist readings, with differing readings. The postmodern reading of Venturi (who was himself a postmodernist) was that ornament and historical allusion added a richness to architecture that modernism had foregone. Some Postmodern architects endeavored to reapply ornaments even to economical and minimal buildings, an effort best illustrated by Venturi's concept of "the decorated shed." Rationalism of design was dismissed but the functionalism of the building was still somewhat intact. This is close to the thesis of Venturi's next major work, that signs and ornament can be applied to a pragmatic architecture, and instill the philosophic complexities of semiology.

The deconstructivist reading of *Complexity and Contradiction* is quite different. The basic building was the subject of problematics and intricacies in deconstructivism, with no detachment for ornament. Rather than separating ornament and function, like postmodernists such as Venturi, the functional aspects of buildings were called into question. Geometry was to deconstructivists what ornament was to postmodernists, the subject of complication, and this complication of geometry was in turn, applied to the functional, structural, and spacial aspects of deconstructivist buildings. One example of deconstructivist complexity is Frank Gehry's Vitra Design Museum in Weil-am-Rhein, which takes the typical unadorned white cube of modernist art galleries and deconstructs it, using geometries reminiscent of cubism and abstract expressionism.

This subverts the functional aspects of modernist simplicity while taking modernism, particularly the international style, of which its white stucco skin is reminiscent, as a starting point. Another example of the deconstructivist reading of *Complexity and Contradiction* is Peter Eisenman's Wexner Center for the Arts. The Wexner Center takes the archetypal form of the castle, which it then imbues with complexity in a series of cuts and fragmentations. A three-dimensional grid, runs somewhat arbitrarily through the building. The grid, as a reference to modernism, of which it is an accoutrement, collides with the medieval antiquity of a castle. Some of the grid's columns intentionally don't reach the ground, hovering over stairways creating a sense of neurotic unease and contradicting the structural purpose of the column. The Wexner Center deconstructs the archetype of the castle and renders its spaces and structure with conflict and difference.

Deconstructivist Philosophy

The main channel from deconstructivist philosophy to architectural theory was through the philosopher Jacques Derrida's influence with Peter Eisenman. Eisenman drew some philosophical bases from the literary movement Deconstruction, and collaborated directly with Derrida on projects including an entry for the Parc de la Villette competition, documented in *Chora l Works*. Both Derrida and Eisenman, as well as Daniel Libeskind were concerned with the "metaphysics of presence," and this is the main subject of deconstructivist philosophy in architecture theory. The presupposition is that architecture is a language capable of communicating meaning and of receiving treatments by methods of linguistic philosophy. The dialectic of presence and absence, or solid and void occurs in much of Eisenman's projects, both built and unbuilt. Both Derrida and Eisenman believe that the locus, or place of presence, is architecture, and the same dialectic of presence and absence is found in construction and deconstruction.

According to Derrida, readings of texts are best carried out when working with classical narrative structures. Any architectural deconstruction requires the existence of a particular archetypal construction, a strongly-established conventional expectation to play flexibly against. The design of Frank Gehry's own Santa Monica residence, (from 1978), has been cited as a prototypical deconstructivist building. His starting point was a prototypical suburban house embodied with a typical set of intended social meanings. Gehry altered its massing, spatial envelopes, planes and other expectations in a playful subversion, an act of "de"construction"

In addition to Derrida's concepts of the metaphysics of presence and deconstruction, his notions of trace and erasure, embodied in his philosophy of writing and arche-writing found their way into deconstructivist memorials. Daniel Libeskind envisioned many of his early projects as a form of writing or discourse on writing and often works with a form of concrete poetry. He made architectural sculptures out of books and often coated the models in texts, openly making his architecture refer to writing. The notions of trace and erasure were taken up by Libeskind in essays and in his project for the Jewish Museum Berlin. The museum is conceived as a trace of the erasure of the Holocaust, intended to make its subject legible and poignant. Memorials such as Maya Lin's Vietnam Veterans Memorial and Peter Eisenman's Memorial to the Murdered Jews of Europe also reflect themes of trace and erasure.

Constructivism and Russian Futurism

Another major current in deconstructivist architecture takes inspiration from the Russian Constructivist and Futurist movements of the early twentieth century, both in their graphics and in their visionary architecture, little of which was actually constructed.

Artists Naum Gabo, El Lissitzky, Kazimir Malevich, and Alexander Rodchenko, have influenced the graphic sense of geometric forms of deconstructivist architects such as Zaha Hadid and Coop Himmelb(l)au. Both Deconstructivism and Constructivism have been concerned with the tectonics of making an abstract assemblage. Both were concerned with the radical simplicity of geometric forms as the primary artistic content, expressed in graphics, sculpture and architecture. The Constructivist tendency toward purism, though, is absent in Deconstructivism: form is often deformed when construction is deconstructed. Also lessened or absent is the advocacy of socialist and collectivist causes.

The primary graphic motifs of constructivism were the rectangular bar and the triangular wedge, others were the more basic geometries of the square and the circle. In his series *Prouns*, El Lizzitzky assembled collections of geometries at various angles floating free in space. They evoke basic structural units such as bars of steel or sawn lumber loosely attached, piled, or scattered. They were also often drafted and share aspects with technical drawing and engineering drawing. Similar in composition is the more recent deconstructivist series *Micromegas* by Daniel Libeskind.

The raw structuralism of constructivist architects Ivan Leonidov, Konstantin Melnikov, Alexander Vesnin and Vladimir Tatlin have also had an impact on deconstructivist architects, notably Rem Koolhaas. Their work, in final form, seems to embody the *process* of construction. They finalize the temporary and transitional aspects of building sites, the scaffolds and cranes necessary for buildings of large scope. El Lissitzky's *Das Wolkenbügel (illustration)*, resembling cranes connected and made habitable, is a good precedent for Koolhaas' China Central Television tower. Koolhaas also takes after Ivan Leonidov in an architecture that seems like a perennial construction site.

Contemporary Art

Two strains of modern art, minimalism and cubism, have had an influence on deconstructivism. Analytical cubism had a sure effect on deconstructivism, as forms and content are dissected and viewed from different perspectives simultaneously. A synchronicity of disjoined space is evident in many of the works of Frank Gehry and Bernard Tschumi. Synthetic cubism, with its application of found art, is not as great an influence on deconstructivism as Analytical cubism, but is still found in the earlier and more vernacular works of Frank Gehry. Deconstructivism also shares with minimalism a disconnection from cultural references. It also often shares with minimalism notions of conceptual art.

With its tendency toward deformation and dislocation, there is also an aspect of expressionism and expressionist architecture associated with deconstructivism. At times deconstructivism mirrors varieties of expressionism, neo-expressionism, and abstract expressionism as well. The angular forms of the UFA Cinema Center by Coop Himmelb(l)au recall the abstract geometries of the numbered paintings of Franz Kline, in their unadorned masses. The UFA Cinema Center also would make a likely setting for the angular figures depicted in urban German street scenes by Ernst Ludwig Kirchner. The work of Wassily Kandinsky also bears similarities to deconstructivist architecture. His movement into abstract expressionism and away from figurative work, is in the same spirit as the deconstructivist rejection of ornament for geometries.

Several artists in the 1980s and 1990s contributed work that influenced or took part in deconstructivism. Maya Lin and Rachel Whiteread are two examples. Lin's 1982 project for the Vietnam Veterans Memorial, with its granite slabs severing the ground plane, is one. Its shard-like form and reduction of content to a minimalist text influenced deconstructivism, with its sense of fragmentation and emphasis on reading the monument. Lin also contributed work for Eisenman's Wexner Center. Rachel Whiteread's cast architectural spaces are another instance where contemporary art is confluent with architecture. *Ghost* (1990), an entire living space cast in plaster, solidifying the void, alludes to Derrida's notion of architectural presence. Gordon Matta-Clark's *Building cuts* were deconstructed sections of buildings exhibited in art galleries.

HIGH-TECH ARCHITECTURE

High-tech architecture, or Late Modernism, is an architectural style that emerged in the 1970s, incorporating elements of high-tech industry and technology into building design. High-tech architecture appeared as a revamped modernism, an extension of those previous ideas aided by even more advances in technological achievements. This category serves as a bridge between modernism and post-modernism, however there remain gray areas as to where one category ends and the other begins. In the 1980s, high-tech architecture became more difficult to distinguish from post-modern architecture. Many of its themes and ideas were absorbed into the language of the post-modern architectural schools.

Buildings in this architectural style were constructed mainly in Europe and North America. After the destruction of many historic buildings in Europe during World War II, repairing them was a difficult matter. Architects had to decide between replicating the historic elements or replacing it with new modern materials and aesthetics.

The scientific and technological advances had a big impact on societies in the 1970s. The Space Race climaxed in 1969 with Neil Armstrong's landing on the moon, and came along with excessive military developments. These advances set people's minds thinking that much more can be achieved with advancing technology. Technological instruments became a common sight for people at the time because of the use of ramps, video screens, headphones, and bare scaffolds. These high-tech constructions became more visible everyday to the average person.

NAME

The style got its name from the book *High Tech: The Industrial Style and Source Book for The Home*, written by design journalists Joan Kron and Suzanne Slesin and published in November 1978 by Clarkson N. Potter, New York. The book, illustrated with hundreds of photos, showed how designers, architects, and home owners were appropriating classic industrial objects—library shelving, chemical glass, metal deck plate, restaurant supply, factory and airport runway light fixtures, movers' quilts, industrial carpeting etc.—found in industrial catalogues and putting these to use in residential settings. The foreword to the book by architect Emilio Ambasz, former curator of design at the Museum of Modern Art, put the trend in historical context.

As a result of the publicity and popularity of the book, the decorating style became known as "High-Tech", and accelerated the entry of the still-obscure term "high-tech" into everyday language. In 1979, the term high-tech appeared for the first time in a *New Yorker* magazine cartoon showing a woman berating her husband for not being high-tech enough: "You're middle-, middle-, middle-tech." After *Esquire* excerpted Kron and Slesin's book in six installments, mainstream retailers across the United States, beginning with Macy's New York, started featuring high-tech decor in windows and in furniture departments. But credit should go to a shop on 64th Street and Lexington Avenue in New York, Ad hoc Housewares, which opened in 1977, for marketing these objects to a residential audience before anyone else. The book went on to be reprinted in England, France, and Japan, and like the original, each edition included a directory of local sources for the objects.

AIMS

High-tech architecture was, in some ways, a response to growing disillusionment with modern architecture. The realization of Le Corbusier's urban development plans led to cities with monotonous and standardized buildings. Enthusiasm for economic building led to extremely low-quality finishes, with subsequent degradation countering a now-waning aesthetic novelty. High-tech architecture created a new aesthetic in contrast with standard modern architecture. In *High Tech: The Industrial Style and*

Source Book for The Home, when discussing the high-tech aesthetic, the authors emphasized using elements "your parents might find insulting". This humour so aptly demonstrates the rebellious attitude.

Kron and Slesin further explain the term "high-tech" as one being used in architectural circles to describe an increasing number of residences and public buildings with a "nuts-and-bolts, exposed-pipes, technological look". There is no need to look further than Roger's Pompidou Centre for an example of this. This highlights the one of the aims of high-tech architecture, to boast the technical elements of the building by externalizing them. Thus, the technical aspects create the building's aesthetic.

For interior design there was a trend of using formerly industrial appliances as household objects, e.g. chemical beakers as vases for flowers. This was because of an aim to use an industrial aesthetic. This was assisted by the conversion of former industrial spaces into residential spaces. High-tech architecture aimed to give everything an industrial appearance.

Another aspect to the aims of high-tech architecture was that of a renewed belief in the power of technology to improve the world. This is especially evident in Kenzo Tange's plans for technically sophisticated buildings in Japan's post-war boom in the 1960s, but few of these plans actually became buildings. High-tech architecture aimed to achieve a new industrial aesthetic, spurred on by the renewed faith in the progression of technology.

But however prominent the industrial look appeared, the functional element of modern architecture was very much retained. The pieces still served a purpose in the building's function. The function of the building was also aimed as not being set. This dynamic property means that a building should be a "catalyst", the "technical services are provided but do not become set."

CHARACTERISTICS

Characteristics of high-tech architecture have varied somewhat, yet all have accentuated technical elements. They included the prominent display of the building's technical and functional components, and an orderly arrangement and use of pre-fabricated elements. Glass walls and steel frames were also immensely popular.

To boast technical features, they were externalized, often along with load-bearing structures. There can be no more illustrious example than Pompidou Centre. The ventilation ducts are all prominently shown on the outside. This was a radical design, as previous ventilation ducts would have been a component hidden on the inside of the building. The means of access to the building is also on the outside, with the large tube allowing visitors to enter the building.

The orderly and logical fashion in which buildings in the high-tech architectural style are designed to keep to their functional essence is demonstrated in Norman Foster's Hong Kong and Shanghai Bank HQ. Besides the technology being the overriding feature of the building, its design is very much functionally orientated. The large interior open space and the easy access to all floors very much enhance the function of being a bank. Also, the elements of the buildings are very neatly composed to achieve optimal orderliness in order to logically solve the problem of the needs of a bank. This can be seen in the levels' structure and in the escalators.

The high-tech buildings make persistent use of glass curtain walls and steel structure. It is greatly indebted to modern architecture for this, and influenced by Mies van der Rohe's corporate buildings. The SOM Sears Tower demonstrates that with glass walls and skeleton pipe structure of steel, a very tall building can be built. Many high-tech buildings meant their purposes to be dynamic. This could best be explained by Günther Behnisch and Frei Otto's Munich Olympic Stadium. This structure made sport in the open possible and is meant to be used for many purposes. Originally an abandoned airfield, it is now a sport stadium, used for various disciplines.

POSTMODERN ARCHITECTURE

Postmodern architecture was an international style whose first examples are generally cited as being from the 1950s, and which continues to influence present-day architecture. Postmodernity in architecture is generally thought to be heralded by the return of "wit, ornament and reference" to architecture in response to the formalism of the International Style of modernism. As with many cultural movements, some of postmodernism's most pronounced and visible ideas can be seen in architecture. The functional and formalized shapes and spaces of the modernist movement are replaced by unapologetically diverse aesthetics: styles collide, form is adopted for its own sake, and new ways of viewing familiar styles and space abound.

Classic examples of modern architecture are SOM's Lever House or Mies van der Rohe's Seagram Building, as well as the architecture of Le Corbusier or the Bauhaus movement. Transitional examples of postmodern architecture are Michael Grave's Portland Building in Portland, Oregon and Philip Johnson's Sony Building (originally AT&T Building) in New York City, which borrows elements and references from the past and reintroduces color and symbolism to architecture. A prime example of inspiration for postmodern architecture lies along the Las Vegas Strip, which was studied by Robert Venturi and Denise Scott Brown in their 1972 book *Learning from Las Vegas* celebrating the strip's ordinary and common architecture.

Postmodern architecture has also been described as "neo-eclectic", where reference and ornament have returned to the facade, replacing the aggressively unornamented modern styles. This eclecticism is often combined with the use of non-orthogonal angles and unusual surfaces, most famously in the State Gallery of Stuttgart (New wing of the Staatsgalerie Stuttgart) and the Piazza d'Italia by Charles Willard Moore. The Scottish Parliament buildings in Edinburgh have also been cited as being of postmodern vogue.

Modernist architects regard post-modern buildings as vulgar and cluttered with "gew-gaws". Postmodern architects often regard modern spaces as soulless and bland. The divergence in opinions comes down to a difference in goals: modernism is rooted in minimal and true use of material as well as absence of ornament, while postmodernism is a rejection of strict rules set by the early modernists and seeks exuberance in the use of building techniques, angles, and stylistic references.

RELATIONSHIP TO PREVIOUS STYLES

New trends became evident in the last quarter of the 20th century as some architects started to turn away from modern Functionalism which they viewed as boring, and which some of the public considered unwelcoming and even unpleasant. These architects turned towards the past, quoting past aspects of various buildings and melding them together (even sometimes in an inharmonious manner) to create a new means of designing buildings. A vivid example of this new approach was that *Postmodernism* saw the comeback of pillars and other elements of premodern designs, sometimes adapting classical Greek and Roman examples (but not simply recreating them, as was done in neoclassical architecture).

In Modernism, the pillar (as a design feature) was either replaced by other technological means such as cantilevers, or masked completely by curtain wall façades. The revival of the pillar was an aesthetic, rather than a technological, necessity. Modernist high-rise buildings had become in most instances monolithic, rejecting the concept of a stack of varied design elements for a single vocabulary from ground level to the top, in the most extreme cases even using a constant "footprint" (with no tapering or "wedding cake" design), with the building sometimes even suggesting the possibility of a single metallic extrusion directly from the ground, mostly by eliminating visual horizontal elements — this was seen most strictly in Minoru Yamasaki's World Trade Center buildings.

Another return was that of the "wit, ornament and reference" seen in older buildings in terra cotta decorative façades and bronze or stainless steel embellishments of the Beaux-Arts and Art Deco periods. In post-modern structures this was often achieved by placing contradictory quotes of previous building styles alongside each other, and even incorporating furniture stylistic references at a huge scale.

Contextualism, a trend in thinking in the later parts of 20th Century, influences the ideologies of the postmodern movement in general. Contextualism was centered on the belief that all knowledge is "context-sensitive". This idea was even taken further to say that knowledge cannot be understood without considering its context. This influenced Postmodern Architecture to be sensitive to context as discussed below.

POSTMODERNISM

The postmodernist movement began in America around the 1960's/70's and then it spread to Europe and the rest of the world, to remain right through to the present. The aims of postmodernism or Late-modernism begin with its reaction to Modernism; it tries to address the limitations of its predecessor. The list of aims is extended to include communicating ideas with the public often in a then humorous or witty way. Often, the communication is done by quoting extensively from past architectural styles, often many at once. In breaking away from modernism, it also strives to produce buildings that are sensitive to the context within which they are built.

Postmodernism has its origins in the perceived failure of Modern Architecture. Its preoccupation with functionalism and economical building meant that ornaments were done away with and the buildings were cloaked in a stark rational appearance. Postmodernists felt the buildings failed to meet the human need for comfort both for body and for the eye. Modernism did not account for the desire for beauty. The problem worsened when some already monotonous apartment blocks degenerated into slums. Post Modernism sought to cure this by reintroducing ornament and decoration for its own sake. Form was no longer to be defined solely by its functional requirements; it could be anything the architect pleased.

ROBERT VENTURI

Robert Venturi was at the forefront of this movement. His book, *Complexity and Contradiction in Architecture* (published in 1966), was instrumental in the postmodernist movement in architecture and was fiercely critical of the dominant Functional Modernism. The move away from Modernism's functionalism is well illustrated by Venturi's witty adaptation of Mies van der Rohe's famous maxim "Less is more". Venturi instead said "less is a bore". Along with the rest of the Postmodernists, he sought to bring back ornament because of its necessity. He explains this and his criticism of Modernism in his *Complexity and Contradiction in Architecture* by saying that:

Architects can bemoan or try to ignore them (referring to the ornamental and decorative elements in buildings) or even try to abolish them, but they will not go away. Or they will not go away for a long time, because architects do not have the power to replace them (nor do they know what to replace them with).

Robert Venturi was possibly the foremost campaigner of the rebellion against Modernist Architecture which became known as Postmodern. His two books *Complexity and Contradiction in Architecture* (1966) and *Learning from Las Vegas* (1972) (although not actual manifestos of Post Modern Architecture) do well to express many of the aims embodied in Postmodernism. The latter book he co-authored with his wife, Denise Scott Brown, and Steven Izenour.

Learning from Las Vegas highlights an aim that ornamental and decorative elements "accommodate existing needs for variety and communication". Here Venturi stresses the importance of the building communicating a meaning to the public (which necessitates non-functional elements of the building). The Postmodernists in general strive to achieve this communication through their buildings. This communication is not intended to a direct narrating of the meaning. Venturi goes on to explain that it is rather intended to be a communication that could be interpreted in many ways. Each interpretation is more or less true for its moment because work of such quality will have many dimensions and layers of meaning. This pluralism of meaning is intended to mirror the similar nature of contemporary society. The pluralism in meaning was also echoed in the postmodern architects striving for variety in their buildings. Venturi reminisces in one of his essays, *A View from the Campidoglio*, to that effect when he says that:

When [he] was young, a sure way to distinguish great architects was through the consistency and originality of their work...This should no longer be the case. Where the Modern masters' strength lay in consistency, ours should lie in diversity.

Postmodernism with its diversity possesses sensitivity to the building's context and history, and the client's requirements. The Postmodernist architects considered the general requirements of the urban buildings and their surroundings during the building's design. For example, in Frank Gehry's *Venice Beach House*, the neighboring houses have a similar bright flat color. This vernacular sensitivity is evident in some Postmodern buildings.

AIMS AND CHARACTERISTICS

The aims of post-modernism, including solving the problems of Modernism, communicating meanings with ambiguity, and sensitivity for the building's context, are surprisingly unified for a period of buildings designed by architects who largely never collaborated with each other. The aims do, however, leave room for various implementations as can be illustrated by the diverse buildings created during the movement.

The characteristics of Postmodernism allow its aim to be expressed in diverse ways.

These characteristics include the use of sculptural forms, ornaments, anthropomorphism and materials which perform *trompe l'oeil*. These physical characteristics are combined with conceptual characteristics of meaning. These characteristics of meaning include pluralism, double coding, flying buttresses and high ceilings, irony and paradox, and contextualism.

The sculptural forms, not necessarily organic, were created with much ardor. These can be seen in Hans Hollein's Abteiberg Museum (1972-1982). The building is made up of several building units, all very different. Each building's forms are nothing like the conforming rigid ones of Modernism. These forms are sculptural and are somewhat playful. These forms are not reduced to an absolute minimum; they are built and shaped for their own sake. The building units all fit together in a very organic way, which enhances the effect of the forms.

After many years of neglect, ornament returned. Frank Gehry's Venice Beach house, built in 1986, is littered with small ornamental details that would have been considered excessive and needless in Modernism. The Venice Beach House has an assembly of circular logs which exist mostly for decoration. The logs on top do have a minor purpose of holding up the window covers. However, the mere fact that they could have been replaced with a practically invisible nail, makes their exaggerated existence largely ornamental. The ornament in Michael Graves' Portland Public Service Building (1980) is even more prominent. The two obtruding triangular forms are largely ornamental. They exist for aesthetic or their own purpose.

Postmodernism, with its sensitivity to the building's context, did not exclude the needs of humans from the building. Carlo Scarpa's Brion-Vega Cemetery (1970-72) exemplifies this. The human requirements of a cemetery is that it possesses a solemn nature, yet it must not cause the visitor to become depressed. Scarpa's cemetery achieves the solemn mood with the dull gray colors of the walls and neatly defined forms, but the bright green grass prevents this from being too overwhelming.

Postmodern buildings sometimes perform the age old *trompe l'oeil*, creating the illusion of forms or depths where none actually exist, as has been done by painters since the renaissance. The Portland Public Service Building (1980) has pillars represented on the side of the building that to some extent appear to be real, yet they are not.

The Hood Museum of Art (1981-1983) has a typical symmetrical façade which was at the time prevalent throughout Postmodern Buildings.

Robert Venturi's Vanna Venturi House (1962-64) illustrates the Postmodernist aim of communicating a meaning and the characteristic of symbolism. The façade is, according to Venturi, a symbolic picture of a house, looking back to the 18th century. This is partly achieved through the use of symmetry and the arch over the entrance.

Perhaps the best example of irony in Postmodern buildings is Charles Willard Moore's Piazza d'Italia (1978). Moore quotes (architecturally) elements of Italian renaissance and Roman Antiquity. However, he does so with a twist. The irony comes when it is noted that the pillars are covered with steel. It is also paradoxical in the way he quotes Italian antiquity far away from the original in New Orleans.

Double coding meant the buildings convey many meanings simultaneously. The Sony Building in New York does this very well. The building is a tall skyscraper which brings with it connotations of very modern technology. Yet, the top contradicts this. The top section conveys elements of classical antiquity. This double coding is a prevalent trait of Postmodernism. The characteristics of Postmodernism were rather unified given their diverse appearances. The most notable among their characteristics is their playfully extravagant forms and the humour of the meanings the buildings conveyed.

CHANGES IN THE TEACHING OF ARCHITECTURAL HISTORY

The rise of interest in history that came as a consequence of the general Postmodernist turn had a profound impact on architectural education. History courses became increasingly regularized and insisted upon. With the demand for professors knowledgeable in the history of architecture, several Ph.D. programs in schools of architecture arose in order to differentiate themselves from art history Ph.D. programs, where architectural historians had previously trained. In the US, MIT and Cornell were the first, created in the mid 1970s, followed by Columbia, Berkeley, and Princeton. Among the founders of new architectural history programs were Bruno Zevi at the Institute for the History of Architecture in Venice, Stanford Anderson and Henry Millon at MIT, Alexander Tzonis at the Architectural Association, Anthony Vidler at Princeton, Manfredo Tafuri at the University of Venice, Kenneth Frampton at Columbia University, and Werner Oechslin and Kurt Forster at ETH.

The creation of these programs was paralleled by the hiring, in the 1970s, of professionally trained historians by schools of architecture: Margaret Crawford (with a Ph.D. from U.C.L.A) at SCI-Arc; Elisabeth Grossman (Ph.D., Brown University) at Rhode Island School of Design; Christian Otto (Ph.D., Columbia University) at Cornell University; Richard Chafee (Ph.D., Courtauld Institute) at Roger Williams University; and Howard Burns (M.A. Kings College) at Harvard, to name just a few examples. A second generation of scholars then emerged that began to extend these efforts in the direction of what is now called "theory": K. Michael Hays (Ph.D., MIT) at Harvard,

Mark Wigley (Ph.D., Auckland University) at Princeton (now at Columbia University), and Beatriz Colomina (Ph.D., School of Architecture, Barcelona) at Princeton; Mark Jarzombek (Ph.D., MIT) at Cornell (now at MIT), Jennifer Bloomer (Ph.D., Georgia Tech) at Iowa State and Catherine Ingraham (Ph.D., Johns Hopkins) now at Pratt Institute.

BIBLIOGRAPHY

Ambrose, Kay (1983) *Classical Dances and Costumes of India*, New York: St. Martin's Press.

Baines, Anthony (1966) Musical *Instruments Through The Ages*. Penguin Books. Banerji, Projesh (1982) *Aesthetics of Indian Dance*, Atlantic Highlands, N.J.: Humanities Press.

_____.(1982) *Khatak Dance through Ages*. New Jersey: Humanities Press. Basham, A. L. (1954) *The Wonder That Was India.*, New York: Grove Press, Inc.

Bhattacharyya, Benoytosh (1993) *The Indian Buddhist Iconography*, Reprint. New Delhi: Asian Educational Services.

Bhavanani, Enakshi (1965) *The Dance of India*. Bombay: D. B Taraporevala Sons & Co.

Bowers, Faubion (1980) *Theatre in the East*, New York: Arno Press.

Brown, Percy (1956) *Indian Architecture* (3rd ed.) Bombay: Taraporevala.

—. *Essays in Architectural Theory* (ed.) (1995) Michael W. Meister, Delhi: Oxford University Press.

—. *The Transformation of Nature in Arted (ed.)* Kapila Vatsyayan, New Delhi: Sterling, 1995.

Chittick, William (1983) *The Sufi Path of Love, The Spiritual Teachings of Rumi*, Albany: State University of New York Press.

Clark, Mary and Crisp, Clement (1981) *The History of Dance*, New York: Crown Publisher.

Coomaraswamy, Ananda K. (1972) *The Origin of the Buddha Image*, Reprint. New Delhi: Munshiram Manoharlal.

Craven, Roy C. (1997) *Indian Art: A Concise History* (Rev.ed.) New York: Thames and Hudson.

Dar, S. N. (1983) *Costumes of India and Pakistan*, Bombay: D. B. Taraporevala Sons & Co.

Dean, Beth, The *Many Worlds of Dance*, Sydney: Murray Publishing Co.

Dehejia, Vidya (1972) *Early Buddhist Rock Temples*, Ithaca, NY: Cornell University Press.

Devendra, D.T. (1958) *Classical Sinhalese Sculpture*, London: A. Tiranti.

Dhanapala, D.B. (1964) *Buddhist Paintings from Shrines and Temples in Ceylo*, New York: Mentor-UNESCO.

Harle, James C. (1986) *The Art and Architecture of the Indian Subcontinent,* Harmondsworth, UK: Penguin.

Huntington, Susan L. with John C. Huntington (1985) *Art of Ancient India: Buddhist, Hindu, Jain,* New York: Weatherhill.

James, E.O. (1959) *The Cult of the Mother Goddess,* London: Thames and Hudson.

Jayakur, Pupul (1980) *The Earthen Drum: An Introduction to the Ritual Arts of Rural India,* New Delhi: National Museum.

Karmay, Heather (1975) *Early Sino-Tibetan Art,* Warminster, UK: Aris and Phillips. Kirstein, Lincoln (1969) *Dance, A Short History of Classical Theatrical Dancing,* New York: Dance Horizons Inc.

Kramrisch, Stella (1965) *The Art of India* (3rd ed.) London: Phaidon.

—. (1983) *Exploring India's Sacred Art; Selected Writings of Stella Kramrisch.* Ed. Barbara Stoler Miller. Philadelphia: University of Pennsylvania Press. —. (1981) *Indian Sculpture* Reprint. Delhi: Motilal Banarsidass.

Lauf, Detlef Ingo (1976) *Tibetan Sacred Art: The Heritage of Tantra,* Berkeley, CA: Shambhala.

Lokesh, Chandra (ed.) (1991) *Buddhist Iconography,* New Delhi: International Academy of Indian Culture and Aditya Prakashan.

Malandra, Geri H. (1993) *Unfolding the Mandala: The Buddhist Caves at Ellora,* Albany: State University of New York Press.

Menon, K. P. S. (1979) *A Dictionary of Kathkali,* Madras: Orient Longman Ltd. _____(1978) *Sufi Sects Saints and Shrines,* Salt Lake City, Utah: Eastern Mysticism.

Moscati, Sabatine (1962) *The Faces of the Ancient Orient.* Garden City, New York: Anchor Books.

Nawab, Vidya Sarabai (1964) *419 Illustrations of Indian Music and Dance,* Ahmedabad: The Diamond Jubilee P. Press.

Rowland, Benjamin (1970) *The Art and Architecture of India; Buddhist, Hindu, Jain.* Harmondsworth, UK: Penguin.

Rawson, Philip(1973) *The Art of Tantra,* Greenwich, CT: New York Graphic Society. Royce, Anya Peterson (1977) *The Anthropology of Dance,* Bloomington: Indiana University Press.

Singh, Madanjeet (1965) *The Cave Paintings of Ajanta*, London: Thames and Hudson.
Singha, Rina (1967) *Indian Dances Their History and Growth*, New York: George Beazillen Inc.

Sorell, Walter (1967) *Dance Through the Ages*, New York: Grosset and Dunlap Publishers.

Spencer, Sidney(1963) *Mysticism in World Religion*, Baltimore: Penguin Books.
Spink, Walter (1967) *Ajanta to Ellora*. Bombay: Marg.

Weiner, Sheila L. (1977) *Ajanta: Its Place in Buddhist Art*, Berkeley: University of California Press.

INDEX

A

Acharyas, 284
Aesthetic needs, 21
Aesthetic underpinnings, 31
Ahimsa, 284
Airavat, 164
Amalaka, 104
Anekantavada, 283
Aniconic phase, 180
Animal motif, 216
Antarala, 113
Anti-historicism, 328
Antiquarians, 15
Apartment blocks, 14
Apsaras, 172
Arabesque, 234
Arabic inscriptions, 229
Aranmula, 126
Architect, 5
Architectural boom, 232
Architectural educators, 32
Architectural profession, 36
Architectural publications, 6
Architectural schools, 26
Architraves, 163
Arhat chaityas, 272
Arthasastra, 278
Artifacts, 178
Asramas, 277
Attached shafts, 304
Avataras, 133

B

Baghdadi, 322
Baolis, 312
Barakat, 241
Baroque cities, 8
Barrel-vault roofs, 64
Bas-reliefs, 160
Bengali Mahal, 262
Bhumija, 88
Blind arcading, 302
Boddhi tree, 162
Bodhisattvas, 159
Bonsais, 271
Brain-shaped design, 326
Brick wall, 46
Brickwork, 25
Buddhapada, 209
Buddhist cults, 184
Buddhist motif, 155
Buddhist sculpture, 153
Buddhist sutras, 154
Buffalo demon, 112
Building styles, 10
Bungas, 286

C

Calligraphic inscriptions, 245
Calligraphy, 54
Carvansarai, 250
Cathedrals, 4, 307
Cave architecture, 50
Cenotaphs, 248
Ceramists, 225
Chaitya- grihas, 179
Chaitya halls, 39, 47
Chakravartin, 166
Chamaras, 189
Chamukhs, 53
Chapels, 182
Charbagh, 256
Chevette, 302
Chhatras, 192
Chhatri, 65
Chubby, 86
Chunam, 56
Circular garden, 267
Circumambulation, 118
Classical antiquity, 339
Clerestory, 301
Cloistered prakara, 115
Coin hoards, 168
Columnar style, 280
Communal meditation, 66
Construction sites, 330
Contemporary architecture, 19
Cosmic dance, 142
Cosmopolitan tastes, 40
Cosmopolitan, 310
Cultural influence, 151
Curvilinear steeple, 279
Cylindrical shafts, 259

D

Dagoba, 183
Darbar, 290
Dargah, 55
Darwaza, 257
Deorhi, 295
Design process, 1
Dhaka, 3
Dharma, 144
Dharma-chakra, 161

Dharmamita, 171
Dharmarajika stupa, 190
Dhyani Buddhas, 145
Domed cupolas, 52
Domes, 228
Dvarapalas, 113
Dvikuta, 78
Dwapara yuga, 136
Dwarapalakas, 143

E

Ecclesiastical buildings, 30
Edifices, 132
Elliptical comics, 291
Emerald Buddha, 170
Equilateral arch, 306
Erotic sculptures, 91
Excavation work, 44
Excavation, 201

F

Female icon, 76
Feminist stance, 21
Figurative art, 156
Fireproof design, 32
Flagstaff, 124
Floral scrolls, 176
Fortified castle, 11
Frieze, 214
Funerary coins, 248

G

Gach, 297
Garbhagriha, 77
Geographical areas, 20
Gew-Gaws, 335
Global aesthetics, 60
Global warming, 37
Golden Duranta, 269

Gopuradwaram, 127
Gopurams, 71
Gothic architecture, 297
Gothic buildings, 22
Gothic tracery, 303
Greco-Buddhist art, 167
Greek himation, 169
Grey friars, 299
Gumbad, 288
Gurudwaras, 287
Gurumattas, 288

H

Hadiths, 226
Haikus, 157
Haram, 234
Hasht bihisht, 242
Hathi pol, 261
Hegemonic style, 24
Hellenistic, 152
Heritage industry, 16
Herringbone inlays, 254
Hieratic style, 38
High-tech architecture, 331
Hindu fundamentalists 235
Hindu mythology, 90
Hindu pilgrimage, 68
Historiography, 17
Human burials, 51
Human figure, 28

I

Indian epics, 114
Indian miniature, 316
Indo-Saracenic style, 308
Indo-Saracenic, 61
Industrial chimney, 58

Inlaid metalwork, 230
Intricate filigree, 109
Islamic art, 223
Islamic design, 229
Islamic dome, 296
Islamic faiths, 319
Islamic invasions, 175
Islamic legacy, 319
Islamic music, 237
Iwan, 233

J

Jagati, 77
Jain ascetics, 285
Jali, 255
Jaratkari, 289
Jatakas, 203
Jharokhas, 324
Jilaukhana, 251

K

Kachcha, 99
Kadamba shikhara, 81
Kalasa, 296
Kalasha, 244
Kalpa sutras, 76
Kalpavriksha, 313
Kalyanamantapa, 96
Kapota, 92
Kharoshthi, 171
Khasarpana, 148
Kinnaras, 217
Kirthimukhas, 80
Kshatrapas, 195

L

Lakshadeepam, 116
Lakshmi, 76
Lancet arch, 305

Linga, 93
Lunatic asylum, 20

M

Madanikas, 110
Mahacaitya, 202
Maharajas, 130
Mahtab bagh, 253
Manasthambhas, 281
Mandala, 65
Mandapa , 49
Manqabats, 239
Massive rock face, 101
Mausoleum, 240
Mehrabs, 224
Metallurgical curiosities, 260
Metaphorical messages, 9
Microcosm, 102
Mihrab, 54
Mihrabs, 249
Minarets, 243
Miniature paintings, 318
Misals, 298
Mithuna, 221
Moderate, 206
Modern technology, 339
Monastery, 46
Monasticism, 299
Monumental architecture, 43
Moonlight garden, 246
Morbidezza, 211
Mounds, 67
Mudras, 38
Mughal creativity, 264
Mukti sthala, 137
Mussammam Burj, 266
Mythological culture, 150

N

Nabhi, 128
Nagara style, 73
Nagara, 41
Nanak shahi, 289
Nandi, 117
Native traditions, 61
Neo-modern, 35
Nishan Sahib, 292

O

Octagonal shafts, 207
Octagonal shikharam, 108
Organic architecture, 34
Oriental motif, 57
Ornamental niches, 69
Ornate shrines, 132

P

Pagoda, 63
Palaki, 288
Pali Canon, 158
Palimpsest, 218
Panca Lenani, 181
Panca mahakshetras, 138
Pancanarayan, 139
Pancatirthis, 275
Paramatman, 274
Parikrama, 188
Pendaka, 204
Penrose, 227
Pietra dura mosaic, 236
Pilgrimage shrine, 135
Pillared halls, 105
Pinjras, 297
Political symbols, 2
Porte da Mer, 55
Postmodern architecture, 334

Pradakshina, 84
Prakaram, 108
Prasadas, 103
Pukka, 100
Pushkarni, 73
Pyramidal towers, 147

Q

Qasidah, 238

R

Radical design, 333
Ragamala, 41
Ragamalas, 317
Rayagopura, 74
Real architecture, 14
Regional kingdoms, 323
Relic caskets, 197
Relief medallions, 39
Rock-cut shrines, 72
Rock-cut viharas, 165
Romanesque traditions, 300
Roofed chhatris, 247

S

Sacred tree, 186
Saivite temples, 07
Sakti, 145
Sakyasimha, 194
Salabhanjika, 79
Sampradaya, 134
Sangam literature, 268
Sangharana, 146
Saptarishis, 125
Scientific principles, 1
Sculptural decoration, 315
Secular architecture, 311

Shah Burj, 265
Shikhara, 49
Shravakas, 274
Shravikas, 274
Shukongoshin, 177
Siblings, 141
Sick building, 12
Siddhas, 120
Skyscrapers, 4
Social rituals, 13
Spatial organizations, 13
Spiritual fusion, 314
Stellate plan, 111
Stellate, 87
Sthambas, 193
Stupas, 45
Sufi shrines, 319
Superstructures, 83
Svelte forms, 219
Symmetrical façade, 338

T

Tactile architecture, 1
Taikhanas, 293
Taj market, 252
Tall spires, 301

Tantric Buddhism, 149
Temple architecture, 115
Temple deities, 75
Terrace garden, 270
Terraced house, 25
Thakats, 288
Tirthankara, 273
Tirthankara, 53
Tiruvaimozhi, 21
Tomography, 325
Tondi, 205
Torana, 63
Torana, 89
Town planning, 42
Traditional crafts, 33
Triple-lobed footprint, 231
Trishul , 95
Tukri, 297
Tutelary deity, 140

U

Udhapata, 208
Unisa, 206
Urban buildings, 337
Urban planning, 30
Urbanism, 27

V

Vastushastra, 62
Vedika, 92
Vernacular buildings, 29
Viharas, 52
Vimana, 70
Vishnu, 76
Votive stupas, 187

W

Warehouses, 7
White Hun, 145
White stone, 258
Womb house, 106
Wooden harmika, 191

Y

Yaksas, 150
Yaksha, 48
Yali, 97
Yalis, 129

Z

Zeitgeist, 23